INTERNATIONAL NEGOTIATIONS

INTERNATIONAL NEGOTIATIONS

Theory, Practice, and the Connection with Domestic Politics

Alexander G. Nikolaev

LEXINGTON BOOKS

A division of
ROWMAN & LITTLEFIELD PUBLISHERS, INC.
Lanham • Boulder • New York • Toronto • Plymouth, UK

LEXINGTON BOOKS

A division of Rowman & Littlefield Publishers, Inc.
A wholly owned subsidiary of The Rowman & Littlefield Publishing Group, Inc.
4501 Forbes Boulevard, Suite 200
Lanham, MD 20706

Estover Road
Plymouth PL6 7PY
United Kingdom

British Library Cataloguing in Publication Information Available

Library of Congress Cataloging-in-Publication Data

Nikolaev, Alexander G.
    International negotiations : theory, practice, and the connection with domestic
  politics / Alexander G. Nikolaev.
        p. cm.
    1. Diplomatic negotiations in international disputes. I. Title.
  JZ6045.N55 2007
  327.1'1—dc22   2007014410

    ISBN-13: 978-0-7391-1758-3 (cloth : alk. paper)
    ISBN-10: 0-7391-1758-0 (cloth : alk. paper)
    ISBN-13: 978-0-7391-1759-0 (pbk. : alk. paper)
    ISBN-10: 0-7391-1759-9 (pbk. : alk. paper)

Printed in the United States of America

∞™ The paper used in this publication meets the minimum requirements of American
National Standard for Information Sciences—Permanence of Paper for Printed Library
Materials, ANSI/NISO Z39.48-1992.

This book is dedicated to my wife Svetlana—
with love and appreciation.

Contents

Contents

Part Four: Culture

List of Tables and Figures

Acknowledgments

I WISH TO EXPRESS MY SINCERE APPRECIATION to all people who made this book possible.

First of all, I would like to thank Dr. Stephen D. McDowell of the Florida State University, whose ideas, intelligence, and constructive guidance were priceless at the early stages of this project.

My sincere appreciation also extends to Mr. Glen Fisher and the Institute for the Study of Diplomacy and the School of Foreign Service of Georgetown University for granting me their gracious permission to use some of their ideas, materials, and other products of their intellectual work in this book.

I want to express my gratitude to my faithful research assistant Julia Hagemann whose diligence and hard work are evident throughout this volume.

My special thanks are directed toward the Department of Culture and Communication of Drexel University and personally to Dr. Douglas V. Porpora who provided me with invaluable emotional and professional support throughout the years I spent working on this project.

Finally, I would like to highlight my exceptional appreciation for my wife Svetlana, whose love, patience, and support became the foundation for everything I have done in my life—including this book.

Introduction

IN THE FALL OF 1997, the president of the International Communication Association, Dr. Stanley A. Deetz, wrote in his annual address to the association's members: "The principal need of our time is to develop the capacity to make mutually satisfying decisions in contexts where fundamental consensus is absent. In this sense, we have entered what is most usefully described as an age of negotiation" (Deetz, 1997, p. 128). It is very difficult to argue with this simple but fair statement. That is why over the last several decades, scholars from many areas of human knowledge have devoted a great deal of attention to negotiation processes.

Negotiation is one of the most important and widespread forms of international communication. Indeed, in the time when unabridged market competition or the use of military forces may be too costly business people and politicians more than ever rely on negotiations to find mutually satisfying solutions to the world problems. Many structural elements of the contemporary political world that affect our everyday life—such as NAFTA or EU—came into being out of long and difficult negotiations. Simultaneously, any failure of such negotiations as the nuclear talks with Iran and North Korea may entail disastrous consequences. At the same time, the international talks process is extremely complex. It includes sociological, psychological, communication, political, and cultural variables. Consequently, a holistic and comprehensive scholarly examination of the process of international negotiations as well as a thorough analysis of the practice of international talks is important and enlightening.

Many theories of negotiation have been created and have made valuable contributions to the general understanding of this process. Simultaneously, they left some room for further interpretations and explanations of specific questions. But negotiation is, first of all, a purpose-oriented process and, ultimately, key aspects of this process matter only so far as they are related to the final outcome of the process. That is why "the basic analytical question for all approaches to answer is: How are negotiated outcomes explained?" (Zartman, 1989, p. 242) The variations in the outcomes of even similar negotiations are so wide and unpredictable that even the best negotiation scholars and practitioners were often puzzled. And this is not amazing because negotiations may occur in an incredibly complex web of political, social, and psychological situations and structures. That is why, when explaining the talks process outcomes, negotiation scholars have frequently borrowed some concepts and even whole theories from other areas of human knowledge. Explanations have been drawn from psychological, sociological, political and other viewpoints, using concepts such as perceptions, interests, and power. Certainly, these theories and concepts were not only adopted, they were also adapted. The flow of ideas and concepts between different fields of knowledge has proved very fruitful for explaining negotiations. Using different kinds of explanations related to various kinds of human activities in which negotiations may go on and by which they can be affected, scholars have been able to solve many problems and answer many questions in this area.

But often practitioner and theoreticians have to deal with quite complex negotiational situations which just one theoretical perspective will not be enough to explain. And one type of such complicated problems is so-called two-stage or two-level negotiations (Druckman's two-type-function or two-model). The two-level situation happens when negotiations go on in both *inter-entity* and *intra-entity* levels. It means that two or more entities (institutions, countries, organizations) have to negotiate an agreement between them and, then, they have to approve that agreement within each entity. Without such approval the agreement cannot come into force.

This type of negotiation is interesting because it does not fall cleanly within any one single discipline-specific theory of negotiation. For example, the outcome of this type of negotiation cannot be explained using only a communication process-oriented approach, one that focuses on the processes of persuasion, influence, compliance gaining, uncertainty reduction, and information transmission. These aspects can help to understand the outcome of negotiations at the *inter-entity* level; but often an agreement is reached and signed at this level and then, it does not go into effect. It ultimately fails because it never obtains approval at the *intra-entity* level. Why does it happen? If an agreement can be reached between different countries or organizations, why are people not capable of reaching an agreement (using the same approaches and techniques as at the inter-entity level) with their group members—citizens or colleagues? Theoretically, it should be even easier, taking into account shared goals, values, and experiences.

The scholarly literature from the field of international relations tells us that one of the answers may be the *structure*. Each organization, institution, or country has its own structure. *Structure* is defined here as the embodiment of the aggregation of interests, of the distribution of resources, and of the distribution of capabilities—that is, the realization of power. This very structure often impedes free flow of information, distorts perceptions, and creates or affects actors' interests. That is, this structure itself may have an independent and strong influence on the process and outcome of two-level negotiations.

Is there a theory that would help to account for the effect of structural variables on the outcome of the two-level negotiations? One theory that was originated in the field of international relations is called the *two-level-game* theory. It was especially designed to analyze two-level negotiations between different countries and within countries. Therefore, it is logical to try to use this theory to account for the effect of structural variables on the negotiations process.

That is, what we will try to do from the theoretical point of view is to take an analytical approach that has been used primarily in one field—international relations—and explore its relevance and application to the analysis of international negotiations from a communication perspective. This particular analytical approach—the two-level-game—is part of a larger approach of the rational actor models and the game theoretic models. The application of a new version of this approach to the field of communication may be helpful in the analysis of some types of international negotiations.

In a broader philosophical sense, this study will address an important issue—the problem of agreement-seeking in the complex modern world. The findings of this study may help to understand and explain some elements and dynamics of this agreement-seeking process. Consequently, these findings could serve as a theoretical framework and practical guide for action in different difficult social, economic, and political situations, such as international conflict management or work of international development agencies trying to introduce changes in Third World countries.

Such a new approach could also help to explain the effects of some institutional structural variables on the communication process in general and on the negotiation process in particular. That is, we will try to understand and explain how, on one hand, communication dynamics affect the two-level negotiations processes and outcomes and how, on the other hand, structural variables affect the negotiations process itself. A structural communication-oriented theoretical model, which is presented in this book, should help to conceptualize this two-way effect.

As was mentioned above, the structural dimension can be important for many forms of international communication—not only negotiations. As long as there is any kind of structure between the sender of the message and the audience or receiver—state, media, social, political, business, etc.—this dimension may shape the negotiation process in several ways. The institutional structure is important for many reasons. First of all, it may impede the flow of information and, consequently, distort actors' perceptions. Second, it may create or affect actors' interests and, consequently, affect their negotiational strategies. It also may dictate the routine procedures (standard operating procedures) organizations have to go through in order to have something accomplished. Finally, it may set overall limits (lower as well as upper) on what actually can be accomplished in a certain structure by a certain kind of individual or group. This volume is intended to demonstrate how some structural variables may affect the outcome of communication processes in negotiations. The new version of the two-level-game theory, suggested in this book, demonstrates that the outcome of this process is heavily affected by the structural context in which it occurs. The theory shows that the final outcome of a negotiation process may depend not only on the argumentation, persuasiveness of the message, or even the degree to which a certain agreement is favorable to one of the parties, but also on the structural characteristics of the environment in which it takes place.

The connection of such two dramatically different perspectives—the communication process-oriented approach and the rational-actor game-oriented point of view—will not be easy. Some adaptation—extension and transformation—of the two-level-game theory will be necessary in order to use it in the communication area. This connection will be a two-way process. Firstly, the two-level-game theory will be transformed through the lens of the communication point of view. Second, it will be applied to a communication area—namely, international negotiations—in order to find out how useful it actually is for understanding and explaining so far unexplained aspects of two-level negotiations outcomes.

It is important to note here that the structural dimension does not exclude or contradict the traditional communication process-oriented point of view—it supplements it. It introduces new tools or ways to analyze the negotiation process. The significance of this work is that it will highlight the importance of the structural dimension in the field of communication and will offer some recommendations and guidelines regarding how to deal with the structural problems through the use of the transformed and extended version of the two-level-game theory.

In 1996, professor Ronald Smith (SUNY at Buffalo) published a review of a book called *Negotiation as a Social Process*. The book is a collection of articles on many different aspects of the negotiation process, some of which may seem quite remote from the field of communication. However, Dr. Smith wrote about the book:

> *Negotiation as a Social Process* will interest the practitioner steeped in the notions that . . . negotiation is an element of that field. . . . Many readers are likely to pass over this book because it seems not to address their practical concerns. . . . But those able and willing to ruminate on the theoretical themes may discover for themselves some interesting conclusions and potential applications. *Negotiation as a Social Process* belongs on the reading list of people who consider themselves thinkers. (pp. 199–200)

The book you are now holding in your hands is theoretical in nature as well and, consequently, is also written for thinkers. But some practical advice will also be offered. Therefore, the author of this volume believes that the model offered in this book will help international communication practitioners, who are involved in problem-solving and negotiations, to raise some useful theoretical claims and point out professional applications for use by professional negotiators.

Structural Elements of the Book

Structurally, the book will include four main elements: a comprehensive and detailed overview of theoretical perspectives on the process of international negotiations; a new (communication-oriented) perspective on the two-level-game theory, a number of international negotiations case studies, and a discussion of the effect of culture on the process of international talks.

Comprehensive theoretical overview of the process

This part will provide a comprehensive and detailed overview of various theoretical approaches toward the process of international negotiations and it will also include a detailed discussion of the origins and features of the two-level-game theory.

Chapter 1 discusses how scholars from different academic disciplines conceptualize the process of negotiations. Various scholars have created a fertile theoretical ground upon which the communication approach was founded. Communication scholars have adopted and adapted theoretical concepts from different fields but finally came up with an unmistakably communication-oriented theory of negotiations. This theory offers many interesting insights into the process, but it also has some drawbacks that are associated mainly with the disregard of the structural context of negotiations.

Chapter 2 covers the two-level-game theory in detail. This theory originated in the field of international relations, and it considers the issue of how the state structure affects the outcome of the two-level negotiations. This theory represents a new step in negotiations studies. It provides new tools for the analysis of international negotiations. At the same time, it has its own problems. The main problem is that the theory is static and disregards informational and communication aspects of the negotiations process. That is why some extension and transformation of this theory is required to account more fully for all the dimensions of negotiations.

New Theoretical Perspective

All the theories covered in the first chapter are as old as the field of international negotiations itself. There was little theoretical development in this area in recent years. Therefore, the need for a fresh look at the field is clearly felt by many scholars.

It is interesting that "Perhaps the most neglected aspect of bargaining has been the role of various kinds of communication" (Jonsson, 1989, p. 258). At the same time, negotiation is inherently a communication process—"without communication there is no negotiation" (Jonsson, 1989, p. 259; see also Fisher and Ury, 1983). That is, the introduction of a new—more communication-oriented—theoretical perspective in the field is capable of providing us with such a fresh point of view.

At the same time, international negotiations are not going on in a political vacuum. Many variables affect the outcomes of such talks. And one of the most important sets of variables is the domestic political situation and structure. This aspect is usually put on the back burner by the international relations scholars. But in fact it is one of the most important aspects in this area. Often talks fail or succeed mainly due to pressure of some domestic groups. So, it is simply unwise to disregard this issue.

One of the relatively recent major contributions to the field of international negotiations was the two-level-game theory. The theory was conceptualized in 1988 by R. D. Putnam in his article "Diplomacy and domestic politics: The logic of two-level games." The purpose of the article was to start conceptualizing the effect of domestic political variables on the process of international negotiations. Almost a decade later, Helen V. Milner (1997) published her book in which she built up on Putnam's theory and developed it further.

One of the main goals of this volume is to offer a new—communication-oriented—model of the two-level-game theory. The author made a new step beyond Milner's model: offered a new (dynamic) model of this theory; conceptualized a new set of variables (although clearly connected to those created by Milner); changed main assumptions of the theory; introduced new concepts (such as "institutional approval" and "side payments"); redefined other concepts (interests, information, institutions). The result is a new and unique model of the two-level-game theory—more lifelike and analytically useful. It will be able to clearly demonstrate how domestic politics affect the dynamics of international negotiations.

Chapter 3 presents this new—extended and transformed—model of the two-level-game theory, where communication dynamics are superimposed on the traditional paradigm of the theory. Such an approach provides an opportunity to analyze negotiations as a process instead of a set of static situations.

Case Studies

The case studies parts of the book—chapters 4, 5, 6, and 7—will carry out several functions. First of all, they will provide different examples of important and complex contemporary international negotiations. They will also demonstrate how different theoretical approaches—sociological point of view, psychological perspective, learning theory, the problem-solving and the joint decision-making approaches—contribute toward a deeper understanding of the outcomes of different international talks. Finally, they will demonstrate the importance of the domestic politics for the process of international negotiations.

Culture

Chapter 8 will discuss the role of cultural variables in the process of international negotiations. It will warn against cultural ignorance and arrogance. But the main thesis of the chapter is that it is not enough to learn superficial customs in order to be able to conduct an effective communicative act from the cultural point of view. It is necessary to delve below those external sets of rituals and understand the deeply seeded cultural meanings that stand behind main philosophical concepts that are under negotiation. Cultural analysis guidelines will also be suggested in the chapter.

Conclusion will discuss in detail the novelty and significance of the new model of the two-level-game theory and also will talk about the analytical benefits this model carries upon itself. But mainly in that part of the book real-world negotiators or negotiation analysts will be able to find some useful recommendations (based on the new model) that will be able to help them in their work.

The appendix part of this book will try to pave the way for a possible practical use of the new model. This model can be extended through quantitative analysis to help communication practitioners to analyze negotiational situations with greater precision.

General Conceptual Overview

In general, this book has three main points at its heart.

First of all, it is clear that recently the negotiations theory field fell into a theoretical stagnation. Scholars working in their separate areas—sociology, psychology, political science, IR, economics—ossified in their concepts and perspectives. And this prevented this field's theory from effectively developing further. Therefore, it was necessary to change some of those ossified assumptions in order to make theoretical flexibility and development possible. The definitions and roles of such ideas as interests, information, institutions, actor-formation, and actor-identity had to undergo thorough revision and reconceptualization. But it was necessary to find a theoretical basis for such revisions. Since some approaches (as, for example, game-theory) are too static for that, it was necessary to find a dynamic theory to serve as the basis for such a theoretical development. And the communication perspective seems to be custom-made for such purposes—it is dynamic and fluent—easily allowing for transformation and adaptation of previously rigid concepts and assumptions to new situations and theoretical outlooks. And through the use of this perspective the author of this book made an attempt at an advancement of international negotiations theory.

The second idea of this volume is that it is not enough to know and be able to use just one perspective on international negotiations. It is absolutely necessary to deeply understand and be able to apply all the possible perspectives. Each of them is capable of providing us with an interesting insight that would not be visible from another point of view. Then, the final solution to a negotiation problem can be put together as a mosaic from different ideas and recommendations. The author calls it *the complex analysis*. The word "complex" has a dual meaning here. First of all, the analysis will incorporate a whole complex of different views and ideas. And second, this analysis is really difficult and complicated as the case studies will demonstrate later in this book.

The third and final purpose of this volume is to show that whatever issue we are dealing with at the international level—it is always useful and enlightening to examine the effect of domestic politics on the problem under consideration. The author of this book is far from saying that all the international politics are actually domestic in nature but, at the same time, it has been proven that domestic politics have a tremendous effect on international negotiations. And even if that effect is not crucial—it is still worth looking into some aspects of internal political issues. They may give an analyst some interesting hints and clues that would not be evident otherwise—if he or she would just look at the international variables.

Therefore, this book is intended to have theoretical as well as practical significance and to be interesting for international negotiations scholars as well as for the practitioners who actually participate in real-life international talks.

I
THEORY

1

The Development of Negotiation Theory
and the Communication Perspective

IN A BROAD SENSE, THIS BOOK WILL ADDRESS an important issue—the problem of agreement-seeking in the complex contemporary world. The questions and claims of this volume may help readers to understand and explain some elements and dynamics of the agreement-seeking process. Consequently, these concepts might serve to contribute to both a theoretical framework and a practical guide for action in difficult social, economic, and political situations. In order to be able to theorize in the area of negotiations it is necessary to thoroughly and deeply understand all the elements and dynamics of this complicated process. The conceptual development of this area and its theoretical origins should be considered. The advantages and drawbacks of different theoretical perspectives, and, consequently, the opportunities for further theoretical developments that are opening up before us must be assessed. This chapter is intended to provide a broad analytical overview of the theoretical dimensions of negotiations.

This chapter will show how scholars from different disciplines have viewed negotiations in general and how they have conceptualized separate aspects of the negotiation process in particular. Many theories have been created in attempts to explain this complex process, and one of them is the cognitive or communication theory. It was born out of the abundance and versatility of previously accumulated theoretical material. This theory adopted and adapted concepts and viewpoints from different fields. At the same time, it bears an unmistakably and distinctly communication character because it emphasizes the communication aspects of the negotiation process. These include interactions between the negotiation parties, message interpretation, information processing, and the exchange of symbols. Cognitive theory provides a new understanding of the negotiation process, explaining many previously unexplained aspects and suggesting interesting ties between communication dynamics and the outcomes of negotiations. At the same time, it is also limited because cognitive theory emphasizes direct communications between the sides and makes its conclusions based exclusively on communication interactions. It places less emphasis on the structure of environment in which a particular negotiation occurs. This structure may have a dramatic impact on the negotiation process changing its dynamics and results. That is why it makes sense to consider structural variables that can influence the negotiation process and its outcomes. These structural variables will be considered at the end of this chapter.

General Negotiation Theories

An extensive body of literature exists on the subject of negotiations. Many different theories and approaches have been designed and used to explain this very complicated process. Before dealing with these theories, some basics of the negotiation process should be defined.

Basics of the Negotiation Process

"Negotiation is a process of combining conflicting positions into a common position, under a decision rule of unanimity, a phenomenon in which the outcome is determined by the process" (Zartman, 1989, p. 242). This is probably the best and most widespread definition of negotiation in the scholarly literature. Most other definitions are modifications or versions of this one, many with very small deviations. Some of them omit the "under a decision rule of unanimity" part, others skip the "outcome is determined by the process" element. But all definitions agree that negotiation is a process of combining conflicting positions into a nonconflicting one through a process of exchange. The problem is that different scholars from various fields have different opinions on what is actually exchanged—symbols, ideas, gestures, information, things of value, perceptions, etc. This aspect will be covered in theoretical parts of this chapter. But in general, the definition above is very appropriate for the purpose of this study.

Every negotiation process starts with the prenegotiation phase: "Policymakers in the White House, the Department of State and corporations need to think in terms of a process which deals with the obstacles *to* negotiation as well as the hurdles *in* negotiation" (Saunders, 1984, p. 47). This phase in turn consists of three stages. The first stage is *defining the problem* when the definition of interests and objectives takes place. The second stage is *commitment to negotiate* when leaders "come to judgment that the present situation no longer serves their interests" (Saunders, 1984, p. 54). The final stage of the pre-negotiation phase is actually *arranging the negotiation.* "Whereas the commitment to negotiate is a political decision which can be made known in a variety of general ways, the effort to arrange a specific negotiation tends to focus on more detailed terms of reference for the negotiation and dealing with those physical arrangements which may have political implications" (Saunders, 1984, p. 56). Only after all the arrangements are made, can the negotiation itself proceed.

The whole negotiation process is usually thought of as a sequence of bids and concessions until a decision acceptable for all the involved parties is reached. The first statement of the negotiation position is called the opening bid. This statement is very important because it shows if the position expressed in that statement is within the latitude of acceptance of the other party. If the point of view expressed is out of the range of acceptability, it simply means that negotiations are not "ripe" yet. In this case, usually, negotiations either do not proceed further or do not start at all. If the opening bid is acceptable for the other party—negotiations can proceed. The opening concession is a response to the opening bid. It shows the first party (who made the bid) what the position of their opponent is and what kind of negotiation dynamics can be expected in the future. And this process is repeated in cycles until an acceptable solution for both parties is found (Bartos, 1978).

Most scholars specify three main functions of the negotiation process. The first of them is *diagnosis*: "trying to find out what the problem is, what the other side is susceptible to in the way of appeals, what the ingredients of the situation are, what the other side wants, and what one wants oneself" (Zartman, 1984, p. 2). The second function is *formulation*: "finding an over-arching principle or formula which will define the problem, since problems can be defined in many ways" (Zartman, 1984, p. 2). Function number three is applying this general principle to a certain situation in an attempt to construct an agreement between the parties.

The negotiation literature also highlights several turning points that occur in any negotiation process. The first turning point is the *moment of seriousness.* "It is the moment when both parties realize that it actually is possible to arrive at a solution to the problems by a joint decision, since their expectations are perceived to be within range of each other" (Zartman, 1984, p. 3). The *crest* or the *hump* happens when the sides become satisfied with the agreement. "Finally there is the closing moment of deadline when it becomes important to the sides to agree before they lose the opportunity" (Zartman, 1984, p. 4).

It may seem strange that such a seemingly simple process has attracted such a great deal of attention from scholars from different areas of knowledge. Literally dozens of books and hundreds of articles have been written on this subject. One of the possible reasons for such a significant level of interest is that, as the world has changed and become more and more interdependent, people came to rely on negotiations more than on any other way of problem-solving. And as the importance and number of different types of negotiations were increasing, scholars and practitioners from different fields started to realize that this process was not as simple as it had seemed. They definitely needed a better understanding of the phenomenon called negotiation.

From the very beginning, the investigation of negotiation did not belong to any particular field of knowledge. People negotiated in all industries and explored negotiations in many different areas of studies. They solved problems specific to their fields using perspectives pertinent to their areas. That is why so many different theories arose in the field of negotiations—because each author tried to analyze the phenomenon from the point of view of his or her discipline. Consequently, most typologies of the negotiation theories have a definite discipline-ordered character. And it is understandable, because this area started as a collection of theoretical concepts taken from different fields. Recently some mixed or interdisciplinary perspectives have also emerged.

Each field's negotiation theory has a specific character and makes very special contributions to the negotiation theory in general. But one aspect unifies them all: "The basic analytical question for all approaches to answer is: How are negotiated outcomes explained?" (Zartman, 1989, p. 242). This question is understandable because negotiation is a purpose-oriented process. Negotiations rarely occur for their own sake. The main purpose for any negotiation is to find a mutually acceptable solution to a common problem. All the elements and dynamics of this process matter so far as they have any effect on the final outcome. That is why basically all negotiation theoreticians have tried to explain the relationship between the outcome and different aspects of the negotiation process.

The purpose of the following review is to summarize the main issues and components in the development of negotiation theory. This review will start (as the whole area did) with discipline-specific theories, such as sociological and psychological theories. It will proceed to more recent models that combine concepts from different fields, perspectives, and approaches.

The Sociological or Strategic Choice Point of View

The first perspective represents what Zartman calls the *sociological point of view*. It carries many very recognizable characteristics of the rational-actor approach used by many social sciences, such as economics or political science. This perspective includes and is based on the elements of the *strategic analysis* and the *process analysis* approaches.

The *strategic analysis* approach is "based on an array of elements, but its structure is one of ends, not of means. Strategic analysis, as portrayed in game theoretic matrices, begins with the assumption that outcomes are determined by the relative array of their values to the parties, under condition of rational (i.e., preferred) choice" (Zartman, 1989, p. 244).

The *process analysis* approach explains the outcome of the negotiation process through a system of concessions. These concessions in turn are determined by a certain element of each party's position. "The particular element varies slightly according to the particular version of the theory; most process analysis is based on a security point theory in some form, although there are also a few other variations used. Process analysis indicates that the party will concede on the basis of a comparative calculation of its own versus its opponent's costs or of its own costs versus some acceptability level" (Zartman, 1989, p. 246).

In general, according to the sociological perspective on negotiations, the negotiator is a rational utility maximizer. The utility function is derived from the structure of payoffs each side expects to get or actually receives from the result of negotiations. The process itself is competitive and is based on the series of bids and concessions. The outcome of the negotiation process should be fair because it is supposed to be based on fair and mutual concessions. "The concessions are fair as long as the negotiators have no need to revise their original expectations about what the ultimate agreement will be" (Bartos, 1978, p. 22). If concessions are not fair "the unfairly treated negotiator should stop making further concessions rather than retract his last concessions" (Bartos, 1978, p. 23). This move is supposed to let the other side know that the negotiations may come to a stalemate or even to an end unless that side adjusts its concession policy.

Often, theoretical conceptualizations of this viewpoint are expressed in game theoretic terms because it is the most convenient way to work with concepts based on the above-mentioned assumptions. "These concepts are developed on the basis of mathematical reasoning rather than upon observation of actual negotiations in the real world of international diplomacy" (Hopmann, 1996, p. 37). All these concepts are parts of and connected to each other by the process of bargaining defined by Young (1975) as "a means by which two or more purposive actors arrive at specific outcomes in situations in which: (1) the choices of the actors will determine the allocation of some value[s], (2) the outcome for each participant is a function of the behavior of the other[s], and (3) the outcome is achieved through negotiations between or among the players" (p. 5).

The values each player receives from the play are called utilities and they are "a summary measure of all of the costs and benefits that collectively may be associated with a particular outcome" (Hopmann, 1996, p. 39).

Another important aspect in such a game is information. It can be either perfect (players know everything about each other's preferences) or incomplete, or absent (players can only guess each other's preferences based on the payoff structure, rules of the game, or previous experience). Given the amount of information players have, they can choose a strategy—"the set of choices that each player will select in the face of all possible contingencies" (Hopmann, 1996, p. 41).

The game analysis proceeds according to the following general assumptions:

> The players are rational in that they prefer to receive the highest possible utilities. In other words, players will try to maximize their gains or, if gains cannot be achieved, at least to minimize their losses. These outcomes are usually expressed in probabilistic terms as expected utility, defined as the probability of each outcome time the utility of each possible outcome, summed across all possible outcomes. A rational actor will choose the action that offers the greatest expected utility. In other words, one may prefer a lower valued, but highly likely, outcome to one that may have a higher absolute value, but where the likelihood of obtaining that value is remote. (Hopmann, 1996, p. 40)

In a simplified form the formula for rational calculations can be represented in this form: $U = P*V$ (where U is expected utility or "payoff" of a certain outcome for a certain actor, V is the value of that outcome for that actor and P is a probability of that particular outcome in real life). This approach in general suggests that people, organizations, and even whole countries consciously or subconsciously actually go through this type of calculation in order to come up with the best decision available for them.

All the games may be divided into two groups—zero-sum and non-zero-sum games. A zero-sum game is one in which "the joint utility of all the players equals zero, that is, where the utility of all the players sums to zero; in this case, the gains of some players must be offset by equal losses to others" (Hopmann, 1996, p. 40). In non-zero-sum games "there are generally no determinate solutions, so that the parties may try to negotiate joint strategies that will improve payoffs for both compared to unilaterally determined strategies" (Hopmann, 1996, p. 45).

The outcome of such games may be Nash Equilibrium, Pareto Optimal, or Hicks Optimal. A *Nash Equilibrium*, named after John Nash (an American mathematician), is a set of strategies, one for each player, such that no player has incentive to unilaterally change his or her action. Players are in equilibrium if a change in strategies by any one of them would lead that player to earn *less* than if he or she remained with the current strategy. An outcome of a game is *Pareto Optimal*, named after Vilfredo Pareto (an Italian economist), if there is no other outcome that makes every player at least as well off *and* at least one player strictly better off. But a Nash Equilibrium does not have to be necessarily Pareto Optimal. In a Nash Equilibrium type of situation the players' payoffs can be increased for one or all of them without hurting any other player. In the Pareto Optimal situation it is impossible. If all players receive their maximum payoffs, then that outcome is Pareto Optimal. An outcome of a game is *Hicks Optimal*, named after John Hicks (a British economist), if there is no other outcome that results in greater total payoffs for the players. Therefore, a Hicks Optimal outcome is always the point at which total payoffs across all players is maximized. That is, a Hicks Optimal outcome is always Pareto Optimal (with some compensation criteria to differentiate between Pareto optimality outcomes).

We will provide here just a few examples of the kinds of games and outcomes discussed above. The games discussed here are the most well-known and illustrative for the rational-actor type of approach.

Probably, the most well-known game is the Prisoner's Dilemma (see figure 1.1). The idea is simple. Two criminals, who have participated together in one crime, are caught and put into different cells by the policy and interrogated. The prison terms they will eventually receive depend on their behavior. They can either squeal on each other or cooperate with each other by remaining silent. One of the main assumptions of the game is that the prisoners have no communication with each other. This is a typical zero-sum game—one wins, the other loses.

The prisoners cannot coordinate their efforts and have to guess each other's actions. In this case, the cost of being cheated (of a defection on the other side) is too high. Therefore, although the cooperation choice (remain silent/remain silent) is quite good, the game usually ends up with mutual defection. Certainly, it will be mostly true for so called "one-shot" or nonrepeated games. If the game is repeated with the same actors—the outcome may change due to the learning effect.

The next scenario is named after the game that used to play out on the back roads of American towns and cities—the Chicken Game. Two young and not

| | | Prisoner 2 | |
		remain silent	squeal
Prisoner 1	remain silent	2/2	0/3
	squeal	3/0	1/1

FIGURE 1.1
Prisoner's Dilemma payoff matrix

| | | Driver 2 | |
		stay	swerve
Driver 1	stay	-100/-100	1/-1
	swerve	-1/1	0/0

FIGURE 1.2
Chicken Game payoff matrix (pride)

very smart individuals are challenged to drive straight at each other on a narrow road. The first to swerve loses face among his peers. If neither swerves, however—both die. Figure 1.2 shows the pay-off matrix for this game.

In the form depicted on Figure 1.2 this game may be used as a metaphor for a situation where two parties engage in a showdown where they have nothing to gain, and only pride stops them from backing down. In some other forms it may be used as a model of negotiations during international crises where pride is not the only consideration. Figure 1.3 shows that version of the game.

Another well-known scenario is the Stag Hunt game. Actually, the idea of this game comes back to the French philosopher, Jean Jacques Rousseau and is quite simple. Two hunters want to catch a stag (a lot of food for everybody) and try to do it by approaching it from different sides. A stag can be caught only through a cooperative effort. But each of them unexpectedly sees a rabbit—a much smaller catch but easier to get. They have to decide each independently what to do. Again, one of the main assumptions of the game is that communication between players is absent.

As we can see from Figure 1.4, there are two pure strategy Nash equilibria in the game and only one of them is Hicks Optimal (stag/stag). Usually, in such situations players prefer to cooperate due to what is called "a universal preference of a stag over a rabbit."

A typical non-zero-sum game is often called "battle of the sexes" but better can be called "family decision" (see figure 1.5). A married couple is trying to decide where to spend a Saturday night. The husband wants to see a boxing match while his wife wants to go to the opera. The only thing they are sure about is that they want to spend this evening together.

| | | Driver 2 | |
		stay	swerve
Driver 1	stay	-100/-100	50/-50
	swerve	-50/50	-10/10

FIGURE 1.3
Chicken Game payoff matrix (crisis)

		Hunter 2	
		stag	rabbit
Hunter 1	stag	10/10	0/5
	rabbit	5/0	5/5

FIGURE 1.4
Stag Hunt payoff matrix

This game has two pure strategy Nash equilibria, one where both go to the opera and another where both go to the football game. In this game, a win for one side does not mean a loss for the other. Besides that, under an assumption that would allow for the information exchange, "the parties may try to negotiate joint strategies that will improve payoffs for both compared to unilaterally determined strategies" (Hopmann, 1996, p. 45).

Certainly, all those matrices can be modified for different political situations and different types of international negotiations and crises.

The rational actor game theoretical approach to negotiations suggests three axioms to serve as a foundation for theories of bargaining:

Axiom 1: In bargaining situations parties will seek optimal solutions, that is, solutions along the frontier beyond which they are no longer able to improve their positions jointly; in other words, all solutions should lie along the negotiation set.

Axiom 2: In bargaining situations parties will not accept agreements that leave them worse off than the results that they could obtain through unilateral actions; that is, they will not accept solutions that fall below their security levels.

Axiom 3: In a bargaining situation, if the payoffs for the two parties associated with nonagreement are unequal, then the solution will tend to favor the outcome preferred by the party with the lower losses from the failure to agree. (Hopmann, 1996, pp. 49–51)

This theoretical approach is the most widespread point of view on the negotiation process in the area of social sciences in the United States. This point of view offers many benefits that can help theoreticians to model different negotiation processes under different circumstances and even to try to estimate

		Husband	
		boxing	opera
Wife	boxing	1/2	0/0
	opera	0/0	2/1

FIGURE 1.5
Battle of the sexes payoff matrix

their outcomes by using utility-oriented functions. But, at the same time, its overreliance on the actors' rationality and abstractly assumed payoff structures limit the theoretical usefulness of this perspective.

The Psychological Point of View

The next perspective represents the *psychological point of view*. It includes and is based on the elements of the *behavioral analysis* approach. In this approach "the terms of analysis used are the personalities of the negotiators, either directly or in interaction. . . . At whatever level, this school of analysis responds to a common belief about negotiation—that 'it all depends on the personalities of the negotiators'" (Zartman, 1989, p. 247).

In general, according to the psychological point of view, any negotiation "can be viewed as a set of personal and interpersonal dynamics that result in outcomes of varying acceptability to the participants" (Spector, 1978, p. 55). One of the main proponents of this approach believes that "Personality factors are likely to influence the toughness or softness of positions that are taken, the strength of commitment to these positions, strategy choice, opening tactics, the potential for compromise and concessions, and the personal need for goal maximization. . . . Perceptions of threat, for instance, may cause some negotiators to retreat to more cautious positions, while others might become more aggressive and hard-nosed" (Spector, 1978, p. 57).

The outcome of the negotiations is determined by:

(1) the individual personality needs of negotiators;
(2) the personality compatibility among negotiators representing opposing parties;
(3) negotiator perceptions and expectations of the opponent—his strengths and weaknesses, his intentions and goals, and his commitments to positions; and
(4) persuasive mechanisms employed to modify the bargaining positions and values of the opponent to achieve a more favorable convergence of interests. (Spector, 1978, pp. 55–56)

Quite a few empirical studies have been completed in this area and it turned out that the above mentioned factors are not always obvious but still may be important. For example, a set of dyadic-negotiation laboratory experiments showed that:

(1) Highly cooperative bargainers who agreed to *share their payoff* with the other side were motivated by self-oriented needs for social approval

and emotional support rather than outgoing needs for cooperation and friendship.

(2) Altruistic bargainers who *transferred payoff* that could have been theirs to the opposing side were motivated by defeatist and harm-approaching needs.

(3) Bargainers who *bluffed and deceived* were motivated by needs for play, seduction, cleverness, and exhibitionism.

(4) Hostile bargainers who employed elements of *coercion* were motivated by the mirror image hostility of their opponents. (Spector, 1978, p. 65)

As we will later see in one of the case studies, such personal qualities as vanity and consequently a self-oriented need for social approval did play a tremendous role in determining the outcome of a very complex and long-term set of international negotiations.

Learning Theory

The idea of negotiation as a *learning process* comes from the field of clinical psychiatry. It was championed by Professor John Gross, who worked for a long time in the area of mental health care.

According to this point of view, perceptions are very important for every negotiation process. "Negotiation is a matter of manipulating perceptions, in a number of different ways" (Zartman, 1984, p. 5). First of all, it is necessary to bring together the perceptions of both sides. The "second aspect of manipulating perceptions concerns the parameters of vision of the two parties. Negotiation does not involve only an exchange of offers and concessions to make the offers finally fit together. Offers are measured against two other notions: expectations of an outcome, and estimates of an outcome without agreement (security points)" (Zartman, 1984, p. 5). By comparing these two points of reference people adjust their perception points: "If expectations are high, a given offer will be less acceptable than if expectations are lower. But this means that one way of making an offer more acceptable is to lower the other party's expectations, if one does not want to improve the offer" (Zartman, 1984, p. 5).

"A third aspect of manipulating perceptions concerns the frills and feelings that surround the parties' vision. If parties were machines, the calculation of results would be quicker and coldly scientific. But human beings are doing the negotiating, which means that they are inefficient because they are unsure of their information and because their feelings get in the way" (Zartman, 1984, p. 6).

Bargaining strategies mostly depend on the parties' perceptions of the opponents' position, values, views, and expectations. As the parties negotiate, their strategies and expectations change according to what they have learned about each other. This adjustment process is the main way of finding a mutually accepted solution to a common problem. Besides that, each negotiator learns not only about the opponent but also about him or herself. Often, people find out that a certain outcome is not as favorable as they expected because either circumstances or their perceptions have changed.

On a larger scale, the concept of *moral-practical learning* is interesting and important:

> Moral-practical learning refers to the process of recognizing the injustice of many of the social and political barriers to involvement in open dialogue, and to the practice of questioning the rituals of exclusion which prevent the features of *communicative action* from being more widely accepted. . . . Moral practical learning refers to the development of more advanced tests of the legitimacy of social principles and political arrangements. (Linklater, 1998, pp. 120–21)

The notion of *communicative action* lies at the heart of the whole moral-practical learning process. This concept puts the learning process theory of negotiations into a larger communication perspective:

> human subjects make claims about the truth, rightfulness, sincerity and intelligibility of their views whenever they are involved in an attempt to arrive at an understanding with each other. A commitment to be guided by the unforced force of the better argument is made whenever subjects bring their respective views before the tribunal of open discussion and explore the prospects for an inter-subjective consensus. . . . they [features of communication] arise whenever human beings cooperate to reach an understanding. (Linklater, 1998, pp. 119–20)

In this context, not only learning but also *unlearning* processes can be relevant: "Human subjects can unlearn the moral relevance of political boundaries and national differences, and learn to cooperate with outsiders in creating new communities of discourse which are authorized to resolve disputes peacefully" (Linklater, 1998, p. 119). This unlearning process is definitely important when people unlearn the barriers that impede progress during a negotiation process.

The speed with which this learning process goes on—the learning rate—may be quite important. Gross (1978) makes the following conclusions:

> If a party's learning rate is high, for whatever reason, the duration of the negotiation will be reduced.
> If a party's learning rate is high, for whatever reason, that party will receive a smaller payoff at settlement time than he would otherwise.

There is a central tendency in the bargaining process which reduces any asymmetries in the parties' expectations which are not reflections of differences in learning rates, utility functions, or in the availability of means for altering the outcome through the use of force. (p. 47)

As we will see, learning theory, with its emphasis on values, views, expectations, and communicative actions, provides a rich theoretical ground for the communication theory of negotiations.

This theory was often applied to many real world noninternational communication problems such as, for example, labor disputes and negotiations. It was often used to explore circumstances in which two leaders had to negotiate not only with each other but also with their constituencies. For example, Cross (1978) discusses such labor negotiation practices as *boulwarism*. This term refers to a practice when the employer outlines to the union what it expects the agreement to be and refuses to move from that position unless the union presents previously unknown facts that can alter the employer's position. Unless the administration learns about some new facts or circumstances, they will not adjust their negotiation position. It means that learning lies at the heart of the negotiation process—no learning means no adjusting the negotiation position. This practice was very often characterized as unfair by the union leaders because it "denies to these leaders the opportunity to appear to their constituencies as having squeezed concessions out of reluctant employers, thus resulting in a severe political liability for them" (Cross, 1978, p. 31). In this respect, this point of view is one of the early precursors of the two-level-game theory and definitely represents a very appropriate approach toward international-level negotiations as well.

The Problem-Solving Point of View

Sociological and learning points of view, based on the bargaining mechanisms, are often contrasted with the *problem-solving* viewpoint.

For the bargaining paradigm, indicators of flexibility include concession rates, initiation of new proposals, and other soft behaviors. For the problem-solving perspective, flexibility is usually indicated by a search for better, mutually beneficial solutions to problems that satisfy the needs, identities, and interests of all parties. . . . Most research tends to reveal that problem solving produces greater flexibility and more frequent, efficient, equitable, and durable agreements than bargaining does. (Hopmann, 1995, p. 24)

Hopmann (1996) believes that the whole field of the negotiation theory in the 1990s "has moved beyond bargaining theory toward an approach that emphasizes the central role of integrative problem solving . . . " (p. 76). The same author also writes that the bargaining approach has been criticized for several reasons. Firstly, bargaining is a single continuum model while most issues are complex and multidimensional. Secondly, bargaining overstates conflictual elements of negotiations. Finally, "the dynamics are largely restricted to making initial offers, making concessions and retractions . . . " and this point of view "seem overly stylized and simplistic" (Hopmann, 1996, p. 76). Hopmann (1996) describes the problem-solving perspective in the following way:

> In traditional bargaining, negotiators usually sit across the negotiating table, facing one another from opposite sides as adversaries. In integrative or problem-solving negotiations, the problem itself is the adversary; therefore, the table may be visualized as one in which both negotiating teams sit on the same side and face the problem head on. Thus, rather than confronting one another, they confront together the problem that creates difficulties for both sides. (p. 77)

According to this point of view, each negotiation process goes through three phases: (1) diagnosis; (2) formula construction; and (3) agreement on details. During the first phase, the sides try to set agenda for attacking the problem and find out the problem's structure. During the second phase, the sides can try to construct agreement formula using one of two broad techniques: "(1) they may try to redefine the issues under negotiation . . . ; or (2) they may engage in creative problem solving or brainstorming, in which they try to create new solutions through a process of trying to work the issue through together" (Hopmann, 1996, p. 80).

The issue redefinition process can go in two directions. The first of them is called *issues disaggregation* and is used when "comprehensive agreement seems to be blocked by some important component, in which case the negotiators may decide to disaggregate the issue and seek agreement only on those components of the problem that are not hopelessly blocked" (Hopmann, 1996, p. 81). The second approach is called *issue aggregation* "in which subissues are linked together to create package agreements out of components that would be nonnegotiable if treated separately" (Hopmann, 1996, p. 81)

The creative problem solving approach is likely to be used when "previous conceptualizations of the problem are discarded and when the parties actually work together to define problem in a new light" (Hopmann, 1996, p. 84). This process starts with determination of the side's interests, that is, each party makes sure that it understands the opponent's as well as its own interests. "The emphasis in this approach is for each party to try to view the problem from the perspective of the other and try to find solutions that meet the other's concerns. In this sense, they try to find the valid points in the positions of the other party, develop empathy, and then seek solutions that seem to incorporate the interests of the other. . . . The essence of this approach is one of converting the negotiation from a zero-sum to a non-zero-sum game" (Hopmann, 1996, p. 89).

Hopmann (1996) illustrates this approach by a little parable about two women who are arguing over the same orange that both want to use:

> They first consider dividing the orange in half, but that way both lose; neither will have enough orange to meet their needs. They begin to discuss their reasons for wanting the orange: one wants to make orange juice and the other wants to make orange marmalade. This discussion of their basic interests reveals an obvious mutually beneficial solution. Instead of cutting the orange in half, they peel it; the entire peel goes to the woman who wants to make marmalade, whereas the entire interior goes to the woman who wants to make orange juice. With this division, they are both satisfied; indeed, each one got as much as if she had obtained the entire orange for herself. (p. 89)

A real world example of such a kind of decision would be the accord signed in 1978 in Camp David, when the Sinai was entirely given to Egypt but, at the same time, was completely demilitarized. Both sides got everything they wanted: Egypt, territorial integrity; Israel, security. It was much better than just splitting the Sinai territory in half.

In short, the problem-solving approach is creative and, therefore, is not simple and obvious. But it is worth the effort because it produces better and more durable solutions.

The Joint Decision-making Process Point of View

Negotiation as a *joint decision-making process* is another point of view widely represented in the scholarly literature. This literature says that there are three major modes of social decision-making. The first is usually called *coalition*— "the process of making a choice by numerical aggregation, involving voting majorities, rules of collective choice, and legislation. Decision by coalition is a 0-sum process in that one side wins and the other loses. . . . There are many parties, fixed values, and a twofold choice (yes or no) on any given proposal" (Zartman, 1978, p. 69). The second mode is called *judification*. This mode stipulates "a hierarchical process, during which parties plead before a single judge or executive who aggregates conflicting values and interests into a single decision that may or may not favor one of the parties more than the other(s). It is hard to conceive of decision-making by a single judging individual in terms of sums; there is one deciding party, variable values which are combined into a decision, and one-fold choice on any given subject . . . " (Zartman, 1978, pp. 69–70). Besides that, the judge is free to come up with his or her own decision on the subject freely combining elements of all the involved sides' positions. That is his or her vote by itself is a decision.

And finally, the third mode of social decision-making is *negotiation*. This mode is different from the previous two:

> It is a *positive-sum* exercise, since by definition both parties prefer the agreed outcome to the status quo (i.e., to no agreement). . . . Both sides come off better in the agreement than in the absence of the agreement, or else they would not agree. . . . There are *fixed parties* and *flexible values*; a decision is made by *changing the parties' evaluation* of their values in such a way as to be able to combine them into a single package, by persuasion, coercion, or force. In the process, the parties exercise a *threefold choice* (yes, no, maybe or keep it on talking). Choice is neither numerical . . . nor hierarchical. . . . (Zartman, 1978, p. 70)

The process of a joint decision-making negotiation goes "through a search for a single formula satisfactory to both sides, followed by a further search for the implementation of this formula through the specification of the details necessary to affect the agreement" (Zartman, 1978, p. 80).

In general this perspective is different from, let's say, the problem-solving approach because the former does not usually contain the element of creativity as the latter does. The joint decision-making paradigm assumes the business type of approach to the problem. The decision is made taking into account structural variables of the negotiation environment, bureaucratic standard operation procedures (SOPs), and cost-benefit analysis. But at the same time it is not as strict as the strategic choice model and allows for such factors as actors' bounded rationality, human information processing flaws, emotional and ideological aspects, and some other limiting factors.

This point of view on the negotiation process will be covered in greater detail below—when Allison's *rational actor*, *organizational process*, and *governmental politics* models of the decision-making process are presented.

Negotiations as Dual Responsiveness Theory

The last theory presented in this section is probably the most important for the purpose of this study. It was offered by Daniel Druckman ten years before Putnam's two-level-game theory—in 1978—and was the direct precursor of that theory. The *negotiations as dual responsiveness* theory addresses the same idea as Putnam's theory, that there are "two types of functions in negotiations: monitoring the other side for evidence of movement and monitoring one's own side for evidence of preferences" (Druckman, 1978, p. 87). It means that there are two general sets of functions every negotiator carries out—*negotiator as bargainer* and *negotiator as representative.* "The negotiator-as-bargainer model assumes responsiveness between opposite-number negotiators.... The negotiator as representative model assumes responsiveness between the negotiator and his constituents" (Druckman, 1978, p. 87).

The behavior of a negotiator when he or she acts as bargainer "can be a direct calculated response to the other's concessions, it can be based on both one's own previous concessions and the other's concessions, or it can be a more complex function of expectations and evaluations.... A negotiator's responses are mediated by expectations that are adjusted through the course of the conference. Information-processing can be presented as a sequence of steps involving the *formation* of, *evaluation* of, and *adjustment* of expectations" (Druckman, 1978, p. 109).

The negotiator-as-representative model is:

> a utility model where the negotiator attempts to balance n-components of value in the process of building a package. He is concerned with maximizing the value of the package in terms of both his own and his agency's priorities. This is essentially a weighting process. The cognitive processes involved consist of defining and ordering the various components of the package and ascertaining his agency's preferences for this ordering.... However, as the number of components increase and as his agency's positions diverge from his own, the information-processing requirements become rather complex. (Druckman, 1978, pp. 109–110)

As we will see, this theory represents the basis for the two-level-game theory. But Druckman was not the only one who saw that bargaining with one's own constituencies played an important role. In 1984 Thomas Colosi conceptually divided all the negotiations into two categories—horizontal (between parties) and vertical (within one's party)—and wrote, "A team is rarely independent of a larger constituency. It is at the negotiating table because it has been sent there to accomplish something. In the context of private sector labor negotiation, for example, management's vertical hierarchy is the company's leadership; for the union's bargaining committee, it is the international union and, most times, ultimately the membership who must vote to decide on the proposed contract" (p. 18).

Recently, this two-level approach was developed even further by challenging the above described *bargainer-representative* point of view. In 1995, Dean Pruitt wrote that thinking about negotiations between organizations "has been dominated by a simplistic model of communication structure: the constituent-representative model" (Pruitt, 1995, p. 38). Instead, he offered the *branching chain* model. His model is depicted on Figure 1.6.

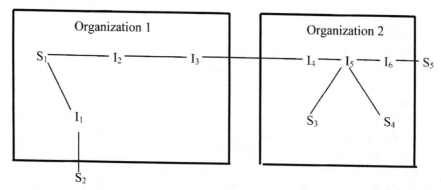

FIGURE 1.6
Pruitt's model of interorganizational negotiations

The intermediaries are shown by the letter I. There are also stakeholders at the ends of the branches on both sides of the chain, who are represented by letter S. Though they may not always recognize it, the job of the intermediaries is to reconcile the interests of as many of the important stakeholders as possible. This means that *bilateral* negotiation is usually better understood as *multilateral* negotiation. . . . Normal communication is from person to person along the chain, with intermediaries presenting the views of the parties on both sides of them to each other. (Pruitt, 1995, pp. 39–40)

An important question here is: What do intermediaries exist for? Why isn't it possible to establish the direct communication between the stakeholders? Pruitt says that there are two main answers to these questions: "First, intermediaries become involved because stakeholders usually do not have sufficient knowledge, access, or resources to deal directly with each other. . . . Second, intermediaries can become involved because of the need to introduce *extraneous policy considerations* into most decisions. . . . Many of the policies introduced by intermediaries reflect the interests of stakeholders outside the primary chain" (Pruitt, 1995, pp. 39–41).

The next question is: Does this long chain distort some information? Are these intermediaries actually weak links of this chain? Pruitt says that there are several answers to these questions:

One answer to these questions lies in the fact that the issues are usually *important* to the participants. Hence they are trying to influence thinking and action down the line rather than simply passing along what they have heard. This motivates them to check to be sure that their messages are transmitted accurately and taken seriously. . . . A second answer lies in the availability of *alternative channels* of communication at most junctures in the chain. . . . A third answer lies in *meetings* that often occur between people from several points along the chain. Such meetings reduce reliance on intermediaries and, hence, help to solve the problem of weak links. (Pruitt, 1995, p. 42)

Consequently, according to this theory, there is a certain set of circumstances that produce successful agreements: "Success is partly a function of the *quality of the relationships* between people who are adjacent to each other along the communication chain. . . . Success is a function of *optimal chain length*. . . . Success is a function of *organizational flexibility*—the availability of alternative channels of communication and the capacity to hold large meetings that cut across significant organizational boundaries" (Pruitt, 1995, pp. 43–44).

Since countries are just big organizations what Colosi (1984) and Pruitt (1995) are talking about is 100 percent applicable to international negotiations. Actually Druckman (1978) wrote that "If the negotiator-as-bargainer model is of the genre referred to as *unitary-rational actor models*, then the negotiator-as-representative model is cut from the class of models referred to as *bureaucratic (governmental) politics*. Whereas the former emphasizes international interactions, the latter focuses on intranational interactions. Together these two types of activities constitute international negotiation" (p. 99).

In short, this point of view offers another suggestion that the negotiation process is a much more complex phenomenon than simply a direct interaction between two or more negotiators. This is because it also involves constituents (or stakeholders) and some structure of relationships within and between different organizations.

Intra-entity Level Interactions

So far this chapter has explored what may be called inter-entity negotiations—that is, interactions between two or more separate organizations, countries, or institutions. But the discussion in the previous section has pointed out that intra-entity interactions—within a certain organization, country, or institution—also matter. These dynamics also have an influence on the negotiation process. That is why it is interesting and may be important to know what kind of interactions, negotiations, and deals occur at the intra-entity level in general. It may help to guide analysis of intra-entity dynamics later in this work.

One way to answer this question is to think about the types of interactions, negotiations, and deals going on in the American Congress. There are several techniques that are usually used to reach an agreement in the Congress that provide useful beginning examples.

Logrolling is a very interesting and important technique of intra-entity interactions. This technique is best described in the following way: "The standard

tactic for a proponent of a public works project is to tell a senator or representative, 'Look, you have a dam in this bill; therefore, you will support the entire
bill. If you don't we'll drop your dam.' The idea is to get the necessary numbers
together so that, regardless of some lemons in the package, everyone who has
a piece of the action will support the entire package. . . . That is logrolling in its
purest form, an art of negotiation" (Derwinski, 1984, p. 10).

A form of logrolling is *coalition-building*. For example, during some international negotiations American counterparts demand that the United States
stop subsidizing its agricultural sector. And they rarely achieve anything.
American farmers represent just 4 percent of the U.S. population. How do
they manage to interact with each other in such a way that their interests are
always protected? Derwinski (1984) describes the process of *coalition-building*
within the United States that later affects the American position at the international level:

> The agriculture people from North Carolina, where agriculture means tobacco,
> discuss their problems with the man representing the rice growers in Arkansas
> or California. The sugar beet growers in Minnesota and sugar cane interests in
> Louisiana and Hawaii and the wheat and corn and soybean and other producers
> just gather together in one big happy family to be sure that there is a subsidy for
> every commodity. They put those numbers together again so that they have at
> least 218 supporters in the House and 51 in the Senate. [Voting rule thresholds]
> A supporter of tobacco subsidy automatically becomes a supporter of the wheat
> subsidy, or the sugar quota, or the soybean subsidy, or whatever else follows. . . .
> The greatest practitioners of this kind of negotiation are the heavily subsidized
> dairy industry interests. You will not find a representative of the dairy industry
> who is not an ardent supporter of the tobacco subsidy. (p. 11)

The next important kind of interaction in the Congress is *staff-level negotiations*. This type of interaction helps to keep senators and representatives
free from any kind of obligations: "One of the inherent problems is that one
cannot tell from talking to a senator's assistant if, in fact, the senator is following the issue at all. The assistant may be striking out on his own. So when
you hear within the State Department that a particular senator favors this or
that legislation or policy, you are never sure that the report is accurate" (Derwinski, 1984, p. 12). This is exactly what is necessary to give the senator some
political position-forming leeway and, in case of a problem, to give him or
her an opportunity to deny that she or he ever supported anything. That is
why in such a type of intra-entity interactions "One of the tricks is to bypass
the staff to get to the member" (Derwinski, 1984, p. 12). This approach also
helps to keep a certain type of negotiations at a low profile if publicity is not
desired.

These internal dynamics are so important that they affect the entire rhythm of political activities in the United States and at the international level. For example, it makes sense to expect major international talks initiatives introduced and major international agreements signed in even-numbered years but real international negotiation progress must be made during odd-numbered years. It is so because "Even-numbered years are political years, election years, in which compromise becomes much more difficult. The general rule followed in Congress is to deal with all the difficult issues in the odd-numbered years and to take on just the bare bones items in the even-numbered years" (Derwinski, 1984, p. 12).

The negotiation theories described above provided rich theoretical material for the approach that emphasizes the process of communication in negotiations—the cognitive perspective. This perspective was a reaction to the fact that the communication process itself remained the most ignored aspect of the negotiation theory (Jonsson, 1989, p. 258). Theorists who conceptualized the communication theory of negotiation borrowed some concepts from some theories (such as the learning theory) and disagreed with others. But nevertheless, the cognitive perspective described below has a very distinctive character and occupies a very special niche in the area of negotiation theory.

A Communication or Cognitive Perspective on the Negotiation Process

The basis for the communication approach to the negotiation process was shaped by Robert Jervis. In his books *The Logic of Images in International Relations* (1970) and *Perception and Misperception in International Politics* (1976), Jervis laid down the foundation for a future communication theory of negotiation. Later on, many other scholars made their contributions to this point of view. In the late 1980s and early 1990s, Christer Jonsson summarized all the previous research in this area in a sound theoretical perspective that is mostly known under the umbrella term of the *cognitive theory*. Indeed, this is a group of theories unified by one common factor—all of them assume that communication is the basis for the negotiation process. It may seem strange, but proponents of other approaches mostly disregarded communication elements in the negotiation process. "Perhaps the most neglected aspect of bargaining has been the role of various kinds of communication" (Jonsson, 1989, p. 258).

In the new perspective, communication becomes a pivotal aspect of any negotiation process because, in this view, "bargaining and negotiation are subclasses of social communication" and are defined as "back-and-forth communication designed to reach an agreement when you and the other side have some interests that are shared and others that are opposed" (Jonsson, 1989, p. 259; see also Fisher and Ury, 1983, p. 33). Jonsson (1990) argues, "the human capacity to acquire, reveal and conceal information then becomes crucial and creates the problem of interpretation associated with communication" (p. 3). This information-interpretation connection lies at the very heart of the communication view of the negotiation process.

As was indicated above, other scholars analyzed negotiations mostly from the game theoretic point of view. In this view, negotiation is seen as "the manipulation of the information of others in the interest of improving the outcome for one's self under conditions of strategic interaction" (Young, 1975, p. 304). Jonsson (1990) calls it *manipulative* (p. 4) approach to the negotiation process. And the game theoretic viewpoint has some other conceptual problems: "Game theory has certain shortcomings as an analytical tool. It is essentially static in nature; it tends to homogenize actors; it 'blackboxes' the information-processing aspects of bargaining; and it envisages unitary and perfectly rational actors" (Jonsson, 1990, p. 3).

That is why, in order to solve those problems, Jonsson (1990) suggests *cognitive* approach to the negotiation process.

> The cognitive perspective, finally, focuses on the belief systems of the bargaining actors. . . . Each actor comes to the bargaining process with a set of beliefs and expectations about himself, the adversary and the bargaining issue, based on previous experiences. As soon as the exchange begins, each actor is in a position to test and either validate or adjust his initial beliefs. . . . The cognitive perspective emphasizes the obstacles to change in bargaining. First, *incompatible beliefs* frequently complicate and aggravate international bargaining. Second, belief systems tend to be *resistant to change.* (p. 5)

This change can be achieved only through the exchange and processing of new information. That is why the information-processing mechanisms are extremely important for the cognitive approach and have to be explored deeper. The following two quotations show why information is so important for the negotiation process. Walton and McKersie (1965) wrote, "When information is low, the result will be a less adequate definition of the problem; fewer alternatives will be generated; and the potential consequences of these alternatives will be less explored. . . . When the information is relatively low, the parties will produce relatively low-grade solutions" (p. 140). Rubin and Brown (1975) wrote, "To the extent that the other party knows both what the first wants as well as the least that he will accept, he [the other] will be able to develop a more effective, more precise bargaining position than would be possible in the absence of this information" (p. 14).

The outcome of the information-processing process, however, depends on how information is perceived. This perception is heavily affected by the social context surrounding negotiations. "*Social context* here refers to the broad constellation of social factors in negotiations" (Thompson, Peterson, and Kray, 1995, p. 7). For example, such factors may include negotiation party configuration (dyad or more), personal relationships between negotiators, constituencies behind each negotiator. These are the simplest elements of a bargaining situation. Other groups of factors are more complex because they deal with knowledge, norms, and communication.

Knowledge refers to information the sides have about each other. "This information may concern another person's preference structure (preferences and priorities), alternatives to agreement, and strategies. . . . Information about other parties may be based on previous experience, reputation, or direct disclosure. In addition to such explicit forms of information, negotiators may have implicit information about parties derived from stereotypes and role and group schemata" (Thompson, Peterson, and Kray, 1995, pp. 8–9).

Social norms is another factor that affects the perception of information. In general social norms are defined as "the beliefs held by members of a particular culture, organization, group, or institution that define acceptable and unacceptable behavior" (Thompson, Peterson, and Kray, 1995, p. 9; see also Bettenhausen and Murnighan, 1985). There are several types of norms that work during every negotiation process:

> *Social interaction* norms prescribe appropriate behavior in social interactions, such as politeness rituals, reciprocity in disclosure, and turn taking. *Decision-making* norms prescribe how decisions should be reached by groups (e.g., majority rule, consensus). *Negotiation* norms prescribe appropriate behavior and the conduct of bargaining (e.g., agendas, reciprocity, good faith bargaining, symmetric concessions . . .) and appropriate outcomes (e.g., focal points, compromises . . .). (Thompson, Peterson, and Kray, 1995, p. 9)

The final set of factors deals with *communicative* aspect of negotiations, that is, with mechanisms by which the parties interact—face-to-face, correspondence, telephone, e-mail, special messengers. "Different forms of communication may affect the way information is perceived, remembered, and acted upon" (Thompson, Peterson, and Kray, 1995, p. 9).

All the above factors affect information processing. This process, in turn, can be subdivided into five major subprocesses—information distribution, encoding, representation, retrieval, and judgment (Thompson, Peterson, and Kray, 1995).

In terms of the first factor (*information distribution*), the decision-relevant information that each of the negotiation parties has, can be divided into two types—*shared* and *unshared.* "*Shared information* is held by all members of the group; *unshared information* is held by only one group member. Information may also be partly shared, held by some percentage of the group members" (Thompson, Peterson, and Kray, 1995, p. 10). These notions are very important because group members have a tendency to discuss shared information more than unshared, and this effect is exacerbated as group size increases. Besides that, shared information is given greater weight in group decision making than unshared information. Within each party, people are likely to concentrate on shared information rather than unshared. On the other hand, between the parties discussion is likely to concentrate on unshared information rather than shared. But ultimately, social norms and strategic considerations determine the patterns of information sharing (Thompson, Peterson, and Kray, 1995).

Encoding is another subprocess which refers "to how negotiators evaluate and interpret information" (Thompson, Peterson, and Kray, 1995, p. 13). This concept is important because people often interpret information in a manner that fits their expectations or they may simply ignore or discard a certain piece of information because it is inconsistent with their beliefs and expectations. Each person's perspective is important here. For example, the other party's proposals always seem to have a catch hidden in them. Besides that, ego-involvement, that is how much a negotiator cares about particular situation or issue, will affect information processing. At the least, the amount of effort to find a solution definitely depends on it. There are also several social mechanisms that help to code information. A person can use the *structural balance principle.* This is used when people do not have enough information about the other party and use simple structural or relational inferences to make conclusions. If evaluation is based on stereotypes of category-based information, this mechanism is called *role-based inference. Correspondent inference process* occurs when people infer unobservable positions and interests on the basis of observable facts. Finally, *individualized target impressions* are based on particular characteristics of a person or a group of people the judgment is made about (Thompson, Peterson, and Kray, 1995).

The next subprocess, *representation,* refers to the structuring of information about a concept, event, people, or issue. "Cognitive schemata, or organized relations between attributes, are used to structure information" (Thompson, Peterson, and Kray, 1995, p. 18; see also Fiske and Taylor, 1991). These relations can be organized in forms of *implicit theories* (internal, personal theories people create to evaluate a certain situation); *judgment tasks* (a set of judgments about negotiations, their parties, self, utilities, outcome, procedures, etc.); or *conflict schemata* (a series of win/lose statements that are supposed to reflect a certain negotiation situation) (Thompson, Peterson, and Kray, 1995).

The subprocess of *retrieval* refers to the acquisition of previously stored information and deals with such aspects as memory organization, storage capacity, and retrieval system (Thompson, Peterson, and Kray, 1995).

"The goal of information processing is the formation of judgments that can be used to guide behavior" (Thompson, Peterson, and Kray, 1995, p. 27). That is why the last subprocess is called *judgment*. It is the most problematic area in any negotiation process. Judgment errors concerning other party's preferences, payoffs, positions, opinions, beliefs, account for the largest number of negotiation failures. One of the big problems here is judgment coordination. Even people with the same interests and beliefs can make different judgments. That is why open communication between all the group members is important. Communication is the key to the whole process.

All kinds of communication serve as the basis for the cognitive theory of negotiation. The basic propositions of this theory are that "Social communication involves the transmission of messages to which certain meanings are attached. These messages can be either verbal or nonverbal. . . . In fact, both behavior and nonbehavior may constitute messages, especially in a negotiation setting" (Jonsson, 1989, p. 259). It is also interesting that the verbal components in a negotiation process, like in any other normal person-to-person conversation, can carry actually less than 35 percent of the social meaning. "Activity or inactivity, words or silence, all have message value: they influence others and these others, in turn, cannot *not* respond to these communications and are thus themselves communicating" (Simons, 1976, p. 50). Actually, "we may refer to *communication* in bargaining situations whenever one actor displays behavior that is perceived and interpreted by another, whether or not it is spoken or intended or even within the actor's conscious awareness" (Jonsson, 1990, p. 10; se also Condon and Youself, 1975, p. 2). That is why such a concept as *tacit bargaining* is important. It is a process "in which adversaries watch and interpret each other's behavior, each aware that his own actions are being interpreted and anticipated, each acting with a view to the expectations that he creates" (Jonsson, 1989, p. 259; see also Johnson, 1974, p. 74). All the above leads to so-called *assumption of intentionality*, that is, the negotiation parties believe that whatever message they perceive in actions or words of another party is the intentional message that party tries to convey.

Finally, in any negotiation situation, there is one predominant kind of communication—persuasion—designed to influence others by modifying their behaviors, beliefs, and attitudes. "Negotiation, then, can be seen as mutual persuasion attempts" (Jonsson, 1990, p. 11).

The traditional approach to the study of communication focuses on the *transmission of messages*. In this point of view, messages move from point A to point B. There are two main concerns of this model: the efficiency of the channels of communication and the accuracy with which messages reach the point of their final destination. "It sees communication as a process by which one person affects the behavior or state of mind of another" (Fiske, 1982, p. 2). If the effect differs from the intended one, this is a communication failure. The main problem in this case is to find the stage of the process where that failure occurred. "This approach highlights the process of exchanging messages while treating the *meaning* of these messages as given. . . . The speaker puts ideas/objects into words/containers and sends them to a hearer who takes the ideas/objects out of the words/containers" (Jonsson, 1990, p. 12; see also Lakoff and Johnson, 1980, p. 10).

On the other hand, there is another school in communication studies. This school is often called *constructivist* and is mostly concerned with the production and exchange of meaning. "Its adherents are concerned with how messages interact with people in order to produce meaning. They see *signification* as an active process and use verbs like 'create', 'generate' or 'negotiate' to refer to this process. In contrast to the traditional approach, this school does not view meaning as an absolute static concept neatly parceled up in the text itself. . . . To the constructivists, communication processes are not transmission of messages but social interaction" (Jonsson, 1990, p. 13; see also Fiske, 1982).

By now "the bulk of traditional bargaining studies adheres to the nonconstructivist view of communication" (Jonsson, 1990, p. 14). The proponents of the communication theory of negotiations believe that this approach is too mechanistic and simplistic, and that it does not uncover all or even main processes and mechanisms of the negotiation process. That is why they base their approach on the constructivist views and the cognitive model of information processing.

The new negotiation theory, a cognitive one, is based on two cognitive approaches to communication—semiotics and attribution theory.

"Semiotics is the study of *signs* and the way they acquire meaning" (Jonsson, 1990, p. 17). These signs are also often called signals. "Signaling is as essential to diplomacy as to a busy airport. The only difference is that there is more scope for ambiguity in diplomatic signaling" (Jonsson, 1990, p. 17). The main problem here is to reduce this ambiguity and uncover the meaning of each signal—meanings that can be deeply rooted in cultural or social traditions of the signal source.

The process through which a sign or a signal receives its meaning is called *signification* and is the main focus of the attribution theory. In general, classic cognitive psychology considers any communication process, including negotiation, as a sender-receiver linear model. But, in the recent decades, this basic assumption has been challenged by scholars who contend that a human being does not simply respond to stimuli but actively shapes his or her communication environment. Every person very selectively searches for, perceives, remembers, and responds to information. The second basic assumption of the classic cognitive psychology point of view is that the human being is a consistency seeker. But other scholars present people as problem solvers or naive scientists. "Where cognitive consistency theorists assume that people see what they expect to see by assimilating incoming information to pre-existing images and interpreting new information in such a way as to maintain or increase balance, attribution theorists are concerned with the individuals' attempts to comprehend the cause of behavior and assume that spontaneous thought follows a systematic course that is roughly congruent with scientific inquiry" (Jonsson, 1989, p. 262). This cause-effect systematic approach lies in the basis of the attribution theory.

There are two other theoretical communication traditions that can be seen as attempts at linking language with attribution and semiotics—symbolic interactionism and social constructionism:

> Attribution theory and symbolic interactionism share an interest in the broad question of how persons attain a subjective understanding of their social environment. The two approaches also share the premise that individual behavior is guided by the subjective construction of reality rather than by the objective properties of external stimuli. . . . Social constructivism eschews the empiricist account of scientific knowledge and seeks for an alternative metatheory. . . . Knowledge is seen not as something people possess somewhere in their heads but as something people do together, and languages are seen as essentially shared activities. . . . Symbolic interactionism and social constructionism join semiotics in viewing signification as a *collective* phenomenon, whereas attribution theory studies signification at the *individual* level. Yet these two perspectives are not necessarily mutually exclusive. A metaphor may be helpful: if we think of the human mind as a computer . . . the heuristics described by attribution theory may be seen as the hardware, and the culturally conditioned codes discussed by semiotics and discourse analysis as the software. (Jonsson, 1990, pp. 27–29)

As the cognitive theory of negotiation states, the main problem during every negotiation is to correctly understand each other's signs and signals and, consequently, to correctly derive from them each other's intentions, ideas, and beliefs. If an understanding is found, the parties will be able to agree. Without it, every negotiation is doomed to failure. There are four main problems that arise during every negotiation and prevent the parties from finding mutual understanding. They are the problems of meaning, categorization, explanation, and credibility. And all these problems, in turn, are rooted in much larger cognitive, cultural, and linguistic issues.

The problem of meaning deals with two questions: "How, then, do ambiguous signals acquire meaning? And how can shared meaning—the essence of communication—be achieved? These questions are basic to an understanding of international bargaining. They are also questions which have been addressed by cognitive theorists and semioticians alike" (Jonsson, 1990, p. 33).

In order to derive meaning from a signal, every person has to process information coming from the signal source. Individuals process information through preexisting structures that scientists tend to label as the structures of beliefs. An incoming signal is matched against these belief structures and either falls within their limits or not. If the signal does not fit the belief structure, a certain set of beliefs should be changed. But, as was mentioned above, human beliefs are resistant to change. Jervis (1976) identified several psychological mechanisms that tend to make beliefs resistant to change:

> The actor may (1) fail to see that new information might contradict his beliefs; (2) see the information as discrepant but reject its validity; (3) discredit the source of discrepant information; (4) admit puzzlement with new information; (5) engage in bolstering—seeking new information to support initial beliefs; (6) engage in undermining—adducing additional elements to weaken discrepant information; (7) engage in differentiation—splitting the object by sloughing off the parts that are causing attitudinal conflict; and/or (8) invoke transcendence— the opposite mechanism from differentiation, where elements, instead of being split down, are built up and combined into larger units. (pp. 291–96)

This kind of the belief preservance effect may also be the result of so-called motivational bias or emotional commitment to certain beliefs. But, in general, it can occur even without such a kind of commitment, "because (a) people tend to seek out, recall, and interpret evidence in a manner that sustains beliefs, (b) they readily invent causal explanations of initial evidence in which they then place too much confidence, (c) they act upon their beliefs in a way that makes them self-confirming" (Jonsson, 1990, p. 34; see also Nisbett and Ross, 1980, p. 192). This belief preservance mechanism applies not only to individuals but also to collective actors.

Another problem of meaning is the metaphorical nature of communication in general and language in particular. "Linguistic and cognitive theorists alike have pointed to the metaphorical nature not only of our language use but also of our knowledge structures. . . . In contrast to the nonconstructivist skepticism, constructivists assign an important role to metaphors in both language and thought, . . . " (Jonsson, 1990, pp. 34-35).

In the intercultural context, this problem is especially acute because each culture has its own set of metaphors. And the term *culture* in this particular context does not necessarily mean national culture, it may be, for example, professional culture as well:

Two sets of subcultures seem to condition communication in international negotiations: the national subcultures of the participating states, on the one hand, and a 'negotiator subculture' on the other. The notion that national subcultures produce national 'negotiating styles' has been developed by scholars and practitioners alike. . . . Most signaling in a bargaining context, though not totally idiosyncratic and arbitrary, is less than conventional and iconic. This, in combination with the existence of multiple subcultures, makes the signification process problematic in international negotiations. When interpreted by members of different subcultures who bring different codes to them, signs may produce different meanings. Negotiators, therefore, have to be content with saying both less and more than they mean: less, because their verbal and nonverbal signaling will never immediately convey their meaning; more, because their signaling will always convey messages and involve them in consequences other than those intended. (Jonsson, 1989, p. 261; see also Pocock, 1984)

This general idea gave birth to dozens of books and hundreds of articles on the subject of the cultural effects on the negotiation process. For example, Moran and Stripp (1991) describe national negotiating styles of Japan, China, South Korea, India, USSR, Germany, France, Spain, Nigeria, Mexico, and Brazil. *The ABA Guide to International Business Negotiations* (Silkenat and Aresty, 2000) describes national negotiating styles of Argentina, Australia, Belgium, Bermuda, Brazil, Canada, Chile, People's Republic of China, Czech Republic, France, Germany, Hong Kong, India, Ireland, Italy, Japan, Korea, Netherlands, Pakistan, Poland, Singapore, Spain, Sweden, Taiwan, United Kingdom, and the United States. Another book actually promises to teach you "how to negotiate anything with anyone anywhere around the world" (Acuff, 1993). Certainly, some of these recommendations are based on rather anecdotal grounds while others are the product of serious research.

The next major problem is the problem of categorization. "Categorization is basic to human thought, perception, action and communication. Whenever we see something as a *kind* of thing, we are categorizing. Without the ability to categorize we could not function in our physical and social environment" (Jonsson, 1990, p. 51). Research demonstrated that "once people have applied a particular label to a given object (and thereby applied a specific knowledge structure to it), their subsequent presumptions about the object are apt to owe too much to the label and too little to any actual observations about the unique object" (Nisbett and Ross, 1980, p. 293). These differences in labeling may be very important for dynamics and outcomes of negotiations. "Carefully calibrated signals most often fail to make the desired impression because they are based on distinctions that seem obvious to the sender but to which the receiver is oblivious" (Lebow, 1985, p. 205). According to attribution theory, the process of categorization involves the reliance on so-called *judgment heuristics*, or rules of thumb, which reduce complex inferential tasks to simple judgmental operations, that is, people try to find some resemblance between the current situation and something in their previous life experience. Any vivid information is more likely to be stored and retrieved in case of need. "In the context of international negotiations, this points to a common tendency among statesmen to think in terms of historical analogies. . . . Translated to international negotiators, this implies that certain traumatic events are readily available and therefore tend to condition their interpretation of moves in the bargaining situation at hand" (Jonsson, 1989, p. 263). The use of national or social stereotypes falls within the same domain of categorization problems and represents a great impediment for every intercultural negotiation process.

The next logical step after a signal has been categorized is to try to explain it. That is why the next major communication problem during every negotiation process is the problem of explanation. "Actors in international bargaining are constantly faced with the problem of looking beyond manifest signals and trying to draw inferences about their adversaries. . . . To interpret signals, the actors have to search for causes and motives. Only by assessing the motives underlying the adversary's proposal, can the actor judge whether it represents a concession or a retraction and decide upon his own response" (Jonsson, 1990, p. 63).

At the same time, not all the events and signals need explanation. Stereotyped sequences of events called *scripts* will make events and signals readily comprehensible. "In other words, there are events and actions which do not elicit explanatory *efforts*. In any negotiation, for example, the parties initially demand more than they expect to obtain. This may be considered part of the 'negotiation script' and is not likely to cause surprise or warrant explanation" (Jonsson, 1990, p. 64).

But most signaling in the negotiation process requires explanation. "A prerequisite for successful bargaining and negotiation is that the common interests of the parties ultimately outweigh their divergent interests. Whether they do or not depends in large measure on the way the parties interpret and explain each other's behaviour" (Jonsson, 1990, p. 64). Unfortunately, very often the sides interpret each other's behavior incorrectly because they attribute each other's behavior to the wrong factors. For example, they attribute their own and other people's actions to different causes. Translated to international negotiations, it means "among adversaries the tendency is to explain one's own 'good' behavior as well as the adversary's 'bad' behavior in dispositional terms. Conversely, 'bad' behavior of one's own side and 'good' behavior by the other are attributed to situational factors. In brief, 'I am essentially good, but am occasionally forced by circumstances to behave badly, whereas you are bad but are occasionally forced by circumstances to behave well' " (Jonsson, 1989,

p. 263). This kind of misinterpretation is called the *fundamental error of attribution*. The same kind of error is made when the parties take credit for all the successes and deny responsibility for failures, regardless of the true nature of the situation. "This kind of bias makes bargaining actors insensitive to how their own signaling feeds into the other side's internal bargaining process" (Jonsson, 1990, p. 64).

Another kind of explanation error is called *punctuation*, which is "instances where two people have different perceptions regarding which act in a sequence is stimulus and which is response" (Sillars, 1981, p. 280). For example:

> In March 1946 the Soviet refusal to withdraw their troops from northern Iran, as they had agreed to do by treaty, caused an American-Soviet crisis. President Truman attributed the eventual Soviet withdrawal to American diplomatic protests (which he wrongly characterized as an 'ultimatum'). In reality, the Soviet withdrawal was the payoff for an Iranian oil concession. (Jonsson, 1990, p. 70; see also Larson, 1985)

In short, "attributional biases frequently entail punctuation, reinforcing the tendency to put the blame for the conflict on the other side" (Jonsson, 1990, p. 71). Needless to say, that these errors create and perpetuate very negative images of each other in the both sides' eyes. And the question is: How are such images broken? Jonsson (1990) believes that "negative images can be eroded by conciliatory actions that (a) involve surprise, (b) are voluntary and costly and thus cannot be attributed to self-interests or ulterior motives, (c) are perceived to involve internal bargaining and (d) are repeated, even if they are not immediately reciprocated" (p. 78).

The last major problem that arises during each negotiation process is the problem of commitment. All the efforts of deriving a meaning, categorizing, and explaining signals may be futile and even dangerous if those signals are false or intentionally misleading. That is why it is extremely important to clearly understand if one can or cannot trust the other side's signals during negotiations. "An actor can lie as easily as he can tell the truth. A signal used to convey an accurate message can also convey a misleading one. It is logically impossible to design a signaling system that does not have this attribute" (Jervis, 1970, p. 66).

How can this problem be solved? The negotiation literature offers several methods and factors according to which one can make a decision if a certain signal is credible or not.

The first one is the system of *indices*. "Signals are issued mainly to influence the receiver's image of the sender. They have no inherent credibility, as they can be used as easily by a deceiver as by an honest actor. Indices, by contrast, are less easily manipulated; they are believed to be inextricably linked to the actor's capabilities or intentions and to be untainted by deception. Indices are used by the perceiving actor to verify or falsify the other actor's signals" (Jonsson, 1990, p. 82). Indices are believed to be "beyond the ability of the actor to control for the purpose of projecting a misleading image" (Jervis, 1970, p. 26).

There are several indices mentioned in the negotiation literature. One of them is actual known capability of one of the parties in a certain area. If one side knows for sure that the other side has certain limited capabilities in the area of negotiations, that side is not going to believe the signals that try to tell them otherwise. Another index is often called the *clandestine channels* index— "information received through illicit channels . . . is often judged to be more credible than open information" (Jonsson, 1990, p. 83). One of the main indices is directly related to the main purpose of this work. It is the political situation within the other side's country, institution, or organization, that is, the second level situation. This situation, as a rule, quite clearly demonstrates actual capabilities and vulnerabilities of all the negotiation parties.

But the indices are not perfect either. They also can be manipulated. "The effective use of indices for credibility estimates requires that the sender is unconscious of the fact that the adversary perceives certain behaviour as an index. Once the sender becomes conscious of this, possibilities of manipulation emerge" (Jonsson, 1990, p. 83). The following is just an example of it.

> The tendency to use the adversary's balance of domestic forces as index can also be manipulated. During the fall of 1989 Boris Yeltsin and other Soviet sources communicated to the Americans that Gorbachev's days could be numbered, implying that an American-Soviet arms deal might help him overwhelm his opponents and remain in power. Similarly, in 1961 and 1962 Soviet diplomats dropped hints to their American opposites in the nuclear test ban negotiations that Khrushchev, failing a success for his "softline" policy toward the United States, was likely to be succeeded by "orthodox" forces who were opposed to concluding and agreement with the United States. (Jonsson, 1990, p. 83)

There are also other factors that people use to evaluate credibility of a signal. One factor is expectations. "The more new information conforms to these expectations, the more credible it will appear. Conversely, information that contradicts expectations will be deemed less credible" (Jonsson, 1990, p. 85).

Another factor is the source credibility. "The credibility of a message is enhanced if it comes from a reliable source. On the other hand, signals from a source who is regarded unreliable are rarely considered to be credible" (Jonsson, 1990, p. 86). And this factor definitely puts some restraints on lying "the most important of which is the loss of bargaining reputation should the deception fail" (Jonsson, 1990, p. 81).

In the international relations literature, Thomas Schelling (1963, 1966) calls the complex of issues associated with the credibility problem the *art of commitment*. He pays a great deal of attention to such issues as threats and rationality. He draws analogy with the infamous automotive chicken game that "illustrates how a commitment becomes effectively credible by demonstrating recklessness as well as lack of control" (Jonsson, 1990, p. 79).

All the above-mentioned four major problems make negotiators commit many perceptional errors that prevent negotiations from being successfully concluded. It is interesting and useful to mention just some of them. For example, there is "a common tendency to see the behavior of the adversary as more centralized, planned, and coordinated than it usually is" (Jonsson, 1989, p. 264; see also Jervis, 1976, pp. 319). Another error is that negotiators usually "see their own behavioral choices and judgments as relatively common and appropriate to existing circumstances while viewing alternative responses as uncommon, deviant, and inappropriate" (Ross, 1977, p. 188; see also Jonsson, 1989, p. 265). The next possible mistake is to attribute the consequences of the other side's actions to one's own actions. Then, negotiators often "underestimate ambiguity and overestimate their cognitive abilities, it is likely that statesmen think that they can draw more accurate inferences from what the other state is doing than in fact they can" (Jervis, 1986, p. 495; see also Jonsson, 1989, p. 266).

As we can see, this cognitive or communication point of view offers very interesting and useful insights and offers many words of caution to prevent negotiators from very dangerous mistakes. At the same time, this approach has its own problems.

The first problem is that the communication approach ignores the basis of the negotiation process itself, that is each side's interests. Negotiation is a purpose-oriented communication process. Every negotiation starts because the sides have in mind some goals that they want to achieve as the result of the negotiation. Those goals are based on the interests of the sides. However, the cognitive approach focuses exclusively on the upper tier of the negotiation process—the communication dynamics. It does not even try to answer the questions: Why do the parties send these particular messages but not others? What do the parties want to say? The only issue that this theory is concerned with is how the parties "say it." As it has already been mentioned above, communicative strategies are based on goals of the communicative act. But the cognitive point of view is concentrated on strategies without even considering goals. This is a very serious drawback because, depending on the goals, the parties will use different communication strategies, derive meaning in different ways, and have different levels of involvement. The cognitive approach does not deal with these issues and possibilities.

Secondly, the communication perspective on negotiations is mainly descriptive. It does not have any prescriptive element to it. It is almost impossible to derive any policy implications from this approach. The theory describes very well what can go wrong during negotiations but does not provide any suggestions or tools to correct any of the perception problems. It claims that there are many things that can be misinterpreted but there is nothing one can do about it. The only thing one can do is to state his or her case as clearly as possible and hope that the other side will understand the message properly. Sometimes, even clear statement is impossible because the other side will interpret at its own will even one's smallest unintended actions and even inactions. One can use indices but they can also be manipulated. To restate, this theory gives an excellent understanding of the problem but does not provide tools to solve it.

Finally, the cognitive approach considers all the communication interactions as if they always go just at the interpersonal level. It never considers the context or structure in which a certain communication action happens. For example, often communication goes through the state bureaucratic machinery or mass media. These organizational or institutional structures may affect heavily the communicative dynamics as well as the final outcome of the communication act. They can distort, delay, or even completely block a certain kind of information. Consequently, final outcomes of communication acts may vary not due to perception and beliefs problems but due to the structural distortions of information. The cognitive perspective does not address this aspect.

That is why in order to open up some possibilities for improvement of the communication theory of negotiations, it is necessary to introduce structural variables into this perspective. The introduction of institutional and interest structures aims at correcting the problems of the cognitive theory mentioned above and, consequently, improving the analytical power of this approach.

The Concept of Structure

Structure Defined

Before covering structural variables, it is important to explain the term *structure*. In the area of social sciences, there are at least two major definitions of structure. One of them belongs to the critical or marxist paradigm. It is mainly concerned with economic and social structure, that is the structure of society (social classes) and the structure of the mode of production (feudal, capitalist, socialist, etc.) both of which are the basis of the structure of the institutions of power and society.

The other definition of structure is rooted in the field of economics and is mainly concerned with the structure based on the distribution of capabilities, resources, and interests. One of the most prominent proponents of this point of view on structure is political science theoretician, Kenneth Waltz. He conceptualized a structural theory of international relations in which political processes depend on both structure of separate states and the general international system structure.

Waltz (1979) writes, "The structure is the system-wide component that makes it possible to think of the system as a whole. . . . A structure is defined by the arrangement of its parts. Only changes of arrangement are structural changes. . . . The concept of structure is based on the fact that units differently juxtaposed and combined behave differently and in interacting produce different outcomes. . . . Structure is not a collection of political institutions but rather the arrangement of them" (pp. 79–81). Drawing from these basic assumptions, he gives his three-part definition of the structure. He argues that any structure is defined "first, according to the principle by which it is ordered; second, by specification of the functions of formally differentiated units; and third, by the distribution of capabilities across those units" (Waltz, 1979, p. 82). Let's briefly discuss each of these three parts.

Waltz (1979) argues that the order of the structural elements "has to be examined in order to draw a distinction between expectations about behavior and outcomes" (p. 81) and that this distinction comes from the fact that "patterns of behavior . . . derive from the structural constraints of the system" (p. 92). These structural constraints, in turn, are the results of the system's element ordering.

The character of the units (part two of the definition) is specified by the functions performed by different units (Waltz, 1979, p. 93). In different structures similar units can perform slightly different functions and these differences, to a large extent, explain the differences between structures themselves. The units' functions are dictated by the rules according to which each structure works. Consequently, such rules are often expressed or explained in the official procedures of that particular structure. That is, the character of each unit is defined by standard procedure according to which a certain structure functions—the standard operating procedures (SOPs).

In terms of the distribution of capabilities Waltz (1979) writes:

The units . . . are then distinguished primarily by their greater or lesser capabilities for performing similar tasks. . . . The structure of a system changes with changes in the distribution of capabilities across the system's units. And changes in structure change expectations about how the units of the system will behave and about the outcomes their interactions will produce. . . . Power is estimated

by comparing the capabilities of a number of units. Although capabilities are attributes of units, the distribution of capabilities across units is not. The distribution of capabilities is not a unit attribute, but rather a system-wide concept.
(pp. 97–98)

This means that the third element of Waltz's definition of structure is actually the distribution of power among the structure's units.

Finally, Waltz (1979) unequivocally says that political structures influence
all the processes going on in these structures: "Political structures shape political processes. . . . Political structure produces a similarity in process and performance so long as a structure endures" (pp. 82, 87). Can this conclusion be
transferred to a different field of knowledge other than political science?
Waltz's answer is yes because "a structural definition applies to realms of
widely different substance so long as the arrangement of parts is similar . . .
because this is so, theories developed for one realm may with some modification be applicable to other realms as well" (Waltz, 1979, p. 80).

According to Waltz (1979), his definition of power "makes it possible to say
what the expected organizational effects are and how structure and units interact and affect each other" (p. 100). That is, Waltz's definition is very important for the purpose of this book because it is one of the main purposes of
this volume to say what the structural effects will be on the process of international negotiations. Waltz's definition ties together power and institutional
structure, which is a very good basis for the definition of power used for the
purpose of this particular work.

There is one remark to be made here. Waltz is talking about two types of
structures—international and state internal. One affects the other in many
different ways. For the purpose of this work although, the term *structure* most
often will not mean super- or general structure—such as the international
system that determines the character of relationships *between* entities. When
talking about structural effects we will mostly mean *intra-entity* interactions—that is, the effect of domestic political structures on international negotiations. That is not to say that the general system in the context of which a
certain entity exists does not have any effect on intra-entity negotiations. Such
a kind of influence definitely exists, but it can be the topic of another book.
But one of the main focus points of this particular study is the intra-entity dynamics—so, we will typically emphasize this particular structural aspect. In
this respect the term *structural influence* will be different from the way Waltz
generally used it. It will not denote the external effect of a general or super-
system on each entity. It will rather denote the internal structural effect, the
effect of the structure of a certain entity itself on the outcome of a negotiation
process.

The term *structure* in this work will mean the structure of institutions as a reflection of the structure of interests because "Political institutions shape the process by which preferences [read: *interests*] are aggregated domestically. Within a country every group's preferences do not have the same impact on politics. Some groups' preferences are weighed more heavily in any decision. . . . Institutions create a mobilization of bias in favor of certain actors" (Milner, 1997, p. 18). As we can see, such a kind of definition of the institutional structure ties together institutional structure, interests (preferences), and resources and capabilities (weight of preferences or power). This definition shows that structure of institutions reflects resource distribution, comparative capabilities among actors, and the structure of interests at the same time. This nonformal and broad approach toward the definition of institutions is useful and parsimonious. First of all, it clearly shows that the institutional structure is realization of the aggregation of interests, the distribution of resources, and comparative capabilities—that is, the realization of power as it was defined by Waltz. Secondly, instead of four terms and, consequently, four different definitions (institutions, resources, capabilities, and interests), it gives us one universal and all-encompassing definition of institutions. Finally, this definition demonstrates that exactly because of its interests (preferences) a certain institutional structure can distort, delay, or block certain information. That is why, for the purpose of this work, the term *structure* will mean the institutional structure defined as the embodiment of the aggregation of interests, of the distribution of resources, and of the distribution of capabilities—that is, the realization of power.

A similar approach to structure has already been used in the area of the negotiation theory.

A Structural Analysis of the Negotiation Process

The structural analysis of negotiations "is based on a distribution of elements—in this case, of instrumental elements of power, defined either as parties' relative positions (resource possessions) or as their relative ability to make their options prevail (or to counter the other's efforts to make its options prevail)" (Zartman, 1989, p. 243).

The concept of power itself can be very important for the negotiation theory and practice. Many types of negotiations are greatly affected by power differences. That is why the structural analysis literature on negotiations covers this particular aspect quite thoroughly.

For example, William Habeeb (1988) came up with a process-oriented definition of power designed especially for the analysis of negotiation processes: "Power is the way in which actor A uses its resources in a process with actor B so as to bring about changes that cause preferred outcomes in its relationship with B" (p. 15). The same author (Habeeb, 1988) also argues that there are several types of power that are important for the negotiation process. The first of them is *aggregate structural power,* which is defined as "the actor's total (or aggregate) resources and possessions" (p. 17). *Issue-specific structural power* "is concerned with an actor's capabilities and position vis-à-vis another actor in terms of a specific mutual issue" (p. 19) and shows what kind of influence one actor can exert over the other in the particular area the negotiation is about. *Behavioral power* is actually the process "by which they [actors] maneuver and use their resources (both aggregate and issue-specific) to achieve preferred outcomes" (p. 23) and, in negotiation, it is revealed "by actors' tactics, which are the means by which an actor exercises power" (p. 23).

The effect of structural power on negotiated outcomes can be very important. For example, Lawler and Yoon (1995) write:

> Structural power establishes the contextual conditions for negotiations between some pairs of actors in a network by providing incentives for them to negotiate repeatedly and to arrive at satisfactory agreements. . . . They [actors] will develop an emotional/affective commitment to their relationship that, in turn, changes the context for future negotiations. Behaviorally, emotional/affective commitment should be manifest in a propensity (a) to give each other benefits without strings attached . . . , (b) to stay in their relationship even if the expected payoff from an alternative actor becomes equal to or better than that of the focal relation, and (c) to invest in a joint venture that takes the form of a social dilemma. (p. 144)

Unfortunately, as we can see, this approach is very limited in its theoretical value because it concentrates exclusively on the difference in power, and ignores such important concepts as interests, resources, standard operating procedures, etc. That is why this perspective practically cannot be used to identify what the expected structural effects on the negotiation process are, which is one of the main purposes of this book.

General Structural Aspects in the Field of Communication

It is interesting and important to explore the extent to which structural variables have been introduced into the field of communication in general. This review may contribute to the foundation on which a structural communication-oriented model of international negotiations can be based. It would also lay out a context in which the new model can be built. Besides that, it will help situate this work in the communication theory literature.

Not much has been done using the structural approach in the field of communication. Nevertheless, there is at least one work that is almost entirely devoted to this issue. Graham T. Allison's (1971) *Essence of Decision* describes in detail the communication and decision-making processes in the United States and the Soviet Union during the missile crisis in October 1962. Allison's main objective is to create a theoretical explanatory model of the decision-making processes in both countries and, by so doing, explain why those events actually happened.

In his book Allison offers three models of the decision-making process— the *rational actor, organizational process,* and *governmental politics* models.[1] The first model is a traditional rational-actor decision-making model that can be found in any economics, psychology, management, or organizational communication literature. The latter two models are so similar that many scholars often unify them into one.

In the *rational actor* model, the actor is a rational utility maximizer. He or she is aware of all the available choices and able to calculate probability and utility of any outcome of any action, which is called *comprehensive rationality.* Although there are some constraints limiting his or her actions, basically, that actor acts at his or her own will and discretion.

Many scholars believe that Allison set up this model just as a "straw-man," with the only purpose to later tear it apart. Indeed, this is exactly what he does. First, he claims that people are never aware of all the choices and information concerning their problem. Second, the rationality of the actor is always suspect because there are many other reasons to act in a certain way, such as anger, jealousy, out of prejudice, etc. Third, a person is rarely able to calculate the utility and probability of every event. The lack of time or misinformation may limit the ability to conduct such calculations. Fourth, people tend to choose not the best but the closest satisfactory option in a time of crisis. Fifth, problems are usually so complex that only a limited number of aspects of each problem can be taken into account. Finally, there are many structural constraints that severely limit the range of choices for any actor under any circumstances. All the above points constitute the reasons for and the definition of *bounded rationality.* Allison says that people, during any decision-making process, are much more likely to utilize bounded rather than comprehensive rationality.

The conclusion that Allison draws is that another, better, model should be utilized to describe how people make decisions in international and organizational settings. He reminds us that in those settings people never act alone and they are never independent actors. They are always a part of some structure, some organization that inevitably shapes the way they go about doing things. That is why he introduces the *organizational process* model.

Allison (1971) argues that (1) organizations break complex problems into parts and attend to them sequentially, (2) they also search for the "good enough" solution instead of the best one, (3) consequently, the order in which the alternatives are turned up is very important, (4) organizations emphasize short run feedback especially in times of crisis, and (5) the repertoire of choices is limited by an organization's properties (ch. 3).

Furthermore, the organizational decision-making process is heavily affected by parochial priorities and perceptions, goals, standard operating procedures (SOPs), solution-search models, and degree of flexibility. Finally, good information is a very expensive thing. Solid information-search and information-processing systems are costly. And cost is a strong limiting factor in relation to how much information can be obtained and how solid that information would be. Even for such big countries as the United States it was and still is an important issue. That is why organizations (including countries) simply cannot have perfect information on any problem—something will always be missing.

Consequently, Allison (1971) writes that it was the Soviet military SOPs, for example, that were to blame for easy discovery of the Soviet missiles in Cuba. On the other hand, the American political structure (role of the military in the government, distribution of power in the Congress, election considerations, pressure from the military-industrial complex, etc.) were responsible to a large degree for the choices made by Kennedy's administration (ch. 3).

Since governments are just huge organizations, the *governmental politics* model is very similar but is mostly intended to explain outcomes by analyzing the political process within government bodies. It emphasizes variables such as power distribution, political struggle, and bureaucratic functions. But the conclusion is the same—government, as a structure, seriously affects, limits, and shapes the actions of all the people involved in any decision-making process (Allison, 1971, ch. 5).

This concept of the decision-making process affected by bounded rationality first made its way into the area of organizational communication. We already mentioned here the works of Herbert Simon. Recently, one of the textbooks in this area describes in detail the so-called "Decision-Making Approach" toward organizational communication (Shockley-Zalabak, 1999, p. 109). Miller (1995) in her textbook pays at least some attention to the organizational decision-making process as well.

In the area of public information campaigns and diffusion of innovations, Everett Rogers (1995) argues that structure of a bureaucratic organization, like a government agency, can affect the process and the outcome of a communication process: "There is a well-developed social structure in such a system, consisting of hierarchical positions. . . . Such patterned social relationships among the members of a system constitute *social structure*, one type of structure. . . . The structure of a social system can facilitate or impede the diffusion of innovations in a system" (Rogers, 1995, pp. 24–25). And a great role in this system plays "a formal, established system of written procedures governing decisions and actions of organizational members" (Rogers, 1995, p. 376). These regulations dictate who is going to make a decision, how, who is going to approve it, the process and requirements of approval—in short, the structural or protocol variables of the communication process.

Communication scholars tried to study this aspect of the organizational communication process, but, as Rogers (1995) put it, such studies "generally become passé" (p. 378). Why does this occur? One answer might be found in the general approaches and, consequently, the designs used by those studies. They used independent variables such as the degree of centralization, complexity, formalization, and interconnectiveness. They gave each organization a score for each of these variables and tried to come up with an explanation for a degree of success of adoption of an innovation using formal modeling. This formal, superficial, and mechanistic approach failed because it did not examine closely the mechanisms of the internal organizational communication process.

Mark McElreath (1997) highlighted the importance of structural variables in the field of public relation:

> A number of structural and functional variables can predict and explain public relations. . . . There most likely will be a set of standard operating procedures (SOPs) for managers to use in resolving the problems. In some bureaucracies, these SOPs would be found in manuals; in others, the SOPs would be built into computer programs, 'kicking out' exceptions so that they are handled separately. Routine technologies are characterized by standardized rules and regulations. In the case of bureaucracies, the rules are necessary because the organization must handle a tremendous volume of requests for services every day; it's the only efficient way the job can get done on time. Public information campaigns and employee relations programs for a routine government agency would be different from public relations activities for a more complex organization such as hospital. (pp. 16–19)

The conclusion is quite clear—to properly understand or moreover predict the outcome of any international negotiation or interaction we must take into account internal (domestic) structural or institutional variables. If we communicate an idea we cannot know how it may be perceived without explaining the structure of interaction. The outcome of the communication process may be far from the intended one. In order to hit the target and reach our goal we have to correctly determine our intended audience (the decision-making actor), channels of information (how our message will go through organizational structure toward that actor), content of the message, and time frame. Now we will try to conceptualize, explore, and understand what those variables are in the negotiation process, how they affect the outcome, how they can be understood, and how they can be used in the course of international talks.

Note

1. It is important to note here that the origins of Graham Allison's ideas can be traced back to the works of Herbert Simon in the 1950s, including the concept of bounded rationality. Simon's 1957 book *Models of Man* laid the foundation for decision-making models different from the ration actor paradigm. But if Simon worked mostly in the organizational communication sphere, Allison applied his models to the international relations field and, in particular, in the area of international negotiations which is the main focus point of this volume.

2

Two-Level-Game Theory

THIS CHAPTER DESCRIBES IN DETAIL the two-level-game theory—its origins, development, and main assumptions. It starts with the explanation of the roots of the theory that come from the field of international relations (IR)—a field dramatically different from the area of communication. It is very important to understand how one group of IR scholars deals with the issues and concepts that have already been discussed in chapter 1, and how they define the main terms that will be used further in this book. This will give us an opportunity to correlate the IR terms and concepts with those used in the field of communication. It is also necessary to understand the general logic IR scholars applied to create this theory, the reason for its being, and the general context in which it is used. That is why this chapter will start with a brief review of international relations literature that deals with these aspects.

Then, the theory itself will be examined in detail. It is very important to understand all the internal mechanisms of this theory—what it responds to, what issues and problems it deals with, how it deals with them, what the main terms and concepts of this theory are, and how the internal logic of this theory connects all its parts. Special attention will also be paid to the main assumptions of the theory.

As will be shown, all the problems covered by these international relations scholars are practically the same as in other negotiation-related literature, including communications. They are also concerned with information flow, credible commitment, interest structure, norms, perceptions, and beliefs. That is why the concepts from the IR field can be easily applied to the communication area.

Two-level-game theory deals with the mechanisms of two-level negotiations and uses several structural variables to conceptualize and model interactions in this particular kind of negotiations. At the same time, this theory has its own problems: it is static, it "blackboxes" the information-processing aspect of negotiations, it disregards interests of the negotiation participants, and it homogenizes very heterogeneous actors. The roots of many of these problems lie in the traditional assumptions of the two-level-game theory and, consequently, can be solved by changing some of these assumptions.

International Relations Literature

Problems of International Cooperation
Related to the Negotiation Process

The issue of international negotiations is closely related to the problem of international cooperation. Needless to say that negotiation is a part of cooperation—people talk to each other only if they want to reach an agreement about cooperation in some area. All the problems on the way toward successful cooperation are similar to those that impede a successful negotiation outcome.

International relations literature that looks at cooperation from the rational actor and game-theoretic point of view tells us that even in the situations when states are forced to cooperate or it is in their best interest to cooperate, they often fail to do so. There are several reasons for such behavior. First of all, people are afraid of cheating by the other party. One of the specific examples of this point would be the Prisoner's Dilemma (PD) game. It exemplifies the situation all of the countries think they are in.[1] If you get cheated—you are the loser and there is no external authority to enforce any agreement. The second problem is the lack of reliable information. This problem is closely related to the first one because one of the main assumptions of the PD game is the complete absence of information exchange between the players. Precisely this absence of communication makes them defect on each other (because of their own defection suspicions) and completely destroys any possibility for their cooperation. The next two problems are very closely related to each other. These are the problems of compliance and credibility. Even if an agreement is reached, can we trust the other side? Is the other side credible? Will it comply? How can we make it comply? Are there any tools available to accomplish this task? Under complete anarchy, the answer seems to be "no." The last problem is the one of relative gains. Some players think that it is not a good idea to cooperate if the other side is getting more than them from this cooperation. This question arises especially when countries deal with so-called fungible resources, that is, the resources that can easily be transformed into another form of gains, such as, for example, military force.

Nevertheless, countries do cooperate and the situation in the contemporary world clearly demonstrates how widespread and important this cooperation can be. How can the problems associated with international cooperation be overcome? The IR scholars working in this area highlight several main ways to promote cooperation under the assumption of anarchy. First of all, it is necessary to reach a cooperative agreement. Then, when the agreement is reached, it is necessary to make sure that all the rules of this agreement will be observed and the system in place will be sustained for some time. There are several ways to do so. First of all, it is important to establish a monitoring system in order to expose violators. The second logical step is to establish a system to punish them. All these actions can change the whole game by changing the structure of payoffs. What might have been profitable to do before all those changes—will be no longer profitable. The best example here would be the taxation system. Certainly, some people do not want to pay taxes and want to leave in their pocket as much money as they can. But the state needs money. In order to get it, the state establishes a system of monitoring and severe punishment for those who don't pay taxes. It changes the whole payoff structure. Before this system, the tax violators received a better payoff by not paying taxes. After this system has been established, the cost of not paying taxes becomes very high and people prefer to pay up.

Another way to promote cooperation is to create a reliable system of information exchange in order to avoid misunderstandings and guarantee all the agreement participants from the breach of promises. "The possibility of a breach of promise can impede cooperation even when cooperation would leave all better off" (Oye, 1986, p. 1). We never know how credible the commitment of our partners is (the problem of credible commitment). The information exchange system will help us to monitor the situation and make informed decisions. This system is supposed to make sure that we will not unexpectedly become a victim of defection. That is why it is very important to establish this information exchange system in order to solve the credible commitment problem.

Besides that, by establishing such an information exchange we change the PD game into another, more cooperative type of game. It happens because we change one of the main assumptions of the game—the complete absence of the information exchange between the players, and, consequently, we change the whole payoff structure and these "changes in the magnitudes of differences in the value placed on outcomes can influence the prospects for cooperation . . . " (Oye, 1986, p. 9).

Finally, we have to increase *shadow of the future*, that is, we have to ensure future cooperation. If countries know that they are going to deal with each other in the future many times—they are more likely to stick to the current agreement. Even in case of the iterated or repeated PD game (without any changes in the payoff structure) the outcome can be quite different from the one-shot game because "in iterated situations, the magnitude of the differences between CC and DD and between DC and CD in present and future rounds of play affects the likelihood of cooperation in the present" (Oye, 1986, p. 9).

Regimes, according to Oye (1986), make sure that there is a shadow of the future over the current cooperation because "states must expect to continue dealing with each other ... and payoff structures must not change substantially over time" (p. 12). In the wide sense, international relations literature defines regimes as "sets of implicit or explicit principles, norms, rules and decision-making procedures around which actors' expectations converge in a given area of international relations. Principles are beliefs of fact, causation, and rectitude. .... Rules are specific prescriptions or proscriptions for action. Decision-making procedures are prevailing practices for making and implementing collective choice" (Keohane, 1984, p. 57). Norms are defined as "standards of behavior, whether adopted on grounds of self-interest or otherwise" (Keohane, 1984, p. 57). That is why, norms, rules, beliefs, and decision-making procedures are the main points for every negotiation. That is, the international relations approach considers many of the same concepts as the communication point of view on the negotiation process does.

Also "multilateral strategies, centering on the formation of international regimes, can be used to alter payoff structures in two ways. First, norms generated by regimes may be internalized by states, and thereby alter payoff structure. Second, information generated by regimes may alter states' understanding of their interests" (Oye, 1986, pp. 10–11). Besides that, regime agreements institutionalize reciprocity which is, according to Oye, another strategy for fostering cooperation. These are three of the main functions of international regimes.

Finally, Oye writes that regimes are necessary because "conventions provide rules of thumb that can diminish transaction and information costs. Second, collective enforcement mechanisms both decrease the likelihood of autonomous defection and permit selective punishment of violators of norms. These two functions of international regimes directly address problems created by large numbers of players" (Oye, 1986, p. 20).

The above discussion of regimes is also important because regimes are a form of international institutions established in certain areas for certain purposes to address certain problems in certain situations. The concept of institutions will be very important for the new model of the two-level-game theory created in this work. Many functions and features of regimes, that have been just covered, will be discussed later on in this study but already as functions and features of a larger concept of institutions.

Traditional Neglect of the Internal or Domestic Politics

International relations literature traditionally deemphasized the effect of internal politics on the outcome of negotiations. One of the main authorities in this area in the IR field—Helen Milner—says that there are two reasons for the neglect of internal politics in the international relations literature. These are the centrality of anarchy as the main condition for differentiating between domestic and international politics and the use of game theory with its assumption of unitary and rational actors. According to Milner, the focus on these two points is problematic because it rests upon a series of assumptions that are made about three areas: (1) the determination of the payoff structure, (2) the strategies available to states to alter systemic conditions, and (3) the capacity of states to ratify and implement cooperative arrangements.

Area 1

Game-theoretic models of international cooperation rest heavily upon the specification of the payoff matrix. These payoffs—exogenous to the models— are simply assumed. At the same time, according to Snidal's quote in Milner's article (1992) "state's preferences may not always be tightly linked to the objective conditions. Perceptions and information processing, as well as organizational or bureaucratic imperatives, may change the relevant payoff for decision makers" (p. 490). Even in such an orthodox, important, and sensitive area as national security "the perception of elites plays a sizable role, whereas in economic issues the international distribution of the costs and benefits of different international policies weighs heavily. On the whole, as Haas also maintains, the internal character of states and their elites is a central element in determining the preferences of states" (Milner, 1992, p. 490).

Milner says that, because of all this, general theories of international cooperation often "slip into inductive case studies dependent on domestic factors. ... Payoffs and hence the likelihood of cooperation depend on the perception of decision makers" (Milner, 1992, p. 491). She gives an example that the outcome of a set of agricultural negotiations was finally determined for the Japanese by their domestic factors—because of their domestic political system, gains to agricultural producers counted more than gains to consumers.

Area 2

In the second area—the strategies available to states—Milner argues that the perceptions of decision makers affect these strategies; that is they are not really structural. "Misperceptions, bureaucratic politics, and vested interests may systematically interfere to undermine—even to reverse—the hypotheses posited. When domestic factors are introduced into the argument, not only may the predicted effects of reciprocity, iteration, and numbers of actors fail to materialize, but the very opposite effects may manifest themselves" (Milner, 1992, p. 492).

Area 3

In terms of the last area—the problem of ratifying cooperative agreement—Milner (1992) writes, "Cooperation may be unattainable because of domestic intransigence, and not because of the international system" (p. 493). She also names many failed international agreements the failures of which are attributed less to concerns over cheating or payoff structure than to the opposition of domestic actors. "It is therefore difficult, if not impossible, to explain any of these cases with reference solely to international factors" (Milner, 1992, p. 493).

As we can see, the problems covered by the rational actor game-theory-oriented IR scholars are practically the same as in other negotiation-related literature, including communications. They are also concerned with information flow, credible commitment, interests structure, norms, perceptions, and beliefs. And now, when we understand better where this theory comes from and what the main concepts actually mean, we can try to apply it to the negotiation process in general. But before that, it is necessary to explain the theory itself in greater detail.

The Origins of the Theory—Putnam's Work

The two-level-game theory was created to solve the problem of disregard of the effect of domestic politics in the study of international negotiations. In his article published in 1988 in *International Organization* Robert Putnam wrote that "Without domestic resonance, international forces would not have sufficed to produce the accord, no matter how balanced and intellectually persuasive the overall package. . . . A more adequate account of the domestic determinants of foreign policy and international relations must stress *politics*: parties, social classes, interest groups (both economic and noneconomic), legislators, and even public opinions and elections, not simply executive officials and institutional arrangements" (pp. 430, 432).

This proposition was a step aside from the state-centric model where the state is the central and unitary actor and it derives its interests mainly from the international situation. Vice versa, Putnam (1988) argues that:

> Even if we arbitrarily exclude the legislature from 'the state' (as much of this literature does), it is wrong to assume that the executive is unified in its views. . . . Central executives have a special role in mediating domestic and international pressures precisely because they are directly exposed to both spheres, not because they are united on all issues nor because they are insulated from domestic politics. Thus, the state-centric literature is an uncertain foundation for theorizing about how domestic and international politics interact. (pp. 432–33)

In order to include domestic variables, Putnam (1988) developed the two-level-game theory. This theory states that, "At the national level, domestic groups pursue their interests by pressuring the government to adopt favorable policies, and politicians seek power by constructing coalitions among those groups. At the international level, national governments seek to maximize their own ability to satisfy domestic pressure, while minimizing the adverse consequences of foreign developments. Neither of the two games can be ignored by central decision-makers, so long as their countries remain interdependent, yet sovereign" (p. 434).

Putnam (1988) defines these two levels as follows:

1. bargaining between the negotiators, leading to a tentative agreement; call that Level I.
2. separate discussions within each group of constituents about whether to ratify the agreement; call that Level II. (p. 436)

The author explains that the actors at the level I are negotiators who represent the state at the international level. "The actors at Level II may represent bureaucratic agencies, interest groups, social classes, or even 'public opinion.'" (Putnam, 1988, p. 436).

The whole two-level game is about the "win-set." "We may define the 'win-set' for a given Level II constituency as the set of all possible Level I agreements that would 'win'—that is, gain the necessary majority among the constituents—when simply voted up or down" (Putnam, 1988, p. 437). There are two main reasons why win-sets are very important for the whole game.

First of all, larger win-sets make level I agreements more likely. "By definition, any successful agreement must fall within the Level II win-sets of each of the parties to the accord. Thus, agreement is possible only if those win-sets overlap. Conversely, the smaller the win-sets, the greater the risk that the negotiations will break down" (Putnam, 1988, p. 438).

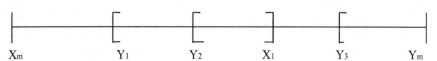

FIGURE 2.1
Putnam's illustration of the win-set concept

Secondly, the relative size of the respective level II win-sets will affect the distribution of the joint gains from the international bargain. "The larger the perceived win-set of a negotiator, the more he can be 'pushed around' by other Level I negotiators. Conversely, a small domestic win-set can be a bargaining advantage: 'I'd like to accept your proposal, but I could never get it accepted at home.' Lamenting the domestic constraints under which one must operate is (in the words of one experienced British diplomat) 'the natural thing to say at the beginning of a tough negotiation'" (Putnam, 1988, p. 440).

Putnam (1988, p. 441) draws a very demonstrative picture to illustrate how the win-set mechanisms work. This picture is shown on Figure 2.1.

Putnam (1988) explains how the system works, saying that it is a simple zero-sum game between X and Y.:

> Xm and Ym represent the maximum outcomes for X and Y, respectively, while X1 and Y1 represent the minimal outcomes that could be ratified. At this stage any agreement in the range between X1 and Y1 could be ratified by both parties. If the win-set of Y were contracted to, say, Y2 (perhaps by requiring a larger majority for ratification), outcomes between Y1 and Y2 would no longer be feasible, and the range of feasible agreements would thus be truncated in Y's favor. However, if Y, emboldened by this success, were to reduce its win-set still further to Y3 (perhaps by requiring unanimity for ratification), the negotiators would suddenly find themselves deadlocked, for the win-sets no longer overlap at all. (p. 441)

Putnam (1988) also gives a very demonstrative example for a deadlock win-set situation: "For example, during the prolonged pre-war Anglo-Argentine negotiations over the Falklands/Malvinas, several tentative agreements were rejected in one capital or the other for domestic political reasons; when it became clear that the initial British and Argentine win-sets did not overlap at all, war became virtually inevitable" (p. 438).

There are three sets of factors that determine the win-sets:

1. level II preferences and coalitions, that is, the size of the win-set depends on the distribution of power, preferences, and possible coalitions among level II constituencies.
2. level II institutional structure, such as form of ratification, etc.

3. level I negotiators' strategies such as so called "Schelling conjecture"[2] at level I and side-payments at level II.

But the win-set is very difficult to determine because of the uncertainty factor. "Governments generally do not do well in analyzing each other's internal politics in crises (and, I would add, in normal times), and indeed it is inherently difficult" (Putnam, 1988, p. 452). That is why the role of the chief negotiator is so important: "In purely distributive Level I bargaining, negotiators have an incentive to understate their own win-sets. . . . On the other hand, uncertainty about the opponent's win-set increases one's concerns about the risk of involuntary defection. . . . Thus, a utility-maximizing negotiator must seek to convince his opposite number that his own win-set is 'kinky,' that is, that the proposed deal is certain to be ratified, but that a deal slightly more favorable to the opponent is unlikely to be ratified" (Putnam, 1988, pp. 452–53).

Putnam (1988) believes that the chief negotiator is motivated by three major groups of motives:

1. Enhancing his standing in the Level II game by increasing his political resources or by minimizing potential losses.
2. Shifting the balance of power at Level II in favor of domestic policies that he prefers for exogenous reasons.
3. To pursue his own conception of the national interest in the international context. (p. 456)

Finally, Putnam (1988) makes a conclusion that "It is reasonable to presume, at least in the international case of the two-level bargaining, that the chief negotiator will normally give primacy to his domestic calculus, if a choice must be made, not least because his own incumbency often depends on his standing at Level II" (p. 457).

Putnam's work was just the first step toward a more complete theorization of the effect of domestic politics on international cooperation. It was just a general idea of how we can organize our thinking about this problem. Putnam had to make some assumptions to simplify the model, such as rational actors and complete information. At the same time, it was clear that in the real world the conditions for the international negotiations are much more versatile and complicated. That is why more in-depth research and theory-building was needed.

Milner's Work on the Two-Level-Game Theory

Helen Milner's 1997 book was the next important step in the development of the two-level-game theory. She starts with the proposition that the international cooperative agreement negotiations are predominantly games about the domestic gains distribution:

> My central argument is that cooperation among nations is affected less by fears of other countries' relative gains or cheating than it is by the *domestic distributional consequences* of cooperative endeavors. Cooperative agreements create winners and losers domestically; therefore they generate supporters and opponents. The internal struggle between these groups shapes the possibility and nature of international cooperative agreements. International negotiations to realize cooperation often fail because of domestic politics, and such negotiations are often initiated because of domestic politics. All aspects of cooperation are affected by domestic considerations because cooperation is a continuation of domestic political struggle by other means. (pp. 9–10)

She believes that three factors are decisive in this game "the policy *preferences* of domestic actors, the *institutions* for power sharing among them, and the distribution of *information* among them" (Milner, 1997, p. 11).

Domestic Actors

Milner (1997) says, "Domestic politics matter because the state is not a unitary actor. Groups within it have *different policy preferences* because they are differently affected by government policies" (p. 16). She believes that the best way to discuss these preferences is to introduce the term *structure of domestic preferences.* "This structure refers to the relative positions of the preferences of important domestic actors on the issue at hand" (p. 16). Consequently, there are three main actors in the game "the political executive (the president or prime minister), the legislature, and interest groups" (p. 17).

The latter term requires some clarification. An interest group is any societal actor that may be affected by an international cooperative agreement. "The preferences of societal groups depend on the *distributional* consequences of international agreements. . . . The distribution of costs and benefits of cooperation provides a map for understanding which group will be for cooperation and which will be against it" (Milner, 1997, pp. 60–61).

These interest groups play two roles in the process of international cooperation: "First, they serve as pressure groups who, through their ability to contribute campaign funds and mobilize voters, directly shape the preferences of the executive and the legislature. . . . Second, they also play a more indirect role by acting as information providers to political actors, especially legislators, who have their own preferences but are not completely informed about the ramifications of policies" (Milner, 1997, p. 60).

Domestic Political Institutions

It is very important to understand how Milner defines "political institutions." In her model, it is not a tangible bureaucratic structure or a part of the state apparatus, but it is rather a set of societal conventions that shape the political process in a country. She defines political institutions in the following way: "Political institutions shape the process by which preferences are aggregated domestically. Within a country every group's preferences do not have the same impact on politics. Some groups' preferences are weighed more heavily in any decision. . . . Institutions create a mobilization of bias in favor of certain actors" (Milner, 1997, p. 18).

This approach gives a deeper understanding of the political process in a certain country because it takes not a formal but a historical approach to political institutions.

The Distribution of Information

The lack of information is another problem and an important feature of the game. The actors do not possess complete information about their counterparts, all circumstances surrounding an agreement, and possible consequences. In Allison's terms, they can exercise only bounded rationality. And again, as was explained in the discussion of Allison's book, the lack of information creates suboptimal outcomes and unequal situations for the players. Certainly, the side that has more information has a much better position.

The role of information has often been neglected by the scholars working in the area of political economy. At the same time, studies in both economics and international security have dealt extensively with the problem of incomplete information and the signaling games it creates (Jervis, 1976). This literature suggests that a state of uncertainty is created by incomplete or asymmetric information and this situation leads to outcomes that prevent optimal levels of exchange or even foster conflict.

Milner supports this point of view and thinks that this situation is also applicable to the two-level-game theory. "Information problems are also important in the two-level game here. In general, incomplete information has two effects. Not only does it create inefficient outcomes, it also confers political advantages" (Milner, 1997, p. 21).

Milner's View of the Game

In order to further develop the theory, Milner introduces the main actors of the game. They are the foreign country, F; the domestic executive (the president, prime minister) or Proposer, P; the legislature or Chooser (personalized in so-called median legislator who casts the decisive vote), C; and domestic interest groups or Endorsers, E. Each of them is assumed to be a unitary, rational, and utility-maximizing actor. Each of the actors has its own position on the issue at hand and that position has its direct effect on other players as well as on the final outcome of the negotiations.

In order to demonstrate how positions of the actors affect the final outcome of a set of negotiations, Milner presents several graphs that try to depict the position of the final outcome of the talks relative to the positions of the actors. She takes a hypothetical situation in a snapshot and tries to explain it in the terms of the two-level-game theory. That is how, for example, the situations under the incomplete information assumption are explained:

> [If] the endorser is less hawkish than the legislature . . . then C knows that E will endorse only proposed agreements that also meet with C's approval. But C also knows that E will not endorse some agreements that C prefers to the status quo—that is, those between E's indifference point and C's indifference point. E's endorsements cover only a subset of proposals that C would like to ratify. Hence when C hears an endorsement, C will know to ratify the agreement. When C hears no endorsement, C has to guess where the proposal lies. If C thinks it is close to his preferred policies, it should be ratified anyway (C is accommodating). If C believes it to be far from c [its point of preference], then C will reject it in favor of q [status quo] (C is recalcitrant). P and F will take C's beliefs into account when offering a proposal. If P and F know that C requires an endorsement before ratification is possible, the closest ratifiable agreement is q [status quo] itself. So P and F offer q, which is endorsed and ratified. (Milner, 1997, p. 87)

In this particular case, the position of a hawkish legislature to some extent dictates the final endorsement position of the interest groups. These two actors have to find a point where their positions may converge. At the same time, because of the lack of information, all the actors have to guess each other's positions, which may create different outcomes depending on the quality of their guesses. In this way, Milner ties together actors' perceptions under the assumption of bounded rationality, the state structure, and the quality of the final outcome of negotiations.

Milner does not try to explain all the possible combinations. Her goal is to demonstrate how international negotiation situations can be analyzed. At the same time, the quote above demonstrates a little problem with her approach. It is extremely "*if*"-reliant. The analyst has to guess what the perception of, for example, C would be in order to predict the possible outcome. And it is clear that trying to guess a possible perception of a very heterogeneous legislature is a very thankless task. Nevertheless, Milner's view of the two-level-game theory indeed gives some useful tools to analyze international negotiations.

In the second part of her book, Milner introduces several case studies where she uses this model to analyze the situations and to suggest how the outcomes of those negotiations might have been predicted. Her analysis is quite interesting and effective. However, even Milner herself admits sometimes that certain aspects in some negotiations cannot be explained by her model. Nevertheless, as a result of her analysis, Milner came up with a set of variables that can help to explain the talks' dynamics and final outcomes. They are *the degree of divided government, endorsement of the agreement by key domestic groups,* and *changes in the ratification process.* These three variables will be at the very foundation of the new model of the two-level-game theory, offered in this book, and will be discussed below in depth.

An Evaluation of Milner's Model—
Theoretical Contributions and Problems

Milner's model definitely represents a step forward as compared with Putnam's version. For the first time she introduced the notion of perceptions and beliefs into the game. As well, the game moved away from exclusively rational calculations toward the direction where "state's preferences may not always be tightly linked to the objective conditions. Perceptions and information processing, as well as organizational or bureaucratic imperatives, may change the relevant payoff for decision makers. . . . Payoffs and hence the likelihood of cooperation depend on the perception of decision makers" (Milner, 1992, pp. 490, 491).

She also was able to offer for the first time a model for the estimation of the final outcomes of the process of negotiations based on the positions and perceptions of the negotiation participants. Although these estimations are quite approximate, because they are based mostly on guesses of the opponent's positions, it is still a step to a more human-oriented view of negotiations and toward creating a model for estimating negotiation outcomes based on some real-life-based parameters.

Therefore, Milner tried to combine the best features of the rational actor model and cognitive points of view on the negotiation process discussed in chapter 1 of this work. On one hand, she modeled different negotiation processes under different circumstances, just as the rational actor approach does. On the other hand, she took into account human information-processing limitations and perception problems, just as the cognitive approach does. It is probably the first attempt in the negotiation literature to combine these two seemingly incompatible approaches.

At the same time, there are five problems associated with Milner's model. First of all, the assumption of three separate but still unitary actors at level II is problematic. Secondly, the level II part of the game is too static. The model provides some snapshots but does not show level II interactions. Third, the whole analysis is concentrated on level I activities, pushing level II actors to the second plan and, therefore, diminishing and underestimating their role. Fourth, it is too "iffy." We have to guess possible perceptions, and therefore, the possible outcomes. Finally, this model cannot account for many important aspects in the real world of negotiations although it provides a very useful set of tools for the analysis. These questions prompt us to ask whether the model needs some fine-tuning, that is transformation and extension, in order to be more useful and comprehensive in application to the analysis of negotiations.

The roots of the theory's limitations lie in its assumptions. That is why it is necessary to take a closer look at those assumptions to find out which of them are problematic and, consequently, which of them can be changed or specified in order to further improve the theory.

The Traditional Assumptions of the Two-Level-Game Theory: Critique

As discussed in the previous section, in Milner's model there are four main players: the foreign country, F; the Proposer, P; the Chooser, C; and Endorsers, E. Each of them is assumed to be a unitary, rational, and utility-maximizing actor. Each actor has its own position on a certain issue at hand and that position has its direct effect on other players as well as on the final outcome of the negotiations.

The assumption of the unitary level II actors is the most problematic one. Milner (1997) herself clearly states that the unitary actor assumption is quite awkward: "Obviously, to claim that the executive branch is unitary is to make a simplifying assumption. Politics within the executive branch may be as complex and consequential as politics between it and the other branches. For heuristic purposes, however, the executive is considered to act as if she were a unitary actor" (p. 34). Milner (1997) also writes "The second actor is the legislator. Again it is assumed to be unitary and rational. Neither of these assumptions is unproblematic. . . . Nevertheless it seems useful to abstract from these considerations. . . . Hence the focus is on the median legislator. The member of the legislature who casts the deciding vote on the international agreement becomes the actor who represents the 'unitary' legislature" (p. 35).

By making this unitary actor approximation, the political struggle, which is permanently going on at each political level and between them, is deemphasized. Subsequently, also deemphasized is the effect that this struggle has on the level I process. Milner (1997) understands it because she writes regarding the interest groups that "they serve as pressure groups who, through their ability to contribute campaign funds and mobilize voters, directly shape the preferences of the executive and the legislature; that is the preferences of interest groups often have a significant bearing on political actors' policy preferences" (p. 60). Even though the diversity of these interest groups is quite obvious, they are also considered a unitary actor in the two-level-game theory. They simply push a unitary government for action and provide a median legislator with the necessary information.

The next two assumptions are not stated absolutely clearly in the two-level-game theory. They are those of rationality and information. The reason that they are not stated may be because Putnam did not go that far and Milner tried to probe in different directions. For example, her book contains complete as well as incomplete information game variants. At the same time, it looks as if she were leaning toward the incomplete information model, as can be inferred from the following passage: "the median legislator is assumed not to be fully informed about the foreign country's most preferred outcomes and thus is uncertain about the exact contents of the proposed agreement. Under asymmetric information the model introduces an additional feature—the presence of domestic 'endorsers'" (Milner, 1997, p. 75).

Consequently, not all of the actors have the same level of information and knowledge about the subject of agreement. It is clear that at least interest groups must be experts in a certain area. Other actors desperately need endorsers or informants. This modified assumption is important for two reasons. First of all, very often the lack of information is one of the main reasons why the government and the legislature do not understand each other. Secondly, the lack of information explains why the first two actors very often turn to the interest groups and, consequently, become vulnerable to their influence. If information were full, equally distributed, and easily accessible for every actor in the game, the ratification process would be much easier.

Now the rationality assumption can be clarified. Since a majority of the game's actors do not possess complete information about the possible effects of the negotiation, they can be assumed to exercise only bounded rationality. They are not typical rational actors—they commit perceptional errors and act out of emotions and ideological convictions as well.

Another important assumption of the two-level-game theory is the divided government assumption. The whole game occurs because the government is divided. Here is how Milner (1997) explains this assumption:

> A divergence between the policy preferences of the executive and the median legislator created divided government. The more divergent these preferences are,

the more divided government is. . . . *Divided government* is a term usually re-served for presidential systems. In this context it occurs when the president's party is not the one in control of the majority in the legislature. . . . It also cap-tures the divergence in preferences that may occur even when the same party controls both but party discipline is low and/or the two agents have divergent preferences because of their different constituencies. . . . In multiparty presiden-tial systems, like many in Latin America, legislative majorities depend on coali-tions of parties, thus making divided government fairly constant. Divided gov-ernment is also an obvious possibility in 'semi-presidential' political systems. (pp. 37–38)

The next important assumption is that the whole game is assumed to be uni-dimensional. It means that "if one were discussing trade negotiations, the pol-icy choice would be a single issue such as the percentage reduction in the trade barriers that all countries would accept. . . . Political actors' ideal points will re-flect the policy that perfectly balances the many preferences of their constituents so that their chances for reelection are maximized" (Milner, 1997, p. 71).

The last assumption is that the negotiations between the government rep-resentatives occur in a sort of international political vacuum. This means that all other international political variables that can affect the course of negotia-tions (such variables as political and military block affiliation, unresolved po-litical disputes, trade policy disagreements, any influence or pressure from a third country, etc.) should be ignored.

As the discussion illustrates, some of the traditional assumptions of the two-level-game theory are problematic and, therefore, limit the capacity of the the-ory. The assumption of unitary level II actors disregards internal political struggles and ignores most kinds of political communication. Another prob-lematic assumption is that of the divided government. It is not a historical or political necessity that there *must* be a divergence between the policy prefer-ences of the executive and the median legislator. Nevertheless, it is one of the main assumptions of the theory. This assumption disregards the fact that it is the interests (policy preferences in Milner's terms) but not the government branch affiliation that underlie the actor's actions. From this point, another problem arises, which is the lack of attention to the interests of the actors. Those interests are assumed to be exogenous to the model, consequently, their origins are not stated or explained clearly. It is assumed that *every* actor has his or her own set of interests (policy preferences). But this ignores the fact that large groups and parties constantly fight *together* for their *common* interests, forming political alliances permeating all the strata of society. And most of the time, the whole dynamic of the game is the struggle between two big alliances, permeating through P as well as C and P levels—those *for* or *against* a certain idea or proposal. Finally, the traditional point of view assumes that the negotiations are divided into two separate stages—levels one and two—forgetting about a possible prenegotiation phase and the ongoing consultations during the negotiation process itself. The assumptions of unidimensionality and international political vacuum are also highly problematic because they almost exclude the use of side-payments, one of the main agreement-making tools.

Outside of questions regarding assumptions, it is absolutely necessary to note that the theory almost completely neglects one of the most important and interesting aspects of any negotiation process—it ignores the communicative dynamics of the negotiation process, which is how deals between the parties are actually completed. This is a serious problem because, without understanding the communication process, it is impossible to see how people can actually agree on anything in the face of so many barriers in the way toward an agreement.

All of the assumptions mentioned above create many problems for the traditional version of the two-level-game theory: it is static, it disregards the interests of the negotiation participants, it unjustifiably homogenizes very heterogeneous actors, and it disregards any communication dynamics in the game. In order to solve these problems it is necessary to change the problematic assumptions.

Notes

1. According to the nonrepeated PD game, cooperation is impossible for two reasons. First of all, there are many incentives to defect. And secondly, the cost of being a victim of a defection is very high.

2. Lamenting the domestic constraints—"I'd like to accept your proposal, but I could never get it accepted at home"—is exactly what is called Schelling conjecture.

3

The Extension and Transformation of the Two-Level-Game Theory

<hr>

T HIS CHAPTER WILL START WITH THE THEORETICAL JUSTIFICATION for the extension and transformation of the two-level-game theory. What we will try to do from the theoretical point of view is to take an analytical approach that has been used primarily in one field—international relations—and explore its relevance and application to the analysis of international negotiations from a communication perspective. This particular analytical approach—the two-level-game—is a part of a larger approach of the rational actor models and the game-theoretic models. The application of a communication-oriented version of this approach to the field of communication may be helpful in the analysis of some types of international negotiations.

One of the main problems is that the two-level-game theory is static, which is exactly what is necessary to avoid. That is why it would make sense to give this theory a more dynamic character—to transform it to increase its fidelity and to make it more analytically useful. In order to lay the ground for this kind of transformation some of the assumptions of the two-level-game theory have to be changed or further defined. One of the sections in this chapter will explain how the main assumptions of the theory can be either changed or further specified. Assumptions such as the unitary actor, the obligatory divergence of interests between the Proposer and Chooser actors, and other assumptions will be changed. Then, the theory itself will be presented in graphic as well as textual forms.

The Theoretical Justification for the New Model

For the communications scholars, negotiation is a communication process, which is the process of exchange of symbols. The symbols can be either words or actions (or even nonactions). They are processed by all the parties and interpreted in a certain way. The interpretations then are matched against the set of initial beliefs held prior to the exchange. As a result of this matching process, beliefs are adjusted and new negotiation positions are formed. Further negotiation actions—bids and concessions—are made based on the new positions. These last actions and their consequences are interpreted by the sides again and the whole process is repeated until a mutually satisfactory solution is found. In this perspective, the informational exchange (communication) is the very essence of the negotiation process. It helps the parties to check their initial beliefs and data, to adjust them, to learn about the situation at hand and about the opponent, make intelligent moves, and, finally, find a mutually acceptable solution. That is how people negotiate according to the communication approach.

This cognitive or communication point of view offers very interesting and useful insights as well as many words of caution to prevent negotiators from making very dangerous mistakes. At the same time, this approach has its own problems. First of all, it ignores the sides' interests. It is exactly the differences in interests that create problems that, in turn, require negotiations to solve them. The cognitive approach focuses exclusively on the upper tier of the negotiation process—the communication dynamics. It does not address the question of why the parties send these particular messages but not others. What do the parties want to say? The main issue that this theory is concerned with is how they say it. To restate, communicative strategies are based on goals of the communicative act, but the cognitive point of view is concentrated on strategies without considering goals. This is a very serious drawback because, depending on these goals, the parties will use different communication strategies, derive meaning in different ways, and have varying levels of involvement.

The second problem is that the cognitive approach considers all the communication interactions as if they always occur at the interpersonal level. It does not delve into the context or structure in which a certain communication action happens. Often communication occurs, for example, through the state bureaucratic machinery or the mass media. These organizational or institutional structures may heavily affect the communicative dynamics as well as the final outcome of the communication act. They can distort, delay, or even completely block a certain kind of information. Consequently, the final outcomes of communication acts may vary, not due to perception and belief problems but due to the structural distortions of information. The cognitive perspective ignores this aspect as well. That is why the introduction of interest and structural considerations into this perspective might help to address these problems and open new possibilities for future theoretical development.

For the rational actor/game theory scholars, negotiation is a game of calculations. By knowing the structural requirements of the system, negotiation parties can calculate their moves so that their payoffs are maximized. They try to tailor their negotiation positions according to what is known about the opponent. The problem is that the information that they have can be either complete or incomplete depending on the rules of the game. If the information is incomplete, positions and moves of the players are based on their best guesses about positions and moves of their opponents: "rational choice involves making guesses about one's own future preferences as well as about future consequences of present actions" (Keohane, 1984, p. 116). If the information is complete, the players can calculate positions and actions of the other party. The positions and actions of all the parties are assumed to be based on the payoff structure and cannot be changed unless the rules of the game are changed. That is, if your opponent has taken some position profitable for him or her, you must tailor your response according to that position without assuming that you can change or somehow affect your opponent's stand. All the calculations are done in an exclusively rational and mathematical way. No wonder that this kind of approach draws criticism for being "essentially static in nature; it tends to homogenize actors; it 'blackboxes' the information-processing aspects of bargaining; and it envisages unitary and perfectly rational actors" (Jonsson, 1990, p. 3).

The latest form of the two-level-game theory also assumes four rational and unitary actors (F, P, C, and E) who tailor their negotiation actions based on their best calculations of their opponents' positions (policy preferences). Some of these traditional rational actor assumptions of the two-level-game theory limit the capacity of the theory. The assumption of the unitary level II actors disregards the possibility of internal political struggle and ignores any kind of political communication. Another problematic assumption is that of divided government. It cannot be certain that there *must* be a divergence between the policy preferences of the executive and the median legislator. Nevertheless, this is often one of the main assumptions in many analytical snapshots of the theory. First of all, the presence or absence of policy divergence depends on a specific institutional arrangement of a particular state. It seems that Milner's version of the theory was specifically tailored for the presidential system, such as in the United States. As was mentioned above, it seems that scholars who make this assumption disregard the possibility that it is interests (policy preferences in Milner's terms) but not the government branch affiliation that underlie an actor's actions. From this point comes another problem—it is assumed that every single level II actor has its own set of interests (policy preferences). This underestimates the fact that big groups and parties constantly fight together for their *common* interests, forming political alliances permeating all strata of society. Cooperation as well as conflict is a part of game-theoretic models. Proponents of major contemporary paradigms in the field of international relations emphasized the significance of interests for cooperation (and negotiation as a form of cooperation). For example, on behalf of the realists Mitrany (1975) wrote that shared economic interests create a demand for international cooperation. On behalf of the institutionalists, Keohane (1984) emphasized not only the fact but also the *need* for cooperation. He wrote that cooperation can "develop on the basis of complimentary interests" (p. 9). Both realists as well as institutionalists believe that people, countries, and institutions often must cooperate in order to survive and that the cooperation is based on the *common* interests of the cooperating parties. That is why the underestimation of the cooperative aspects in the two-level game weakens the theory's exploratory and explanatory powers.

To summarize, it can be said that interests can serve as the basis for cooperation as well as conflict—common interests can produce cooperation, different interests may create conflict. The affiliation with a certain branch of government or an administrative body means less for the negotiation process than the actors' interests—that is, officials and managers from different branches can cooperate if their interests are similar while people belonging to the same administrative body can be in conflict if their interests are different.

As any game-theoretic approach, as was mentioned above, the two-level-game theory almost completely ignores the most important and interesting aspects of any negotiation. These are the communicative dynamics of the negotiation process, that is, how the deals between the parties are actually completed. If the positions of the parties were so hard and unchangeable, professions such as lobbying or public relations would not exist. In real life, people can and do persuade or pressure each other to change or adjust their positions. The section in chapter 1 regarding negotiation tools used by the members of the American Congress is the best confirmation of this point. Additionally, the effect of a new piece of information or a new argument can be tremendous. For example, learning theory, also described in chapter 1, argues that during every negotiation process people learn not only about their opponents but also about themselves. The latter can be even more important than the former. People adjust their positions according to what they have learned, that is, their positions are not hard and unchangeable. Ignoring the communication aspects of negotiations is like ignoring traffic signs on the road—it can be confusing and even dangerous. That is why the introduction of communication considerations into the two-level-game model might help to address some of these problems and open new possibilities for future theoretical development.

As we can see, both theoretical perspectives have something to offer to each other. The application of the two-level-game theory to the field of communication will help to take into account the effect of the structural variables on the two-level negotiations. Systematic structural analysis of the two-level negotiation process is something missing from the communication literature: "Little systematic analysis has been done on the communication aspects of international bargaining and negotiation" (Jonsson, 1990, p. 9). But this analysis is very important if we want to know how different types of structures affect the process of the two-level negotiations. It may also shed some light on some previously unexplained variations of outcomes of negotiations.

On the other hand, it does not make sense to use a static model for a dynamic phenomenon because our main goal is to avoid the static character of the traditional game paradigm. That is why the application of the two-level-game theory to the communication field cannot be done without transforming and extending this theory from the communication point of view. It is essential to explore how communication processes work in a certain structure. For this purpose, it is necessary to take the two-level-game structure and superimpose the communication dynamics on it. The result of this process should be a new communication-oriented model of the two-level-game theory. In order to lay the ground for this kind of work it is necessary to change and specify (to explain more fully what was not stated clearly previously) some of the assumptions of the two-level-game theory.

Changing and Specifying the Theory's Assumptions

The Unitary Actor Assumption

Certainly, the first assumption to be changed is the assumption of the unitary level II actors. And, of course, the first actor—the executive or Proposer—is, probably, the most interesting one. For the Americans or the French, who live in presidential systems, the assumption of the unitary executive actors may look quite acceptable, although even in this kind of systems the situation is far from simple.

Even Milner (1997) herself says that "Obviously, to claim that the executive branch is unitary is to make a simplifying assumption. Politics within the executive branch may be as complex and consequential as politics between it and the other branches" (p. 34). Frederick Mayer (1992) echoes Milner saying that all the actors "are not unitary actors but rather are composed of domestic factions which share power but which differ in their interests" (p. 794). It is important to remember the last word—*interests*—that is going to be the key concept for the whole logic of the new model. The previous quote demonstrates that in terms of the Proposer the assumption of the unitary actor can be relaxed and this actor may be represented as a collection of executive interest groups struggling to advance different political and economic interests.

It means changing the character of the game players. We do not assume any longer that the Proposer is just one person—whether, let's say, the president or the prime minister. We assume that the Proposer actor consists of many heterogeneous groups, structures, or institutions that can each have their own opinion what is the best for a country, company, or a city.

Mayer (1992) gives several excellent examples from the field of international relations that show how these intragovernment groups interact and make deals in order to come up with some unified position which can be presented at the international level. One of the examples is as follows:

> More often, internal side-payments must be made in the coin of a nonmonetary issue linked to the internal negotiations. For example, to compensate the U.S. Joint Chiefs of Staff for agreeing to support the first strategic arms limitations talks treaty (SALT I) as negotiated with the Soviet Union, President Nixon linked an arms procurement issue and agreed to support production of the new Trident submarine with multiple warhead missiles. Congressional supporters of arms control tended to oppose the Trident, but a sufficient number understood that Trident was the price they had to pay for ratification of SALT I. (p. 806)

In this case, the American President had to make a deal with another executive body, the U.S. Joint Chiefs of Staff.

Mayer (1992) provides another interesting example of the internal trade within the Proposer actor group of the U.S. government, but a case which occurred *after* the preliminary international agreement had been reached:

> Henry Kissinger, frustrated with the lack of progress in the talks, took matters into his own hands by dealing directly with the Soviets in a secret 'backchannel'. There he cut a deal that traded ABM parity and limits on SLBMs for limits on Soviet intercontinental ballistic missiles (ICBMs). The trade having been made with the Soviets, Kissinger then had to sell the agreement at home. Success required the support of the Joint Chiefs of Staff. As part of his strategy to gain that support, Kissinger made a side-payment: a new generation of submarines and SLBMs. (p. 814)

Some readers may say that the two examples above demonstrate variables that are more situational rather than institutional. This objection is confronted by three arguments. First, interests—the very reason for the necessity for making deals—are situational, as it will be explained later on in this chapter. Second, the composition of actors within the Proposer group is actually a structural dimension. Finally, these examples illustrate that within the Proposer branch itself there are varying groups that have different interests and make deals with each other.

That is why it is useful to assume that the Proposer actor is not unitary, but may consist of several interest groups that make deals among them before, during, and after the inter-entity negotiations. This kind of proposition changes the whole flow of the two-level-game theory logic. Instead of having two steps in the negotiations process we have three:

1. preliminary negotiations at the P actor group level in order to find a proposal acceptable for all of these groups to present at the inter-entity level;
2. inter-entity negotiations;
3. post-inter-entity negotiations between the P actor groups in order to find a way to approve the inter-entity agreement at the intra-entity level.

The assumption of the unitary actors can be also easily changed for the other two actors—the Chooser (C) and Endorser (E)—because it is quite clear that neither, for example, interest groups nor the legislature, that usually consist of the representatives of different parties, can be considered unitary without extreme oversimplification.

Different interest groups can push for absolutely opposite policy choices concerning a certain set of positions under negotiations. Jeffry Frieden (1991) demonstrates that during monetary policy negotiations the import-competing producers of tradable goods for the domestic market usually push to the direction absolutely opposite to that of the international traders and investors; at the same time, the policy choice of the producers of nontradable goods and services is usually absolutely opposite to that of the export-oriented producers of tradable goods; and finally, all these four points of view are very different from one another.

The relationships between the players are difficult not only at each player's group level (P, C, or E) but also in the relationships between the levels. A player can find an ally at another level and play with him or her against another alliance. Those alliances may be quite simple and obvious (like a legislator and his or her constituency) or quite complex and even strange-looking (established through invisible ties of deeply covered interests). In the latter case the relationships between the players can become quite complicated.

Putnam (1988) gives an account of one of the complicated and difficult U.S.-Japanese negotiations. It is remarkable how each of the actors is internally divided and self-interest-oriented, and how complex the interactions between the participants are:

> In Japan a coalition of business interests, the Ministry of Trade and Industry (MITI), the Economic Planning Agency, and some expansion-minded politicians within the Liberal Democratic Party pushed for additional domestic stimulus, using U.S. pressure as one of their prime arguments against the stubborn resistance of the Ministry of Finance (MOF). Without internal divisions in Tokyo, it is unlikely that the foreign demands would have been met, but without the external pressure, it is even more unlikely that the expansionists could have overridden the powerful MOF. (p. 429)

In many other works, authors highlight in particular the interaction between the intra-group actors as a crucial factor for the outcome of the negotiations. For example, Ernst Haas and Karl Deutsch (1957) emphasize especially the impact of parties and interest groups on the process of European integration.

Robert Strauss (1987), an American representative at the Tokyo Round trade talks, writes: "During my tenure as Special Trade Representative, I spent as much time negotiating with domestic constituents (both industry and labor) and members of the U.S. Congress as I did negotiating with our foreign trading partners" (p. vii).

John Conybeare (1991) tries to understand "whether members of Congress are 'single-minded reelection seekers' representing constituency interests or whether they are maximizing something else, such as party loyalty or ideology" (p. 64). He found the following:

> Party identification itself measures constituency interests. [However] a member of Congress will appeal to the largest sectional interest in the represented district and electoral safety will be a function of the homogeneity of interests in that district. Though voters are ignorant and often just vote on the basis of party labels, representatives have two reasons for acting as though constituents respond to their voting record. The first is risk aversion (only a small swing in votes may be necessary to defeat a representative), and the second is the high cost of defeat (the loss of high fixed costs and the waste of specialized human capital). (p. 64)

Now it is time to make some initial conclusions about the assumptions of the two-level game model. The main assumption that can be modified for the purpose of transforming and extending the two-level-game theory is the assumption of the unitary actors. Instead of this we can introduce another assumption, that *the main actors at all three actor group levels of the game (P; C; and E) are separate individuals, groups, or institutional bodies whose actions are the function of their institutional, personal, or group interests as they understand them. The understanding of their interests is a function of information they acquire and process.* As it can be seen from this definition there are three main concepts around which the whole new model will be built. They are *interests, information,* and *institutions.*

Interests

The term *interest* is one of the most differently interpreted and differently used terms in the scholarly literature. For example, Milner (1997) writes, "Domestic actors' preferences are primordial" (p. 33). In the very next paragraph she writes, "The *policy* preferences of actors in domestic politics derive from their basic interests. Actors are assumed to have certain fundamental interests, captured by their utility functions, which they attempt to maximize" (p. 33). There is an apparent confusion here. First Milner says that preferences are primordial, that is, they are basic. Then she says that those policy preferences are derivatives from some kind of other *basic* or *fundamental interests.* This confusion about the terms and concepts of preferences and interests goes though the entire book without ever being clarified.

A clue to the answer to such a puzzle can be found in Keohane's 1984 book, where a clear difference is made between *objective interests* and so-called *myopic self-interests* (pp. 99, 132). Objective interests are basic or fundamental, such as survival or security. "Myopic self-interest refers to governments' *perception* [italics added] of the relative costs and benefits to them of alternative courses of action with regard to a particular issue" (Keohane, 1984, p. 99). Keohane (1984) also notes that *objective* and *myopic self-interests* sometimes may appear to be in conflict with each other.

The reason for such an apparent conflict can be conceptualized in the following way. There are two groups of motives working in many situations. The first group of motives may be defined as basic or fundamental. For example, all of the western democracies declare that the principle goals of their policies are democracy, prosperity, and security. All these goals are based on the fundamental values of freedom, human rights, survival, etc. Consequently, we will call these the *values* of a certain society.

At the same time, achieving the realization of these values is a long and difficult process that poses many everyday challenges for politicians. Often, a certain situation requires some actions that appear to be in contradiction with the values of an actor. For example, the American government proclaimed long ago that worldwide democratization was one of the main goals of its international policy because democracy itself is one of the fundamental values of the American society. At the same time, the American government has quite often supported nondemocratic regimes (such as, for example, the Samosa regime in Nicaragua) because some politicians believed that in that particular situation it was in the American interests (to stop the expansion of Communism in Latin America).

The reason for this apparent conflict is highlighted in italics in Keohane's quotation above—the word *perception*. As the learning and cognitive theories indicate, people's actions are based on their perceptions of each situation. For example, Haas (1983) says that learning is important because it can define and redefine perceptions of values and interests. People form their perceptions according to the information they receive, their ability to process that information, and their previous beliefs. Different combinations of these factors can produce very accurate evaluations of a certain situation as well as really dangerous mistakes—such as the punctuation error and the fundamental error of attribution. For example, one of the most famous perceptional errors was made by the vice president Richard Nixon when he, after a very short meeting, proclaimed Castro a communist. Definitely, the lack of information and Nixon's own prejudice affected his perception of Castro. Consequently, instead of helping Fidel's Cuba to establish a democratic government, the United States started subversive operations against that country pushing it right into an alliance with the Soviet Union. This happened because Nixon believed that by containing a dangerous communist Castro he would save democracy in Latin America. In reality, by his actions, Nixon just helped to boost the communist movement all over Latin America. He *believed* that he acted to advance the American values while indeed he acted in conflict with them.

It is not simply the case that perceptional mistakes alone explain the conflicts between values and actions of some actors. Often situations themselves demand actions that may seem to be incompatible with the values of the actor. These situations may seem clear and obvious. At the same time, when people make mistakes, they may think that they are in such a clear and obvious situation while indeed they simply lack some information and misinterpret other information. That is why perception and, consequently, information and communication are so important for the formation of interests.

In general, *values* are presented here as fundamental. At the same time, *interests* are situational and perceptional. *Interests* are based on the *values*. Paraphrasing Keohane in this discussion, *interests are actors' perception of the relative costs and benefits to them of alternative courses of action with regard to a particular issue or situation.* Another useful definition of interests would be that *interests are actors' perceptions of the way to reach a certain goal, which is in turn based on the actor's values, in a particular situation.* Interests are formed by the processes of communication and information-processing by the actor.

Interests are important because "shared economic interests create a demand" for cooperation (Keohane, 1984, p. 7). This means that shared perceptions must lie in the very basis of any cooperation. That is why "actors may fail to cooperate even when their interests [read *values*] are entirely identical" (Keohane, 1984, p. 65). People may simply fail to perceive a situation in the same way. It may happen because of the differences in their belief systems— the interpretation problem. Or this may happen simply because of some fundamental failures in the communication process. Speaking metaphorically, Keohane (1984) argued that ultimately a simple failure in communication— "the inability of Friar John to deliver a message" (p. 66)—led to failure of Romeo and Juliet's plan and the death of both lovers. That is why the communicative or informational aspect of the problem is extremely important. The next section of this chapter will address this issue. Before that, the term "interest" will be defined in a particular and applied way for the use in the new theoretical model developed in this book.

There are many things that can actually motivate each actor and affect his or her perception of a certain situation at each certain moment (Baldwin, 1985; Coughlin, 1985; Conybeare, 1991). That is why for the purpose of this book, in the applied sense, the term *interest* will be understood very broadly— it may be financial interest, interest to be reelected and, consequently, the interest of the constituencies (or rather perception thereof), even the desire to cover the last scandal with something positive is going to be considered as an interest. This definition includes also emotional interests such as desire for respect, recognition, revenge, etc. The actors may be rational utility maximizers, trying to estimate their payoffs according to some utility functions, or may not be. It is not important for the new model. Since the emotional factors are not excluded, the actors can simply follow their "wants" that in some cases may become their interests. That is why for the sake of parsimony the interests in the new model will be defined simply either as *pro-* or *counter-* a certain idea or proposal. It means that an actor positioned himself or herself either as *pro-* or *counter-* a certain proposal or idea, depending on his or her values, as well as the amount and quality of information, interpretation, and, consequently, the perception of the situation. Such an approach unties our hands and opens the opportunity for deeper, broader, and more realistic situational analysis.

Information

During the negotiation process information has three main functions (that is, it is used in three main ways)—interest formation, interest adjustment, and identity (or actor) formation.

The interest formation aspect of information was discussed in the previous section. The game-theoretic approach also takes into account this function of information. In all the rational actor games, the actors form their interests according to the information they have and act accordingly. Since interests are situational, information about a certain situation may help to develop actor's interests in that particular situation. In order to be *interested* in an issue, an actor has to realize that this particular problem has something to do with his or her values. Then, one has to find out if the current course of events is going in the direction that promotes one's own values or the other way around. Elements, such as the classification of other players (friendly or not), ways to participate in the process, and some possible effects of different courses of events, are vital pieces of information that help to form an actor's interests in a certain situation, all with communication components.

The interest adjustment process is covered by the learning and cognitive theories of negotiation. Interest adjustment happens when people adjust their position according to the new information they receive. In this case, the actors do not have to try to estimate their own and their opponent's positions and actions based on some static payoff matrix assumed in advance. They can actually go ahead and ask about it or dig for more information on the issue. The more information the players can obtain—the better the estimates of the sides' interests. In theory, such an approach should produce better estimates and better outcomes.

The last function—identity formation—has not been covered well enough by either game-theoretic or communication literature. Keohane (1984) says that because of open communication between different organizations "informal coalitions of like-minded officials develop to achieve common purposes" (p. 101). The process of forming these coalitions or actors—identity formation—is going on simultaneously with the process of interest formation although it is a very special one. At the same time, when people realize that they have certain interests in a certain situation, they realize two other important things. First of all, they realize that there are other people who have similar interests in that particular situation (regardless of whether they share their values or not). It usually happens when or if people receive information that such other people exist. Secondly, all these people realize that there are certain things they can do *together* in *that particular situation* to defend, protect, or promote each their own values (again, regardless of whether they share their values or not). It happens when or if they receive information how to do so. At that moment, people realize that they involuntarily formed a certain *group* that can *act united* in order to protect, defend, or promote each their own values in a certain situation, regardless of whether they share those values or not. That is, they become a part of an *actor group*. That is why this process can be called the actor or identity formation process.

In this respect, almost all social and political actors are collective actors in some sense (even some individuals such as, for example, the President, because the presidency is an institution—the President has advisors, the staff, people who influence him, etc.). After an *actor group* formation, communication and development of shared symbols and meanings allows the members to identify themselves with that group. Later, they define common perceptions and understandings (only in relation to a particular situation!)—that is, they form a common (*but temporary!*) identity. That is why communication and information are very important for the formation of the game actors themselves. We have to understand here that, let's say, in the Prisoner's Dilemma game "the prisoner" is a temporary identity for each actor that exists only in relation to that particular situation—at another time they may be hostage-takers, consumers, family members, etc.

A good example of this identity formation process would be the anti-World Trade Organization (WTO) protests in Seattle, Washington, in 1999. All of the participants in those protests were identified as simply the anti-WTO movement. At the same time, this so-called movement included dramatically different groups—environmentalists, human rights activists, political groups, and so on. They had different values. But in that particular situation they had one common interest—to voice their discontent over actions and even the very existence of the WTO. They acted as one organized actor although indeed this actor was internally very diverse. This movement was organized through a network of grassroot communication. First of all, people learned about the upcoming WTO meeting. Secondly, they learned that there were other people who planned actual actions against that organization. At that moment, people with very different values realized that they wanted to be a part of those actions. That is, they identified themselves as members of the anti-WTO movement—a new "actor" on the American and world political scene. That is a member of the so-called anti-WTO movement was a temporary identity for many actors who identified themselves so at that particular time in relation to that particular event.

This example also indirectly supports one of the ideas of this book—practically every actor in the game can be considered as a collection of sub-actor groups who have to negotiate their place and role within that actor. Besides that, the concept of identity formation opens an opportunity for recognizing the role of communication in actually creating actors or entities. Indeed, if agents can provide enough information and persuasion power, they can convince people, even with different value systems, to become a part of a certain actor for a certain situation (for example the "coalition of the willing"). That is where political communication, public relations, propaganda, organizational communication, and even advertising come into play. All these forms of communication can be and often are used to convince people that, in a certain situation or in relation to a certain issue, it is in their interest to do certain things. In this respect, communication practitioners often try to form supporting actors for their plays.

During a negotiation, as in any game, the quality, amount, and distribution of information are also crucial. "It is commonly argued that uncertainty—that is, incomplete information—is inimical to international cooperation" (Milner, 1997, p. 68). Keohane (1984) actually argues that uncertainty creates a demand for cooperation because cooperation reduces uncertainty through establishing of the channels of informational exchange. "It is universally suggested that the result of misperception is conflict that would have been otherwise avoidable" (Stein, 1990, p. 58). When people try to solve their problems through negotiation they try to correct their own as well as each other's misperceptions through providing each other with important and relevant information. "If all the actors knew each other's preferences and capabilities, then concerns over credibility, cheating, and so on, would be moot and conflict unlikely" (Milner, 1997, p. 69).

When information is not complete "the less-informed group must worry about being exploited and hence will often reject agreements that have been concluded by the better-informed partner" (Milner, 1997, p. 83). But the main problem is not simply the asymmetry of information but rather systematically biased patterns of information, what is called *quality uncertainty*. "Awareness that others have greater knowledge than oneself, and are therefore capable of manipulating relationship or even engaging successful deception and double-cross, is a barrier to making agreements" (Keohane, 1984, p. 93).

But even if there is enough information available to make a decision "a cacophony of messages may render all of them uninterpretable" (Keohane, 1984, p. 95). That is where the issues of information selection and interpretation arise. It has been noted above how difficult it is to derive even one's own interests correctly. And certainly, it is even more difficult to estimate the interests and, consequently, possible tactics, strategies, and actions of the other side.

In the case of the rational actor model perspective, players can derive the other side's as well as their own interests directly from a game's payoff matrix (certainly, only during theoretical game exercises—not in real life). But this kind of estimation is based on the amount and quality of information the players have. In case of a lack of information, such estimations are susceptible to serious calculation errors. It would be a good idea to receive more information but the game rules are static—they do not allow players to go for additional information—you have to act with what you have.

If the actors had unlimited time and unlimited access to information sources they would always receive the optimal outcome. But, certainly, this is not the case. Information is costly and difficult to obtain. In the contemporary international relations and communication theories "limits and costs of information are introduced, not as psychological characteristics of the decision maker, but as part of his technological environment.... Now he needs to compute not only the shapes of his supply and demand curves, but in addition, the costs and benefits of computing those shapes to greater accuracy as well" (Simon, 1979, p. 504). Under such circumstances, people have to "economize on information by searching only until they find a course of actions that falls above a satisfactory level—their 'aspiration level'" (Keohane, 1984, p. 112). All this leads us back to the notion of bounded rationality.

Facing "limitations on her capacity in calculation," an actor "cannot calculate the costs and benefits of each alternative course of action on each issue. On the contrary, they need to simplify their own decision making process in order to function effectively at all" (Keohane, 1984, pp. 111, 115). As will be argued below, one of the best ways to simplify this process is to negotiate, that is, to give each other necessary information voluntarily. Negotiations make it easier and cheaper to receive necessary information. As a matter of fact, negotiation is a very good source of information by itself. Certainly, for example, every government has other sources of information, such as research and intelligence. But negotiations give something with which to compare that information. Having compared several sources of information, every decision maker would be more sure about the decision he or she makes. That is, negotiation is a very good way of reducing uncertainty and, by so doing, of producing solid decisions. Certainly, not every negotiator is ready to provide the other side with all the honest and complete information. That is why actors need such indices as intelligence or research to check the information received. But in general, negotiation, as a form of open, easy, and cheap communication, is a very important part of every institution's decision making. Keohane (1984) actually used the reduction of uncertainty through the process of negotiations as a justification for the very existence of international regimes and other types of institutions. For this reason, institutions add still another level to this discussion.

Institutions

As explained above, the neoliberals argue that actors establish institutions because they have some shared interest in them. The purpose of an institution may be either promotion or protection of such *common* interests.

Institutions are also structures. And as any social structures, according to the definition of the structure given in this work, institutions embody the aggregation of interests, distribution of resources, and distribution of capabilities.

There are different points of view on what institutions actually are and what their roles are. In the *structural functionalist* point of view, institutions fulfill functions important for survival or maintenance of some kind of order. The order is necessary in any society, consequently, institutions are essential for the survival of that society. The wholeness and unity of the society depends on institutions (Bull, 1995, p. 72). In the structural functionalist perspective, every institution is a system where the whole has primacy over its parts and the nature of these parts depends on what they contribute to the needs of the whole. In this point of view, every political institution is an open and adaptive system that strives for internal equilibrium. As any open system, institutions use input from the outside to alert, modify, or adjust their internal structure. Finally, institutions produce outputs that are essential for the survival or maintenance of a society (Easton, 1965, pp. 17–33). That is why, according to this perspective, institutions are needed to carry out some important societal functions.

Some scholars, who undertake a more historically descriptive approach to institutions, criticize the structural functionalists' point of view. They say that the society "does not display the kind of wholeness or unity that would give point to explanations of this sort" (Bull, 1995, p. 72). They also argue that some social phenomena, such as, for example, international politics are "better described as a state of war" (Bull, 1995, p. 73). They also emphasize that scholars have to be very specific and cautious using terms such as functions and needs.

The discussion above is very important for the two-level-game theory in general because it places institutions into a larger context, such as the state system or international community. This may be important for level I as well as level II negotiations because the dynamics of talks between as well as within different institutions may depend on and may be affected by the relationships between these institutions and the larger context. It may be important if the broader system is strong and well-structured or weak and loose. This may determine what kind of roles are played by each of the institutions within that system, what demands (if any) that system places on these institutions, etc. Depending on a particular context, institutions may be either required to do certain things, or constrained from certain actions, or they may be quite free to act at their own will. This aspect will be touched upon later on in this book. For instance, legislators may be required to take a very special type of vote in relation to a certain initiative or proposal because that type of vote is required by the Constitution or any other sort or regulatory documents. In this case, the greater system places this particular demand on that particular institution. In other cases actors may proceed at their own will, hardly affected by the constraints of a larger system within which they operate. In general, it seems that each situation should be considered on the case-by-case basis. That is why this relationship—between a decision-making institution and its larger context—is quite important for the two-level-game theory.

For the purpose of this book, institutions are structures (as "structure" was defined above) created for the purpose to promote or protect certain common interests. That is why it is also important to consider other definitions of institutions.

For example, Young (1980) defines institutions as "recognized patterns of practice around which expectations converge" (p. 337). Keohane (1984) defines regimes (as a specific approach to institutions) as "rules, norms, principles, and decisionmaking procedures" (p. 8). Decision-making procedures are, to a large degree, recognized patterns, rules, and practices of the movement of information within an institution from one actor to another. These two definitions of institutions, working together, are very important for the new communication-oriented model of the two-level-game theory.

Institutions play many roles. They "facilitate agreements by raising the anticipated costs of violating others' property rights, by altering transaction costs through clustering of issues, and by providing reliable information to members" (Keohane, 1984, p. 97). They exclude certain groups from or include them in the circle of people who have the access to information and/or the right of participation in important discussions. They also manage conflict and, ultimately, crystallize power relations. But there are three roles of institutions that will be especially important for the purpose of this book. They are interest aggregation, information distribution, and information flow regulation.

The interest aggregation role of institutions was discussed in the "Interest" section of this chapter. The only thing that will be added here is that, through the process of interest aggregation, institutions will also play a role in the process of actor formation. Since institutions define certain roles for their members, they, consequently, indirectly define points of view from which these members perceive issues and problems.[1] All this, as explained above, may have an effect on, for example, which group a certain person (or a group of people) decides to join in case of a problem, or whether they decide to join a group at all. Finally, certain incentives or paths for collective action are encouraged within certain institutional structures.

As was mentioned in chapter 2, many neoliberal institutionalists, especially Keohane, believe that one of the main roles of institutions is the distribution of information. An institutional role in distributing information is important for many reasons. It serves as a safeguard against the fear of defection, helps to expose violators, insures the prospects of future cooperation, etc. Institutions make it cheaper and easier for actors "to get together to negotiate an agreement" (Keohane, 1984, p. 90). They also give the actors "incentives to reveal information and their own preferences fully to one another" (Keohane, 1984, p. 92).

At the same time, institutions regulate the flow of information. The institutional structure limits the access to information for the outsiders, establishes time-limits for information processing according to standard operating procedures (SOPs), and prevents information overflow by filtering out unnecessary data and leaving in only relevant information. Therefore, the institutional structure may impede the flow of information, distort it, or completely block out some types or pieces of information.

Taking into account all the above, we can quite confidently say that institutions reflect not only arrangements of interests but also informational arrangements or arrangements of the communicative practices and procedures. In this respect, negotiation itself is an institutionalized form of communication. Negotiations are regulated by special protocol procedures. These procedures usually regulate the order and the time frame in which negotiations occur. It is important to know who participates in negotiations because actors try to negotiate primarily with other important actors—that is, with the decision makers. Information exchanged during negotiations is the information produced by one organization or actor and required by the other organization or actor participating in the negotiations. These and some other aspects of the negotiation process can be considered to be institutionalized.

To summarize the three previous sections, information affects the processes of actor formation, interest formation, and interest adjustment. Interests and actors, in turn, are aggregated into institutions that, then, regulate the distribution and the flow of information and, consequently, also affect the processes of actor formation, interest formation, and interest adjustment again. As we can see, these three elements of the negotiation process—interests, information, and institutions—are very closely interrelated and intertwined and that is why they will be very important for the new model.

Other Assumptions

As was mentioned above, the assumptions of the previous version of the model will have to be either changed (such as, for example, the unitary level II actors assumption) or more precisely specified. The latter means that the assumptions that were either not stated clearly or not covered at all in the previous model will have to be explained in more detail here.

The actors in the new version of the game are assumed to act according to their interests as they were defined above. The more information they can receive from different types of communication—the better the quality of their estimates of the payoffs will be. They also can affect their opponents' positions by providing the other side with additional information. At the same time, the actors do not always calculate their payoffs based on a utility function. Some steps may leave them worse off in terms of purely rational considerations but if the same step satisfies some of their emotional needs, they still may make it. That is why the best way to estimate actions of the other side is to obtain as much information about the opponent as possible, that is, to become involved in information exchange or negotiation with your opponent as well as with other actors in the game.

We also assume strictly asymmetric information flow. This does not mean unlimited information. Factors such as the information search cost, the ability to process only certain amounts of information, time constraints, and others come into play here as well. Therefore, some actors—with better information search and processing capabilities—will be better informed than others. Consequently, all actors are able to exercise only bounded rationality, which means some of the actors (namely, Proposer and Chooser) do not have full information on the topic under consideration and are not aware of all the available choices. That is why they are susceptible to the Endorser's influence. The Endorser actors provide them with the necessary information and, by so doing, affect their interest formation and adjustment processes.

According to the new model, the main actors are separate individuals, groups, or institutional bodies acting at three actor group levels—Proposer, Chooser, and Endorser. All the mechanisms of the bargaining process at the inter-entity level described in the literature (for example, as presented in Milner's 1997 book) will remain intact. It basically means that such concepts as "win-set" will also be applicable to the new model.

Besides that, the negotiations are not assumed to be entirely unidimensional—at least to the extent that some deal-making side-payments may come from adjacent or even entirely unrelated areas. Consequently, the assumption of theoretical political vacuum in which negotiations are taking place has to be modified as well because definitely such factors as political block affiliation, trade disputes, unsolved political problems as well as third party pressure may play a significant role in the game.

Finally, the term "divided government" will be redefined later in this work to reflect the new approach to the problem and new character of the game.

The New Model—A Communication Perspective

Problems of the Traditional Form of the Two-level-game Theory

From the communication point of view, every negotiation is traditionally considered as a process, that is, something dynamic and constantly changing.

The two-level-game theory as it exists today, on the other hand, is a set of static situations that occur under certain circumstances. This absence of dynamism is the main problem of this theory. But it is possible to address this problem if it is recalled that "bargaining in general and negotiation in particular can be seen as communication superimposed on the game" (Jonsson, 1990, p. 3). It means that it is necessary to superimpose communication dynamics on the traditional paradigm of the two-level game.

The second problem is that the two-level-game theory "treats constituents as a black box, failing to acknowledge that they usually are parts of complex organizations involving many individuals and groups who communicate and negotiate with each other about the issues under discussion" (Pruitt, 1995, p. 39). In order to address this problem we have to expose and emphasize *intra-entity* rather than *inter-entity* differences and contradictions.

Finally, the discrete point of view that divides negotiations into two separate levels is another problem.

> The model draws a misleading distinction between *inter*organizational negotiation . . . and *intra*organizational . . . negotiation. . . . In reality, negotiation is found in all these arenas, and usually many more, within the organizations. Furthermore, preparation for negotiation *within* organizations is often found in discussions *between* the organizations. . . . Indeed, the main resistance to agreement, and hence the main focus of preparation for negotiation, may lie deep in one organization, at a considerable distance from the boundary between the organizations. (Pruitt, 1995, p. 39)

In order to address this problem, it must be noted that ratification is not the only type of *intra-entity* interaction that is important for a two-level negotiation process. Internal bargaining before negotiations, consultations during negotiations, and different types of internal interactions after inter-entity negotiations are very important factors as well. In this case the discrete picture of the game can be transformed into a unified one that emphasizes internal communication dynamics.

The solution to all three of these problems should create the new *communication-oriented* model of the two-level-game theory.

Approval—An Institutional Perspective

Before introducing the new model, it is necessary to explain a new concept that lies at its very heart. It is the concept of *institutional approval.* Until now, most researchers interested in the effect of the intra-entity variables on the inter-entity negotiation process focused their attention on the ratification process as key at level II. But it would be much more logical to say that ratification itself is just a final point in a very long and complex internal approval process.

Ratification is simply an institutional standard operating procedure (SOP) that dictates what institutional body must give the *final* approval to what kind of decisions using what kind of processes. The key word here is *final*. The whole process consists of three main stages. First of all, a certain initiative must be approved at the Proposer level. If that initiative has too many opponents at this level, the Proposer may not push the initiative ahead strongly enough to reach the ratification level. The initiative will simply die within this actor group level. Next, the initiative should get the approval of some interest groups. These groups are those whose interests were aggregated into a certain institution, and they can be either external or internal in relation to this institution (like stakeholders in Pruitt's 1995 model). The main point is that there must be at least one powerful interest group that will be willing to provide favorable support for the initiative. Otherwise, how would the Choosers know that this initiative is in their interest (in the interest of their constituency) or in the best interest of the whole institution? Though some already may have their positions formed, some of them may not. Additionally, even if the position of some of the Choosers is not favorable toward the initiative, according to the communication point of view, their positions can be adjusted by providing them with more favorable information toward the initiative (or the other way around—favorable to not favorable).

Only after the above issues have been resolved does the ratification process usually comes into play, but not always. Often the Chooser simply refuses even to consider a document already signed at the inter-entity level. It means that the document failed to be approved at one or more other intra-entity levels. It shows that ratification is not the main point, but usually just the final point in this process. Besides that, ratification may never formally happen in a certain country or institution only because the other side failed to ratify the agreement before that. But it does not mean that the approval process in the first institution or country failed. Had the agreement been put forward for ratification— it would have passed. That is why, the formal emphasis on ratification is a misconception which skews the analysis. But the concept of institutional approval is much more logical and encompassing.

The whole internal institutional approval process may be expressed as follows:

Internal Approval = Proposer + Chooser + Endorser

This formula actually shows us the three main variables of the new model— *the degree of division at the Proposer (P) level; favorability of the situation at the Chooser level (or the degree of division at the C level); and the presence of*

Endorsers at the E level. These three variables are supposed to help explain the outcome of the whole internal approval process that is either *pass* or *fail.*

Before actually introducing the new model, it is necessary to clarify some terms. When discussing the inter-entity levels of the two-level-game theory, the terms *level I or level II* or *the first level* or *the second level* will be used. When the discussion is about the interactions at each of the model's intra-entity levels—P, C, or E—the term *actor group level* will be used.

The New Model

The traditional two-level-game model assumes four separate unitary actors F, P, C, and E. All these actors are independent but calculate their negotiation actions based on their estimates of actions and positions of other actors in the game. This approach is graphically depicted on Figure 3.1.

According to this model, as soon the game is finished at the first level—it starts at the second one: after inter-entity negotiations—it is time for ratification bargaining.

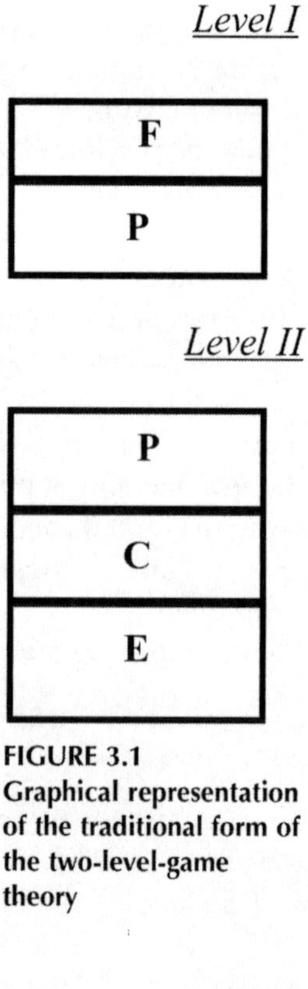

<u>*Level I*</u>

F
P

<u>*Level II*</u>

P
C
E

FIGURE 3.1
Graphical representation of the traditional form of the two-level-game theory

As indicated above, the creation of the new model has to be accomplished through finding appropriate solutions for the three main problems of the two-level-game theory. We will be working backwards and start with problem number three—the discrete point of view of the game.

First of all, it is necessary to point out that the two-level-game model assumes the following sequences of events—the agreement is reached at the inter-entity level and only after that is it ratified by the Chooser. It is a discrete point of view on the negotiation process. It provides for two distinct and separate negotiation stages—stages of level I and level II. But Putnam (1988) writes, "at the national level, domestic groups pursue their interests by pressuring the government to adopt favorable policies . . ." (p. 434). It means that negotiations may be initiated not by the Proposer but by the interest groups who pressure the P level actors to start negotiations about a certain issue. In this case, the real first stage of the negotiation process is not between P and F but between P and E actors.

At the same time, the influence of the Chooser actors and interest groups on the negotiators is a continuous variable—it never stops. As a rule, formal as well as informal consultations between all the internal actors go on simultaneously while the inter-entity talks progress. That is why these are not exactly two separate steps. Since the whole essence of the new model is to better express interactions between the actors—this new, more interactive scheme is being suggested:

1. preliminary negotiations between the Proposer groups (within the P level only) or Proposer and interest groups (between P and E) in order to find an acceptable proposal for all of these groups to present at the inter-entity level;
2. inter-entity negotiations, that may go on for years, along with consultations with the intra-entity actors that also do not stop at that time;
3. post-inter-entity negotiations between the intra-entity actors at all the actor group levels in order to make sure that the current version of the document is acceptable for all of these groups;
4. sometimes, an amended or completely transformed agreement goes back to the inter-entity level for further negotiations (*optional*).

As we can see, this is actually not a clear-cut two-stage pattern but rather a complex interlocked process. This process is depicted on Figures 3.2 and 3.3.

Figures 3.2 and 3.3 depict the game in a unified model. Each of the rings represents a country with its own Proposer, Chooser, and Endorser groups. The rings are supposed to demonstrate that all three groups of actors at the intra-entity level interact with each other at the lines of juncture in a permanent

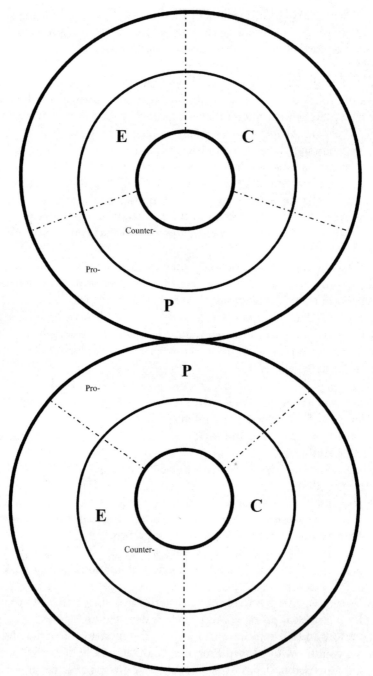

FIGURE 3.2
A graphical presentation of bilateral negotiations

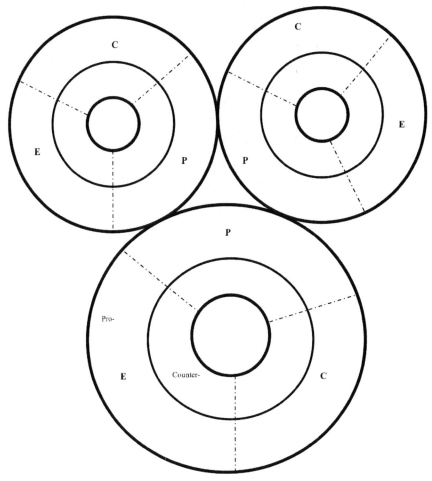

FIGURE 3.3
A graphical presentation for multilateral negotiations

manner and there is no break or any distance between them at any time. The traditional rectangular diagram may create the false impression that the Chooser separates the Proposer and the Endorser actors one from the other which is not the case. There is as much continuous interaction between Proposer and Endorser actor group levels as between Proposer and Chooser or Endorser and Chooser. The second false impression that may be created by a rectangular diagram is that it represents some kind of hierarchy in the system. Again, this is not the case. Each actor group level is equally significant in the game. There is no actor that is considered to be superior to another. The circular shape helps to solve these problems. It clearly shows that there is no hierarchy among the internal actors. It also demonstratively shows that there is no separation between the actor group levels. In the circular form, we clearly see that P interacts with E and C, E—with P and C, and C—with P and E at the junction lines. There is no top-to-bottom drop-down process of approval. There is a continuous circular discussion process. It is not necessary to argue what actor to put at the top and what actor goes at the bottom.

The Intra-entity Interaction Model

In order to solve the second problem of the two-level-game theory—it treats constituents as a black box—we have to uncover the composition of actors at each actor group level. From the communication point of view, communication is impossible without at least two entities that communicate with each other— one entity cannot communicate with itself. That is why, the unitary actor assumption automatically eliminates any possibility of communication at the actor group levels. At the same time, we know that active communication processes go on at each of these levels. It means that there is more than one actor or group of actors at each level. The problem is how to define them. The answer has already been given above—they will be defined according to their interests— *pro* or *counter* a certain idea or proposal. This broad and general approach has at its roots the concept of *interests* and should uncover the principal differences, contradictions, and interactions that take place at each actor group level.

In the new model, there will be the same acting groups—Proposer, Chooser, and Endorser—as we saw in the classical two-level-game model. But in this case the real actors are members of these groups who act according to their interests.

The transformed version of the situation at the intra-entity level of the new model is depicted on Figure 3.4.

Regardless of some similarities between the new model and the classical one, they are dramatically different. Comparing the two diagrams depicting the models, in the first one (traditional—Figure 3.1) there are three separate actors. They interact but also act independently, and that is why they are divided by solid lines. In the second model (new—Figure 3.4), following the solid lines pattern, there are just two main groups of actors—*pro-* and *counter-*, acting at three actor group levels—Proposer (P), Chooser (C), and Endorser (E). This represents a different point of view regarding the intra-entity level of the negotiation process. It is supposed to show that actors' interests matter more than the actor group affiliation.

This may be demonstrated using the American state structure as an example. Often, the members of Congress who belong to the president's party give the chief executive almost unanimous support in all his initiatives. This pat-

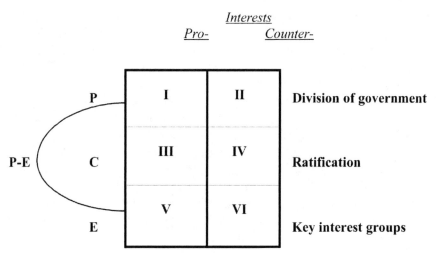

FIGURE 3.4
The intra-entity composition of actors in the new model of the two-level-game theory

tern may be partially explained by the party affiliation (discipline) and, therefore, political interests. Even deeper, it can be explained by the system of beliefs and shared values that underlie the party affiliation. It does not matter
here. The main fact is that within the groups formed by interests, the actors
have much more in common than within the same actor group level—P, C, or
E. At the same time, it would be a mistake to suggest that the agreement goes
strictly along party lines. There may be people from the other party who support the same initiative. It depends only on the interests of a particular politician in a particular situation. For example, in the parliamentary system (with
stronger party discipline), had the agreement always gone along the party
lines, there would not have been any ratification problems. But it is not always
the case. Even the members of parliament of the same party affiliation as the
prime minister may have their own interests in relation to a certain issue or
situation. Their interests can be rooted in their constituency's interests, personal interests, or something else. And in some cases, they may protect these
interests regardless of the prime minister's position. That is why the interest
variable is a key one in the new model.

The same is true for every country in the world and basically for every sector of international relations. Let's take, for example, the debates concerning
the degree of openness of the domestic market. It is axiomatic that right-wing
governments tend to open markets while the left-wing ones try to close them.
(The same kind of debate can be seen between the supporters and opponents
of market openness at every actor group level.) It means that the bargaining

between the Proposer and the Chooser mainly occurs between cells I and IV—
and much to a lesser extent between cells I and III. (Please, refer to Figure 3.4.)
It does not mean that there are no negotiations at all between I and III, but
those negotiations are conducted just to polish up the details of their common
position against cells II and IV.

The same is obviously the case for the C-E interaction. "Politicians want to
please their constituents and will attempt to manipulate the trade policy to
further this goal" (Conybeare, 1991, p. 57). "Elected officials choose policies
that disproportionally favor their supporters" (Cowhey, 1993, p. 304). The legislators will try to "please" the people who give them votes and financial support. Actually, they often form their political positions directly based on the
position of their underlying constituents (that is III on V's interests and IV on
VI's interests). That is why, again, most of the deals and side payments will be
made between cells III and VI—but not between cells III and V. (Please, refer
to Figure 3.4.)

The P-E arc on the diagram above demonstrates the relationship between
the Proposer and the Endorser. Here we can find the same—P level actors will
be very vulnerable to the demands of the interest groups with similar economic and political interests and will be arguing or bargaining only with their
political opponents. Again, the deals will be made mostly between the cells I
and VI—and very rarely between cells I and V. (Please refer to Figure 3.4.)

That is why, on the diagram the division between Proposer, Chooser, and
Endorser is denoted by just dotted lines while the division between the vertical groups of interest is a thick solid line. It means that the actor group affiliation (P, C, E) explains much less of the political behavior than the group of
interest affiliation.

In short, it is one of the assumptions of the new model that, since actors are
grouped according to their interests, communication within each interest
group is less important than between groups. At the same time, the author of
this work understands that this assumption is a simplification. Often, communication, persuasion, and even side payments are necessary within each interest group in order to mobilize supporters or opponents of a certain document, idea, or proposal. It may be important. In a situation in which every
actor is bombarded with new information and persuasive messages, it is necessary to hold each interest actor group together and prevent defections. But
this kind of dynamic is beyond the scope of the main idea of the new model.
Besides that, the introduction of this kind of dynamic into the new model
would make it unreasonably complex.

But the new model is not complete yet. It is static and does not explain the
dynamics of the whole process. Let us consider again the following passage
from Milner (1997):

[If] the endorser is less hawkish than the legislature . . . then C knows that E will endorse only proposed agreements that also meet with C's approval. But C also knows that E will not endorse some agreements that C prefers to the status quo—that is, those between E's indifference point and C's indifference point. E's endorsements cover only a subset of proposals that C would like to ratify. (p. 87)

According to this description the situation is static—the Chooser is more hawkish than the Endorser. In this case, the Endorser takes this situation as something given and can endorse "only a subset of proposals that C would ratify" (Milner, 1997, p. 87). But the last statement does not make a lot of sense in the real world. Certainly, the interest groups can take into account the position of the ratifying body but they are not bound by it. What if they need something that the "median legislator" would not endorse? Would they give up? Certainly, they would not. The real world answer is that they would try to persuade the legislators to support their initiative. They would get involved in activities such as lobbying and public relations. Milner herself admits this in other places in her book where she says that the Endorsers are influential information providers for the Choosers and that such information does influence the Choosers. But in her actual game calculations she makes it sound as if the position of the Chooser level actors is set is stone, unchangeable, and it is the final law and that the interest groups have to tailor their position according to the opinions of the members of the ratifying body. But in that case, what would the Endorsers provide all this information for? In that case, lobbying and public relations would not simply exist, yet these activities are very important for public affairs and decision-making.

In order to solve this apparent serious controversy it is useful to draw upon the communication point of view. Communication can adjust the sides' positions, and hence "hawkishness" may be a temporary state of mind. That is where it is useful to talk about a process rather than a state. This problem shows the usefulness of superimposing communication dynamics on the static game paradigm. According to the learning theory of negotiations covered in chapter 1, negotiation is a bargaining process. Bargaining strategies depend on the parties' perceptions of the opponent's position, values, views, and expectations. As the parties negotiate, their strategies and expectations change according to what they have learned about each other. This adjustment process is the main way of finding a mutually accepted solution to a common problem. Besides that, each negotiator learns not only about the opponent but also about himself, herself, or their group. Often, actors find out that a certain outcome is not as favorable to their group as they expected because either the circumstances or their perceptions have changed. It means that even if the perception of their own interests by the

Choosers was "hawkish," different negotiation activities can change either the circumstances or the Chooser level actors' perceptions.

According to the communication point of view, in any negotiation situation there is one predominant kind of communication—persuasion—designed to influence others by modifying their behaviors, beliefs, and attitudes. Communication is "a process by which one person affects the behavior or state of mind of another" (Fiske, 1982, p. 2). By the process of persuasion the actors' positions can be changed. "Negotiation, then, can be seen as mutual persuasion attempts" (Jonsson, 1990, p. 11). It means theoretically that the position of every actor can potentially be changed which, in turn, changes all the game calculations and the final outcome. If the positions of the game actors are not static, Milner's calculations are not going to work anymore. Another approach to the whole process is needed, a dynamic approach. Demonstrating the degree of bargaining and political struggle at each actor group level can help in understanding the differences in the final outcome within the limits of the same political system. In other words, it is useful to superimpose the communication dynamism onto the general game paradigm. To represent the dynamic potential of communication the central line dividing interests needs to be moveable and, moreover, moveable separately at each actor group level.

To illustrate this, let us consider Figure 3.5.

In a hypothetical country the President pushes forward a certain international monetary policy proposal. But the Central Bank of this country op-

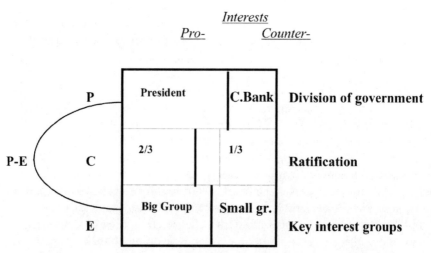

FIGURE 3.5
The intra-entity negotiation dynamics in the new model of the two-level-game theory

poses this kind of policy. The agreement needs to be ratified by two-thirds of the upper chamber of the country's parliament (dotted line at the C level) but, as we can see, the current distribution of the votes (solid line at the C level) is approximately 50/50. Therefore, it does not favor the new policy proposal. At the same time, there is a large group of import-competing producers of tradable goods for the domestic market who want this policy adopted. Simultaneously, there is a small group of the international traders and investors who do not like this policy at all.

It may look like this bill has few chances to pass because at one of the crucial levels—ratification—there are not enough votes to support it and there are endorsers on both sides. The classical two-level-game model might lead to just that conclusion. But the new model makes it possible to consider the issue more deeply and see that there are quite a few chances for this bill to pass and come into effect. Indeed, within the executive actor group, the President can make some side payments and, consequently, make some deals with the Central Bank. At the same time, he or she can keep bargaining with the opposition representatives in the parliament and try to persuade them that they have to support the bill or put some pressure on them. The large group of endorsers can also influence the members of the parliament. If they manage somehow to move the solid line on the diagram at the C level up to the level of ratification (dotted line)—they will be able to pass the bill. The old model does not recognize this opportunity because there is no interest border in the scheme.

As we can see, the primary goal of the supporters of a proposal in the new two-level game is very intuitive and simple—to move the vertical borderline of interest at each actor group level as far to the right as possible and, by so doing, to capture as many supporters as possible. At the same time, by moving that line to the right, they squeeze the opponent's territory to the greatest extent possible. Simultaneously, the opponents of the bill will try to move the border to the left. The winner is the side whose sum of P + C + E (the approval formula above) is greater.

According to the old model, as long as the government is divided, the ratification process has been changed, and there are endorsers on both sides (three key variables in Milner's classical model)—the bill has very few chances to succeed. That is why the old scheme gave some incomplete explanations for the results of some international negotiations. But the new model offers a new perspective on the process and therefore new analytical capabilities as well. The emphasis on interests—the new key variable—and the moveable vertical interest border help to account for more variations in possible outcomes.

A question remains: How can the players move the interest border? The obvious answer would be communication. And a very special role will be played by a particular tool called the side-payment.

Side-payments

This is the part of the model where communication dynamics really come into play. People support or oppose certain actions or initiatives because they believe that those actions or initiatives run for or against their interests. According to the communication perspective, there are several ways to change such beliefs. The first is to provide some additional information that would show to a person that a certain action is much more favorable toward him or her than that person has previously believed. The second way is to present some logical arguments. These arguments may be intended to persuade a person that a certain action is in his or her interests even if it is not obvious for that person right away. Another set of arguments may be intended to explain that, although a certain action is not in the interest of this particular individual, it should be taken anyway because of some other overriding interests (such as common good, etc.). All these types of communication can be used in negotiations to change actors' positions.

But the problem is that all of these communication methods may not be very effective. As mentioned above, positions are formed based on interests, and even the best arguments in the world may fail to persuade people to change their opinion and act against their interests as they see them. The overview of the communication approach toward negotiations provided in chapter 1 stated that human beliefs are resistant to change. People may fail to see that new information contradicts their beliefs, may reject the validity of the new piece of information, may discredit the source of discrepant information, may engage in seeking new information to support initial beliefs, or may start adducing additional elements to weaken discrepant information. That is why one way to shift beliefs is to shift people's interests. Simply speaking, if a person realizes that he or she is going to receive something positive from a situation that has been previously considered negative, this person can adjust his or her point of view on that particular situation. (Another approach is to let that person know that he or she will avoid something negative.) That is, other actors must give to that person something positive; this is the action known as the side-payment. The side-payment is one principle tool for making people adjust their positions regarding policy-related issues.

The literature on side-payments is scarce, but the author was able to find some important information that is directly related to the topic at hand and will help to understand the side-payment tool much better.

Milner (1997) writes in her book about side-payments:

> Side payments refer to a broad range of tactics that have one common element. As the name implies, side payments involve an actor giving up value on one issue in exchange for other actors giving up value on another issue. Thus side pay-

ments may be viewed in a broader sense to include such practices as logrolling, vote trading, compromise, concessions, reciprocity, bribes, and issue linkage. All these tactics involve the same general principle that is the centerpiece of side payments: an actor gives up value on one issue of lesser importance in order to gain value from others on an issue of greater importance. (p. 109)

The reason that side payments are used is that different actors have different preferences or different intensities of preferences across issue areas.

Milner (1997) also says that types of side payments differ in many important aspects. First of all, the value exchange may occur simultaneously or sequentially. Second, side-payments may be implicit or explicit. Third, side-payments can be made in different currencies, such as money, votes, future policy choices, political appointments, a territory, etc. Finally, Milner believes that even threats may be a part of the side-payment strategy (although she admits that it is not a well-accepted point of view).

In relation to two-level-game theory Putnam (1988) writes about side-payments:

In a two-level game the side-payments may come from unrelated domestic sources . . . or they may be received as part of the international negotiation. The role of side-payments in international negotiations is well known. However, the two-level approach emphasizes that the value of an international side-payment should be calculated in terms of its overall value to recipient nation. What counts at Level II is not total national costs and benefits, but their *incidence, relative to existing coalitions and procoalitions.* An across-the-board trade concession . . . is less effective than a concession (even one of lesser intrinsic value) that tips the balance with a swing voter. (p. 450)

An institution is a form of interest aggregation. A side-payment is an exchange of values. Thus, the use of side-payments in the institutional context will involve an increase in the value of a certain interest for some actors. That is, by making a side-payment we add some value to a certain interest of the other side. If the payment is important and big enough, the opponent's interest in a certain initiative may increase enough to change his or her position from opposition to support (or at least neutrality).

The tangible value of side-payments does not undermine their communication character. People often use tangible objects (like gifts, for example) for communication purposes (such as, for example, gratitude or respect). Even a small and symbolic side-payment may convey a message of readiness to negotiate and flexibility. Often, side-payments are the main topics and the main arguments during negotiation communications.

In addition, side-payments are not always tangible. Guaranties and assurances can be used as side-payments as well. The only effect these symbolic gestures can achieve is to create a sense of security. If something goes against an actor's interests, that actor will be somehow protected from that adverse effect. The same can be said about assurances that may promise some tangible value in the future but for now they provide just a perception that a certain actor will receive that value. This creates a cognitive effect of a sense of an increase in payoff value rather than an actual increase in payoff value for that particular actor. Promises are also important because there are time limits imposed on the negotiation process by institutional structures. Often, it is important to reach an agreement now, because of those constraints, even if the actual actions will be undertaken much later. That is why promises can also provide the sense of satisfaction—"the deal is finally done"—even if the actual value will be received in the future. Guarantees, assurances, and promises are major types of arguments in communication and, simultaneously, they are major types of side-payments in the negotiation game.

The perception of constituencies is another important aspect. Often politicians have to appear to have squeezed an important concession out of the opponent, otherwise, they will be perceived by their constituencies as weak and ineffective leaders. In this case, the side-payment is a "face-saving" device, a way out of a deadlock. The side-payment may also be a symbolic message of respect: "You are not at the negotiation table but you are important enough for us to listen to your concerns and to pay you for your support." This kind of message can calm down the opposition and help to neutralize one of the *counter* cells in the new game's diagram. This kind of message can change sides' perceptions of each other from "enemies" to "strategic partners" with whom a future agreement is possible. Sometimes, side-payments are purely emotional—status-oriented. For their concessions people may be given a title of count, earl, a rank of general, a symbolic position of an advisor to an important person. All these side-payments express nothing but a perception of respectability and importance—vain but powerful emotions. And for these intangible payments often very tangible values are given up. That is why the side-payment is a communication tool. And this tool will help the two-level-game players to move the vertical interest border at each actor group level.

Questions to be Addressed by the New Model

Now, when the new model has been comprehensively introduced, several questions related to the structure and dynamics of the new model can be identified to further guide the analysis.

It is interesting and important to explore how interactional dynamics between game actors affect negotiation outcomes. These negotiational dynamics are based on actors' interests and go on at three actor group levels—P, C, and E. The discussion will focus on how interactions between players with different interests at each actor group level affect the outcome. What level of support and opposition is necessary for what type of outcome—that is, the success of failure of an agreement or initiative? That is why the first three main questions will address the degree of division at each actor group level:

1. How does the degree of division at the Proposer (P) level affect the outcome of the negotiation process?
2. How does the degree of division at the Chooser (C) level affect the outcome of the negotiation process?
3. How does the presence of supporter groups at the Endorser level affect the outcome of the negotiation process?

It was also assumed that the side-payment will be the main tool which actors will use to affect the actors' positions and, consequently, the game's outcome. Thus, question number four will be as follows:

4. How does the use of side-payments affect the outcome of the negotiation process?

The last question comes directly from Milner's book. She was interested in how the type of ratification procedure affects the negotiation outcome. It makes sense to assume that the easier the ratification procedure—the better the chances for success. The type of ratification procedure is an institutional variable. Since institutional considerations are a large part of the new model, it is necessary to explore this variable as well. Institutional standard operating procedures (SOPs) may indeed have a serious effect on the outcome of negotiations. If the situation at the Chooser level is difficult, the ratification procedure may finally determine how much communication and how many side-payments are necessary at this level in a particular situation in order to achieve a success. That is why the last question will be as follows:

5. How does the type of ratification procedure affect the outcome of the negotiation process?

Explaining the Main Dynamics of the New Model

In order to ultimately clarify the model, it is necessary to make several remarks about the dynamics at each actor group level (Proposer, Chooser, Endorser).

First of all, the moving border is a metaphor or allegory rather than a really moving dividing line at least at two levels (except, probably, for the Chooser level).

At the Proposer level, it is not always possible to move the line to the right and make supporters out of the opponents. Often, the institutional structure prevents it. If a certain department loses something as a result of a particular agreement, an actor may offer to that department a side-payment that may make the situation more tolerable. But to drag the whole unit from the opposition side to the supportive position is almost never possible. For example, the U.S. Pentagon did not like certain arms reduction treaties. But it received permission to build several new submarines in exchange for its neutrality on these treaties, and started to perceive the whole set of circumstances in a new way (that it received at least something from a very bad situation). In short, the only possible approach in this case is to make a set of side-payments and neutralize the opposition. These opponents do not disappear and they may still not like the agreement, but they will be silent. The borderline stays where it was but the right-hand cell becomes simply neutral, not negative.

This example shows how institutions affect actor formation and interest formation processes, mainly through the distribution of resources. As a result of a certain agreement, every actor either gains or loses something. That is how interests are formed. The affiliation with a certain structural unit itself may also affect the actor's interests. If the larger unit loses, a smaller unit (a subunit or a person) loses too. That is, the interests of the game's actors may be connected to the interests of the structural unit with which they are affiliated and, at a larger scale, with the shape of the institutional structure as a whole. In general, all this comes back to the notion that the institutional structure by itself may provide some motives, incentives, or disincentives for the actions of the game's actors (for deeper understanding and additional information see the diagram of the "Theoretical Model of Factors Involved in the Taking of Organizational Roles" in Katz and Kahn, 1978, p. 196).

At the Endorser actor group level, the dividing line may not be movable at all. It stays where it is. The groups who oppose a bill may oppose it forever unless the Proposer can offer something extraordinary. In some cases, the mechanisms at this level will be similar to the Proposer level ones. At the same time, what is important here is that this line stays at a different position for each different policy proposal. Milner (1997) writes that "the legislature need consider at most two endorsers. . . . Increasing the number of endorsers beyond two does not add to the analysis" (p. 95). What this basically means is that the number of endorsers is not very important here. The only aspect that does matter is the presence or absence of the endorsers because "ratification will not occur without at least one, and often two, endorsements" (p. 95). At the same time, the power of endorsers may be important. For example, the NRA is definitely more powerful than a local vegetarian association. And this is exactly what the position of the vertical interest line at the Endorser level is supposed to symbolize the power of the endorser.

At the Chooser actor group level the situation is a little bit different. Basically, with regard to each proposed policy there are three groups—supporters, opponents, and undecided (or the "swamp"). Persuasion theory says that it is extremely ineffective to try to persuade the die-hard partisans to change their opinion. The only thing one can do is to try to shift the undecided voters or the "reasonable" opponents. That is why the two-cell system at the Chooser actor group level is an approximation. Indeed, we could introduce a multicell system at the C level (die-hard supporters, reasonable supporters, "swamp," reasonable opponents, die-hard opponents) but this would make the model unnecessarily complex.

Certainly, the mechanisms will differ across different systems. For instance, if we take as an example different nation-states, political institutional interactions in the U.K. will be very different from those in the U.S. In Great Britain, where the prime minister is the leader of the party with a majority in the Parliament and the Parliament is not required to vote on every international agreement, the whole interaction process will be very special and the outcome may heavily depend on the Endorser groups. (This is another place where institutional structural arrangements come into play.) But even in this case it is important to remember that the support for the prime minister in the Parliament is not guaranteed because a divergence in interests may occur even within the same party (Milner, 1997, pp. 37–38).

So far the model has been discussed with the goal of providing a theoretical understanding of the two-level negotiation process. But it is interesting to see if this model can offer a valuable way of understanding and explaining real world cases. And the following case study—U.S. negotiations of voluntary restraint agreements in steel—will help us to see how the new model can be applied to the real world negotiations and how effective it is in analyzing such a type of material. At the same time, in the appendix part of this book the reader will be able to find an attempt at paving the way for a possible practical use of the new model. The model can be extended through the use of quantitative analysis to help communication practitioners analyze negotiation situations with greater precision. And an example of such an analysis can be found in the appendix part of this volume.

A Two-Level-Game Case Study

The main purpose of the analysis presented below is to see if the dynamics and elements found in the real world negotiation material are consistent with the dynamics and elements of the new model.

Clarification and Explanation of
Some Important Terms in the Analysis

Before starting the analysis, it is necessary to clarify some terms. The definitions and understanding of those terms will be a little bit different from how similar terms may have been used by other negotiation scholars—like, for example, Putnam or Milner.

For example, a concrete definition is required for what belongs to the Proposer actor group level. Milner did not specify that clearly. But it is very important to define the Proposer clearly for the purpose of this book.

For the purpose of international negotiations analysis, a certain body belongs to the Proposer level (or the executive branch of the government) if:

1. it is not a purely commercial organization,
2. it is managed by a bureaucrat appointed by the government,
3. it carries out essential functions of regulating certain areas of the state economic or political structure.

Under this definition, the Central Bank of a country will be a part of the Proposer actor group level but not an interest group as, for example, Milner defined the German Central Bank in one of the case studies in her book.

Another term that should be clearly defined is the notion of division. When it is said that "the government was divided," it will not mean that it was divided in the traditional sense (when the cabinet and the legislature are controlled by different parties) but in the sense that "the divergence in preferences that may occur even when the same party controls both but party discipline is low and/or the two agents have divergent preferences because of their different constituencies" (Milner, 1997, pp. 37–38). The same divergence may occur for the same reasons within the executive branch of the government alone. In this case, the words *the government was divided* will mean exactly that and will have nothing to do with the legislature. When the situation at the Chooser level will be described, the words *the legislature was divided* will be used. In both cases the word *divided* will mean the division of interests at each actor group level.

U.S. Negotiations of Voluntary Restraint Agreements in Steel[2]

By 1984 "the U.S. steel industry was in grave difficulty. The Soviet Union, Japan, and the European Economic Community (EEC) all produced more steel than the United States, which in 1985 accounted for only 11 percent of global steel production" (Walters, 1994, p. 2). Old big American steel companies faced intensive competition from two sources: domestic "mini-mills" and imports. Penetration of the foreign steel in the American market was facilitated by high prices of the domestic product: "Decades of tight oligopolistic control over domestic steel markets led to a regime of high wages and administered prices that secured labor peace in the industry from 1959 to 1986, but which also helped push U.S. steel prices above those in the world market" (Walters, 1994, p. 3). The lack of investments also prevented the industry from modernizing its production facilities.

At the same time, representatives of the big U.S. steel industry claimed that unfair trade practices had damaged their market position. They said that foreign companies dumped their products on the American market below fair market prices in order to squeeze the American share of the market and, eventually, drive them out of business. "Consequently, if these 'unfairly traded' steel products were kept out of the U.S. market, the domestic industries earnings would be sufficient to capitalize the modernization and structural adjustment necessary to restore the financial health and international competitiveness of U.S. steel firms" (Walters, 1994, p. 4). The U.S. largest companies, such as USX and National Intergroup, appealed to the American government to help them to restrain the foreign competition. Through the years, the American government made some efforts to alleviate the difficult steel market situation for the U.S. producers.

Between 1969 and 1974, the U.S. employed a trade protection instrument known as voluntary export restraints (VERs). "This policy device reduces imports threatening U.S. industry in a manner that keeps the United States formally in compliance with its international trade commitments under the General Agreement on Tariffs and Trade. Exporters to the United States 'voluntarily' curtail their shipments to certain levels, which are determined through negotiation, in order to avoid facing more restrictive quota and/or tariff barriers unilaterally imposed on them by the United States" (Walters, 1994, p. 5). This practice turned out to be just marginally effective because of the enforcement issues and many regulation loopholes. That is why in the late 1970s the Americans changed this practice.

Between 1977 and 1982, the American government used a tool called Trigger Price Mechanism (TPM). Under this mechanism

U.S. trade officials estimated the average production costs of Japanese steel (product by product) and specified prices of Japanese steel products entering the U.S. market that would cover production costs, shipping charges, and a fair profit (8 percent). Any foreign steel entering the U.S. market below this price would trigger an investigation of dumping by the Commerce Department. In return, the U.S. steel industry agreed to withdraw and hold in abeyance their anti-dumping and countervailing duty suits against all foreign steel products. (Walters, 1994, p. 6)

This policy was quite convenient because it could be administered under existing trade laws and, therefore, would allow the United States to remain in formal compliance with GATT. But in 1981 this policy was abandoned as unworkable by the American steel industry because it "in effect legitimized the dumping" (Walters, 1994, p. 6) by less effective European producers. That is why in 1985 a special U.S.-EEC Steel Pact was signed. This pact "would limit exports of steel in ten specific product lines to an average of approximately 5.5 percent of projected U.S. consumption" (Walters, 1994, p. 7).

By 1984–1985, the steel market situation became even more complex because many other, smaller, countries entered the U.S. market with their products. Such countries as South Korea, Brazil, Spain, Mexico, Sweden, and South Africa took a larger share of the American steel market. Besides that, the problems with the U.S. steel industry went much deeper than just these import challenges. Such factors as "labor and raw material costs, age and location of production facilities, adoption of technological innovations, availability and cost of investment capital, and relations with labor and government" (Walters, 1994, p. 8) put the Americans in a position of competitive disadvantage. Besides that, many legislative loopholes let many countries avoid many regulations. That is why the U.S. steel industry pushed for more import limitations.

In 1984 powerful organizations such as the United Steelworkers of America (USW) and the American Iron and Steel Institute (AISI) started a large-scale public relations and lobbying campaign to obtain even more trade protection for the industry. "State and local political officials in traditional steelmaking regions . . . joined the USW and AISI in mobilizing support for steel import restrictions and in putting political pressure on Congress, the trade agencies in the executive branch, the White House and the Republican and Democratic parties (which were both gearing up for the 1984 congressional and presidential elections) to enact such measures" (Walters, 1994, p. 9). As a result of this pressure, legislation was proposed in Congress. This bill would establish formal quotas limiting all steel imports from all sources to 15 percent of the U.S. market for five years. This legislation "enjoyed the active support of the Congressional Steel Caucus, which comprised 160 members of Congress—most of whom were standing for reelection in 1984 and were facing challengers for whom revitalization of the steel industry was a primary campaign issue" (Walters, 1994, p. 9). Besides that, many members of Congress wanted to use Section 201 of the main U.S. trade law—the escape clause. "Escape clause actions provide import relief to a U.S. industry found by the U.S. International

Trade Commission to have suffered injury due to increases in imports—whether fairly or unfairly traded" (Walters, 1994, p. 9). And indeed, the ITC found that some sectors of the American steel industry producing certain products were damaged by imports and it "recommended a combined program of increased tariffs and quotas to remedy injury from imports to these steel products" (Walters, 1994, p. 9). But all these measures were not in compliance with the U.S. international trade commitments under the General Agreement on Tariffs and Trade and, consequently, may have required complex negotiations and a more difficult ratification procedure (if treated as a treaty). President Reagan had either to accept the ITC's recommendations or to develop an alternative proposal.

At the Proposer (P) level, the situation was very complex and difficult. There was a deep division between the President's advisers. Powerful officials like Secretary of State George Shultz, Secretary of Treasury Donald Regan, Secretary of Defense Caspar Weinberger, and many others opposed any protectionist policy because they believed that such measures would just prolong current industry problems without offering any actual remedy. The President himself was on this side because he traditionally "espoused liberal economic philosophy with its preferences for market solutions to economic challenges" (Walters, 1994, p. 10). Besides that, these officials were concerned that other GATT countries would retaliate against U.S. exports. Finally, they were supported by the American steel-using industries (such as car manufacturers) who wanted to buy steel as cheaply as possible.

On the other side of the vertical interest border at the Proposer level, there was the U.S. Trade Representative William Brock, Secretary of Commerce Malcolm Baldrige, and Secretary of Labor Ray Donovan. They favored limiting imports "considering that such a policy could have beneficial implications for the stability of overall international trade if it were successful in preventing steel from continuing to be a contentious issue repeatedly poisoning trade relations with the closest economic partners in Europe" (Walters, 1994, p. 11).

The situation at the Chooser (C) level was quite simple. Congress was very protectionist. It supported policies that "would offer meaningful support to steelworkers—that is, support that would be sufficient to relieve the pressure being exerted on Congress by the industry, labor, and communities dependent upon steel" (Walters, 1994, p. 14).

On 18 September 1984, President Reagan announced his decision to reject the ITC's recommendations involving Section 201 and, consequently, not to impose unilateral tariffs and quotas. Instead, he decided to negotiate a comprehensive array of bilateral voluntary export restraint agreements (VERs). These agreements had to cover all the steel products imported in the United States and all the countries involved in this kind of trade. It was a side-payment to those segments of the steel industry that had not been included in the original ITC's recommendations (the original ITC plan included only five steel products). The VERs would be enforced only for five years—from 1984 to 1989—"providing a sufficient, but limited, breathing spell to aid U.S. steelmakers in adjusting to rapidly evolving international and domestic steel markets" (Walters, 1994, p. 15). This term limitation was a side payment to steel-using industries who wanted to limit protectionist measures as much as possible. In order to address the steel industry's complaints about the previous VERs' loopholes, the new steel program did not rely completely on voluntary compliance by foreign partners: "Export licenses were to be verified by the U.S. Customs Service and were required for all steel imports to enforce the negotiated quota limits (a feature adopted from the 1982 steel trade agreement with the European Community)" (Walters, 1994, p. 15).

The Reagan administration negotiated bilateral VERs with seventeen countries and the EEC. This VER program was a success. It reduced steel imports' penetration level and "was widely supported among U.S. trade officials and among industry and labor officials in the private sector" (Walters, 1994, p. 17). Besides that, this program "was successful in largely defusing the steel issue as a highly contentious question of domestic politics and international trade relations" (Walters, 1994, p. 16). As was mentioned above, the contentious character of the steel trade issue was one of the main concerns of some members of the American administration.

Now it is time to try to use the new model of the two-level-game theory to analyze this case study. But the question is: How can such a complex problem with more than one possible solution be analyzed? The answer is to break this case into parts and analyze each solution separately. The Section 201 solution is shown in Table 3.1.

It seems that the internal approval process in that case failed because the administration did not support it. At the same time, supporters of this kind of solution did not make any side-payments to the P actors and, consequently, failed to draw more actors to their side.

The solution for the program of bilateral VER agreements is shown in Table 3.2.

The internal approval process for the bilateral VER agreements solution succeeded because the Proposer supported it, there was a substantial group of endorsers, and several side-payments were made. Even members of Congress were not very antagonistic toward the VER idea because they received at least something to talk about during their election campaigns. Finally the "fast-track" ratification procedure chosen for this option definitely helped tremendously in this situation. It is much easier to reach the simple majority thresh-

TABLE 3.1
The Section 201 Solution to the U.S. Steel Problems

Variables	Situation
Situation at the Proposer (P) level	The government was divided. But the President opposed this type of protectionist solution. That is why the situation at this level may be rated as "somewhat unfavorable" to the escape clause solution.
Situation at the Chooser (C) level	The situation was favorable because Congress was protectionist and needed support of constituencies of the steel producing parts of the country for the upcoming elections
Presence of supporters (positive Endorsers) at the interest groups level (E)	Large steel companies, USW, AISI, steel producing regions.
Type of ratification procedure chosen	2/3 qualified majority in the Senate (if treated as a treaty, a part of GATT).
Side-payments made	None
Result	Failed

old (even in two houses) than to drag the vertical dividing interest border all the way to the two-thirds-required qualified majority level. In short, this choice succeeded overwhelmingly.

This case study shows clearly the main significance of the new model to the two-level-game approach in general. All the old versions of the theory would fail to explain the outcome of this particular situation. Indeed if we just focus on ratification (majority and procedures)—the Section 201 solution simply could not fail. Most of the legislators supported it and the ratification procedure was not changed (using Milner's variables). Besides, that solution had powerful supporters—large steel companies, USW, AISI, etc. At the same time, the VERs Program solution had to inevitably fail—choosers did not support it and the ratification procedure was changed. But in reality, exactly the opposite happened. There is no explanation for this in the old models. But the new model provides plenty of explanations and even some prescriptions.

Both Putnam and Milner talk about how level I actors try to estimate positions and actions of the level II actors and try to negotiate a deal that would be approved at that level. But neither of them actually mentions how to estimate the level II actor's reactions. Milner says that if a level I actor knows that a position of level II actors is such that a certain agreement is going to fail the

TABLE 3.2
The VERs Program Solution to the U.S. Steel Problems

Variables	Situation
Situation at the Proposer (P) level	The executives were divided. But the majority of them, including the President, supported this kind of solution. Therefore, the situation at this level may be rated as "favorable."
Situation at the Chooser (C) level	The situation in Congress was more complex. On one hand, the members wanted more. On the other hand, they still could use this kind of solution as something positive in their election campaigns. That is why the situation at this level may be rated as "somewhat unfavorable".
Presence of supporters (positive Endorsers) at the interest groups level (E)	Large steel companies, USW, AISI, steel producing regions—it was not everything they wanted but it was at least something. Steel using industries—they avoided stronger restrictions and received a 5 year limit on VERs.
Type of ratification procedure chosen	Simple majority in both houses (*fast-track*)—treated as a congressional-executive agreement.
Side-payments made	Steel using industries received a 5 year limit on VERs. Steel producers received licensing enforcement in order to avoid the previous VER loopholes. These agreements had to cover all the steel products imported in the United States and all the countries involved in this kind of trade. It was a side-payment to those segments of the steel industry that had not been included in the original ITC's recommendations.
Result	Passed

internal approval process, this level I actor tries to tailor or negotiate such a level I document or an agreement that it could be approved at level II. But the question is: How does he or she *know* what is going to succeed and what is going to fail? The internal approval process is very complex. It involves many actors. It may seem that the traditional two-level-game approach assumes that the level I negotiator knows everything—that is, he or she has absolutely perfect information, knows and understands all the level II actors, and is capable of rationally and perfectly calculating the outcome of the level II approval process. Otherwise, how does he or she *know* that outcome? It is clear that the authors of the two-level-game theory did not make such an assumption. The problem is that level II interactions were underestimated and did not receive the proper attention. But this aspect is crucial and vital for the main idea of the two-level-game theory—coordination of the level I and level II positions. How can an inter-entity negotiator coordinate level I and level II positions if he or she is not actually sure what is going to fail and what is going to succeed at level II? With what particular level II actor does the negotiator have to co-ordinate the level I position—P, C, or E? If with all of them, what is the model tying all these three actors together in a consistent and logical pattern? The new model of intra-entity negotiations offered in this book is supposed to help him or her to better understand and better estimate the final outcome of the internal approval process. Using Putnam's concept of the win-set and its graphical representation presented in chapter 2 of this book, we can say that the new model can help to estimate positions of Y1, Y2, and Y3 points on the win-set continuum and, consequently, to tailor the level I proposal accordingly.

The steel agreement case gives us an example of how to use the new model. First of all, there should be several solutions or several courses of actions. Then, it is necessary to collect information about all the variables, actors, and interactions at the intra-entity level concerning each of them. Using the new model we can estimate the outcome of the internal approval process for each of them and choose the course of actions that would be approved internally. Then, we can use Milner's and Putnam's calculations to negotiate the level I agreement.

In case of either level I negotiation failure or our initial discontent with the choices that would get approved at level II, the new model can help us understand what can be done to adjust the level II situation. For example, there may be a situation when a decision maker sees that only the policy choices that he or she does not like would get approved and the choices he or she likes are going to fail at level II. In this case, the new model suggests that it will be necessary to make some side-payments to unfavorable actor group level cells, recruit supporters, or make the ratification procedure in the case of the policy choices we like easier and, consequently, increase the chances of success for such policies. Certainly, the across-the-board type of sweeping concessions as side-payments would not be efficient. Side-payments must be made only in crucial areas and in the size that is just enough to tip the balance in favor of the policy option we like. If the level I negotiation failed because the proposal did not fall within the win-set limits, it is possible to come back and, using the new model, try to find another version of the document that would meet requirements of the win-set. If a certain policy or document has already been agreed upon at level I, but has some difficulties at level II, the new model can help to find ways to affect the level II situation so that the chances for the internal approval success are maximized.

Certainly, in the case of the steel agreements, it was not done formally. But the analysis of the case study shows that it could have been done. If the decision makers had formally analyzed both policy options from the point of view of the new model, they would have seen that ultimately the VER program had as many chances to succeed as the Section 201 option, although the latter had much more chances to succeed initially. The President liked the VER option, there were some powerful supporters behind it, some effective side-payments were available, and the ratification procedure could be made easier. So, the main thing is to start communicating and moving the interest borderline in the direction that favors your political preferences. The old models do not see such possibilities because they are static. But the new model gives quite effective prescriptions what to do in difficult situations.

Besides that, what this case study clearly shows is that the method of "knowing" the domestic approval process outcome would not work because, in this particular case, nobody *knew* what would get approved and different advisers gave different advice to the President of the United States. The intra-entity approval process is so complex that it should be estimated based on some sort of model of the level II relationships and dynamics. That is why this new model is offered to explain these relationships and dynamics.

At the same time in the appendix part of this book the reader will be able to find an attempt at paving the way for a possible practical use of the new model. The model can be extended through the use of quantitative analysis to help communication practitioners analyze negotiation situations with greater precision. And an example of such an analysis can be found in the appendix part of this volume.

The next several chapters will not concentrate exclusively on the two-level-game theory dynamics. They will rather demonstrate the method and approach of the *complex analysis* mentioned in the introduction of this book. The main idea behind this approach is that it incorporates a whole complex of different points of view and theories considered earlier in this volume. Each of those perspectives is capable of providing us with an interesting insight that would not be visible from another point of view. Then, the final solution to a negotiation problem can be put together as a mosaic from different ideas and recommendations.

As you will see, in this type of analysis domestic factors will also play a major (and often decisive) role. Some two-level-game dynamics will be clearly seen and highlighted in the case studies below. Therefore, all the theoretical concepts and ideas discussed so far in this book will be useful and necessary for the analytical method and the material presented further in this volume.

Notes

1. You can find more information on the factors involved in the taking of organizational roles in Katz and Kahn, 1978.

2. A substantial part of the information for this case study comes from Case # 107 of the data base of the Institute for the Study of Diplomacy and the School of Foreign Service of Georgetown University in Washington, DC. The official document's reference information is *U.S. negotiation of voluntary restraint agreement in steel, 1984: Domestic sources of international economic diplomacy*, Robert S. Walters, (Washington, DC: Institute for the Study of Diplomacy, Georgetown University, 1988). The author wants to thank the Institute and the authors for their permission to use their data.

II

INTERNATIONAL NEGOTIATIONS
WITH KNOWN OUTCOMES

4

Negotiations on the Admittance of Russia into the World Trade Organization

O NE OF THE MOST RECENT AND INTERESTING CASES of international trade negotiations is a set of US-Russia talks on the admittance of Russia into the
World Trade Organization (WTO). By the end of 2006 only one country was
still resisting Russia's entrance into this international institution—the United
States of America. All the other interested members had already signed off on
the Russian membership application. This is where, after twelve years of negotiations, multilateral talks turned into bilateral. We will try to analyze the
negotiations—see what the main problems were and what steps were taken by
both sides to make the successful outcome of the negotiations possible.

General Information

The World Trade Organization (WTO) appeared on the international scene
on January 1st, 1995. It is a direct descendent of the General Agreement on
Tariffs and Trade (GATT) which was first signed in 1947. WTO sets rules of
international trade for its member states and resolves disputes between them
if necessary. The main idea behind WTO is that this organization is supposed
to promote free trade at the global scale and theoretically, by so doing, to provide valuable economic benefits to all its member states. By June of 2007 the
organization had 150 members.

Russia applied for membership in 1994 (still under Yeltsin's rule). According to WTO's rules and regulations every new applicant has to negotiate its
membership conditions with a group of countries that have unresolved trade

issues with the new candidate. In the case of Russia, there were fifty-eight of such countries—the largest number in the history of the organization. After twelve years of negotiations Russia signed agreements with all the interested countries (including the European Union) except for the United States. That time became a sort of proverbial "moment of truth" for the Russians—the talks reached the point when they actually started considering giving up the very idea of their WTO membership because many of them began doubting the possibility of reaching any acceptable agreement with the Americans. It is important and interesting to see how the two sides got to this point and what kind of problems made the situation so difficult.

Sides' Interests

Russian membership in WTO is a very hot and contentious political topic for the Russians themselves. This issue divided the political elite into two radical camps—proponents and opponents of the idea. A slight majority represents the opposition group while just a little smaller but more powerful minority supports the initiative (mostly for ideological and not economic reasons). For the opponents, WTO means some uncertain benefits for very few industries in the future and unbearable difficulties (even possibly death) for numerous and most important industries right away. They believe that in this case Russia will forever remain simply the "big world's" source of raw material. But supporters say that WTO will help to remove all the barriers against Russian products on the global market and it will also mean modernization of many of the Russian industries. The arguments of the both sides can be summarized as follows:

WTO advantages for Russia:

- free access for all the Russian products to the global market;
- free access to the mechanism of international trade dispute resolution;
- favorable climate for foreign investments into the country's economy;
- improvement in quality of domestic products as a result of direct competition with foreign goods;
- participation in the process of international trade rule-creation which will help protect national trade interests.

WTO disadvantages for Russia:

- cheap imported agricultural products will put domestic producers out of business;

- the amount of state subsidies for domestic agricultural producers will be limited;
- many important industries will not survive a direct competition with foreign manufacturers (among them such industries as food processing, textile, auto, aviation, agricultural machinery, and many others);
- international banks and insurance companies will put out of business their Russian competitors and entirely take under their control the whole domestic financial system of the country.

Americans have a definite advantage in this situation—they are already a member of the organization (and an important member) and it is basically entirely up to them whether to let the Russians in or not. Consequently, they are vigorously trying to protect their national trade interests and even, hopefully, to obtain some additional advantages in the newly negotiated agreements. Slowly, their interests took a final shape and became quite well defined. This is what they demand from the Russians:

- free access of the direct branch offices of their banks and insurance companies into the Russian market;
- a significant decrease of import duty tariffs for American airliners bought by Russian resident companies for the Russian civil aviation market;
- elimination of quotas and a significant reduction of import duty tariffs for American agricultural products (namely, meets and poultry);
- a significant reduction in the number of agricultural products that require obtaining sanitary inspection certificates prior to their importation into the country;
- a significant improvement in laws regulating copyright and intellectual property rights issues as well as an actual effort to strictly enforce them.

Some Information from the History of Negotiations

As it was mentioned above, the multilateral WTO negotiations for Russia started in late 1994. At that time, the country was officially ruled by Boris Yeltsin, but in reality by Boris Berezovsky. The economic system was in complete disarray—country produced absolutely nothing. The country was torn apart by poverty, hunger, and civil war. The only way the government survived was by taking multi-billion credits in foreign currencies all over the world and buying literally everything abroad. Certainly, under those circumstances any idea of entering an organization that was supposed to help Russian products to sell better on the global market (the products of which there were none) could be considered only as a sick joke. But it was not a joke—it was a political statement. It was supposed to show foreign sponsors of the regime that the country forever subscribed to the liberal market ideology and was willing to go all the way on that path.

After Putin came to power in late 1999, the Russian economy started slowly turning around. There appeared some industries that were quite successful not only on domestic but also on the international market. Russians significantly increased their export of timber, oil, and natural gas—their traditional products. Some other industries were resurrected and started to play once again a significant role on the world market. For example, metallurgy became afresh an important industry in the country. The problem was that the metallurgical products sold by the Russians on the market were still very low-tech—at the beginning of the technological cycle. The only world-class hi-tech area working in the country was the space industry. At the same time, Russia inherited yet from the Yeltsin era a huge number of newly born domestic banks most of which were absolutely unreliable and closely connected to the criminal underworld. After disintegration of the only official Soviet airline—the "Aeroflot"—Russia became a record-holder for the number of airlines in one country. Certainly, the condition of the airplanes they operated was disastrous.

Vladimir Putin, as a reformer, took an approach different from his predecessor. He was still an advocate of the free market economy system but he also was a patriot. Being from Saint Petersburg, he clearly saw himself as a sort of new Peter the Great—maybe not that brutal and radical, but a patriotic reformer. He believed in the potential of the country and dreamed of the tremendous success Russian hi-tech products one day would enjoy on the global market. He believed that at some point Russian computer software, automobiles, airplanes, space crafts, banks, and even agricultural producers would be competing on the global market as equals. Certainly, in this case other countries would want to protect themselves from the Russian expansion. It meant only one thing—the Russians just had to become WTO members in order to remove future trade barriers that would threaten future success of the future Russian products.

So, in the early 2000s he reenergized the process of Russia's application for WTO membership. The problem was that he underestimated how close "the future" was. His fantasies at that time took him too far. The economic progress in the country was very difficult and very slow. There was an apparent contradiction between the reality and the purpose of the process. He was pushing toward WTO so hard as if the Russians already had thousands of hi-tech products to offer on the global market. But they did not. If WTO had opened its doors to the Russians at that time—Russia would have had nothing to benefit from but the Russian economy would have been devastated by the foreign giants. In short, he did not realize that his dream was appropriate for a very remote future—when the Russian economy strengthens enough to offer something valuable (besides oil and natural gas) on the global market. But at that time WTO would have spelled a complete disaster for the country.

Nevertheless, in the early 2000s he started to try to actively integrate Russian economy into the world market. In 2002, when 75 percent of all the Russian civil airliners had already worked out their safety resource, Russian WTO negotiators were talking about completely doing away with import duty tariffs for foreign-built planes. Putin was even glad when the Americans promised to organize the production of some small details of the landing gear for Boeing 777 in some Russian aviation factories. (That was a little bit humiliating for the Russian aviation industry able to produce civil supersonic airliners such as TU-144 and intercontinental bombers such as TU-160.) The same year he appealed to the Americans to abolish the Jackson-Vanik amendment that linked the freedom of Jewish immigration from the Soviet Union to the issues of trade. The Americans were seemingly ready to entertain such an idea.

But troubles in the free trade paradise started quite soon. The problem was that Putin decided to show the rest of the world his commitment to the idea of free trade. With that in mind, the Russians voluntarily took upon themselves some obligations that usually only WTO members were supposed to take. Immediately some crucial parts of the Russian economy started failing. And the worst situation was in agriculture. The situation was so bad that between March of 2002 and early months of 2003 some import quotas were gradually introduced to stem the tide of imported meat and poultry products. Specifically, the import volume of poultry products was cut by 30 percent, pork by 22 percent, and beef by 16 percent. Besides that, it turned out that the quality of some meat and poultry products imported into the country (including from the US) was below any food safety standards. So, the border sanitary food safety control was also strengthened.

Americans immediately protested such Russian "protectionist" measures. Besides that, they offered the Russians what they thought was a big carrot. In exchange for abolishing all the agricultural import barriers the Americans promised to abolish the Jackson-Vanik amendment. For some reason, Russians were not extremely interested anymore.

In 2003 Americans also joined the Europeans in their demand that the Russians made the price of natural gas (extracted from the Russian soil) the same for domestic users as for export purposes. The Europeans argued that it would level the playing field for all the companies competing on the Russian market. The Russians responded that, first of all, it was their gas and they could do with it whatever they wanted and, secondly, that their poor companies would not be able to pay the same price as rich foreigners. After some debates, both sides (the Russians and the EU) agreed that the Russians would slowly raise the price of natural gas for the domestic market but still not to the export price level. For example, in 2003 European companies had to pay for Russian natural gas $100 for a thousand cubic meters while Russian companies paid just $25–$30. The Russians agreed to charge their domestic companies $45 for a thousand cubic meters for the next (2004) year and eventually to raise the price up to the level of $60–$70 which was jointly (Russia/EU) determined as the threshold price for the Russian entrance into WTO. But the Americans were still not completely satisfied with that decision.

Americans also initially joined the Australians in their demand for free access to all the Russian natural resources. Certainly, it was a long shot and both countries ultimately stopped raising that issue after the Russian government assured them that they would be able to either form joint ventures with Russian companies to exploit natural resources or would be able to develop and exploit certain gas and oil fields under the licensing option (like it's being done in Sakhalin 1 and 2 projects).

In the year 2005, the aviation issue became one of the central topics. The problem was that out of five thousand civil aviation planes flying that year in Russia 50 percent were good enough only for spare parts as the Minister of Transportation of Russia Igor Levitin said himself. By the years 2010–2012 two types of Russian short- and medium-range airliners (TU-134 and TU-154) were supposed to be phased out of service completely and there was nothing to replace them with. Something had to be done urgently. That is why the Russians easily agreed to cut import duty tariffs for new airliners in half—from 20 to 10 percent. (The civil aviation spare parts import tariffs were supposed to drop down to the level of 5–6 percent.) The same was suggested in terms of the import tariffs for new cars. The Russians were ready to cut import duty tariffs in this area from 25 to 15–17 percent. But the Americans were not satisfied with the Russian offer. They demanded either deeper cuts or a complete removal of all import duties in some areas.

The negotiations reached the critical point in the second half of 2006. In July of that year a G-8 summit took place in Saint Petersburg, Russia. The Russians hoped that by the beginning of the event they would be able to complete their WTO talks with the United States and pompously sign the official agreement right at the meeting on the Russian soil.

But after twelve years of negotiations the Russians knew that it would take a lot of persuading to reach that goal. So, they started preparing the ground. Just eleven days before the summit Putin said on Russian TV that if no agreement with the Americans was forthcoming soon his country would refuse to fulfill its obligations taken voluntarily prior to its entrance into the WTO. He again and again highlighted the fact that in many areas Russia had been using voluntarily WTO standards even though it was not a member of that organization. He further expressed his opinion that the Russian economy was functioning in a more open and liberal manner than economies of some WTO member states.

In addition, he openly put the blame for the negotiational problems on the Americans. He claimed on Russian state-run TV that he received from them a list of trade issues that had to be resolved and that the list included some items he thought had been agreed upon a long time before that. He accused the Americans of artificially slowing down the talks.

At the end, the Russians were disappointed—President George Bush refused to sign any WTO documents in Saint Petersburg. The post-meeting press conference was a cold one. Putin vowed to fight for the Russian economic interests while Bush admitted that the Americans were "difficult to negotiate with" but explained it in a traditional-in-such-situations way—he lamented the Shelling Conjecture. He said that he always had to look over his shoulder and see what type of agreement would be approved by the US Congress.

After that shock the Russians became really frustrated (they indeed were hoping for a positive outcome at the G-8 summit). That time became to some extent a turning point in the negotiation process—since that moment on the Russian officials more and more often started to express what looked like sincere doubts about the value of WTO for their country. In September 2006 a presidential aid, Igor Shuvalov, finally openly proclaimed that the negotiations reached the critical point when none of the sides seemed to be able to move from the currently occupied negotiational positions. He also lamented the Shelling Conjecture. He said that the Russians could not change their position because at the domestic level no further concessions would be approved.

Even Russian newspapers that used to support the WTO idea jumped into the discussion with angry articles. For example *Izvestia* accused the Americans of intentionally preventing the Russians from joining WTO. Several publications wrote that the Americans like magicians pulled out of their sleeves some claims and complaints about the subjects that had been settled previously. For example, they wrote, the Americans complained about high import duty tariffs for yogurts—the product the Americans never exported to Russia.

But the really crucial point came when Putin himself broke down. In frustration he publicly said literally the following: "They just talk about free trade but indeed over there [abroad] everything is closed, it is impossible to get through in there [foreign markets]." It was really shocking to hear a statement like that from a former fan of free trade. It seemed that the reality finally caught up with him and he at last realized the difference between the idea and the truth.

After their boss broke down, many Russian bureaucrats felt free to express their real attitude toward WTO. They started talking in the press about the fact that Russia's membership in WTO might bring many real economic problems to the country. The Minister of Agriculture Alexey Gordeyev simply called WTO a "harmful organization."

It is interesting to see here how internal struggle within the Russian government manifested itself in public debates. For example, an adamant supporter of the WTO plan German Gref (The Russian Minister of Economic Development and Trade), having seen the collapse of his dreams around him, tried to save the initiative by convincing everybody that under any circumstance WTO is a good option for the country. For example, he said that in order to join WTO the Russians would have to reduce import duty tariffs from the average level of 10.5 percent down to 6–9 percent for consumer goods, however, not right away but over the following seven years and even under those circumstances the level of market protection in Russia would be almost twice as high as in economically developed countries.

His arguments might have had an effect but the Americans started tying Russia's WTO membership with some political issues that further frustrated and alienated the Russians. First, the Americans wanted the Russians to make a general pledge to reduce the role of the state in domestic economic activities. The US Secretary of State Condoleezza Rice linked the WTO issue with such problems as Iran (building of the nuclear power station in Bushehr) and Russian relations with Georgia (a former Soviet republic in the Caucasus region).

In September 2006, the Chairman of the Council of Federation of the Federal Assembly of the Russian Federation (the Russian parliament) Sergey Mironov met in New York with Henry Kissinger (who represented at that meeting the Council on Foreign Relations) and was surprised by the fact that Kissinger was absolutely sure that the Russians would have to make substantial concessions (economic and political) to enter WTO in the near future. The reaction was strong, unequivocal, and immediate. The same day, in response to Kissinger's remarks, Boris Gryzlov, leader of the United Russia (UR) party and chairman of the State Duma (and likely Putin's successor) sturdily indicated that there should be no further concessions at all.

Alexander Shokhin, President of the Russian Union of Industrialists and Entrepreneurs, expressed quite well the opinion of many business leaders in Russia. He said that in his opinion Russian membership in WTO became a political and not an economic issue.

Finally, the Russians created a self-imposed deadline for the whole process—the end of October 2006. On October 21, 2006, Vladimir Putin personally told Condoleezza Rice that Russia might stop its WTO application process if there would be no further progress in WTO negotiations some time soon. And there was none.

At that time, everybody (politicians and the media) started saying that Russia would not have to become a member of the WTO because this institution, if not already dead, was slowly dying. They mostly referred to the failed Doha Round of WTO talks. Their logic was as follows.

The Doha Round of WTO negotiations failed and it was doubtful it would ever resume. The main problem was that one of the key players—the European Union—refused to participate. Then, the analysts noticed a trend toward bilateral or regional agreements (ASEAN, Mercosur, Eurasec, etc.). They saw the reason for such a trend in three factors. Factor number one was that, in their opinion, WTO was simply manipulated by world leading economic powers to help them achieve the goal of their economic domination in the world. The second factor, they believed, was that the organization used the same standards for everybody without deep consideration of underlying differences. Finally, they said, as a dispute resolution mechanism WTO was at least problematic and, at most, ineffective. Those analysts believed that WTO was not vital for the world trade. They said that even after its death (imminent as they believed) the world trade was not going to stop because the huge arsenal of rules and mechanisms of international trade had been created and nobody was going to entirely discard it. But cooperation in the world without WTO would occur mostly at the regional level or in the form of bilateral treaties. Maybe later on WTO could be reborn but that would be a different organization. It would be transformed into an institution that would consist of independent trade blocks, separate treaties, and regional alliances, and organization where there would be no obvious domination of the strong over the weak. So, they argued, why don't we (the Russians) wait and for now, instead of trying to fight the Americans, concentrate seriously on our own regional trade organization—Eurasec.

One way or another, by 2006 four issues became central in Russian-American WTO negotiations. They were intellectual property rights, import duty tariffs for civil aviation industry, financial institutions (banks and insurance companies), and import duty tariffs and quotas for American agricultural products (namely meats and poultry). And these issues proved to be so difficult that both sides were almost ready to abandon the negotiations altogether. Let's try to analyze the situation in each industry separately and see where the sides stood and what could be done to resolve the dispute.

Industry-by-Industry Analysis

Aviation

By the year 2006, 75 percent of five thousand civil aviation planes in Russia had already worked out their safety resource and 50 percent of them were good enough only for spare parts. At that time, the Russians had an unusually large number of small airlines that were so poor that they were able to use only either very old Russian-made planes or almost as old foreign-made airliners. Most of foreign-made planes came to Russia from the "second-hand" market and were not in good shape either. But the airlines could not even afford spare parts—so, they bought cheap counterfeits that directly led to a series of deadly crashes in the mid-2000s. Those crashes made the government seriously consider the issue of air travel safety.

The Russian government decided to work in two directions. The first one was consolidation of smaller airlines into a smaller number of bigger ones. The second measure was the resurrection of the Russian domestic aviation industry.

Indeed, over several years quite a few small aviation operators went bankrupt or were put out of business by strict government safety regulations. Simultaneously, some big operators bought out smaller ones. All this led to a much smaller number of quite reliable operators with significant financial resources—such as "Sibir," newly formed in 2006 "Russia," and certainly reborn "Aeroflot." Some of those companies were at least 51 percent state-owned. The largest one—"Aeroflot"—was 51 percent state-owned and operated almost one hundred planes flying over three hundred flights daily from Moscow. It handled almost 40 percent of all the international flights from the country. It was rich enough to buy new planes abroad and did it quite often. The import duty tariffs for new foreign-built planes were standing at that time at about 20 percent and still the big companies were buying those planes in bulk, ordering dozens at a time. (For example, in September 2006 "Aeroflot" announced their decision to buy forty-four new planes abroad.)

The second goal—the resurrection of the domestic aviation industry—was supposed to be accomplished through a consolidation of devastated and scattered remains of formerly formidable Soviet aeronautic industry. In order to save the know-how, production facilities, and lives of innocent air travelers, the Russian government decided to organize a 75-percent-state-owned aviation holding which would include all the aviation-related research institutions, design bureaus, and production plants in one huge company able to compete with Boeing and Airbus.

Although the country's aviation industry was in bad shape due to decades of neglect and funding starvation, some of its companies were doing quite well. World-famous producers of jet fighters such as MIG or Sukhoi were doing well selling their products on the world arms market. But the civil aviation manufacturers—such a Tupolev or Ilyushin—were not in such good shape. There were even some people in the country that called for complete abandonment of any production of civil airliners in Russia because, as they said, the industry was so badly destroyed that it was impossible to save. But Putin thought otherwise. He ordered to prepare all the documents for consolidation of almost twenty different aviation-related companies into the holding. And all the giants mentioned above—MIG, Sukhoi, Tupolev, Ilyushin—were among them. He also funded the research and development of new Russian planes such as TU-334 and the Russian Regional Jet or RRJ (the latter was supposed to be designed by Sukhoi in cooperation with Boeing).

So, by October 2006 the battle lines were drawn. By that time, almost all of the new planes flying in Russia were produced either by Boeing or Airbus. And big Russian companies were buying them regardless of the 20 percent import duty tariff. They had to buy them because there was nothing else available. It is difficult to estimate what exactly was the American share of the Russian civil aviation market but it was very big. Only in 2005, 60 percent of all the civil aviation planes bought by the Russian companies were of foreign production—Airbus or Boeing. And the Russians usually bought them 50/50—half American and half European—not to offend anybody (for example, "Aeroflot" bought exactly twenty-two planes from Boeing and twenty-two from Airbus). Therefore, the American share of the market was at least 30 percent. But anybody who has ever been at a Russian airport would say that indeed the share is much higher—maybe 40 percent or even higher.

After several deadly crashes, some people suggested removing all the import duty barriers and, by so doing, to enable Russian companies to buy new foreign planes cheaper. Putin refused because, first of all, such a step would kill instantly the Russian aviation industry and, secondly, because he put all his hopes into the new aviation holding that was being formed at that time. Nevertheless, he was genuinely concerned with the problem of air travel safety and he also wanted Russia to become a WTO member. Therefore, the Russians made the following offer to the Americans. In order to become WTO members they were ready to drop their import duty tariff for new airliners from 20 to 10 percent over a seven-year period and they were also ready to reduce the import duty tariff for spare parts all the way down to the level of 5 or 6 percent.

It was actually a very good offer. Even at 20 percent the Americans controlled a huge share of the Russian aviation market and were selling their planes there like hotcakes. So, cutting the tariff in half would only increase their sales. And the spare parts agreement would definitely help a lot. Consequently, the status quo was very good for the Americans and the suggested changes would make the situation for them only better. But what was the alternative to success of the talks?

And it seems that initially the Americans answered that question incorrectly because of their indestructible feeling of technological superiority. They were not happy with the Russian offer and wanted to get more out of the Russians. They thought that even if they did not receive any more concessions and the talks simply failed—nothing terrible—the Russians would still keep buying American planes at the same pace. That was a mistake.

The Russians were buying foreign planes not because they liked it—the time of romantic purchases of whatever foreign was available passed pretty quickly. They also did not buy them because they were more reliable than Russian planes—the propaganda one can hear a lot in the West. Actually, Russians are afraid of flying on, let's say, Boeing 737 and especially on Airbus 320 (after a series of crashes involving these two types of planes). They would prefer their own airliners that they consider to be safer because of their military design background—more redundancy and sturdier construction. They had to buy foreign planes for two reasons. First of all, nothing else was simply available. Secondly, some European environmental regulations (sound level, pollution) did not allow some types of old Russian-built airliners to fly to Europe. But if Putin was to be successful with his United Aviation Corporation (UAC) the situation would have to change dramatically. And it was already changing.

First of all, the Russians already had several projects that were able to enter production very soon. For example, a new short-haul Tupolev TU-334 was ready to enter production any day. There were two problems holding it—domestic political intrigues and lack of funding—both of which would be fixed momentarily by the appearance of UAC. The second short-range airliner—RRJ (or now they call it SuperJet-100)—was still on the drawing board but there was a powerful lobby pushing that project ahead. For example, "Aeroflot" had already agreed to buy at least 30 of them with the price tag somewhere between 30 and 35 million dollars each. This project could be finished very quickly. That is why the Russians were already marketing that airliner all over the world quite actively. In general, Russians believed that quite soon they would be able to capture up to 20 percent of the world's short-haul airliners and cargo-planes market (consequently, taking it away from other manufacturers).

On the long-range front, the Russians almost completed the new version of their long-standing IL-96 line—IL-96-400. The main feature of that airplane was that it would satisfy all the European ecological requirements. It would also be as economical and technologically advanced as, for example, Boeing 777 or Airbus 350. They were also feverishly working on improving their medium-range TU-214 (previously a big disappointment for them). Many countries in Latin America, Africa, and Asia (including China and India) would be able to buy them quite soon. The only things the Russian manufacturers needed were the state support (including domestic market protection and tax breaks for buying domestically-built planes) and funding—both of which would become available if WTO negotiations had failed and UAC had come into existence.

And the Russians decided to show to the Americans that they were not kidding and were ready for the WTO failure option—that is, they were ready to work in this sector independently and aggressively. Just three days after the self-imposed end-of-October deadline (on the 3rd of November) the Russians officially announced that the United Aviation Corporation had been formally created (a clear signal to the Americans in relation to their WTO negotiation position). The company was supposed to start working at full swing in 2007. They also announced that this holding would receive the state financial support in the next few years in the amount of up to 1 billion dollars. Only civil aviation projects would see their funding doubled. The person who was appointed to lead the new company was Alexey Fedorov—former president of Sukhoi and MIG companies. These two brands were extremely successful. The Russians were selling dozens of fighters of each of these two brands every year taking a solid market share from the Americans. They hoped that Fedorov would be as successful marketing Russian civil airliners and cargo planes on the world market. The Chinese already expressed a big interest in designing and producing jointly with the Russians a new generation of airliners. Actually, the Chinese had already agreed to buy quite a few of Russian TU-204-120 cargo planes and in late 2006 placed a request with Russian authorities for more machines of that type. That is why 20 percent of the world's cargo planes market is not actually such a difficult task for the Russians known for their expertise in this area.

As of the end of 2006, Russians were going to replace literally thousands of aircraft on their domestic market. And if Russia had not eventually become a WTO member—its government would have found a way to help domestic producers and prevent others from taking over the place. For a while they would have left the import duty tariffs alone. But by 2010–2012—when all the above mentioned Russian planes are supposed to go in full-scale production—one could have expected further rises of import duty tariffs for new and used foreign-built planes as well as for the spare parts. And that would have meant big losses for the Americans on the Russian market. Besides that, the Westerners do not have to underestimate the Russian ability to take away in the future a big share of their world aviation market (like they have already done it in the arms-trade area).

That is, in late 2006 the situation for the Americans was good and could have become even better if the tariffs would be cut in half and Russia would become a WTO member that would prohibit them from further protecting their civil aviation market in the future. But had the talks failed—the American losses would have been tremendous.

It is important to make one note here. In general, one of the negotiation strategy problems that Western negotiators experience talking to the Russians (and to some extent to the Chinese) seems to be the fact that the Westerners have an unwarranted feeling of arrogance and technological superiority. They keep pushing their counterparts sincerely believing that those will not be able to do things that the Westerners do. Americans still believe that the Russians (as well as many other nations) will still be buying American things because they are better or simply because they are American. This is a sadly outdated point of view. The world automotive market shows how quickly Detroit's market share is shrinking even in the area of technology which was traditionally considered the American field of expertise. In other hi-tech industries, Russians not only caught up with the Americans but left them far behind. In the mid-2000s they were holding over 50 percent of the world's space-launch industry. In 2005–2006 by some measures they became the largest seller of weapon systems in the world—overtaking even the United States. Their aggressive marketing and high level of technological innovations are doing it for them. In space and arms areas the Russians have technologies that the United States will probably have only by the year 2025 (maybe not). It is not the Russians who buy rocket engines from the Americans but the other way around. Americans bought over one hundred Russian rocket engines ($1 million a piece) because they would not have anything technologically comparable for the foreseeable future. And nothing prevents the Russians from using this expertise and know-how in their aviation industry. (That is why former MIG and Sukhoi officials are now going to work in the civil aviation area.) And it means that another sector of the world economy (and trillions of dollars) could be lost for the Americans. Therefore, it would be in their interest to accept the Russian offer in this area while it is still standing.

Financial Issues

The next problematic issue was the one of the freedom of financial operations for foreign entities on the territory of the Russian Federation. The Russians argued that they gave enough freedom to foreign banks and insurance companies but the Americans insisted that nothing short of complete and unabridged freedom for their financial institutions on the Russian market would satisfy them. So, it is again necessary to consider the actual situation on the Russian financial market to figure out what would be the right course of action for both sides to achieve an agreement.

I want to start with some personal observations because many years ago the author of this book worked for a big foreign-owned bank in Russia. At that time—mid-1990s—huge, solid, and reputable foreign banks were a new thing in the country. They were working under heavy regulations. It is necessary to note that since then most of those heavy rules have been removed. But one regulation is still in place—foreign banks were not allowed and still are not allowed to open their direct branch offices but can only create their daughter Russian-registered resident banks.

These two forms of organization have quite a few subtle differences but the main difference is the set of laws and regulations the bank must go by. A direct branch office is a native part of the foreign bank and considered to be a foreign entity on the Russian market. A local daughter bank (even if it has 100 percent foreign capital) is registered on the Russian territory, according to the Russian laws and, consequently, is considered a Russian resident bank that is supposed to obey all the local laws and be accountable to Russian authorities. Only daughter banks have been allowed in Russia. The Russians argued that they needed to have a complete control over all the banks on their territory in order to manage their economy, fight inflation, and combat criminal activities (such a money laundering).

The Russian financial market in the mid-1990s was full of newly born private banks. Most of them were tiny, all of them were critically unstable, and most of them were direct decedents from criminal structures. Neither Russian businesses nor the Russian citizens trusted them. Everybody kept their money (in US dollars) under their mattresses. So, when such giants as Credit Lyonnais or Dresdner Bank opened their daughter banks in the country—that was a sensation. Everybody—from gray-haired ladies trying to save their pennies from robbers, to the real giants of the Russian economy—rushed to those banks. The immediate problem was that they were not simply capable of processing so many customers and deal with such a flow of capital. The whole country wanted to give them their money.

Therefore, immediately the service was limited only to business clients and only to elite business clients. Probably, only CIA scrutinizes its future employees as thoroughly as the clients were scrutinized by those banks. Every simple request for a meeting with a bank representative was considered very thoroughly and most of them were declined. To open an account with a bank like that took a series of high-level meetings, a lot of time, and tons of papers. Only the richest and most reliable (often with high-level government connections) clients were among the lucky few chosen to be a part of each bank's elite network. And the terms and conditions they had to endure just for the privilege of dealing with those banks were draconian—fees were through the roof. But the Russians did not care—they just needed reliable banks to do their business.

Out of hundreds of requests for loans only one or two were chosen and mostly under the guarantees of the local or regional or even federal government (that is why government connections were so important).

And still foreign-owned banks went through some rough times. And there were many reasons for that. Besides obvious—weak ruble, high inflation, unstable economy, criminal activities—they often simply did not orient themselves too well on the Russian market at that time. For example, they could give a loan or invest into a project under the guarantees of any type of government and still lose their money. They did not consider a simple fact that most of the government bureaucrats were closely connected with the criminal underworld and, besides that, (as everybody connected to the Yeltsin/Berezovsky regime) did not even think of returning any money at all. They considered any cash their own—a sort of endless flow of honorariums for their governmental services. Under this level of corruption and chaos (and in the face of the default of the Russian economy in 1998) some foreign banks even decided to withdraw completely from the Russian market.

So, when some people say that the daughter-bank system did not work in the past—they are either cunning or do not know what they are talking about. The problem was not competition or regulations (although the latter was very tough at that time)—the problems were the economic situation and the Yeltsin/Berezovsky regime. Under exactly the same regulations but under a different government and in a different economic situation foreign banks could have achieved a dizzying success.

By late 2006 the situation in Russia changed significantly. It does not mean that it was completely fine—the ruble was still quite weak, inflation was quite high, economy was not completely stable, and money laundering was still a part of day-to-day business for some Russian banks—but still it was very different from what it used to be before. The ruble was weak but because the federal government made a lot of effort to keep it down trying to protect the interests of Russian exporters. Inflation was high as compared to the United States and European Union but it was not any more estimated in hundreds of percentage points every year as it used to be. Actually, in 2005 and 2006 it held on at the approximately 10 percent a year level (9 to 11 percent). The economy was growing not very rapidly but steadily and with minimal disturbances. The only troubling fact was that it still heavily depended on oil prices that made it potentially unstable.

But the last issue—criminal involvement in the banking business—was still a problem. Putin's government made a substantial effort and progress in that area but even the very evidence of that progress were, to put it mildly, troubling. It seemed that the criminal element in the banking business really felt the pressure from the government because in the fall of 2006 there had been a series of high-profile murders of high-level Russian government officials and businessmen who were involved in the fight against banking crimes (all together, sixteen bankers were killed over a ten-year period). The physical elimination of those people was the only way for the criminals to somehow relieve the pressure on them. On the other hand, it still showed how powerful and dangerous the criminal groups were in that area.

And even many years later and after all this progress, Russian people still did not completely trust Russian banks. After the default of 1998, numerous bank scandals, and the collapse of even such seemingly indestructible giants as Incombank—they still preferred to keep their money under the mattress or invest it in real estate that was more reliable and profitable. The only bank that the Russians trusted (and still do) unconditionally was Sberbank—the largest and oldest (established in 1841) state-owned bank in the country that was well known to everybody yet from the Soviet times. Although there appeared a group of some Russian relatively big and reliable banks—Alfa Bank, Vnesh-torgbank, Gazprombank—the Russians were still careful with their money. They were slowly getting used to having bank accounts but because they had to—not because they wanted to. Most of them were simply paid through ATM machines that belonged to certain banks. That is Russians did not choose their bank themselves—their employers chose banks for them. But most of the Russians every month emptied their accounts completely, bought US dollars or Euros and put them back under their mattresses—very few of them dared to invest or give anything to a Russian bank (except for Sberbank—the old Soviet giant). In 2006 only 25 percent of the Russians had a bank account. And 60 million Russians (over 40 percent of the whole country's population) lived in the areas that were entirely out of reach of any banking services.

But big foreign banks were a different story. First of all, Russians trusted such names as CitiBank or Chase Manhattan. Secondly, it became a sign of prestige to have an account in a solid foreign bank or to carry around a credit card issued by one of these banks. So, in this sector the problem was that Russian people and businesses would love to work with American banks but it was the banks that often could not process such a huge number of clients or were simply reluctant to enter such a dangerous and unstable market. Therefore, competition, form of organization, or regulations were not the problem here. The problem was the banks themselves.

The banks did not actually rush to invest in the Russian market. Even when they were allowed just 25 percent participation in the foundation charter capital, they rarely ever actually used up their entire 25 percent quota. In late 2006, there were just forty-three banks in the whole country that belonged to foreigners. The share of international market giants in the aggregate capital of the entire Russian banking industry went from 6.19 percent just up to 11.15 percent between the years 2005 and 2006. Foreign banks did not even usually spend money on actually establishing a daughter bank in Russia. They were more and more simply buying out different Russian banks in trouble (often from each other). For example, such big players as Société Générale or GE Consumer Finance preferred to buy a troubled Russian bank from another foreign entity and see what was going to come out of it.

Subsequently, for the Americans to request a greater access for foreign banks to the Russian market was the same as to request a greater access to a wide open field where very few people actually wanted to go. In this case why did the Americans demand that? The answer seems to be quite simple—ideology and politics. Actually, quite a few Russian officials noted that negotiation dialogue in this area turned into a political debate rather than an economic discussion.

For the Americans the freedom of trade, first of all, is a complete and unabridged freedom of the flow of capital. That is why imposing any limitations on banking activities is considered a serious offense. The second reason may be purely political and pragmatic. Some Russian analysts believe that the Americans simply did not want to create a precedent for future negotiations so that other WTO candidates would not be able to point to the Russian case and demand similar privileges.

The Russians usually presented two reasons for their position in this respect. They said that the system they insisted on could actually help them to fulfill the conditions set up for their WTO membership. One of the conditions was to reduce the rate of inflation and the Russians argued that exactly this form of organization of international banking activities would allow them to exert a significant influence on the rate of inflation because daughter banks were regulated by the Russian authorities. The second important condition—to fight crime in the banking area—also could be achieved only if all the bank activities were transparent to the Russian law enforcement authorities. "Otherwise, how are we supposed to fight crime and money laundering if we do not control and do not have complete information about all the financial activities in the country"—they argued.

One way or the other, it seemed that Putin had a strong opinion on this issue (especially after the murder in September 2006 of Andrei Kozlov—a member of his government, his ally, and a known crime fighter in the field of banking). In January 2006 Putin said on Russian TV that for Russia direct branch offices approach was not acceptable because it did not let the Russians control the flow of capital.

In relation to the insurance industry, we can say that it was almost nonexistent in Russia. The old giant Gosstrah was the only company the Russians were ready to deal with. But in general the population was not used to having insurance policies, considered it a waste of money, and bought insurance only if they absolutely had to (like, for example, mandatory auto insurance). And their experiences with the nascent Russian insurance industry only increased their apprehension. That is, probably, why the Russian government did not consider this particular industry as something very important and could make substantial concessions in this area. Consequently, they were frustrated by American attempts to bundle the insurance issue with the banking problem.

After all this analysis, the course of action to reach an agreement is very clear. First of all, it is necessary to separate two issues—banking and insurance. In this case the Russians may be willing to make substantial concessions in the insurance area. At the same time, it is unwise for the Americans to continue insisting on the direct banking branch offices approach and agree on the Russian condition of American-owned but Russian-registered resident daughter banks. They are not going to lose anything because this field is still widely available for exploration and the Russians did a lot to make it easier (regulation-wise) for foreign-owned banks to operate on the Russian market.

But for that the Americans have to abandon their purely ideological and political position and return to a solid and purely economic basis. And the main question here is: How important for the Americans is the banking issue (the question that is not actually vital for them but for the Russians it may be crucial in terms of their ability to control inflation and fight crime)?

Agricultural Issues: Meats and Poultry

By the end of summer 2006, Russian market of meats and poultry was completely dominated by American products. It happened to a large extent because a year earlier the two countries signed an agreement that stipulated a special preferential treatment for American agricultural products and raised the US import quotas up to 1,252,000 metric tons of poultry, 450,000 tons of beef, and 502,000 tons of pork.

In August 2006 the Minister of Agriculture of the Russian Federation Alexey Gordeyev said that out of 1,150,000 metric tons of poultry and meat imported into Russia—800 tons came from America. As anybody can easily calculate, that amount constituted a staggering 70 percent of the entire poultry and meat segment of the market. Only in this segment the Americans earned that year approximately 1 billion dollars.

The poultry market import breakdown at that time looked like this:

USA—40 percent
Europe—10.5 percent

Russia—46.2 percent
Other—3.3 percent

So, if we take only the poultry segment, the Americans controlled 40 percent of it. Consequently, Russian poultry producers were very unhappy about
this situation and often appealed to the Russian government to protect them
from what they believed to be unfair dumping practices by the Americans. But
the government mostly ignored them because it still believed that such a preferential treatment for the Americans would help the Russians to enter WTO
sooner.

But the Americans were still not satisfied. In 2005 they demanded from the
Russians to fix state subsidies for agriculture at the level of $3.5 billion a year.
It was strange because during the early years of the Yeltsin government agricultural subsidies in Russia stayed at the level of about $10 billion a year. So,
the Russians saw this demand as an application of different standards depending on what type of government was in power in Moscow. It seemed to
them that the US used not economic but political considerations depending
on whether or not they liked a particular Russian government.

Russians made some concessions on some agricultural products. For example, they substantially reduced import duty tariffs on such goods as tropical
fruits, wines, and vegetables (the latter only in the wintertime). But still the
whole set of negotiations was moving nowhere.

Finally, by late summer 2006 the Russian frustration with the lack of
progress in their WTO bid reached a critical point. And they chose agriculture
to clearly demonstrate it to the Americans.

In August 2006 the Russians announced that they were ready to cancel the
2005 agreement on importing poultry, beef, and pork into Russia and that
was supposed to work until 2009. German Gref, Minister of Economic Development and Trade of the Russian Federation, said then that the government would not be able under such circumstances to decline further demands of the Russian agricultural producers to reconsider the current import
poultry and meats tariffs established earlier for American products. He also
suggested that in case of a poultry products deficit such countries as Brazil
would be able to easily fill that gap. Certainly, Brazilian products were 5 to 10
percent more expensive but that was not economic only a political statement.
The Russians decided to show the Americans how it feels when politics overcome economics.

And the Americans did not like it a bit. Now it was their turn to complain
that the Russians renege on their promises and try to reconsider accords that
had been agreed upon previously. But the Russians said that the agreement
was not a part of the WTO talks.

The level of political activity around Gref's announcement in Washington, DC showed the importance of the agricultural area for the Americans. Not only politicians but many organizations got involved immediately. For example, the USA Poultry and Egg Export Council (USAPEEC) immediately issued a statement that they strongly believed that the 2005 import quotas agreement was impossible to reconsider at all because it was signed and was supposed to expire only in 2009. And such a reaction was understandable because poultry was the largest American agricultural import article brought into Russia (and one of the most profitable too).

After all those moves and countermoves some negotiational progress in the area of agriculture was reported but no specific information was initially released. But good advice for the Americans, certainly, would be to try to clinch their existing advantages on the Russian agricultural market and try to explore them to the fullest extent instead of annoying the Russians with further demands and, by so doing, pushing them to undertake measures that definitely would not be to the advantage of the United States.

Intellectual Property Rights

Russia is indeed one of those countries where certain problems in the areas of intellectual property and copyrights do exist. And the American adamant insistence on Russia fighting this problem seems logical and reasonable. But there is one problem here: What does it exactly mean to fight this type of crime? What standards have to be adhered to and what goals are to be achieved? This part of the negotiations was intangible and extremely fuzzy.

Russians did not argue that it was not important to combat intellectual property crime—after all, many Russian know-hows were (and still are) used all over the world without license or permission (for example, production of AK-47 automatic assault rifles). But what exactly did the Russians have to do to satisfy the American rigor? No clear answer had ever been received.

The Americans asked the Russians to make their legislation tougher on this type of crime but the Russians argued that their legislation was already 99 percent compliant with all the WTO standards. The Americans said "Show us the effort and the results." In response the Russians said that only in 2005 there had been thirty-five thousand raids against the producers of counterfeit products and 223 enterprises had been closed. Only in one year 3,860 criminal and 19,000 administrative proceedings were opened by the Russian authorities in the area of copy- and intellectual property rights. But was it enough? And here even the Americans themselves did not exactly know what to say.

And in such a standardless discussion the Russians got suspicious—was the United States really interested in what they were doing or was just using the issue to make trouble for them. It was indeed suspicious because it was very convenient to use such types of issues to keep the discussion rolling forever without ever been formally obligated to admit that certain goals were achieved and certain requirements were satisfied.

That is why some Russian officials were complaining that the Americans were simply picking on them. After all, the situation with intellectual property rights in China was even worse but the Americans signed a treaty with them. The situation in this area in the Ukraine was no better but the Americans did not emphasize that question in WTO negotiations with them.

So, the only option that existed in that area was that the Americans had to conduct an expertise of the pertinent Russian legislation and establish clear standards and goals for them in this field or simply admit that the Russians were making a reasonable effort in this area and move on to different issues. Otherwise, their negotiational behavior in relation to this particular topic indeed looked suspicious.

Theoretical Analysis of the Situation

The Rational Actor Approach

If we take a purely rational approach to the issue and set aside all the political and emotional aspects we can clearly see that the fastest possible entrance of Russia into the World Trade Organization is in the best interests of the United States. Taking into account the passion of game theorists for matrices, the game is summarized in Figure 4.1.

Before explaining this matrix it is necessary to make some remarks so that the reader could understand the logic behind it. By the end of 2006 it became clear that the Russians had a very limited number of products to offer on the world market. The lion's share of their export was the products that had been traditionally brought by them on the world market for the last thousand years—raw materials. Such commodities as timber, oil, and natural gas repre-

		United States	
		No WTO	WTO
Russia	No WTO	n/a	+95/−75
	WTO	n/a	−95/+95

FIGURE 4.1
The game-theory payoff matrix for Russia's membership in WTO.

sented according to some estimates up to 70 percent of their export. But anyway everybody needs these products and their sales on the market have nothing to do with WTO.

Another set of products could be characterized as traditional Soviet goods—all types of weaponry (including hi-tech), aviation and space industries, and to a lesser extent automotive industry. Recently metallurgy experienced certain resurgence in the country. These products could be theoretically affected by Russia's WTO membership. But this was pretty much the exhaustive list of products that Russia could offer on the world market.

But the problem here is that in general there is no such thing as the "world market." This purely theoretical entity in fact consists of many different types of markets that actually function each in its own special way. For the purpose of analysis here we will highlight three kinds of markets—domestic, developed, and third countries' market (or Thirds World markets which will include China and India).

The Russians have nothing to look for on the developed countries' market. And it is not because they have nothing to offer but because there is no way the Americans, Japanese, or Europeans will let Russian products on their markets. Putin is right here—these are the best protected markets in the world. They will find a way to keep Russian products out of their countries—using environmental, technological, and other regulations. This is an old trick and WTO will not help here. The Russian products and services they are currently buying will remain on their market no matter what. For example, the Americans are buying Russian rocket engines. They will be buying them anyway because they are the best in the world and the Americans are not going to have a comparable technology for the next twenty years at least. It is more efficient to buy them than to develop them with ever-rising cost of R&D in the United States. The Europeans will be using Russian space-launch services no matter what because it is the most reliable and cost-efficient way to get their satellites into space. But only a very naïve person can think that if the Russians enter the organization the Americans, Japanese, or Europeans will allow Moscow to significantly increase the sales of Russian metallurgical products on their markets.

Quite an interesting example for this proposition came in late 2006 when a Russian magnate Roman Abramovich wanted to buy one of the American West Coast companies—Oregon Steel Mills. Immediately, the United States Congress launched an investigation on the national security aspects of such a deal. So, if WTO regulations will allow him to do it—probably, national security will not. That is, it is easy to find an excuse for not allowing the Russians on the American market. And WTO will have very little effect on this issue.

The competition is and will be going on only on the Third World's and domestic markets. There the Russians are and will be successful with their weapons, space services, and, probably in the future, with planes and cars. In 2005 and 2006 they became the number one weapons seller in the Third World overtaking the US and France. People buy or use their products on those markets using considerations that again have nothing to do with WTO. The Russians are very successful in these areas and already are taking a big share of that market from the so-called developed countries. WTO will not help them but it may definitely harm them in a bad way because, for example, it will require them to open their market for cheap Chinese cars that can put out of business Russian domestic automotive industry.

At the domestic level the situation is even more clear-cut. The situation as it exists is quite bad—the Russian market is dominated by foreign (mostly by American and European) products. To keep it this way is bad enough—to open the market even more may be a complete disaster. If it is done immediately and entirely, it will spell out the death of the aviation and automotive industries, killing on the way all the farmers and steel workers.

Putin's dream of a country that will be exporting a lot of hi-tech products has so far not come true. And the best example of this is the collapse in late 2006 of Sitronics, a company that was positioned as Russian Siemens. The company was producing native Russian computers, car radios, LCD TV sets, MP3 and DVD players, audio equipment, and even cell phones. It turned out that Sitronics could not compete with either sophisticated Japanese and European products or with cheap Chinese and Malaysian goods. Therefore, the Russians actually practically do not have any products that would require WTO's interference. That is the products they do successfully trade on the world market have nothing to do with WTO but the products that are usually affected by WTO regulations are not quite developed yet in Russia and may never get developed if the trade barriers are removed and subsidies are cancelled.

Even German Gref, the Godfather of the WTO idea in Russia, had trouble explaining specific advantages of WTO for his country during hearings in the Russian parliament in September 2006. He could not name specifically a single one of them and said that nothing special would happen and that advantages and disadvantages would not be felt right away. The Russian members of parliament were a little bit scared by that answer. If he cannot answer this question—who can?

Consequently, in the matrix above the "no-WTO" option for the Russians is evaluated at +95. If they avoid this organization, they will lose almost nothing on the world market. But they will win at the domestic level. Without WTO they will be able to institute some market protection measures that will allow them to develop and nurture many of their still weak industries. The WTO option is set at −95 because it will give them practically no advantages at the developed or developing markets but may destroy their domestic economy as a whole and may eventually lead to the collapse of the country itself.

For the Americans the situation is different. If Russia becomes a WTO member, the Americans not only get to keep all of their current privileges but can obtain some additional ones (not only on the Russian but also Third World market). Their possible losses would be minimal. Their domestic market will not be affected at all. The payoff is +95. But if the Russians abandon the WTO idea and, following their disappointment and frustration, institute tough protectionist measures—they may lose up to three quarters of what they currently have in Russia—whole industries. So, the payoff is −75.

The final remark in this section may seem to someone heartless and cynical but this is the rational actor segment and emotions are prohibited here (as well as ethical considerations). The Americans have to keep in mind that the Russian economy is slowly and painfully but steadily developing. They are already threatening the American domination in some parts of the world (such as Latin America) and in some industries (such as weaponry). If they are allowed to continue to develop further unchecked—they may soon become a really serious competition on the world market—something the United States does not really need now or in the future. And Russia's membership in WTO is, probably, the only chance the Americans may get to strangle some still weak Russian industries (such as the aircraft industry) before they become a real threat to the Americans. In ten or fifteen years it may be already too late. The opportunity that is presenting itself now to the US is unique and may be gone soon.

The Learning Theory and Perceptions

So, what have both sides learned in the course of these negotiations? How did they adjust their positions according to the new pieces of information they received? What kind of perceptions played the main role in these talks?

It seems that the Russians learned quite a lot and adjusted their position substantially. They seem to have learned that there is no such thing as free trade and that some former partners quickly become bitter rivals when it comes to business. This is where the words of Putin about no freedom of trade and heavily protected Western markets came from. They learned about harmful effects that their WTO membership may entail and modified their position. They started talking a lot about their national interests and about protecting some industries from foreign invasion and expansion. They have also learned that the Americans are not idealists fighting for principles but cutthroat business people who are fighting for their profits and economic interests. The whole understanding of the situation changed from a common march toward the bright future of global free trade to a contentious quarrel over cents, ounces, inches, and percentage points. The idealism of dreams is almost gone—the bitter reality is slowly taking over the Russians.

The Americans seem to have learned surprisingly little. They do not even seem to entirely realize what kind of benefits Russia's WTO membership will bring them and what kind of problems may arise if negotiations fail. They completely fail to understand that Russia of 2006 is not Russia of 1994. It is much stronger and more independent. The Americans still believe that the Russians will eventually give up and surrender all of their national interests as they used to do under the Yeltsin/Berezovsky government. For a long time they could not realize that introduction of political demands into trade negotiations was counterproductive. In this case business and politics did not mix too well. Besides that, these political demands annoyed the Russians and made them even more skeptical of the very idea of the Western model of democracy and, consequently, of the idea of free trade. Many American politicians (especially some members of Congress) still have the Cold War mentality and try to fight the Russians instead of talking to them. They introduce some political bills that make the Russians angry and, consequently, make negotiations more difficult but in reality have nothing to do with trade issues. They are stubbornly doing the same things—linking political issues with trade. Such steps almost pushed the Russians to the point where they were seriously considering abandoning the WTO idea all together.

So, it is always good advice to update your information and perception database, to try to learn more about the opponent, and not to be shy to adjust your own position.

Psychological Point of View and Domestic Politics

The psychological point of view emphasizes personal characteristics of negotiators and that is why in this case it is convenient and appropriate to combine it in one section with the domestic political considerations.

As was mentioned above, Putin used to be the main driving force behind the idea of Russia's membership in the World Trade Organization. Then, he seemed to be having second thoughts. Fortunately for the Americans, there were several powerful figures who were unyielding supporters of that idea. The main figures were German Gref, Minister of Economic Development and Trade of the Russian Federation, Alexei Kudrin, Minister of Finance of Russia, and Maxim Medvedkov, head of the Russian negotiating delegation and director of the trade talks department at the Ministry for Economic Development and Trade. They sincerely believed that WTO would bring their country economic prosperity and power. It was them who kept Putin excited about the organization.

The problem is that the idea of Russia's membership in WTO is very unpopular in the country. It is even more important that there are members of the Russian business and political elites who are ready to fight it. Most Russians like Putin. That is why they were ready to tolerate that idea for so long and applauded when Putin started having doubts. But the same people really dislike the members of his government who support the idea—namely, German Gref and Alexei Kudrin. These two officials conduct disastrous economic and financial policies—starving the Russian economy of the financial resources it so desperately needs for investment and development. Without them the Russian economy could have grown much faster but they do everything to slow down that growth. So, they are as popular in Russia as Donald Rumsfeld or Dick Cheney are in the United States. Therefore, in 2008, when Putin is gone, these two ministers will probably be the first ones to go too. And after these two locomotives of the WTO proposal are gone there will be very few other government officials willing to support the plan. The two possible Putin successors—Sergey Mironov, Chairman of the Council of Federation of the Federal Assembly of the Russian Federation and Boris Gryzlov, leader of the United Russia (UR) party and chairman of the State Duma are not big fans of the initiative and will not be pushing it forward if they see a heavy opposition to it. That is why, both of them made sure to go on record to express their concern over the level of protection of the Russian trade interests during WTO talks. To summarize, the chances of ratifying the agreement after the 2008 Russian presidential elections will drop dramatically.

In late 2006, when Putin still generally supported the plan and his party (United Russia) was in complete control of both chambers of the Russian parliament, the ratification of the WTO agreement was likely. Many deputies (this is how members of the parliament are called in Russia) were eager to please Putin and show the party unity. Putin is a strong and charismatic leader and he would find a way to push the accord through the country's top legislative body.

In general, the domestic political situation in Russia in relation to a possible WTO agreement is shown in Table 4.1.

In the United States the situation is quite unsure. Until mid-2006, neither American government nor the parliament considered it a priority issue. The government appeared not to be able to see all the advantages of the treaty and still believed that the Russians needed it and it would be some kind of favor to them if the Americans let them in. So, they kept tying political demands to this issue and did not seem to be ready to sign the agreement as it was.

Since it was considered to be an unimportant issue, it is logical to suggest that the absolute majority of the American members of Congress had not really thought about the problem and, consequently, had not formed their opinion by then. They seemed to share the government's perceptional errors and

TABLE 4.1
The WTO Initiative in Russia

Variables	Situation
Situation at the Proposer (P) level	The President and a couple of key ministers support it. But strong opposition also exists. So, the situation can be characterized as slightly favorable.
Situation at the Chooser (C) level	Putin's party controls the parliament (2/3 is no problem) and has strong party unity and discipline. But some opposition still exists. So, the situation at this level can be characterized as favorable.
Presence of supporters (positive Endorsers) at the interest groups level (E)	Metallurgy and some parts of the chemical industry.
Type of ratification procedure chosen	Qualified majority—2/3.
Side-payments made	Long transitional periods, keeping some import duty tariffs in place, strong food safety regulations, keeping subsidies for the agricultural sector, full protection for Russian banks.
Result	Under all the conditions above—the agreement would succeed.

liked to play politics around the topic. Besides that, in the United States it is always difficult to collect enough members to vote "for Russia."

The problem is that the names of two countries—China and Russia—usually provoke inadequate reactions among American elected politicians. Having some kind of inexplicable prejudice, they find it difficult to vote "for" if the name of one of these two countries is attached to a bill. They cannot vote "yes" even if the bill is 100 percent favorable to the United Sates. (It is enough to recall how much effort the START treaties ratification required.) The Congress people have an incomprehensible urge to "be tough" on these countries even if such a definition is not applicable in that particular situation. They have a mysterious tradition to feel like they are selling out their country if they vote in support of Russia or China doing anything. Then, during election campaigns, they always say "I was tough on Russia and China during such and such negotiations and my opponent voted for them." They feel proud of that even if it was a foolish thing to do. And in this case, since they mistakenly believe that the Russians badly need it, it would be difficult to make them vote for it. The government would have to apply a lot of pressure on them to achieve this goal but the Bush administration was passive and unwilling to put too much work into this project at all until the end of 2006.

Certainly, the interest groups (the Endorsers) could be willing to put some pressure on the politicians but even they seemed to be content with the current situation and raised their concerns only when the Russians threatened to withdraw their privileges.

The next question is: Will anything change after the American presidential elections in 2008, especially if the Democrats will come to power? The answer is again—"who knows." If the Republicans remain in power—the current course is likely to continue. If the Democrats come to power the situation may even get worse.

The problem is that the Soviets and later Russians traditionally had more stable relationships with the Republican governments. The Republicans are more pragmatic and business-oriented. So, they prefer not to rock the boat and keep normal relations with the Russians (except for the Reagan administration)— stability is good for business. The Democrats are more political and ideological (as they would, probably, define themselves—more idealistic). Historically, they tend to have more political problems with the Russians. Therefore, a history-savvy political analyst would predict more political demands from the Democrats and, consequently, a lower probability of fruitful cooperation under this type of government.

Problem-solving and Joint Decision-making Points of View

These two approaches emphasize joint effort of both parties of the negotiations to reach a mutually acceptable solution free of political games and ideological fog. In this perspective both sides are supposed to work together against the common problem. But the problems in this case were different for the two sides.

The problem for the Russians was exactly the ideological fog that abstracted their economic vision and prevented them from seeing the obvious—they did not need the agreement at all. Therefore, if the Russians had gotten rid of their liberal-market ideological prejudice and looked at everything in a sober manner—the negotiations would have simply stopped.

For the Americans the problems were, first of all, their traditional anti-Russian political orientation and, secondly, the fact that they wanted to get too much when they already had a lot. For them to solve the problem—it was necessary to get rid of their political prejudices and realize that it was them who needed that agreement and soon. Cold economic calculations would show them that the situation was already good for them and could get only better if the agreement was signed and that the Russian offers in all areas were very reasonable.

For example, in the civil aviation area the situation for the Americans was good and would become even better if the tariffs would be cut in half and the Russians would become a WTO member that would prohibit them from protecting their civil aviation market stronger in the future. But if the talks failed—the American losses would be huge.

In the banking area the course of recommended actions to reach an agreement was very clear. First of all, it was necessary to separate two issues—banking and insurance. In this case the Russians could be willing to make substantial concessions in the insurance area. At the same time, it was unwise for the Americans to continue insisting on the direct banking branch offices approach. It would be much better to agree on the Russian condition of the Russian-registered and regulated resident daughter-banks option. In that case the Americans were not going to lose anything because this field was still widely available for exploration and the Russians did a lot to make it easier for foreign-owned banks to operate on the Russian market.

But for that the Americans had to abandon their purely ideological and political position and return to a solid and purely economic basis. And the main question here was: How important for the Americans was the banking issue in general—as the agreement-making (or breaking) problem?

In the agricultural area, good advice for the Americans, certainly, would be to try to simply clinch their existing advantages on the Russian agricultural market and to try to explore them to the fullest extent possible instead of annoying the Russians with further demands and, by so doing, pushing them to undertake measures that definitely would not be to the advantage of the United States.

In the intellectual property rights area, it could be recommended to the United States to conduct a review of the pertinent Russian legislation and establish clear standards and goals for them in this field or simply admit that the Russians were making a reasonable effort in this area and move on to other issues. In any case, it would be nice to have the Russians to sign some kind of document in addition to the bilateral WTO agreement that would put some type of additional obligations on them in relation to this particular issue.

Final Agreement and Ratification

When this case study was already finished, sensational news came—quite unexpectedly for many people, Russia and the United Sates signed the bilateral WTO agreement. The agreement was signed by the Russian Minister of Economic Development and Trade, German Gref and the American representative at the WTO talks, Susan Schwab on Sunday November 19th, 2006 in Hanoi, Vietnam.

After signing the agreement, Russians explicitly thanked President Bush for his help in making it happen. A couple of months after the summer 2006 G-8 summit in Saint Petersburg, President Bush officially announced that he was personally taking the course of these negotiations under his personal control. Why the change of heart—from indifference to support? The answer can be found in the appearance on the scene of such an organization as the Coalition for US-Russia Trade which includes such giants as the Boeing Company, Cargill, Caterpillar, Chevron, Ford Motor Company, General Electric, Intel, and Procter & Gamble. It seems that when it almost came to the breakdown of the negotiations, the American business finally realized two things. First of all, they understood that negotiations from the position of force were not going to work anymore and if the same strategy continued—the talks would simply die. But, at the same time, they realized the second thing—if the talks died they would lose a lot. So, they put some pressure on the administration to make the deal with the Russians.

After analyzing the final agreement, it can be said that it could serve as a textbook example of the situation when both sides managed to put aside their political prejudices and did everything possible (including many reasonable compromises and concessions) to make this accord possible. A lot of joint work went into that agreement—every detail was thoroughly considered, negotiated, and documented. The whole document is over 800 pages long and covers 100 sectors of economy (including pharmaceutical, chemical, automotive, financial services, communication, audiovisual, and other industries). But the most pleasant fact for the author of this book is that the parties followed almost to the point recommendations outlined earlier in this case study. Let's really quickly go over the final document.

In the civil aviation area, Americans indeed decided to simply accept all the Russian offers without any changes and, at least for the foreseeable future, to clinch their advantages on the Russian aviation market. After Russia becomes a WTO member, the import duty tariffs for American civil aviation planes will be reduced from currently 20 percent down to 10 percent. This number for spare parts will drop even lower—it will be an average of 5 percent. Conditions for leasing foreign-made airliners will become more favorable as well.

In the financial sector, the parties (as it was recommended) decided to disintegrate the two industries—insurance and banking. The Russians agreed to let on their market direct branch offices of the American insurance companies but only after a nine-year transitional period.

At the same time, in the banking area Americans made serious concessions. Russia received a rare privilege not to allow direct branch offices of American banks on the Russian marker—only Russian-registered resident daughter banks will be allowed. And even under these conditions all the foreign-related banks in the country all together will not be allowed to exceed the 50 percent capital quota mark in the aggregate capital of the entire Russian banking industry.

In the agricultural sector Americans again decided to make some concessions in order to secure their current domination of the Russian agricultural market. Russia kept its right to impose import quotas on meat and poultry products from the United States. The import quotas for meat products will remain the same at least until the year 2009 and may be extended even after that but, probably, at a lower level. All this is a little bit unusual. But this issue will be further discussed further by the two countries in 2008.

Russia also decided to establish a strict veterinary safety control over pork and beef products brought into the country from America. Russians will be able to inspect American meat products manufacturers and certify or accredit them to allow them to sell their products on the Russian market. Every year they will be able inspect 50 percent of American meat suppliers accredited in that particular year and 15 percent of suppliers certified earlier. In case of safety violations the supplier will be taken off the approved importers list. Special safety laboratories on the Russian border will be better equipped to conduct express safety and quality analysis of all the meat and poultry products entering the country from the US. Americans, on the other hand, agreed to guarantee quality of all such products intended for the Russian market. Actually, the government of the United States gave the government of Russia official guarantees that American beef and pork will satisfy all the requirements of the international sanitary standards. A separate document will also be signed on the issue of genetically modified foods.

Import duty tariffs for other types of agricultural products were also discussed and agreed upon by both parties. They will drop from the previous average level of 21.5 percent down to an average level of 18.9 percent. The tariffs mostly will be reduced on agricultural products not usually generated by the Russian agricultural industry—oranges, bananas, grapes, etc. For the products grown in Russia in the quantity sufficient to satisfy the domestic market—import duty tariffs will not be reduced at all. For the seasonal products that are produced in Russia the tariffs will go down only in the Winter/Spring season but for the Summer/Fall period special higher rates will be established. The one-year transitional period is specified in accord for all the agricultural tariff changes.

The matter of the state subsidies for the Russian agricultural sector will be further clarified at the multilateral phase but so far the level of subsidies, that was reportedly agreed upon by the Russians and the United Sates, stands at about 9 billion and 200 million US dollars. It is four times as big as the level of state subsidies for the Russian agricultural industry by the end of 2006. The Russians seem to be happy and the Americans don't mind.

In the intellectual property rights area, Russians agreed to sign a special separate document in which they would take upon themselves special obligations to strictly regulate this issue and enforce all the international standards in this respect on their territory.

There are also other interesting elements of the agreement. For example, Russia agreed to reduce import duty tariffs for American cars from 25 percent down to 15 percent within five years after its entrance into the organization. For SUVs with big engines this number will go down to 12 percent but within seven years after the event. At the same time, it seems like at least some level of protection of the Russian automotive market will remain in place for the foreseeable future.

Russian main concessions came on the issue of the price for natural gas— one of their main export commodities. They agreed to raise their gas prices for the domestic market 5–10 percent every year and, by the year 2011, domestic and export prices for this particular article of trade will be equalized (but only for industrial and not residential Russian users).

Import duty tariffs will be reduced for medical equipment and drugs, consumer electronics, and computers from 10 to 6 percent on average. In general, import duty tariffs will drop dramatically for many food products and almost all consumer products within two years after Russia's eventual entrance in to the organization. But even after all that, as some Russian officials argue, the level of the market protection (tariff-wise) in some sectors of the economy will be almost twice as high as it is in Europe or in other developed countries.

In short, everybody got what they wanted. Russians got the agreement and some market protection measures (at least, for some time). The Americans lured the Russians into the organization and secured their dominance on the Russian market in many important sectors of economy. But now the next phase is starting—final multilateral talks and ratification.

By itself the concluding multilateral stage is hardly that important. It would be a sure bet to say that Russia will eventually become a WTO member (unless ratification fails). The only aspect that is quite important here is time. For example, it took China twenty months to finish this final stage. In the Russian case the negotiations may take even longer. And this is where some problems arise.

First of all, Putin will leave in 2008 and many other supporters of the WTO idea are likely to leave with him. For now, he can secure support of two-thirds of the Russian parliament to ratify the agreement. He is a strong and charismatic leader and under his rule the accord will be ratified without much trouble. But, if the final multilateral stage of the talks goes beyond 2008, the agreement may stall in Russia. As it was mentioned above, the WTO idea is not very popular in the country. A weaker leader may not be able to push the accord through the Russian top legislative body.

In America the situation has already gotten worse for the accord. In November 2006 the Democrats took control over both chambers of the American parliament. The majority is slim but still a majority. After years out of power, Democrats are determined to exercise their authority at full swing. That is why the form of the ratification procedure is important here.

Usually, Americans ratify trade accords as congressional-executive agreements (CEA)—simple majority in both chambers. It will be even better if they could use what is called the Trade Promotion Authority (or simply "fast-track") procedure. Under this rule the legislators cannot introduce any amendments to the document and have to accept it "as is" and strict time limits for voting procedures are established. But if the qualified majority Senate option is used for some reason and the amendments are allowed—the agreement may die in the Congress quite easily.

If the simple majority is used, Bush personally and organizations like the Coalition for U.S.-Russia Trade could lobby some legislators and still pass the bill. But it would be very difficult to get through the democratically dominated Senate a bill that would require a two-thirds majority and might be considered "Russia-friendly." Besides that, some amendments introduced into the document may not be acceptable for the Russians. Even minor alterations and modifications to the accord could kill it. The fast track is, perhaps, the only procedure able to push the bill through while Bush is still in power. The next president may be a Democrat and the situation may become even worse.

As was mentioned above, Democrats are usually much more ideology-oriented than more business-oriented Republicans. That is why even without a Democratic president, Russians already anticipate problems in the American Congress. They fully expect attempts to tie the ratification of this agreement to such favorite Democrats' issues as democracy, human rights, or something else of that nature. Any such issue may again kill the agreement because in the eyes of the Russians the American legislators lack moral authority to lecture anybody in the World on human rights and democracy.

And the first personnel indicators are not very favorable for the agreement. For example, two early favorites in the 2008 presidential race—Senators John Edwards and John McCain—are extremely anti-Russian and against any economic and political cooperation with Moscow. They are against any Russian membership in any "civilized world" international organizations, including G-

8 and WTO. The position of the chair of the key Foreign Relations Committee in the Senate will be occupied by Senator Joseph Biden well-known for his negative attitude toward the Russian membership in the World Trade Organization. The position of the chair of the House Committee on International Relations will be taken by Thomas Lantos who was one of the co-authors of the congressional resolution demanding to suspend Russia's membership in G-8. And these people will have to introduce the accord in the Congress for ratification. All this indicates a tough road ahead for the agreement if it ever comes up for ratification in the United States at all.

Certainly, all this can be avoided if the document is considered in the US an *executive agreement* an'd, in particular, an *agreement pursuant to treaty* (in this case—the general WTO set of regulations). But even in this case the Congress can request the document for consideration from the administration and start making problems anyway.[1]

That is why such aspects as timing, form of ratification, involvement of endorsers, and side-payments to specific legislators are slowly becoming the key factors for those who are actually interested in the question of whether Russia will ultimately become a member of the World Trade Organization or not. Although the bilateral Russian-American agreement is a done deal (at least, it is negotiated and signed at the executive level) the final outcome of the whole process is still unclear.

Finally, the author wants to note that these negotiations can serve as an almost perfect example how two sides—if they want to agree—can work together to find a mutually acceptable solution to a problem through reasonable concessions and compromises. But the irony of the whole situation is that the Russians have been working for so many years so hard for an agreement they actually don't need. Literally one and a half industry—metallurgy and some parts of the chemical industry—may benefit from that accord but the rest of them will or may suffer. So is the power of ideology. Whether it is Communist or Liberal Market ideology—does not matter. And this is something that rational actor game theorists do not take into account, although, they should have. And the case studies like this one and others below will show that, although some degree of rational calculations is definitely always present at every set of talks, very often quite different considerations and emotions become really crucial for the final outcome of negotiations.

Note

1. In this case it is very important to take into account one peculiarity of the American approach toward international agreements. From the American point of view

their domestic laws take precedent over any international treaty. And especially in the case of international executive agreements (that may be finalized without formal Congress's approval)—they are not considered to be binding for the next President. So, the next President can theoretically call off the signature of his predecessor under the agreement and start reconsidering it all over again.

5

START I: The First Nuclear War Won by the United States

Introduction

THE STRATEGIC ARMS REDUCTION TREATY (START) number one represents an interesting case of security negotiations. The main point of interest here is that the treaty was under negotiation for nine years. And those years proved to be crucial in the history of the Soviet Union. The talks started in 1982, during the period that was later called in the Soviet Union "the stagnation," under the rule of Leonid Brezhnev. The treaty survived two other Soviet leaders (Chernenko and Andropov) and, finally, was signed by the first (and the last) Soviet President—Michael Gorbachev, in 1991. It is quite amazing that the treaty went through all the Russian political troubles and ultimately was successfully signed, ratified, and came into effect. Usually, when political situations change that dramatically—treaties die somewhere on the way because they do not usually satisfy anymore the requirements and the needs of the new era. But START I survived and succeeded, and the most interesting thing is that it was signed exclusively due to domestic political changes in the Soviet Union.

In the late 1990s, the US Department of State declassified dozens of previously secret documents concerning the START I treaty negotiations. The author of this work used this opportunity to take a close look at the negotiations process and, by so doing, to try to understand how and why such a lopsided document, which had very few chances for success at the beginning, was signed and came into effect.

Before the Talks

Everything started on May 9th, 1982, when, during his commencement address at Eureka College, President Ronald Reagan announced that he had sent a letter (dated May 7th) to the Soviet Communist Party Secretary-General (Leonid Brezhnev) suggesting that the United States and the Soviet Union should begin arms reduction negotiations at the end of June of that year. President Reagan stated that his intentions for START I were to enhance deterrence and achieve stability with significant reductions.

For a dilettante, the proposal looked very attractive—and especially so for the general American public. But all the professional diplomats and weapons experts had the absolutely opposite opinion about it. Strobe Talbott, a prominent American diplomat and a participant of the START I talks, describes the first impression of Reagan's proposal on him and his colleagues:

> Haig warned that if the U.S. went forward with a proposal that was dismissed as cynical and implausible the result could be 'a military and political catastrophe'—politically catastrophic because it would create a backlash against the Administration both at home and abroad and military catastrophic because it would cause a loss of support both in Congress and among the NATO allies.... The President's proposal had also elicited skepticism about negotiability. (Talbott, 1984, pp. 251, 275)

Nobody was able to understand how the President of the United States could possibly step forward with a proposal that had no chances for success whatsoever.

But everything became clear during the first meeting after the proposal announcement between the President and his staff. "The words with which he struggled to make his point betrayed the President's basic innocence in this arcane world" (Talbott, 1984, p. 250).

But what was Reagan so "innocent" about? The answer is—the global nuclear strategic balance situation, which was not very simple at that time.

Traditionally "Russia was a land power (compared to the US which was traditionally a maritime power and in modern times an air power), and the Russian military had accordingly always worshipped artillery as the 'god of war'. ICBMs[1] were the artillery of the nuclear age" (Talbott, 1984, p. 213). That is why the US "has chosen to deploy a majority of its warheads on sea-based forces.... The Soviet Union therefore maintains a majority of its warheads on land based ICBM forces" (Kartchner, 1992, p. 2).

Another START I talks participant, Robert J. Einhorn, describes the military nuclear buildup process which had been going on before the START I negotiations began:

TABLE 5.1
START Acronyms

ABM	Antiballistic Missile; the United States and Soviet Union signed the ABM Treaty in June 1972.
ALCM	Air-Launched Cruise Missiles; the limits in START apply to bombers that carry long-range (greater than 600 km) nuclear-armed ALCMs.
ICBM	Intercontinental Ballistic Missile.
INF	Intermediate Nuclear Forces Treaty; the United States and Soviet Union signed the INF Treaty in December 1987.
MIRV	Multiple, Independently Targeted Reentry Vehicles; this refers to ballistic missiles that carry more than one warhead, with each warhead capable of attacking a different target.
RV	Reentry Vehicle; the device on the front end of the missile that contains a warhead.
SALT	Strategic Arms Limitation Talks; SALT I concluded with the signing of two agreements—the ABM Treaty and the Interim Agreement on Offensive Arms—in 1972. SALT II concluded in 1979 with the signing of a treaty limiting strategic offensive weapons. The United States never ratified the SALT II Treaty.
SDI	Strategic Defense Initiative; the program established by President Reagan to conduct research and development on ballistic missile defense technologies.
SLBM	Submarine-Launched Ballistic Missile.
SLCM	Sea-Launched Cruise Missile.
SRAM	Short-Range Attack Missile; these are carried on heavy bombers.

The Soviets have now surpassed the United States in many of the familiar numerical indicators of strategic capability including, significantly, a number of categories that have become key units of limitation in arms control negotiations: strategic delivery vehicles, ICBMs, heavy ICBMs, MIRVed ICBMS, ICBM warheads, and ballistic missile warheads and throw-weight.

During this period, the United States was also adding to its strategic strength, and it has maintained numerical advantages in several categories of strategic capability on which it has traditionally relied more heavily than the Soviet Union. In particular, it continues to hold a numerical lead in SLBM warheads, heavy bombers, bomber weapons, and bomber payload. (Einhorn, 1985, p. 25)

The situation was finally shaped "by signing the SALT II[2] treaty, [when] the United States accepted the legitimacy of Soviet preeminence in prompt counterforce weapons (ICBMs) as a trade-off for US dominance in less capable second strike weapons (bombers and SLBMs)" (Kartchner, 1992, p. 61).

In short, the strategic nuclear situation in the early 1980s did not represent actually a perfect balance of forces but rather an agreed upon by both sides strategic disbalance with which both sides were relatively comfortable for technological reasons. But still some American experts were not happy about such a situation. For example, Kerry M. Kartchner (1992) wrote: "The USSR is ahead of the United States in deployment of mobile ICBM systems.... The Committee on the Present Danger expanded and reiterated these conclusions, finding that a hypothetical Soviet surprise attack in the 1984–1985 time frame would result in destruction of 80 to 90 percent of U.S. strategic force capabilities, 'leaving us with an inadequate and inflexible response capability'" (pp. 14, 23).

Strobe Talbott (1989) also writes: "The Soviets had about three-to-one advantage in the number of nuclear weapons on ICBMs" (p. 241). (It seems that he actually meant the throw-weight ratio here.) The ratio between the Soviet warheads and the U.S. military targets was "6,000 to some 3,000" (Committee on Armed Services, 1988, p. 44), which guaranteed complete and sure destruction of almost the entire American military potential as a matter of minutes.

During 1988 congressional hearings before the Defense Policy Panel of the Committee on Armed Services, Mr. Harold Brown, Chairman of the Foreign Policy Institute at John Hopkins University said: "Some rearrangements of this sort in the US force is required to avoid worsening the present ratio of Soviet hard kill warheads to US silos, though I think that ratio is already bad enough so that making it worse might not matter a lot" (Committee on Armed Services, 1988, p. 92).

And exactly at this time there appeared Reagan's proposal, the whole essence of which was as follows:

> It was dogma in the Reagan Administration that ballistic missiles—'fast-flyers', as President Reagan called them—were bad; they were weapons of aggression and preemption; therefore, they were the things to be limited. They also, not coincidentally, happened to be the Soviet specialty. Bombers and cruise missiles—'slow flyers'—were good; they were instruments of retaliation and safeguard of deterrence. They were to be protected in START. Again, not coincidentally, they were American specialties. . . . Reagan was, in his fashion, supporting an approach to START that would concentrate on limiting land-based ballistic missiles while virtually exempting the two other, supposedly more benign legs of the triad, bombers and submarines. (Talbott, 1984, pp. 241, 250)

President Reagan had no idea about some simple facts that were very well known to all the weapons experts in the world—for example, the fact that "A bomber is itself as much a launcher as an ICBM silo or a tube on a submarine insofar as it can be used to fire a short-range attack missile or long-range cruise missile at a Soviet target, or drop a bomb on it" (Talbott, 1984, p. 241).

Certainly, everybody understood that the Soviets would never accept such a proposal. Nevertheless, in May of 1982 the START I talks began and both sides had their own reasons to get involved in such a hopeless enterprise. Both parties had their big concerns and, consequently, serious objectives to reach as the result of the negotiations.

Sides' Objectives

American Objectives

American objectives were quite clear from all the above: to try to damage as much as possible the core of the Soviet strategic nuclear forces—ICBMs—and, at the same time, to preserve the backbone of the American nuclear strategic forces—SLBMs, SLCMs, and ALCMs. (It is necessary to take into account that the Soviets had a solid superiority in the number of warheads because many of the Soviet missiles were so-called MIRVed ones, that is, they were capable of carrying several independently targeted warheads.) These objectives were reflected in at least four dimensions of the US START I Policy:

> (1) U.S. proposals for limits on Soviet heavy ICBMs; (2) U.S. proposal for ICBM and SLBM warhead sublimits separate from bomber weapon limits (including initial refusal to consider bomber weapons within aggregate warhead counts); (3) U.S. proposals for throw-weight reductions that excluded bombers throw-weight; and, (4) U.S. refusal to treat bomber and missile weapon equally, including initial U.S. resistance to bomber limits at all, and proposal for rules that 'discounted' bomber weapons. (Kartchner, 1992, p. 35)

Many experts were very candid talking about START I objectives. For example, James R. Schlesinger (Counselor, Council or Strategic and International Relations) and Robert C. McFarlane (former Assistant to the President for National Security Affairs) respectively said:

> Mr. Chairman, in my judgment, the priority in our START negotiations should have been on the reduction of Soviet counterforce capabilities. . . . Simply put, we faced in 1982 the reality that we had been reduced to competing with the Soviet Union in offensive systems in ways in which they had the comparative advantage. . . . We intended to reorient our . . . strategy to emphasize an area where we had the comparative advantage. (Committee on Armed Services, 1988, pp. 110–11)

Harold Brown, secretary of defense in the Carter administration put it bluntly: "I believe that we should lock in the considerable advantages in the START treaty" (Bunn, 1992, p. 258).

Soviet Objectives

But why did the Soviets get involved in the START I negotiations? The answer to this question may be found in one of the formerly secret papers released in the late 1990s by the US State Department. In the paper called "Gorbachev's Private Agenda" (which was supposedly written for the Geneva Summit in November 1985) the US foreign analysts wrote for President Reagan: "We continue to believe that Soviets view the status quo in strategic weapons as acceptable and they are less eager than the U.S. for an agreement in this area. However, they recognize that a START accord is the price they must pay to establish limits on SDI, which continues to be their main goal" (The U.S. Department of State, Gorbachev's Private Agenda). And Reagan's Strategic Defense Initiative (SDI—or how it was also called "The Star Wars" project) is exactly the answer to the question of why the Soviets decided to participate in the START I talks.

The situation was as old as the world of politics. The best classical example is the second or big Peloponnesian War in the fifth century B.C. On the two sides of the bipolar Greek political system there were two superpowers— Sparta and Athens. The former was a land-oriented state while the latter was definitely a sea-oriented power. As a defense measure, Athens constructed a huge wall that had to protect the state from a land invasion. This wall was a major element in Athens' defensive system. In 432 B.C., when the political and military situation on the Peloponnesian peninsula got very hot, Sparta demanded to pull down the wall because it perceived the very existence of this defensive device as a major threat to Sparta's security system. Athens rejected Sparta's ultimatum, and Sparta attacked in 431 B.C. The logic of the whole situation is very well explained by Joseph Nye (1997):

> Under anarchy, independent action taken by one state to increase its security may make all states more insecure. If one state builds its strength to make sure that another cannot hurt it, the other, seeing the first getting stronger, may build its strength to protect itself against the first. The result is that the independent efforts of each to build its own strength and security makes both more insecure. It is an ironic result, yet neither has acted irrationally. Neither acted from anger or pride, but from fear caused by the threat perceived in the growth of the other. (p. 12)

That is why, regardless of the defensive nature of SDI, the Soviets perceived it as a major threat to their national security at that time. Indeed, the whole deterrence strategy was based on the concept of Mutual Assured Destruction (MAD). The SDI defensive wall might have dropped from the MAD acronym the first or the second letter, and therefore, might have reduced motivation for the Americans not to strike first.

By getting involved in the START I talks, the Soviets tried to use the American state structure and the American domestic political dynamics to their advantage. The explanation for their logic may be found in the speech delivered by Dr. Richard Garwin, IBM Fellow, during congressional hearings:

> For instance, the Strategic Defense Initiative Organization has stated that it would count itself successful if it could find a way to reduce the number of military targets in the United States that the Soviets could destroy with their nuclear weapons from the present 6,000 to some 3,000. Clearly, this can be accomplished by a 50 percent START reduction in Soviet strategic forces, without the delay and expenditure for an SDI defense, even if one could be built. (Committee on Armed Services, 1988, p. 44)

The key phrase is the last one. START I treaty could be perceived as an alternative to the very expensive SDI program and, consequently, as long as it was possible the US Congress was reluctant to finance SDI and even possibly could cancel it. So, by participating the Soviets wanted to take the approval of the United States Congress and, consequently, the source of funding away from the SDI.

"Each Soviet modification in its negotiating position intended to address U.S. concerns was coupled either directly or indirectly to the Soviet effort to block SDI" (Kartchner, 1992, p. 269). And the whole process of negotiations is one big proof that the SDI program was the only reason for the Soviets to participate in the talks.

Negotiations Process[3]

The whole process of negotiations may be divided into two phases—before and after March 12th, 1985 (when Gorbachev resumed the negotiations after almost a two-year break provoked by the US deployment of intermediate-range missiles in Europe), or simply before and after Gorbachev took over the Soviet Union.

Kerry M. Kartchner (1992) has a slightly different opinion on the specific date: "Soviet acceptance of the principle of deep cuts in strategic weapons did not occur until November 1985, after Gorbachev came to power" (p. 57). (November 21st, 1985, is the date of the first Gorbachev-Reagan summit in Geneva.) But, in any case, it happened in 1985 when Gorbachev already ruled the country.

The First Phase

The recently declassified documents, that can be accessed through the US State Department's electronic reading room, give us a great opportunity to restore the whole process step by step and see how events developed in the real world—without spin of memoirs.

The START I negotiations began in Geneva on June 29th, 1982. The basic American proposal was presented that day by the US representatives. And the Soviets responded quite quickly. Initial Soviet position for the negotiations is outlined in one of the formerly classified papers:

> The Soviet position presented in Geneva ignored warheads and focused only on launchers, although a more significant measure of capability involves the question of warheads. The Soviet side insisted on including the arms of the United Kingdom and France in the balance. (The U.S. Department of State, 1982a)

The beginning of the talks was not easy. Americans tried to tie START with other political issues. They thought that in such a way they would be able to receive some concessions:

> I will make sure he [Gromyko] understands that we remain committed to strategic arms reductions and are continuing our preparations, but that arms control cannot be isolated from international events such as those in Poland. (The U.S. Department of State, 1982b)

Fall 1982: A new proposal was presented by the US which included a limit of 210 MIRVed ICBMs with 4 or more warheads, and a sublimit of 110 heavy ICBMs (Soviet SS-18). A proposal to limit heavy bombers at their current aggregate level was also added.

January 2, 1983: The Soviet Union released a statement outlining its START position. A ban on all cruise missiles with a range greater than 600 kilometers was proposed (mostly American ALCMs and SLCMs).

March 29, 1983: Another Soviet proposal called for limits on missile launchers and bombers, without limits on warheads.

July 7, 1983: A new Soviet proposal again did not specify a limit on warheads. At the same time, the Americans accepted a limit of four hundred heavy bombers with no more than twenty ALCMs per bomber. That was a victory of strong Russian diplomacy. By that time, the Americans had not made any significant progress toward their objectives.

December 1983: The Soviets refused to continue negotiations in response to the US deployment of intermediate-range missiles in Europe, the Soviet

Union refused to set a date for resumption of the START talks. Indeed, the American deployment made the whole START process senseless because there was no sense in conducting negotiations about arms reduction while one of the sides violated future agreements in advance.

The key Soviet figure at the talks was Andrey Andreyevich Gromyko—the Soviet Foreign Minister at that time. He was so firm that the Americans were ready to abandon their intention to break the backbone of the Soviet strategic forces and were even ready to consider an asymmetric alternative. We can find a confirmation for this in a formerly classified memo addressed to the President of the United States:

> With regard to START, I conveyed your desire to move forward and to explore the possibilities of trade-offs among systems where each side had advantages given the asymmetries in force structures. (The U.S. Department of State, 1984)

Only in January of 1985, when the parties agreed to start a separate set of INF negotiations (the Intermediate Nuclear Forces Treaty), the Soviets agreed to reopen START talks.

The first phase in general may be characterized as follows:

> It has primarily been the United States that has been interested in limitations or reductions of existing weapon systems (including systems not yet developed that would be permitted under an agreement). . . . The Soviets have had a much stronger interest in heading off new U.S. programs and capabilities than limiting the size of existing ones. (Einhorn, 1985, pp. 23, 38)

During the first phase, Soviet diplomacy was very firm and strong. Soviet Foreign Minister Andrey Gromyko was so "unforthcoming" (Talbott, 1984, pp. 241, 350) that even Shultz (very experienced and smart diplomat) was not able to make any progress in the direction the United States wanted to move.

The Second Phase

Everything changed when Gorbachev came to power. His diplomacy was not as good as Gromyko's, although everything started in quite a traditional way.

March 12, 1985: Negotiations resumed. No progress was reported. The Soviet Union linked reductions in strategic offensive weapons to a ban on research that might lead to the development of space-based weapons for SDI.

Officially, Americans rejected the Soviet proposal to include SLCMs into START as "unverifiable" (The U.S. Department of State, 1985a).

But still remembering Andrey Gromyko, they were nevertheless ready for some concessions:

> [We] recognize your concern over ALCMs. U.S. ready, in context of significant cuts in ballistic missile warheads, to limit ALCMs to levels well below those implicit in 1983 START proposal. . . .
>
> The trade-off we are seeking to negotiate would address our concern over your ballistic missile force and your concern over our bomber/ALCM force in manner that takes account of and accommodates asymmetries in the sides' force structures. . . .
>
> Moreover, if our concerns are met on reduction in ballistic missile RVs and destructive capability, we could envisage associated limits on ballistic missiles and bombers, the total number of which would be in the range implied by Soviets. (The U.S. Department of State, 1985b)

But later on, Americans understood that Gorbachev's diplomacy was different and they would never again even think about any concessions anymore.

November 1, 1985: The US proposes a ban on the modernization of heavy ICBMs, and a ban on mobile ICBM (both of them were mostly Soviet specialty). The United States would not include heavy bombers or cruise missiles under a single limit.

Geneva Summit, November 21, 1985: Presidents Reagan and Gorbachev agreed on the principle of a 50 percent reduction in strategic forces.

Reykjavik Meeting, October 11–12, 1986: The Soviet Union conceded to the US position of not counting gravity bombs and SRAMs under the six thousand limit. The countries established the bomber counting rule that counted so-called non-ALCM bombers as one delivery vehicle and one warhead. The Soviets acknowledged the need for cuts in heavy ICBMs. Those were the first several major concessions made by Gorbachev. But he again linked all that to a ban on testing of space-based defensive systems.

July 31, 1987: The Soviet Union tabled a draft treaty where it accepted a 50 percent reduction in heavy ICBMs, but it did not include sublimits on ballistic missile warheads or a ban on mobile ICBMs, or a limit on throw-weight. The Soviets continued to tie the 50 percent reduction in offensive forces to a Defense and Space agreement that would restrict research, development, and testing of space defensive systems.

Washington Ministerial, September 15–17, 1987 (the Soviet Union was represented by Eduard Schevardnadze): The Soviet Union agreed that 50 percent reduction in heavy ICBMs would apply to warheads as well as launchers. It also said it would accept a 60 percent sublimit on ICBM warheads, within the limit of six thousand warheads. These were already quite serious concessions.

Washington Summit, December 7–10, 1987: The Soviets agreed that throw-weight would be cut by 50 percent. (That was already a really huge concession.) The countries continued to disagree on the range that would be used to define long-range ALCMs. They also disagreed on the method of counting ALCMs on bombers—the Soviets wanted "maximum capable," the United States wanted ALCM-capable bombers to count as six warheads, regardless of the number they were equipped with.

Washington Ministerial, March 22–23, 1988: The United States altered the ALCM counting rule from six ALCMs per bomber to ten ALCMs per bomber. The Soviet Union continued to insist on counting ALCM-capable bombers as the maximum number of ALCMs they were capable of carrying.

Early 1989: The new Bush administration delayed the resumption of START talks while it conducted its strategic review.

Jackson Hole Ministerial, September 22–23, 1989: The Soviet Union finally dropped its link between the START treaty and the SDI program. That was the game-winning moment for the Americans. Since that moment on, the whole START process became senseless for the Soviets because they abandoned their only objective.

In 1985, the Americans promised Gorbachev to consider the space defense issue seriously. Even a special set of negotiations called "Defense and Space Talks" was formally started. At that point, Gorbachev believed that the Americans took the problem seriously and dropped the main Russian demand for the START I talks. Certainly, no space defense agreement was ever signed but it was not important for Gorbachev anymore. Flattering remarks in all the Western media made him feel like a historical figure and a great peacemaker. And he pushed his diplomats to sign the treaty in any form as soon as possible. That day, the Soviet diplomacy completely collapsed. The following events can be only characterized as a diplomatic massacre.

Moscow Ministerial, February 8–10, 1990: The Soviets withdrew their insistence on an escape clause that would have stated that the Soviet Union would have a right to withdraw from the START regime if the United States did not remain in compliance with the ABM Treaty. The Soviet Union also agreed to the US proposal for counting ALCMs—a much lower number than the number of ALCMs American heavy bombers were equipped to carry—as long as the actual number of deployed missiles on each bomber was also limited.

Moscow Ministerial, May 16–19, 1990: The Soviet Union accepted the US proposal for ALCM-capable bombers counting rules—US bombers could carry up to twenty long-range nuclear-armed ALCMs but count as ten; Soviet bombers could carry up to twelve (later changed to sixteen) but count as eight (The U.S. Department of State, 1990a).

Washington Summit, May 30–June 2, 1990: The countries outlined a framework for START. All the details had been already negotiated during the previous Moscow Ministerial meeting (The U.S. Department of State, 1990a).

Early December of 1990: The Soviets agreed to limit the number of their Backfire bombers to five hundred in a side-agreement and to restrict their fueling capacity. They also agreed that heavy ICBM modifications could continue but new Soviet missiles would not have a total launch weight, throw-weight, and the numbers of warheads greater than those that Soviet SS-18 missiles already had at that time.

London Economic Summit, July, 1991: Bush and Gorbachev agreed upon the ultimate verification procedures to make sure that the Soviets simply would not be able to cheat with the throw-weight limitations. Russian ICBMs had to undergo a serious downgrading procedure that made them much weaker. American victory was full—devastation was complete.

Moscow Summit, July 30–31, 1991: President Bush and President Gorbachev signed the START I treaty on July 31st, 1991.

One of the State Department's formerly classified internal theme papers described very well how American diplomacy worked to sign this treaty and how the Americans received all the Soviet concessions:

> But they were secured by agile policies on our part that exploited the changes and kept the pressure up when we needed further Soviet movements. (The U.S. Department of State, 1990b)

In the same paper, American analysts give an adequate evaluation of the political situation in the Soviet Union at that time: "The Soviet leadership seems to be losing confidence in its ability to control events affecting the USSR's most basic interests" (The U.S. Department of State, 1990b).

And this situation was used by the Americans to sign the treaty that would never have been signed under any other Soviet leadership.

Analysis of the Treaty[4]

The treaty, which was finally signed, reached all the American objectives stated in the START policy paper described earlier in this chapter. When the policy was created, in 1982, nobody could possibly imagine that in nine years there would be signed a treaty that would satisfy almost exactly all the document's requirements. Nevertheless, it happened.

START I permitted the United States and the Soviet Union to deploy up to 6,000 accountable warheads on their strategic nuclear forces, with no more than 4,900 warheads on their ballistic missiles (the Russian specialty). Both countries would be able to add new weapons if they eliminated older systems.

The United States would be able to deploy all the 18 earlier planned Trident submarines and 75 new B-2 bombers if it eliminated Poseidon submarines and Minuteman II missiles. The Soviet Union could either continue to modernize its ICBM forces (but with all the limitations on throw-weight and number of warheads applied) or it could deploy a greater number of ballistic missile submarines (where Russian technology was inferior). Regardless, the number of ballistic missile submarines in the Soviet fleet would decline sharply from more than sixty to fewer than thirty, and possibly fewer than twenty (Congressional Research Service, 1991a).

START I would reduce the number of weapons deployed on both the US and Soviet strategic nuclear forces. However, because most weapons on heavy bombers would not count against the limits in the treaty (American area of expertise), both countries would be able to deploy more than 6,000 weapons. It basically meant that the American nuclear air forces were out of the limitations of the treaty. The treaty would attribute only one accountable warhead to heavy bombers that are not equipped to carry ALCMs, regardless of the number of weapons that could be on short notice deployed on those bombers. For bombers that could carry ALCMs, START I would attribute a number of so-called accountable warheads that is exactly half of the number of actual ALCMs deployed on those bombers; that attributed number was ten for US ALCM bombers and eight for Soviet ALCM bombers (Congressional Research Service, 1991a). Throw-weight of Soviet ICBMs would be cut by 50 percent. In the treaty itself, there were no definite limitations on the mainstay of the American strategic nuclear force—the SLCMs.[5] That is the Americans indeed managed to exempt half of their Air Force and their entire Navy from under the limitations of the treaty.

Tables 5.2, 5.3, and 5.4 summarize all the changes. If we take a closer look at the columns called "Percent Change" in Table 5.2, we would immediately notice big differences between the volumes in reduction in the US and Soviet forces. The next two tables clearly demonstrate the Soviet deepcuts and, consequently, the advantages START I gave to the Americans in the areas of heavy ICBMs, their war heads, delivery vehicles (Table 5.3) and bombers (Table 5.4).

Before starting to analyze the treaty in general, it would be appropriate to say a few words about the throw-weight problem, which may not be clear for everyone. "At the beginning of START, the Soviet Union had a three to one superiority over the United States in total ballistic missile throw-weight" (Kartchner, 1992, p. 21). It was a real problem for the US because "the throw-weight on a missile affects both the range it can fly and the payload it can carry" (Congressional Research Service, 1991b). By reducing throw-weight, the Americans made Soviet ICBMs carry only as many warheads and fly only as far as the United States wanted. The reduction of throw-weight required substantial constructional changes that could not be undone easily. On the other hand

TABLE 5.2
Changes in U.S. and Soviet Strategic Forces under START

Category	U.S. Forces			Soviet Forces		
	1991	1999	Percent Change	1991	1999	Percent Change
Accountable Warheads	9,577	6,000	37%	10,194	6,000	41%
Deployed Weapons	12,902	9,360–10,232	20%–27%	11,247	7,180–8,072	28%–36%

TABLE 5.3
Comparison of START Limits and 1991 Situation

Category	START Limit	U.S. Forces	Soviet Forces
Delivery Vehicles	1,600	1,896	2,504
Heavy ICBMs	154	0	308
Accountable Warheads	6,000	9,577	10,194
Ballistic Missile Warheads	4,900	7,890	9,383
Heavy ICBM Warheads	1,540	0	3,080
Mobile ICBM Warheads	1,100	500	660

"The United States will not have to reduce its throw-weight under START. In fact the United States could increase throw-weight by 1,230 metric tons" (Committee on Foreign Relations, 1992a, p. 17). So lopsided was the treaty.

In order to be as objective as possible the author will yield the stage to American experts in order to show the real bias of the signed treaty.

Really briefly the treaty can be summarized in the following passage: "It promotes a shift from missiles to slower-flying bombers. . . . In emphasizing reductions in long-range missiles, warheads and throw-weight, the Treaty has discounted nuclear-armed gravity bombs; it has limited air-launched missiles only partially; and it has left sea-launched cruise missiles practically unconstrained" (Goldblat, 1994, pp. 69–70). That is it did everything to the advantage of the United States.

These are some testimonies of American experts in relation to the treaty.

Spurgeon M. Keeny Jr., former Deputy Director, United States Arms Control and Disarmament Agency, President and Executive Director, Arms Control Association, Washington, D.C.:

I believe the Senate should promptly approve the existing START Treaty without amendments since despite the dramatic changes in the political and military environment, the treaty continues to be strongly in the security interests of the United States. Let me briefly outline the advantages that I believe the START Treaty holds for the United States.

TABLE 5.4
Comparison of START-Accountable Warheads and Deployed Weapons

Category	U.S. Forces		Soviet Forces	
	Accountable Warheads	Deployed Weapons	Accountable Warheads	Deployed Weapons
Ballistic Missiles	7,890	7,890	9,383	9,383
Bombers	1,687	5,012	811	1,864
Totals	9,577	12,902	10,194	11,247

First, the treaty substantially reduces the number of nuclear warheads Russia can deliver against the United States. Without listing the many qualitative and quantitative restrictions the treaty places on Russian forces, I would simply point out that the overall limit of 6,000 accountable warheads will reduce the overall number of deployed Russian strategic warheads on all delivery vehicles by more than 30 percent.

More important, the sublimit of 4,900 on ballistic missiles warheads will reduce this particularly threatening component of Russian strategic forces by almost 50 percent from the levels existing when START was signed last summer. Most significantly, the treaty specifically cuts the Russian force of SS-18 missiles, the largest and most accurate Soviet ICBMs each armed with 10 warheads, by 50 percent, or from 308 to 154 missiles. (Committee on Foreign Relations, 1992b, p. 268)

Harold Brown, Chairman, Foreign Policy Institute, Johns Hopkins University, said about the treaty:

It would then require 1,800 Soviet warheads, of high precision, two per silo, to destroy those U.S. ICBMs with high confidence. That number would represent more than the total SS-18 force allowed by the tentative agreed numbers, and more than half of the total Soviet ICBM warhead inventory. (Committee on Armed Services, 1988, p. 92)

Now, let's look at how the American military evaluated the treaty and, in particular, at the assessment given to the treaty by the Joint Chiefs of Staff.

Colin Powell, the Chairman of the Joint Chiefs of Staff:
I and my colleagues in the Joint Chiefs of Staff believe that the START treaty achieves our original 1982 strategic arms reduction goals. . . . When we examine the mixed weapons in the case when all of our forces are generated to full alert, we determined that even though the aggregate number of weapons declines, the percentage of survivable [American] warheads increases because of the higher number of submarine and aircraft warheads compared to ICBM warheads.
Of the land-based and sea-based missiles on a day-to-day alert, the percentage of survivable [American] warheads will also increase in the post-START force. (Committee on Foreign Relations, 1992a, p. 13)

General Merrill McPeak the Air Force Chief of Staff said: "The original objectives of the START negotiations . . . have been not only achieved, they have been surpassed" (Committee on Foreign Relations, 1992a, pp. 13–14).

Admiral Kelso, the Chief of Naval Operations, expressed similar views saying: "I support, without reservations, the START treaty. I am satisfied that it is militarily sound" (Committee on Foreign Relations, 1992a, p. 14).

General Gordon R. Sullivan, the Army Chief of Staff, said: "My endorsement is offered without reservation. The ratification of the Strategic Arms Reduction Treaty is in the best interest of the United States" (Committee on Foreign Relations, 1992a, p. 14).

General John R. Dailey, Assistant Commandant of the Marine Corps stated: "The Treaty is in the national security interests of the United States. It retains the objective of deterrence against nuclear aggression, meets our commitments to our allies, and supports the U.S. arms control objectives of increased security and stability" (Committee on Foreign Relations, 1992a, p. 14).

A very enthusiastic unanimity among the members of the American military is self-evident.

The congressional report on the START I treaty gives the following general evaluation of the effect of the treaty on the Soviet (or CIS—the Commonwealth of Independent States) forces:

> In order to comply with the START limits, the CIS will have to make significant qualitative and quantitative reductions in its arsenal of ICBMs. The Commonwealth will have to cut its throw-weight by 46 percent, reduce its force of heavy ICBMs by 50 percent and reduce the number of warheads deployed on ICBMs and SLBMs by 48 percent. (Committee on Foreign Relations, 1992a, p. 20)

The same report gives the following general evaluation of the treaty in terms of the American objectives:

> The United States pursued four specific objectives: (1) to reduce the number of SS-18s; (2) to reduce the aggregate throw-weight of the Soviet ICBM force; (3) to reduce rather than cap the number of deployed weapons; and (4) to promote a more stabilizing force structure. In large measure these goals were achieved. (Committee on Foreign Relations, 1992a, p. 15)

But how did the Americans do it? Was it excellent American or terrible Soviet diplomacy? It seems that mostly the latter. Some experts call the changes that happened in the Soviet START I policy in 1985, after Gorbachev came to power, "startling" (Committee on Armed Services, 1988, p. 25).

All of a sudden, the Soviets started to accommodate all the American concerns:

> During the course of negotiations, the Soviets successfully accommodated major U.S. concerns in START, eventually agreeing to exclusion of INF without a compensation for French and British nuclear forces, fifty percent reductions in heavy ballistic missiles and ballistic missile throw-weight, and favorable counting rules for bombers and ALCMs to offset Soviet advantages in air defenses and land-based ICBMs. . . . Finally, SDI forced the Soviets to reconsider the role and value of extensive silo-based ballistic missile forces, just as the Reagan administration had intended when it set out its initial START position in May 1982. (Kartchner, 1992, p. 269)

George Bunn in his book *Arms Control by Committee* very well sums up the last stage of the START I talks process and gives some excellent connections to the future events which may be considered as a direct outcome of the treaty:

> Soviet Foreign minister Schevardnadze reported domestic criticism for engaging in "unilateral" disarmament, some of which was unreciprocated unilateral steps and some unreciprocated concessions in treaty negotiations. . . .
>
> During the 1980s, Gorbachev took many steps unilaterally—asking, but not awaiting (and mostly not receiving) U.S. reciprocation. His opposition at home, many of them leaders of the August 1991 coup, criticized him for giving away the store. (Bunn, 1992, pp. 258–59)

Indeed, START I was the turning point for anti-Gorbachev opposition in the Soviet Union. Many Soviet leaders were outraged by the treaty. And they (many of them were military) conceived and executed the August 1991 coup that led directly to the collapse of the Soviet Union just four months later.

The Americans won, probably, the most important diplomatic war in the history of the United Sates. By signing the START treaty they destroyed the whole structure of the Soviet strategic nuclear forces and made them inferior.

The Russians had to reduce their forces much more than the Americans because the reductions mostly had to be done in the areas where the Soviet Union had advantages or had a lead in technology. In some areas the United States were not required to make any changes in their strategic nuclear forces at all (like throw-weight or SLCMs).

The Americans broke the backbone of the Soviet strategic nuclear forces—the system of ICBMs. Moreover, America made a huge structural shift in the Soviet strategic nuclear force toward the areas the U.S. had as its comparative advantage (ALCMs and SLCMs).

The throw-weight limitations became the decisive point. American air-weapons were counted not as the maximum number of weapons the American bombers were capable of carrying but as half of the possible payload and no constructional changes for American bombers were stipulated. At the same time, severe constraints were imposed on refueling capabilities of the nuclear-capable Soviet Backfire bombers. That is even in the same category (let's say bombers) America managed to put limitations on the Soviets and to avoid any themselves. The Soviets were required to reduce the throw-weight of their remaining ICBMs by half, for which they had to make serious constructional changes in the missiles. It means that, in case of a conflict, the Americans would be able to quickly load additional ALCMs in their bombers to violate their treaty obligations while the Russians would be stuck with the inferior missiles or with new missiles but still limited by all the START I regulations. It is important to mention here that American SLCMs were not regulated in the treaty at all.

All the above reminds us of the restrictions and limitations imposed on the German armed forces after World War I. The situation looks as if the Soviet Union lost a huge war. All the features of a great defeat are in place: the core of the enemy forces is almost completely destroyed, future limitations are imposed, and the enemy regime perished (the Soviet Union collapsed). The history has seen very few volunteer agreements between practically equal countries that were so lopsided.

The first major full-scale nuclear war in the history of humankind, which lasted for nine years, was won by the Americans. It shows that a nuclear war may be won if it is fought by diplomats through negotiations. American diplomats did what no military strike would have been ever able to accomplish.

Theoretical Examination

The main question for an analyst here is: But how could all this possibly happen? Is there any theory out there that would help us explain such an outcome? As it was indicated above, the best way to analyze negotiations is to try to apply all the theories to a certain situation and see which ones work the best. We will try to do exactly the same in this case.

Certainly, no rational actor model can explain such an irrational outcome of the negotiations. There is no payoff matrix in the world that would produce any type of positive result for the Soviets from these talks. So, this theory is not going to work here.

Some other theories are not applicable here either. For example, the learning theory would tell us what the sides learned as they were negotiating about each other and about themselves and how they adjusted their positions and why. So, the Soviets learned only one thing—Reagan was stubborn and inflexible. The Americans learned exactly the same thing about Gromyko. It was not a good beginning for newly started negotiations. Neither of the sides substantially adjusted their positions (at least, during the first phase) because they knew exactly what they wanted and did not learn any new information that would make them change their stands. Only at the end, the Americans learned that Gorbachev was a "softy" and started pushing him around, strengthening their position even more.

The problem-solving or joint decision-making theories are not working here either because of the obvious historical context at that time. To take either of these two points of view the two sides had to work jointly solving a common problem. But that was the Cold War times. This war mentality made both sides work not together but against each other. The only common problem they had was the very existence of each other. They were not working on solving a problem—they were working on destroying each other. Under these circumstances no compromises or creative solutions can be expected. And there were none.

As we can see from the description above—no external (or global-level) economic or political variables seem to have interfered with the process either. So, the only area where we could find an explanation for the outcome is domestic politics. Besides that, the psychological point of view, with its emphasis on psychology of the main talks' participants, can also provide us with interesting insights.

As we know, at that time, the main domestic disturbances were happening in the Soviet Union while the United States remained relatively stable with regard to internal politics. So, it is the USSR where we have to look for explanations.

Many Western analysts believe that the roots of all the Soviet troubles lied in the economic area and that it was exactly the arms race that bankrupted the USSR. This explanation is extremely superficial and utterly incorrect. This explanation exposes their clear inability to think "out of the box" and their general ignorance about the Soviet economic system. They uncritically accept the assumption that the logic of the liberal market economic patterns can be applied directly to the Soviet type of economic systems—but there is nothing further from the truth. It is like trying to apply Newton's laws of physics to the space travel world of the Einstein's laws. It is like understanding an alien logic—even the most basic of our concepts may not work on another planet. So, the Western economic laws did not work in the Soviet Union. Even more, it was exactly the uncritical acceptance as well as misguided application of Western economic concepts to the socialist economic system by dilettantes in the Soviet (and later Russian) government what led to the collapse of the Soviet economy.

The Soviet economy is classified by really smart economists as *paternalistic* economy. For people who have no understanding of what it might be—it also can be characterized in a simpler way as a "family economy." In the absence of an open market of services and labor force the relationship between work and payment is different from the traditional capitalist model. To make it easy to understand we can use the following metaphor. Your mother may ask you to wash windows in the living room but she will end up feeding you anyway regardless of whether you indeed washed the windows or not or whether you did it well or not. She has a family obligation to feed you and she will. The Soviet government had similar obligations in the face of the Soviet citizens—to feed them under any circumstances. To continue our analogy, your mother can give you some domestic self-made paper money for your work (some American families practice this type of educational tool to teach their kids the value of money). But the money in this case would play a purely educational and symbolic role—and this is exactly the role money played in the Soviet economy.

The government directly established all the prices, printed as much money as they needed, and were able to withdraw from circulation as much money as they needed if it was necessary. That is why people in the Soviet Union did not even know the word "inflation." The purchasing power of the ruble stayed exactly the same for decades. Soviet managers did not understand the very concept of inflation: "How can you run an economy if the values of the means of exchanges changes so quickly." It was so because for the Soviet money was just that—a purely symbolic means of exchange at the domestic level.

Such a system may fail in small countries that are dependent on the outside world market for some important resources. But in huge countries with all the natural resources in the world—it can go on forever. The Soviet Union was not closely integrated in the world economy and did not depend on any outside source for anything. It was an isolated circular system where the money was rotating in a strongly controlled environment and was worth exactly as much as the government wanted it to be. This well controlled circular isolated system cannot go bankrupt by definition.

The Soviet paternalistic economy can be also compared (to use another metaphor) with a nineteenth century mid-Western American farmer family that makes its own cloths, shoes, plows, has its own cattle, lives in relative isolation far from the closest town and, most importantly, eats its own food produced entirely on the farm. So, in that system as long as people work—they will be fine—equally fine but not rich. But when they stop working at the farm and start fighting and stealing (like it happened during Gorbachev's rule)—the problems arise.

Certainly, the country was not completely isolated—they had to buy some things abroad (for example, large diameter pipes for their oil pipelines from Germans and Japanese, or some grain from Canada) and they also had to subsidize for political reasons Eastern block countries (by buying from them products that could have been easily produced in the Soviet Union much cheaper). But we don't have to forget that the Soviets sold quite a few things on the world market—cars, weapons, oil and natural gas, timber. So, at the end, everything balanced out.

The proponents of the financial theory of the collapse of the Soviet Union argue that the country collapsed because of an economic crisis. One coincidence favors them—when the USSR collapsed the country indeed was in the state of economic crisis. Some people may ask whether the very fact that the economic crises were possible in the Soviet Union undermines the idea that it was "unbankruptable." The answer is an emphatic No. Any system can go bankrupt under bad management. And the order of the events provides the support for this statement—first Gorbachev started his *perestroika* and only after that the country spiraled down into economic crisis. It took six long years to destroy the strong Soviet economy.

Could our nineteenth century mid-Western American family farmers go bankrupt? Certainly, if the family patriarch (this is why the system is called *paternalistic*) loses control and lets family members fight with each other, drink heavily, and idle about—the family will go bankrupt and eventually collapse. It was exactly what happened to the Soviet Union.

The Soviet economic system required a strict command and control structure that was destroyed by Gorbachev and his people. But some people would say that the system had to be reformed (or even destroyed) because it was not working well in the form it existed. There are three counter arguments against that. First of all, the country fell into a deep crisis only after several years of Gorbachev's rule. Secondly, certainly, the Soviet economy had to be modernized in many areas but the Chinese experience shows that it was possible to do without completely destroying it. Finally, the standard of living of an average Soviet family by the mid-1980s (when Gorbachev took over) was much higher than many people in the West would think. In order to understand it we have to factor into the income of an average Soviet family such things as housing subsidies (or simply free housing for many), food subsidies, free education at all levels, free pre-school day care system, free health-care and (if necessary, free resort services for really sick people, veterans, and elderly), cheap subsidized public transportation and utilities, and many other things. It was an absolutely normal thing for an average Soviet family at that time to have a car, an apartment in a city, and a country house (the famous "dachas"). Therefore, the system that provides its citizens with too much can hardly be called "not working."

There were some shortages of some products but they were compensated for by the workplace distribution system where one could get a deficit product by being on a waiting list at his or her workplace (such things as cars or washing machines were usually bought that way). Some exotic food products (such as caviar or expensive types of fish) were not readily available in stores but were accessible several times a year (mostly for holidays) through the same workplace distribution system. (And we have to remember that employment was guaranteed—there was no unemployment in the country.)

Certainly, there were famous Soviet food store lines and there were no Levi's blue jeans in the country. But the government had to decide what was more important—free education and health care or Nike sneakers—and the government chose the former. Therefore, if one takes as a standard of living the actual well-being of an average family (but not some abstract market exchange index)—the Soviets were doing pretty well. That is, the system was not perfect (and which one is?) but it was working quite well and definitely was reformable.

Besides that, we have to take into account that the military industry was actually the locomotive of the country's economy. Each economic system has its own industry that drives the economy. The American society is called *consumerist* not just for propaganda purposes—it is its technical economic definition. The more Americans spend in malls and Wal-Marts—the more money they put into their economy and the better the economy functions. In this case military spendings take away money from consumers and, by doing so, hurt the economy. In the Soviet Union it was the military industrial complex that was the main source of technological innovations, production power (even washing machines were produced at military factories), high-salary jobs and, consequently, the purchasing power. That is the more resources were put into this industry—the better Soviet economy was doing. That is why the peak of the well-being of the Soviet people coincided with the peak of its military spendings at the peak of the Cold War.

Only after having read all this, a Western reader may be able to understand two things. First of all, the collapse of the Soviet Union can be attributed only to failed Gorbachev's policies (including domestic economic policies). And secondly, the collapse of the Soviet security and military system had nothing to do with money—it was a direct consequence of the general collapse of the Soviet political and economic system caused by Gorbachev. America with its economic system could go bankrupt because of the arms race while the Soviet Union was much less adversely affected by increasing military spendings and even often benefited from them.

But if the Soviet Union did not go bankrupt as many in the West erroneously thought—what happened? The answer is directly coming from the discussion above. The name of Gorbachev has come up several times already—this fact provides us with a hint to the answer. The answer is that in the mid-1980s in the Soviet Union came to power a group of people who hated the system and, sometimes, even the country they lived in. Using all of their powers (including state-owned media) they did everything to destroy the system and the country—and they succeeded. The next question is: Why did the Soviet people let them do it?

It is imperative to note here an important feature of the Russian national character. Throughout the last thousand years they got used to a strict centralized command system. They easily accept whatever comes from the ruler of the country (may it be a czar or a communist leader). And the new policies were accepted with the same type of attitude: "They know up there in Moscow better. Our business is to do it." And they did it without being able to realize the whole global set of consequences. Besides that, we have to remember that it is very easy to stir up in human beings such basic emotions as greed, envy, or hatred. And if the whole policy is based on them—it is easy to lead people with such a type of appeals to a civil war.

So, it was people ruling the country who were to blame for many disasters in the Soviet Union including the START I treaty. And it is psychological approach that deals with people—their motivations and emotions. And it remains the only theory not explored so far in relation to the START I treaty negotiations. Let's try to use it and construct psychological profiles for the two main actors during phase two of the talks on the Soviet side—Gorbachev and Shevardnadze. It is important because the group of people who ruled the country at that time was not homogenous—it consisted of people who had very different and even often opposite values and goals.

Michael Gorbachev (the Secretary General of the Communist Party of the Soviet Union) had the best of intentions for his country. He was relatively young (for such a high-level politician in the Soviet system) and wanted to use his ideas and energy to make the life of Soviet people even better. But he was far from the idea of destroying the whole system or even from the idea of modifying it substantially. The problem was that he was a weak and not particularly bright individual. As one of the Russian political analysts (Michael Leontiev) put it recently, he had the intellectual horizon of a foreman of a team of herdsmen—not enough to run a big country. He started the chain of events that he could not possibly deal with and the consequences of which he simply did not have a mental capacity to foresee. But one of his character flaws was especially visible—vanity.

As Al Pacino's character says in the famous movie: "Vanity is my favorite sin." And it is a sin for a politician, especially, if it leads him to forget national interests for the sake of his own emotional gratification. He wanted to be considered by the rest of the world a great reformer and one of the great world leaders. All these desires made him very vulnerable to basic flattery. When all the Western media and leaders heralded him as a great historic figure, he was ready to do everything to please the West even more—to deserve even a greater praise—he was ready to sign any treaty at any cost. He was received in all the capitals in the West as the world's hero and he failed to see the real reason behind such a warm reception.

START I was just one of several disastrous international agreements he signed during his tenure. But, not being a very smart politician, he miscalculated the situation. The START I aroused a special indignation among the members of the Soviet military. And those military were among the leaders of the August 1991 coup that led directly to the collapse of the Soviet Union in December of the same year. So, Gorbachev led directly to his own demise.

The second important figure of phase two of the START I negotiations was Eduard Shevardnadze (the Minister of Foreign Affairs of the Soviet Union). He was almost exactly the opposite of Gorbachev. Shevardnadze was smart, strong, and absolutely hated the country he lived in. As any smart person he used the Soviet system to his advantage and eventually reached the highest levels of the Soviet hierarchy.

He showed his real face only after the collapse of the Soviet Union when he became the dictator of Georgia. He finally officially and openly proclaimed his hatred for everything Soviet and Russian and officially declared Russia his enemy.

On his territory (in the Pankissi Gorge) he harbored thousands of international terrorists (including Al-Qaeda-associated). His forces trained them and helped them to cross the border into Russia where the terrorists murdered Russian women and children before coming back into their safe haven under Shevardnadze's wing. So, speaking of the START I talks, it is the same as if Osama bin-Laden was negotiating on behalf of the United States.

Shevardnadze conducted a series of horrifying domestic repressions against anybody who even mildly supported normal relations with Russia. He conducted a series of disastrous domestic wars against several of Georgia's ethnic minority regions (Southern Osetiya, Adzharia, and Abkhazia) that were more inclined to live in peace with their northern neighbor. He also needed those wars and repression to maintain public support for his regime. His government through corruption turned one of the richest republics of the Soviet Union into one of the poorest countries on the face of the planet. Even in the capital, people did not have electricity, heat, or running water. So, he had to find enemies (domestic and external) to mobilize public support for his regime—the device as old as the history of human kind.

But, of course, his family members did not have to live in poor and war-ravaged Georgia. Quite a few of them now live in the United States—exactly the country with which he negotiated the START treaty. It is clear that he, being a smart person and feeling the upcoming demise of Gorbachev and the whole system, was more preoccupied with working off American green cards for his family members than with any security interests of the Soviet people.

He was so much carried away with trying to earn American favors that he even destroyed some Soviet weapons that did not fall under any treaties or agreements. For example, in 1989 he secured Gorbachev's consent for the destruction of the SS-23 Spider—a Russian tactical missile system very much feared by NATO. That system was out of bounds of any Russian-American or any other international treaty. But, nevertheless, 360 of them were destroyed (blown up) in the fall of that year at a remote test-ground in Kazakhstan.

Now it is not difficult to explain the outcome of the negotiations if we take into account that Shevardnadze was Gorbachev's point man at the talks. Gorbachev did not want to disappoint the West (especially after receiving the Nobel Peace Prize). And the last concern for Shevardnadze was the security of the Soviet people.

So, we have our answer—now we know what went wrong for the Soviets at START I. We did it by eliminating one-by-one theories and reasons that did not provide us with clear explanations for the outcome we observed. Finally, we found the theory the use of which gave us the clear, reasonable, and logical answer (in this case the psychological point of view). This is how negotiations are supposed to be analyzed—theory by theory—slowly and thoroughly until the answer is found. Therefore, it is necessary to know all the theories and approaches covered above in order to get the right answer. You have also seen how much information must be obtained (information that sometimes may even seem irrelevant) and how deeply and thoroughly it must be processed. Every now and then, we have to reject long-standing but still erroneous explanations. There are no easy answers. There are no universal theories or one-size-fits-all matrices that could summarize the whole complexity of such talks. Only the *complex analysis* methodology with painstakingly deep examination of all the facts and constant acquiring of new information can help us to give the right answer to the main question of the talks science— "Why did it happen?" And, as we could see, it is always a good idea to look at the domestic politics a little bit deeper—it may really help.

Notes

1. For acronyms, refer to Table 5.1.
2. SALT II treaty was signed in June of 1979 in Vienna by the US and USSR.
3. For a more detailed description of the negotiation process, see U.S. Congressional Research Service. (1991b). *CRS report for Congress—START: Chronology of major events.* (The Library of Congress). Retrieved April 28, 1998, from the U.S. Department of State Electronic Reading Room: www.foia.state.gov/
4. For deeper analysis of the treaty, see: U.S. Congressional Research Service. (1991a). *CRS report for Congress—START: Effects on U.S. and Soviet forces.* (The Library of Congress). Retrieved April 28, 1998 from the U.S. Department of State Electronic Reading Room: www.foia.state.gov/

5. "Accountable warheads" refered to those weapons that would count against the treaty limits. Because all the weapons on the U.S. and Soviet strategic forces would not count against the limits, the number of actual weapons would be greater than the number of accountable warheads. "Deployed weapons" refered to both the accountable warheads and the uncounted weapons deployed on the US and Soviet strategic forces.

III

NEGOTIATIONS WITH STILL UNKNOWN OUTCOMES

6

The North Korean Nuclear Problem

THE NORTH KOREAN NUCLEAR PROGRAM is a very complex issue. It is complex politically, technologically, informationally, and even emotionally. Both major players—North Korea and the United States—sincerely believe that they are right and the other side is not only wrong but in principle does not even have a right to exist (the old confrontation between "scary red Communists" and "evil Western imperialists"). Under these circumstances, it would be very difficult to find any common ground.

To help these two players find a solution to the problem four other countries got involved into negotiations—China, Japan, Russia, and South Korea. And the involvement of these countries, so different politically and culturally, made the talks multilateral and, consequently, even more difficult to analyze. In order to simply start to understand what is going on we will have to analyze many issues—political, technological, informational, and others. Maybe, by the end of this process, we will be able to come up with some recommendations as to how to make the positive outcome more feasible. But let's start with a simple historical outline of the problem.

Some Information from the History of the Problem

North Korea established its nuclear energy research program in the mid-1960s. Initially, they used a Soviet-supplied nuclear research reactor in their atomic energy exploration center in Yongbyon. They learned a lot from that reactor and were even able to independently modernize it.

Because of the closed nature of the North Korean regime it is difficult to determine exactly when their nuclear weapons program started but most experts agree that it began in the 1980s. Nevertheless, in 1985 the country signed the Treaty on the Non-Proliferation of Nuclear Weapons (NPT). At the same time, North Koreans did not allow the International Atomic Energy Agency's (IAEA) inspectors to work in the country until 1992. Finally, in 1992 they allowed the IAEA team in but did not allow the experts to inspect two facilities that were considered "undeclared" or "unreported" by the agency. The scandal that followed those events led directly to North Korea's announcement of its intentions to withdraw from the treaty on March 12th, 1993. But in June they "suspended" their withdrawal from NPT.

Simultaneously, the North tried to normalize its relation with the South. In 1991 both countries signed some major agreements—The Agreement on Reconciliation, Non-Aggression, Exchanges and Cooperation, and the Joint Declaration on the Denuclearization of the Korean Peninsula. The latter also stipulated mutual inspections of nuclear facilities in both countries. But the inspections regime had never been agreed upon and the whole process stalled in late 1992.

The international community reacted strongly to North Korea's threat to withdraw from the nonproliferation treaty. In May 1993 the UN Security Council passed a resolution urging the DPRK to cooperate with IAEA and South Korea (they meant the inter-Korean denuclearization accord). At the same time, the United States threatened to impose tough sanctions on the North. Under all this pressure Kim Il-sung decided not to strain further his diplomatic relations with the rest of the world. So, in June and July of 1993 he held political-level negotiations with the United States. But simultaneously he was continuing nuclear research activities in the country. After learning that North Koreans unloaded some fuel from one of their reactors (what could be considered as a preliminary stage for making material for nuclear weapons) the Americans stopped the talks and pushed for UN sanctions. A large-scale crisis was brewing.

Only interference of former US President Jimmy Carter in June 1994 helped to solve the problem. He managed to convince Kim Il-sung to freeze his nuclear program and come back to the negotiating table. The talks were supposed to resume in July but the sudden death of the North Korean leader prevented that from happening at that time. Nevertheless, the negotiations resumed in August of the same year and led to what was called the Agreed Framework. The document was signed in Geneva on October 21st, 1994.

The four main points of the agreement were as follows:

- North Korea was supposed to freeze its nuclear program and eventually dismantle its nuclear facilities,

- in return, a consortium of countries called the Korean Peninsula Energy Development Organization or KEDO (whose primary members were the United States, South Korea, Japan, and European Union) agreed to provide the North with two light-water reactors (LWRs) that were promoted as "proliferation-resistant" (although many experts agreed that even they theoretically could be used to obtain nuclear material for atomic weapons),
- the United States agreed to move toward full normalization of political and economic relations with the North,
- finally, both sides agreed to work together for peace and security on the Korean peninsula and strengthen the international nuclear nonproliferation regime.

In addition to all this, in January 1995 the Clinton administration decided to provide North Korea with five hundred thousand metric tons of heavy oil. The oil was supposed to be used for electrical energy production. In this way the United States tried to compensate the DPRK for the loss of electrical energy that would have been produced by the North Korean nuclear reactors stopped due to the Agreement's provisions. The shipments actually started in October 1995 with the first installment of one hundred thousand metric tons. Also, in accordance of the terms of the Agreement, the United States eased some economic sanctions against North Korea. The Clinton administration also seriously considered sending some unconditional food aid to the North.

Unfortunately, both sides failed to entirely live up to their commitments. DPRK indeed stopped and mothballed its energy-producing nuclear reactors but did not stop its atomic research program. On the other side, the two LWRs have never been delivered although a groundbreaking ceremony was conducted in August 1997 at the site where they were supposed to be built. No normalization of economic or political relations took place over the next few years either. But still, an uneasy peace held on up to the moment when the administration of George W. Bush came to power in the United States.

George W. Bush almost immediately put North Korea on the list of so-called "rogue states" and a member of the "axis of evil" and called its leader—Kim Jong-il—a "pygmy" whom he "loathed" (Barnaby and Ritchie, 2004). In response, the DPRK threatened to restart its nuclear reactors to compensate for the loss of electricity caused by delays in the construction of the promised two light-water reactors.

In October 2002, Assistant Secretary of State James Kelly visited Pyongyang and came back with sensational allegations. He not only announced that the United Sates became aware of a secret North Korean highly enriched uranium (HEU) research program but he also alleged that the DPRK delegation privately admitted to him the existence of such a program. At that time, Pyongyang denied all those allegations.

Nevertheless, right after that visit, the US stopped supplying oil to North Korea. In response, in December 2002 the North removed monitoring IAEA seals and cameras from its nuclear facilities and restarted its reactors. (Partly it was done because of a real need for energy and partly as a retaliatory move against the United States.) They also ordered IAEA inspectors to leave the country.

In January 2003, Pyongyang officially announced that they were withdrawing from the nuclear nonproliferation treaty (NPT) and this time they actually did it. It meant that since that time on the Kim Jong-il regime was left unchecked to run its nuclear program as it wanted—not an appealing perspective for many countries in the region. But Bush categorically refused to open direct talks with the North and resorted to threats of military action.

The world community was forced to react to the dangerous behavior of both leaders. So, in August 2003 multilateral negotiations were initiated. The six-party talks included representatives of China, Japan, Russia, South Korea and certainly North Korea, and the United States. The talks did not produce any significant progress due to hard-line positions of the two principle parties—Pyongyang and Washington. The Americans demanded a complete, unconditional, and 100 percent verifiable dismantlement of the entire North Korean nuclear program (including research and civil energy production) even before they would agree to start talking to DPRK. The opposite party in their turn demanded first a non-aggression pact with the United States and a promise not to undertake any action to undermine the existing North Korean government. Neither side was able to move from their deeply entrenched positions. At the same time, the Bush administration started a program of a "regime change" in Pyongyang. Citing this "hostile policy" and a lack of progress, North Korea officially dropped out of the six-party negotiations in 2005. In February of the same year they finally officially and publicly proclaimed that their country possessed nuclear weapons. Although it was suspected for a long time it was still a shock to the international community. But many experts actually doubted that it was entirely true. They argued that it might have been a desperate attempt on the North Korean part to scare the United States and spare themselves the fate of Iraq. That is, everybody knew by then that Kim Jong-Il had acquired enough material to make a couple of nuclear weapons, but the question was—how functional they were. Were they actually usable?

In order to support its claim, on October 9th, 2006, Pyongyang conducted a suspiciously well-advertised nuclear weapons test. And although experts are still arguing what actually happened that day in North Korea (an actual successful small-scale nuclear explosion, an unsuccessful nuclear test, or just a large-scale conventional explosion) the international community decided to react swiftly. On October 14th (just five days later) the United Nations Security Council unanimously accepted Resolution 1718 that stipulated some political and economic sanctions against North Korea.

Due to the Chinese and Russian pressure the resolution turned out to be quite soft in essence although quite firm in its tone. The resolution demanded complete destruction of all the nuclear weapons already built by Pyongyang and a freeze on all the ongoing weapons research programs. It also stipulated a series of sanctions mostly directed against the North Korean weapons' design agenda. For example, no nuclear or missile-related technologies would be brought into DPRK from other countries. All the visits by specialists and scholars into or from the country would be banned in order to stop the flow of advanced knowledge in these areas. The document also contained just a recommendation for possible inspections of North Korean transports that might carry weapons of mass destruction (WMD) or their elements in or out of the country. At the same time, no specific economic sanctions were mentioned in the resolution. And although the imposed sanctions did not have any specific expiration date, they could be removed if North Korea would officially come back to its former nonnuclear status and renew the six-party talks.

Even such a soft resolution was considered by DPRK representatives in the United Nations a "declaration of war." The whole delegation left the meeting room as a sign of protest against what they called "double standards" used by other countries against them.

But those who had been involved in the negotiations understood that sanctions alone were not going to solve the problem of nuclear weapons in DPRK, they would just make the lives of ordinary citizens of the country even worse. Therefore, they continued talking to Pyongyang trying to persuade it to come back to the negotiating table. The two countries that cared the most about what was going to happen in the North, its two neighbors—China and South Korea—undertook especially active efforts in this respect. And on the last day of October 2006 several world news agencies reported that North Korea agreed to resume its participation in the six-party talks.

The negotiations indeed resumed in December 1996 in Beijing, China and, as it was expected, went nowhere. Americans kept tying the issue of denuclearization of North Korea with the problem of democracy in that country. They also continued to insist on a complete, unconditional, and 100 percent verifiable dismantlement of the entire North Korean nuclear program before they would even consider any of DPRK's demands. North Korea, on the other hand, demanded from the United States to unfreeze their assets in Banko Delta Asia in Macao, China. In 2005 the US froze $24 millions dollars in that bank as a unilateral sanction against the North and effectively, by so doing, blocked a great deal of DPRK's international financial activities. Pyongyang refused to move ahead with the talks under, as they put it, "conditions of financial blockade."

The North Koreans also formulated their main conditions for curtailing their nuclear program (certainly, if their first demand of unfreezing of the financial assets is satisfied first). First of all, they want the United States to officially reject their belligerent policies against their country and to move toward normalization of relations between the two nations. Secondly, they want the two LWRs promised to them in 1994. Finally, they asked for heavy oil shipments that would be used for electrical energy production to compensate for the loss of electrical production capacity in the country if the existing energy-producing nuclear reactions are stopped and mothballed. In short, they exactly reproduced the provisions of the 1994 Agreed Framework that was signed under President Clinton and collapsed after the Bush administration came to power. Pyongyang also, as a gesture of good will, expressed its readiness to once again accept IAEA's inspections of its nuclear facilities but not on a permanent basis just yet.

The lack of progress frustrated other participants of the talks—especially, the Chinese and the Russians who put so much effort into convincing DPRK to come back to the negotiation table. Despite the attempts of their representatives to be diplomatic it was quite clear that they blamed mostly the United States for the lack of progress. They diplomatically noted that in these circumstances Washington should have been more flexible and ready to compromise. They expressed their confidence that if Washington had been more cooperative and unfrozen the Macao assets of North Korea—they (China and Russia) would have been able to ultimately obtain substantial concessions from Pyongyang on the nuclear issue.

South Korea also expressed its disappointment with the results of the Beijing talks. They suggested acting according to the formula "action-counteraction"—when one concession of one party is reciprocated by one concession on the other side. But the unwillingness of both sides to make the first step made this approach so far ineffective.

Later on some tentative agreements were reached but they were highly superficial. They stipulated just stoppage of the nuclear reactor in Yongbyon in exchange for some shipments of heavy oil. There was nothing said in the document about an actual disarming of the North. On the other side, nothing was said about security guarantees for OPRK, normalization of relations, the building of the LWRs or who would pay for them. It is not clear how such a document could lead to a serious agreement. And the political comedy surrounding the unfreezing of the North's money in Macao puts in major doubt the seriousness of some talk's participants.

One thing is clear, the two main actors in the game have to adjust their positions substantially if they actually want to reach an agreement. But the next questions are: Is it possible? And what can be done to reach the positive outcome of the negotiations? In order to answer these questions we have to examine related problems and the sides' interests. And the rest of this case study will try to do exactly that. But even before we can start considering sides' positions and interests we have to explore and try to understand a multitude of technological, political and other problems that collectively (all added together) constitute this big and complex issue of the North Korean nuclear ambitions.

Issues Involved

Technical and Technological Issues

North Korea is a very secretive society. That is why it is very difficult to evaluate what kind of actually threatening WMD capabilities they may have. Are they just bluffing? And if no, how dangerous is their nuclear force in reality?

There are some things that are well-known and those that are just suspected about the DPRK's WMD programs. Clearly-known facts can be summarized as follows:

- they have enough plutonium for one or two nuclear weapons (between seven and eleven kilograms);
- they have a relatively advanced medium- to long-range ballistic missile program;
- they have restarted their Yongbyon reactor and soon may have more material for new nuclear warheads.

There are also things that are widely suspected by many weapons experts all over the world. They can be summarized like this:

- they have reprocessed enough material for three to six plutonium-based nuclear weapons;
- they started their own highly-enriched uranium (HEU) program;
- they have secret underground nuclear research, production, and testing facilities (one of them was exposed during the October 9th, 2006 test).

In order to understand the meaning and dangers of the above points it is necessary to explain some technological subtleties of the nuclear weapons design.

There are two types of nuclear weapons—plutonium- and uranium-based. Each of these two methods has its own advantages and problems.

As was mentioned above, it is known that North Korea already has several kilograms of weapons-grade plutonium at their disposal. They obtained it by removing fuel rods from their *Yongbyon-1* reactor and reprocessing it at their secret reprocessing facility. This is the most efficient way for them to receive plutonium for their weapons—from their electricity-producing nuclear reactors. That is why the world community was so concerned about their nuclear energy program and wanted to replace their reactors with the light-water reactors (LWR) that are somewhat less suitable for obtaining material for nuclear weapons. In exchange for a promise to provide them with LWRs Pyongyang mothballed their *Yongbyon-1* reactor for several years but restarted it in January 2004. That is why they still have a relatively small number of weapon-grade plutonium but that is why they also can soon have more of it.

For a plutonium-based weapon one needs about six to eleven kilograms of the material but with the use of a reflector or tamper the amount can be reduced down to just three or four kilograms. "The first American nuclear weapons test, called Trinity, and the Nagasaki bomb each used 6 kilograms of plutonium; each produced explosive yields equivalent to that of 21,000 tonnes of TNT" (Barnaby and Ritchie, 2004). North Korean reactors (if not stopped) can produce between 200 and 280 kilograms of plutonium a year that can be enough for 65 nuclear weapons. And this is already a solid and dangerous arsenal.

But the reactors can be taken out by, let's say, an air strike. Therefore, it seems that recently DPRK started an "insurance" weapons program—the one based on highly enriched uranium (HEU).

The HEU technology came to North Korea from Pakistan. Famous Pakistani nuclear scientist Abdul Qadeer Khan provided them with it in exchange for North Korean missile technology.

One does not have to have a reactor to make a bomb out of uranium. It is necessary to obtain a substantial amount of uranium ore and enrich it. There are several ways to enrich the raw material. The cheapest and technologically accessible for Pyongyang is the use of gas centrifuges. That is, probably, why they are using this one.

Natural uranium contains only about 0.7 percent of U-239—the isotope that is the main driving force behind the nuclear explosion. In order to receive a weapons-grade material it is necessary to enrich uranium to the level where it contains 93 percent of U-239. For a HEU bomb one needs about fifty-six kilograms of the enriched material. But this amount can be scaled down to the level of about twenty kilograms with the use of a reflector or tamper. For a strategically significant nuclear force of, let's say, six weapons they will need at least two hundred kilograms of HEU. And the next question: Can they get that much?

Most experts (for example, Barnaby and Ritchie, 2004, or Federation of American Scientists, 2004) agree that in order to obtain that much material they will need about five thousand centrifuges to produce enough HEU for six bombs. The problem is that it will take them up to five years to do it. All those centrifuges (with 40 percent of them on the repair reserve) will be able to produce only about forty kilograms of HEU a year. That is why for two hundred kilograms they will need about five years.

But on top of that, one has to add at least another five years to build a cascade of five thousand centrifuges. Until recently, many experts believed that such a feat was not feasible for North Korea because it would be too expensive to build such a huge cascade and they would not have enough electricity to operate it. (It takes about one thousand kilowatt-hours to produce just one gram of HEU.) But in late 2006 Pyongyang officially announced that they started a small number of centrifuges to enrich uranium. Still, many experts believe that it was a propaganda step rather than an actual attempt to produce a somehow significant amount of HEU. Those experts argue that DPRK does not have the recourses to build more of the centrifuges and does not have enough electricity to operate more of them.

One way or another, nuclear weapons must somehow be delivered it to the target. The North does not have aircraft or submarines suitable for this task. Therefore, they prefer land-based ballistic missile force to potentially carry their weapons into battle.

The North Koreans have the *No-dong* missile that theoretically can carry a nuclear weapon. It is a medium-range missile with a range up to 1,200 kilometers (about 750 miles). Pyongyang has about one hundred of them. It is an old Soviet design but in a North Korean version it is quite unreliable and imprecise. Syria, Iran, Pakistan, and Libya reportedly bought them from DPRK. The Pakistani *Ghauri* and the Iranian *Shahab*-3 are derivatives of this design.

The *Taepodong-1* missile is still considered to be medium-range but its range is already up to 2,000 kilometers (about 1,250 miles). It is a two-stage design that can carry a payload up to 1,200 kilograms. It was tested in 1998 and flew over Japan, which created a panic on the islands, and it is exactly the weapon the Japanese are mostly afraid of.

The *Taepodong-2* version is supposed to be a two-stage long-range missile with a range of up to 6,000 kilometers (3,750 miles) and a payload of 1,000 kilograms. Theoretically it can reach some parts of the United States—some islands, such as, for example, Guam—but *not* the continental part of the United States. But it has not been tested yet and many experts agree that it is still in the early stages of development and it will be years, if not decades, before it can become operational.

In the mid-2000s North Korean missile sales dropped dramatically because nobody wanted to buy any more quite unreliable and inaccurate weapons. It shows the level of technology DPRK possesses in this area.

But it is not enough to have warheads and missiles. It is also necessary to be able to marry them to produce a functional weapons system. And it is not easy. The warhead has to be able to withstand extreme forces of the launch and delivery processes. And most of the experts believe that it is doubtful that the North has the technology to put their nuclear warheads on their missiles or will have it in the forseeable future.

Finally, it is important to know that nonnuclear high explosives are used in nuclear weapons in so-called explosive "lenses." In 2002 North Korea already conducted several high-explosive tests for the purpose of their nuclear weapons program. It is important to know because this fact may shed some light on the events of October 9th, 2006. As it was mentioned above, many experts until now have no idea what exploded in the North that day. But according to some measurements and estimates it may have been a detonation of such a type of high explosives that was intended to fool the world. But the most possible version of the events is that it was simply an unsuccessful nuclear test.

Now we can summarize. The North Koreans already may have a couple of nuclear weapons but they are, probably, not functional (what the October 9th test may have shown) and cannot be put on top of a missile (that is, they are undeliverable). It is unlikely that their HEU program will produce anything serious soon. And even if they find somewhere enough money and electricity—it will take decades for their centrifuges to produce a somehow significant amount of HEU. But if their currently existing reactors are not stopped—they may have rather soon enough plutonium to build several more weapons. That is why it is extremely important to convince them to stop those reactors again and to provide them with alternative sources of energy.

The North Korean missile program is rather primitive—their missiles are imprecise and unreliable and, probably, they in reality cannot carry actual nuclear warheads just yet. With these missiles they could strike South Korea and maybe Japan but not the continental part of the United States. But anyway, their technology is so primitive that it will not be able to overcome the US Ballistic Missile Defense system that can shoot down at once a small number of unsophisticated ballistic missiles.

That is, so far North Korea does not represent a serious threat to anybody (except for, probably, South Korea). But if they are given more time, their reactors are not stopped, and their missile-improvement program continues—in a decade or two the situation may change. Therefore, it is a good idea not to procrastinate and to start looking for an effective and mutually acceptable solution already now.

Other Issues and Problems

One of the main difficulties that North Korea experiences is the *energy problem*. Experts say that "the county's electricity consumption in 2000 was only two thirds of that in 1991" (Barnaby and Ritchie, 2004). As was already mentioned above, the deal with two light-water reactors that were supposed to be supplied by the Korean Peninsula Energy Development Organization (KEDO) fell through. And, as it will be explained below, that was not North Korea's fault. It was a big money debate originated by the United States and South Korea that led to the failure of that project.

Pyongyang stopped their reactors but the new ones never came and the oil shipments from the United States were also discontinued. All that led directly to the restart of the old North Korean nuclear reactors that represent, as it was shown above, a security threat. So, if we do not want the North Korean people to suffer and the regime to have more plutonium at their disposal—we have to solve the energy issue as soon as possible. And there are several effective ways to do it. What is remarkable here is that all those methods are not just abstract ideas but well thought through and well-calculated actual proposals that have been on the table for years. The solution is readily available and the only thing that is needed is the political will to implement it.

The first one, of course, is to renew the KEDO deal. It is not to say that LWRs are absolutely proliferation safe. But there is a solution to the problem. The solution is the fact that "North Korea will have to secure enriched uranium fuel for light-water reactors from outside North Korea. This, the officials claim, will give the United States leverage on the supply of fuel if North Korea should violate the Agreed Framework. . . . [E]xercising U.S. leverage over the supply of fuel would require that potential suppliers of fuel like China and Russia coordinate their policies with the United States" (Niksch, 1996). And the Russians already agreed to supply nuclear fuel to the North and take it back across the border after it has been used. The main requirement for this type of cooperation is that all the spent fuel is returned back. The Russians agreed to make sure that not a gram of the spent fuel remains in North Korea.

All this sounds like a reasonable offer but other countries keep saying that there are problems (for example, money) on the way of this solution. But it sounds ridiculous that the entire European Union, the richest countries on Earth—the United States and Japan (plus North Korea)—cannot find $4.5 billion dollars to provide the North with safer reactors. And this is where suspicion arises: Do they actually want to do it? Is there a political will to solve the problem at all?

The other (or rather additional) option is to provide the North with more fuel for their electricity producing facilities. And there is a couple of interesting proposals on the table in this respect. The Russians, for example, are ready to supply the North with gas and electricity if South Korea is ready to help Pyongyang pay for it. Also, China is planning a gas pipeline into South Korea that will go through the North. Therefore, Kim Jong-Il will be entitled to a substantial transitional fee. He could take it in money or gas. But the main advantage of such an approach is that it would incorporate the North into the regional gas market and, by doing so, involve them into international cooperation and business transactions.

The next problem has already been mentioned above—the *money*. Everybody seemingly wants to solve the problem but nobody wants to pay for it. And everybody is using domestic politics as a pretext for doing nothing. This is how the Federation of American Scientists show why the KEDO deal failed:

> South Korea, which has promised to bear the lion's share of the reactor project cost estimated at US $4.5 billion, is asking the United States to put up at least a symbolic amount. The US administration, however, has said it can make no contribution to the construction cost as Congress has not appropriated the necessary budget. An official in Seoul, however, said that South Korea cannot drop its demand simply because of domestic problems in the United States. The US Congress has been delaying approval of the cost for the reactor project. South Korean officials said the US refusal to share the reactor cost would make it difficult for them to obtain approval from the National Assembly for the South Korean share. (Federation of American Scientists, 2004)

It seems that cooperation among the allies is not going smoothly. That is, probably, why the negotiations in general are not going well either. The North Koreans are not sure whether they will get what they were promised or the whole program will abruptly end in the middle leaving them without electricity but with a lot of problems. Besides that, they do not see a united front talking to them but a collection of quarreling actors fighting only for their parochial interests. In this situation they see an opportunity to play their own game and they are doing it pretty well.

Certainly, all this makes sense only if the next step is made—the dismantlement of the old North Korean reactors. If they continue to exist in their operational form and can be easily restarted—it does not provide any stable security guarantee for the international community. The fuel also must be removed from those reactors and safely stored. Unfortunately, Pyongyang cannot handle it on its own—it is very expensive and this is where the world will have to chip in. These are the estimates of how much the entire dismantlement operation would cost:

> The South Korean Government, however, reportedly estimates that the cost of safe storage of the fuel rods will be about $30 million. . . . Other South Korean experts reportedly place the costs of storage and removal higher, around $200 million. . . . Administration officials have not estimated the cost of dismantlement and from where the money would come. South Korean government experts reportedly estimate that dismantlement of the 50 and 200 megawatt reac-

tors will cost about $500 million but that dismantlement of the radioactive five megawatt reactor and the plutonium reprocessing plant will require a much higher cost. (Niksch, 1996)

In short, the politicians have to make their choice—either they want security and will pay for it or they continue to play politics and blame the other side for all the negotiational failures.

But there is another problem here. All that assistance may be impossible from the legal point of view because the United States put North Korea on the list of states that sponsor terrorism. It also makes it very uncomfortable for American representatives to talk to the North Koreans because they are not supposed to be negotiating with terrorists. That propagandistic action has very real consequences. Therefore, in order for the negotiations to develop further it is necessary to remove Pyongyang from that list. Propaganda is propaganda but business is business and security is security. All the experts in the world know that, despite some mischief, North Korea has nothing to do with terrorism as a normal person would define that phenomenon. "In spite of the impression given by the Bush administration, there is no firm evidence that North Korea is linked to terrorist acts. . . . Following September 11 a North Korean Foreign Ministry spokesman voiced regret and reiterated North Korean opposition to all forms of terrorism. It is not known to have engaged in any form of international terrorism in the 1990s and beyond and has no known links to al-Qaida" (Barnaby and Ritchie, 2004).

There are also other problems associated with the issue. One of them is the problem of North Korean transparency and the disarmament verification issue. Certainly, very solid verification procedures must be stipulated by any agreement with Kim Jong-Il. And making him commit to such procedures and fulfill his obligations is a problem on which the international community has to work as a united front (which is something that has been missing so far). And the role of Pyongyang's allies and neighbors—China, Russia, and South Korea—is very difficult to overestimate.

There are also some rather *perceptional* problems affecting the issue. For example, the rest of the world believes that the policies of the Bush administration in relation to North Korea are too hostile and provocative. Many believe that it was exactly those policies that gave an excuse to the North to behave the way they did because they could always claim that they were under attack (or about to be attacked) and had to protect themselves. On the other side Kim Jong-Il is considered to be dangerous and unpredictable. Unfortunately, very few people know what he is really like.

Finally, the Japanese enormous fear of North Korea makes the problem even worse. Because of that fear they panic and start making statements and steps unhelpful for the progress of the talks. The Japanese position themselves against North Korea in a very belligerent way and then they are afraid that Pyongyang will attack them. It is a little bit illogical. If you want somebody not to attack you—try to become his friend. Such a behavior on the part of the Japanese again gives a chance to Kim Jong-Il to complain about unfair treatment and a belligerent environment for his country. It is also a great domestic propaganda tool for him: "Look—Japanese militarists raise their heads again. Therefore, we have to be strong to protect us from what happened during World War II." The Japanese fear is understandable but during negotiations cool heads have to prevail.

Since we have started talking about separate countries it makes sense now to consider positions, interests, and options of the main participants of the negotiations. We will try not to just show but to understand them as deeply as we can.

Participants and Actors

The United States of America

The United States has three official concerns over the North Korean nuclear problem. First of all, it is anxious that Pyongyang could use nuclear weapons against American troops and allies in the region. Secondly, the possession of the nuclear weapons by DPRK almost surely will lead to further nuclear proliferation in the region. (Japan is already threatening to consider acquiring a small atomic arsenal.) Finally, Washington claims that they are afraid that Kim Jong-Il will provide nuclear weapons or technology to terrorists.

The first two are very reasonable and correct concerns. The third one is a propaganda trick rather than a genuine problem taking into account no connection between DPRK and any known terrorist organization. It is clear that terrorists have much easier access to nuclear technologies through corrupt Pakistani scientists or Iran.

But to be completely fair it is necessary to admit that such a remote possibility exists under two sets of circumstances. The first one is if the United States attacks DPRK and Pyongyang decides to use a terrorist organization as an alternative weapons delivery system. The second situation is if America corners the Kim Jong-Il government to such an extent that it is about to collapse. In this case, as a last desperate act, North Korea can give nuclear weapons to terrorists as an act of revenge. And since we know that destroying Kim Jong-Il's regime is an official policy of the United States and they are actively working in that direction, it would be unwise to discard such a possibility altogether. But a reasonable person can easily see the cause-and-effect flow in this case. It is the United States who can trigger such a course of events and hardly the other way around. So, it is rather the North Koreans who have to be afraid of such an option because the retaliation upon them would be swift and horrendous.

For decades, America tried to keep Pyongyang's nuclear program in check. It was mostly done through a system of sanctions. It is possible to argue for a long time whether those sanctions were successful or not. Some would say yes because until now Kim Jong-Il has just two weapons (and they may not even be functional) and quite a few but very bad missiles. Others would say that the main fact is that regardless of all those sanctions they nevertheless managed to acquire and master nuclear and missile technologies and are improving them slowly but steadily. One way or another, North Korea survived over fifty years of American sanctions.

The United States imposed a total embargo on trade with North Korea in June 1950 including a complete ban on all financial transactions between the two countries. However, since 1989 the US slowly eased sanctions against Pyongyang. The US now allows a wide range of commercial and consumer products to be exported to the communist country without a special export license. It also allows some North Korean imports into the United States but this can be done only after a special approval process. America permits some direct personal and commercial financial transactions between USA and DPRK residents. Restrictions on investments also have been eased. The American government now allows commercial US ships and aircraft carrying American goods to call at North Korean ports. All these measures nevertheless have resulted in little economic activity.

But all this easing of sanctions does not affect counterterrorism or non-proliferation areas. Until now any US exports of nuclear, military, and sensitive dual-use technologies into the communist country is prohibited. Most types of American assistance are also inhibited by various statutory restrictions. North Korea does not enjoy normal trade relations with the United States. Therefore, any goods manufactured in North Korea are subject to higher import duty tariffs upon their entry into the United States.

Experts agree (for example, Barnaby and Ritchie, 2004) that in relation to the current crisis America has several options:

- Military action;
- Hard-line approach or containment (including different types of sanctions);
- Negotiations;
- Accepting status quo.

Military action is the most sensational media-discussed but in reality least possible option. Taking into account all the troubles America is having in Iraq, it is unlikely that they will want to deal with a million-man strong Korean army which is armed with old but heavy weaponry—tanks, heavy artillery, rockets, submarines, etc. So-called limited military strikes (the Yugoslavia style) are also unlikely taking into account the character of the Korean regime. Any military action is likely to unfold into a full-scale and large-scale war.

Let's try to start with the so-called *"limited precision strike"* solution—to take out only North Korean nuclear facilities. First of all, the retaliation upon American forces in the region will be imminent which will entail a big war. Secondly, North Koreans are hiding such facilities quite well and we cannot be sure that even a series of air strikes will destroy them all. Third, if the Americans manage to hit and destroy functional nuclear sites—the radioactive fallout will be catastrophic for China, Russia, South Korea, and Japan. And there is no way to predict how Russia and China would behave in this case. Finally, the Korean army is not as small as, let's say, the Yugoslavian army was and it cannot be destroyed quickly—it is just too big.

If we talk about *full-scale invasion*—it is even more problematic. On top of all the problems just mentioned above we can add quite a few additional ones. South Korea and Japan strongly oppose this option because they will be the first casualties of that war. Retaliation against them is imminent. The situation will be especially grave if North Korea (feeling completely cornered) uses chemical or biological weapons. In this case experts estimate that fatalities will be counted in hundreds of thousands if not millions (Barnaby and Ritchie, 2004). In general, it would be a humanitarian crisis at a catastrophic level. And all the refugees from the North will flee to China—not a lucrative prospect for the Chinese.

But even if the operation is an astounding success—who is going to pay for reconstruction? Allies are fighting over a couple of billion dollars for the light-water reactors. Who is going to pay billions and billions to rebuild both of the demolished Koreas? Finally, what if the victory produces what can be called the "Iraqi result"—when the new regime can handle the situation worse than the previous one (especially, in terms of corruption, security, banditism, and terrorism)?

The next option is the so-called *hard-line approach* or *containment*. This is basically a set of very belligerent policies implemented against North Korea including tough economic sanctions. This option has its own drawbacks.

First of all, South Korea and China do not support this option. For the Chinese, North Korea is their traditional ally. And South Koreans want to peacefully integrate the North into the world community with a hope that eventually it will entail a peaceful reunification of the two countries. Certainly, tough sanctions, that will alienate Pyongyang even more, are not on their priority list.

Sanctions would demonstrate the unity of the world community but they are difficult to enforce and would only harm the people of the North, not the regime. The US has been using them against the communist government for decades and they did not seem to have any serious effect on their nuclear and missile programs. And again, if the economic situation in Kim Jong-il's country becomes unbearable China will be flooded with millions of refugees, something they are not going to let happen.

Because all the options above look so unattractive, inefficient, and implausible, some experts (Barnaby and Ritchie, 2004) even consider a situation where the United Sates will have to accept the *status quo* and unofficially recognize North Korea as a small nuclear power. "Unofficially" basically means that America keeps threatening the North but actually does nothing. On the other side, Kim Jong-Il keeps talking about negotiations to satisfy the world public opinion but does not disarm. That is exactly what has been going on for quite some time now. The same experts say that, after all, America has been living with North Korea having a couple of nuclear weapons at their disposal for years. So, it may continue in the future for quite a while especially if the US missile defense system comes on-line soon. But this idea has a right to exist only if Pyongyang will remain a small nuclear power. If it will want to become too big—neither China nor the United States will let it happen.

The final option the US has is *negotiations*. That is, they will have to convince North Korea to give up their nuclear weapons and research programs in exchange for something. What can that something be? Experts (for example Federation of American Scientists, 2004 or Barnaby and Ritchie, 2004) believe that the "something" may be:

- signing a nonaggression pact;
- promise not to undermine Kim Jong-Il's regime;
- removal of economic sanctions;
- supply of food, oil, and electricity.

(Unfortunately, the Bush administration considers all the above as rewarding the North for "bad behavior.")

Certainly, in return North Korea has to make reciprocal steps:

- freeze all the nuclear-related activities (including mothballing their nuclear reactors that eventually, after the final deal is reached, will be dismantled);
- allow IAEA inspections of all their nuclear-related facilities;
- provide guarantees that it will not attack South Korea or Japan;
- pledge to accept the deal made at the six-party talks.

The United States, as a stronger party, has to make the first step ahead by dropping their insistence on complete, verifiable, and irreversible disarmament as a precondition for even starting negotiations. But so far, the US is not only unwilling to start bilateral negotiations with North Korea but is generally unwilling "to take on the burden of responsibility for making any such agreement work" (Barnaby and Ritchie, 2004).

Besides all, the United States has a serious hurdle to overcome on the way to a strong and lasting agreement with Pyongyang—American domestic politics and, especially, the US Congress as the embodiment of such a kind of politics. The Congress has to approve any agreement reached at the negotiations and ratify it before it can come into force. But so far, American legislators were less than helpful in working in this area.

As was mentioned above, they refused to allocate necessary funds toward the light-water reactor deal. They also created some problems for the heavy oil program:

> A certain role for Congress will involve Administration requests for appropriations to help finance the costs of the various benefits to North Korea. Moreover, Congress under law will have to review a prospective U.S.-North Korea nuclear agreement, which the Administration will have to negotiate before light-water reactors with U.S. technology can be sent to North Korea. . . . Securing funds to implement the Agreed Framework continues to challenge the Administration. The estimated cost of the light-water reactor (LWR) project has risen from $4.5 billion to nearly $6.0 billion. . . . The Administration also has had difficulty in securing money to provide North Korea with 500,000 tons of heavy oil annually. The foreign operations appropriations bill for FY1996 grants the Clinton Administration's request for $22 million for U.S. funding of KEDO operations, including $19 million for 500,000 tons of heavy oil to be shipped to North Korea in 1996 under the Agreed Framework. . . . However, initial House action on the FY1997 foreign operations appropriations bill has cut the Administration's request of $25 million to $13 million. (Niksch, 1996)

That is, they are ready to provide $13–$19 million a year when only dismantlement of the fifty and two hundred megawatt reactors will cost about $500 million. At this pace, the dismantlement process will take over twenty-five years—a quarter of a century. And it is just one of many programs that have to be implemented if any solid type of agreement with North Korea is to be reached.

But at the same time, Congress is willing to spend money on something that makes the negotiations more difficult. For example, on March 24th, 2004 the North Korean Human Rights Act passed in the Congress. The bill authorized the appropriation of $124 million each year over the 2005–2008 period for subversive actions within North Korea for the purpose of overthrowing the Kim Jong-Il regime. Such actions not only make officials in Pyongyang feel unsafe but they also serve as a great propaganda tool for them. It also provides them with an excuse and pretext for inadequate actions. Citing exactly that bill, North Korea withdrew from six-party talks in 2005.

In short, besides all the external problems, the US Congress will provide a formidable challenge to those who would want to reach any kind of agreement with DPRK. So far, they are willing to give just $13 million for aid to North Korea but spend $124 million every year for subversive actions in that country. In short, their priorities are quite clear—hostility over cooperation.

North Korea

For the North there is one and only one interest in the negotiations—the survival of the regime. The invasion of Iraq in 2003 and the North Korean Human Rights Act of 2004 convinced them that the United States would not rest until the regime is gone. That is, as they see it, it is their very survival as a system that is at stake in this game. Under these circumstances they are weighing every step very carefully and are not going to make any concessions that make them more vulnerable in their view. Certainly, all this is nothing new for them. They have been feeling under siege since the 1950s. Since that time they have been seeing right on their border dozens of thousands of American troops poised to strike them any minute.

They are afraid of two things—direct military attack and internal subversive actions. These are the two things that an enemy can do to overthrow a government. And they know that the Americans are good at both of them. They are not even sure that the Americans in reality want to negotiate with them. They are afraid that what they see is a sort of Iraq version of the events when one of the parties (namely, the United States) used negotiations as an international public relations tool in order to use later on the failed talks as a pretext to attack the other side. That is, what they are mainly looking for is a confirmation that the talks are real. So far, all the actions of the United States are pointing in the opposite directions—refusal to directly negotiate with them, numerous preconditions, etc. There are many similarities with the Iraq situation in the early 2000s. If the United States believes that Kim Jong-Il uses negotiations to buy some time to improve his nuclear weapons, North Koreans on their part believe that the Americans use the talks to alleviate their problems in Iraq and to eventually attack them. That is, the main two things that must be done to convince them that the talks are real are to sign a nonaggression document with them and to stop subversive operations within their borders.

We have to remember that the whole nuclear program was started to guarantee their survival in a hostile environment (as they saw it). They are afraid to disarm and later being attacked and to have nothing to defend themselves with (like Saddam Hussein). That is why no disarmament on their part or even no serious negotiations can start before they receive their security guarantees.

And this is where other countries (including the United Sates) make a perceptional mistake. They think that such incentives as normal trade relations, food, oil, and energy can bring Pyongyang to the negotiation table. What they do not understand is that for the regime its survival is much more important than the well-being of its citizens. Indeed, the economic situation in the country is really bad but all this is a distant second consideration after the survival of the system. For them, peace guarantees come first and food—maybe later. And this is exactly what the United States are not willing to give them. But the Americans have to understand their logic which goes like this: "They are giving us food in return for disarmament and when we take this bait—they will attack us." That is why nothing will bring about serious negotiations on the part of North Korea but the security guarantees.

When they are sure that they are not going to be attacked (and under pressure from China, Russia, and South Korea) they may be willing to consider economic incentives and proposals that would definitely make their life better. They have already undergone some changes: implemented some very limited market reforms; allowed some foreign investments in the country, opened several joint ventures with South Korea. That is, they are willing to do something if they do not feel threatened. They already once stopped their reactors and allowed IAEA inspectors in the country and they can do it again if they feel safe, if the incentives are serious and actually forthcoming (for example, LWRs are actually built). But, so far, they were promised a lot of things but very few of them were actually delivered (just some oil and a little bit of food).

Besides that, the belligerent attitude toward them has to be replaced by a more reconciliatory tone. When they are talked to in a normal tone of voice they seem to understand what they have to do. Carter managed to convince Kim Il-sung to cooperate but "loathing" of Kim Jong-Il did not help a bit. It may be exactly the mistake that can prove crucial for the whole problem.

In the West, propaganda paints Kim Jong-Il as a sort of madman whose sick will has to be overcome in order to bring about a progress in this area. But, at the same time, some Russian sources who met him personally, found him to be an intelligent, highly cultured, reasonable person—a sort of much softer version of his father. They believe that he would be willing to negotiate and even institute some limited economic reforms but it is the military who prevent him from doing so. He would like to do more for economic recovery in his country but "some in the military who handle the issues do not [want it to happen], since it could undermine their authoritarian power" (Barnaby and

Ritchie, 2004). The generals did not like him from the beginning as a "softy." After the death of Kim Il-sung in 1994, it was three years before Kim Jong-Il took over the leadership of the ruling Korean Workers' Party. It is difficult to say what happened in those three years but he probably had to prove to the generals that he would be able to run the country the way it was run under his father. That is, it would be a good idea to talk to Kim Jong-Il personally (preferably, out of the country—sometime, for example, during his trip to Russia) and offer him some help in dealing with his domestic political and economic problems in exchange for future cooperation. Instead of this, the West demonizes and insults him and threatens his country with war. In this situation, they are definitely not helping moderate-thinking politicians in DPRK but, probably, already managed to convince even Kim Jong-il himself that his generals were right. That is the West may be kicking the very person they could talk to.

Certainly, a lot must be done by North Korea itself to increase its own credibility at the international arena. Besides the measures mentioned above (freezing of the nuclear programs, allowing IAEA inspections, guaranteeing security for the South) it also has to deal appropriately with the issue of Japanese citizens abducted by the North Korean secret service, to increase transparency of the process of distribution of food, medical aid, and oil supplied to Pyongyang. But all these steps should be secondary issues and not preconditions for talks. When trust is established—it will be much easier to talk about these problems. But what kind of transparency can we talk about when the other side is about to attack them (as they see it)? And again, for them, survival of the system comes first and food—distant second.

Survival is the reason why the whole nuclear weapons program was started and if the international community can show them the way to survive without nuclear weapons—they may be willing to abandon that idea. But for that it will be necessary to abandon the regime change plan. Bringing democracy is a noble cause but it can be done differently—without often undemocratic and subversive operations. It can be better done with what can be called the German way—through peaceful reunification with the South. Therefore, let's see what is going on in that part of the Korean peninsula.

South Korea

The situation in the South is simple and complex at the same time. The complexity comes from a big perceptional generation gap that exists in the country in relation to the United States. The older generation who can still remember the war (even if they were just children at that time) have a great sympathy for the United States. They believe that America saved them from the communist aggression and that the alliance with the US is an important element of their country's security strategy. A younger generation (that does not remember the war) often believes that it is time for the American troops to go home and that the United States have to respect their country more and, consequently, give them more flexibility in dealing with important issues of international politics.

But one simple thing unites the two generations—their feeling toward the North. On one hand, they are a little bit afraid of the neighbor but, on the other, they love them and feel sorry for them. They feel as if they are their brothers held in captivity, their own flesh and blood suffering from oppression, poverty, and injustice. That is why they have chosen what can be called the German option—a peaceful reunification and tolerance.

It is not easy for them. Multiple border incidents annoy and upset them but they are still holding firm to that path and are not going to abandon it. And lately they were not afraid to contradict the United States and take a stand against their ally in this particular issue. For example, when in November 2006 President Bush asked South Korean President Roh Moo-hyun to support the Proliferation Security Initiative—a voluntary international program that calls for stopping ships suspected of trafficking weapons of mass destruction—the South Korean President politely refused saying that they supported the principles and goals of the program but were not going to participate in it.

Some in the West see in Seoul's actions just the fear of war and retaliation by the North. The fear is definitely there as well. But if one talks to the South's citizens—it is clear that it is just a secondary emotion. The main consideration is the eventual and peaceful reunification of the Korean nation. And any step that may work against that goal is unacceptable for them. Even when they are thinking of a possibility of a war, it is not only the fear of casualties and destruction but also an uncomfortable feeling about the Americans (however close an ally they may be) killing their brothers and sisters in the North. And this emotion does not sit well with the South Koreans.

Actually, the South has a clear plan that they have been executing for years and have been amazingly successful. They managed to convince the North authorities to institute although extremely limited but still economic reforms. They were working on creating joint ventures with DPRK's state-owned enterprises. They finally organized programs where relatives can travel across the border and visit each other. A sensation happened during the 2006 Winter Olympic Games that gave hope to all the people on Earth. The participants from both states marched together during official ceremonies as one team of one nation from one country.

South Korea's plan in relation to the North is clear: to open them bit-by-bit by involving them in international trade and cooperation, to widen contacts and promote their way of life in DPRK using culture and economy rather than subversive operations. That is why they like so much Chinese and Russian proposals of incorporating the North into the entire peninsula's gas and electricity energy systems. They believe that it would be a great step toward eventually getting Pyongyang involved into normal trade and business activities. The ultimate goal is to achieve a peaceful and volunteer reunification of the entire Korean peninsula the way it was done in Germany. (We have to remember that East Germany was also a tough state with strong military and Stasi—but was successfully and peacefully integrated into the democratic world.) And every setback on this way is very painful for the South Koreans because they worked so hard and have already achieved so much. That is why when they hear that somebody says that one cannot talk to the North—they start thinking that, probably, that person just does not want to talk to their neighbor.

Japan

Japan is one of the countries whose involvement into the process made it, probably, more difficult than it should have been. The main motivator behind their actions is fear of a nuclear attack that is absolutely understandable from the historical point of view. But the problem is that the fear they experience reached irrational, almost paralyzing proportions. The whole nation is in panic. In 2006 in Japan the mostly sought after types of houses were those that could withstand a nuclear blast—that was the level of hysteria and fear over the DPRK's nuclear program. And, of course, when panic is taking over it is very difficult to think straight and to analyze the situation calmly and logically. It is much easier to take a belligerent stance and to start threatening the opponent. And this is exactly what they have been doing.

They threatened to reconsider their constitution and to increase their military force. They reiterated many times that they would not shy away from using it against the North. In 2006 they started talking about acquiring nuclear weapons themselves. They have been supporting the toughest economic and political sanctions against Pyongyang. They actually imposed their own unilateral and independent sanctions—full ban on North Korean imports into Japan, no Japanese visas for DPRK officials, and no southern ships in Japanese ports or territorial waters. In short, such a position usually does not create the necessary environment of trust and security.

In one respect they are right—North Koreans indeed do not have very warm feelings toward them. But the roots of those emotions are not ideological but historical. If we remember what kind of atrocities the Japanese committed in Korea during World War II we will understand those emotions. But

Japan never admitted any fault and never apologized for what they did. In 1990 they expressed regret for their actions during World War II but never officially apologized. Their school history textbooks do not even cover the subject of the carnage they caused in that part of the world that makes angry not only the Koreans but also the Chinese.

And this is where North and South are absolutely united. South Korean President Roh Moo-hyun in 2006 asked Japan to apologize and consider paying compensation for what they did in the past. But again no response came from Tokyo. And the North Korean missile that flew over their country in 1998, perhaps, made them think about a payback for their sins of the past. But instead of apologizing and trying to find some solution to the problem they became extremely aggressive scaring actually both Koreas into thinking about a resurgence of Japanese militarism. Definitely, such an idea does not help the cause of disarmament.

Certainly, the Japanese have their own grievances against the North. For example, the problem of the Japanese citizens abducted by the DPRK's secret services must be solved in accordance with all the international laws and Pyongyang must come clean and release all the information pertaining to the issue. But the problem is that Japan ties this question to the subject of nuclear disarmament. And this is not an appropriate thing to do. After all, the North does not require Japanese World War II-related apologies before it starts talking about their missile program. Tying such contentious issues to a serious problem makes, as a rule, that problem practically unsolvable. This problem must be solved later on with the involvement of international community but only after the nuclear disarmament agreement is reached and trust and cooperation are established. Then it will be possible, appropriate, and much easier to do.

In 2006 the tensions between North Korea and Japan became so bad that they threatened the negotiation process itself. Actually, DPRK said that it felt uncomfortable seeing Japan at the negotiation table citing their aggressive position and their historical role in the region. To some people, it may sound strange but it may be a good idea to make Japan sort of a silent partner in the negotiations keeping their face-to-face contact with both Koreas' representatives to a minimum. Such an approach is not going to hurt Japanese interests but it may help the process of negotiations.

First of all, the Japanese position is too aggressive to help the talks. Secondly, their point of view is well known to everybody and entirely coincides with the position of the United States on the subject. Finally, (as a consequence of the second point) the Japanese have an ally at the negotiation table who can protect their interests—the Americans. They have already provided an actual missile defense for the Japanese—so, they can also look after their interests at the negotiating table. It may be similar to the Iranian nuclear negotiations where

Israel (an interested party) is not officially a part of the talks and is not present at the negotiating table (to avoid annoying Iran) but is a silent partner whose interests are protected by the United States of America.

Other Countries

China has three reasons for participating in the talks: to prevent a war and a possible nuclear fallout right on their border, to avoid millions of refugees that would flood the country if something bad happens in the North, and to help their traditional ally—the DPRK. Definitely, they are not going to support any military action that could lead to a war or to any serious economic sanctions that could lead to a humanitarian crisis in Pyongyang. They provide the North with many things that actually keep that country alive—oil, electricity, some important food products, etc. So, one would assume that they would have a substantial leverage over DPRK's foreign policy. So, have they thought until recently. But the North Koreans turned out to be more stubborn than had been expected, trying to slip out from under Chinese influence.

Certainly, it would be effective if China could be a guarantor of the North Korean safety and security. But it would require on the Chinese side a commitment to go to war with the United Sates in case the North is attacked. And this is something the Chinese are not willing to do for two reasons. First of all, they do not exactly trust their ally. They are afraid that if Pyongyang feels the "big guy's" support behind its back it can do something foolish and draw them into a war. Secondly, looking at the Bush administration's actions they sincerely believe that the Americans can easily start a war as well. And according to some recent public pronouncements by some Chinese generals—the Chinese are quite afraid of the American military power and consider themselves inferior to the Americans in this respect. For example, one of the high-level Chinese generals said that China would not have any chance to win a conventional war against the United States and, therefore, would have to use its nuclear weapons to fight the US.

Finally, recently the Chinese have been frustrated by the DPRK's position toward their common history. They lost literally hundreds of thousands of solders during the Korean War fighting for the North. But recently, Pyongyang's interpretation of those events amazed them. In their textbooks Koreans diminish the significance of the Chinese contribution to the war effort and made it look as if they "won" that war on their own. This is something that upsets the Chinese quite a lot. And, as we will see a little bit later, this is not the only historical dispute that plays a role in this very contemporary problem. That is why we could say that the Chinese security guarantees for the North would be very helpful but, probably, are not forthcoming.

Russia entered the negotiations for two reasons. First of all, they want to be involved into something that is going on right on their border. (They share a tiny border with DPRK—just nineteen kilometers or less than twelve miles.) The second reason is the one of prestige. They want to convince the rest of the world (and partly themselves) that they are coming back into the superpower league and that everybody has to take their opinion into consideration. At the same time, they have almost no leverage over North Korea. They suggested to provide it with some energy resources but only if the South will pay for them.

What is interesting here is that the general mood in the country is quite anti-American and pro-North Korean. After what happened in Kosovo and Iraq, most Russians sincerely believe that the most dangerous country on Earth is the United Sates and not Iran or DPRK. They honestly think that since the US is attacking everybody the only thing Pyongyang can do is to sacrifice the last piece of bread for the security of the country. (And nobody knows better about sacrificing the last piece of bread for security than the Russians. Throughout their history they had to do it a lot.) Therefore, they are feeling quite strong sympathy for the North Koreans. They look at them as David fighting Goliath. There were even calls from some nationalists to help Pyongyang to develop nuclear weapons.

Fortunately, the Russian government maintains its policy of nonproliferation and insists on the nuclear disarmament on the Korean peninsula. But, at the same time, it is difficult to expect any real help from them (they cannot and, probably, do not want to do a lot). They will, definitely, not support any tough measures against DPRK. They would rather emphasize peace, diplomacy, and cooperation. They also support the idea of the peaceful reunification of both Koreas. This is where they found a strong alliance with the South.

European countries are not officially a party to the six-party talks but they participated in some aspects of the process. For example, the European Union is an official participant of KEDO. Having analyzed the European press, it is interesting to note that it is very hard to find any serious debates, opinions, or statements on the North Korean problem. If North Korea is mentioned, it is usually in the same sentence with the Iranian nuclear program. It seems that the geographical location of the problem may have an effect on the degree of involvement of the Europeans into the issue. Since Pyongyang's missiles cannot reach them—they feel safe and do not care about the problem too much. In Great Britain, for example, it appears if there is more concern about the human rights situation in North Korea than about their nuclear program. Also, there was a lot of material in the European press about the problem up to the year 2003. However, after that, Europe's attention to the issue gradually decreased and by mid-2006 it was hard to find any actual statements pertaining to the topic in the European media. It seems that this problem was put on the back burner in that part of the world. Therefore, it is difficult to expect from them any active participation or actual help (for example, in the form of financial contributions) on the subject matter. They are also all against any type of military solution of the problem but for economic sanctions and further negotiations.

Theoretical Analysis

The Rational Actor Model

It is very difficult to use the rational actor model to find a solution to the problem of North Korea because, as it was shown above, there is very little rational about the behavior of all the parties involved in the issue. The use of game-theory matrices is practically impossible here. The problem is that estimates of parties' payoffs in those matrices often represent nothing more than personal biases and convictions of the people who draw them.

The author of this book saw quite a few matrices depicting the North Korean problem in Western literature (mostly American because they are the biggest fans of this type of analysis). If one looks at those matrices he or she would definitely get the impression that the North Koreans are either really very stupid (because they are not capable of seeing their own interests) or inherently evil (because regardless of clear advantages of disarmament they keep making problems to the world community). Generally speaking, according to such matrices the nuclear disarmament would bring the North a payoff of +100 because they would get safety, food, oil, and maybe even democracy. At the same time, getting nuclear weapons would get them a payoff of −100 because it would mean isolation, sanctions, hunger, and even probably military action. How can't they see it? Indeed how?

The problem is that those analysts just put their prejudices in the numerical form without any regard for reality. They fail to see that even when Pyongyang cooperated the flood of goods promised by the other side never materialized—even the two promised LWRs were not delivered. Secondly, they definitely do not know (or do not want to know) how people of the North feel—scared, angry, cheated. The North Koreans would draw a different matrix if they could or would want to do such a thing. For them, having nuclear weapons means safety and respect (+100 payoff) while disarmament means fear and possibly death (−100 payoff). They are sure that the "evil imperialists" (American and Japanese) will deceive them, attack them, kill them, and enslave them (as they recently did with Iraq). Under these circumstances they see nuclear weapons as the only guarantee of their independence, security, and freedom (however misguided from our point of view it may be). That

is they are not stupid or evil—they simply have their own historical and political experiences and their own logic.

In short, it would be nice to be able to use the rational actor model in this
case and find a solution in a two-by-two matrix but it is simply impossible. In
this highly irrational and emotional dispute we will have to use alternative
ways of analysis trying to find a solution.

Cognitive and Learning Theories

What the main sides have learned so far about each other is not encouraging for both of them (Americans and North Koreans). Consequently, if their
perceptions changed at all—unfortunately, they became even more negative,
extreme, and polarized. The main sides did not stick to their commitments
and violated agreements quite a few times. Both expressed mistrust and even
hatred for each other. Both parties learned that it would not be a good idea to
trust the other side and that concessions would not, probably, lead to recipro-
cation. They do not understand and do not want to understand each other's
positions, ideas, and perceptions. The process of demonization of the enemy
is going at full swing in both countries. At a larger scale, they do not even recognize the right of the other side to exist (as a political system). But the worst
thing is that the further negotiations are going—the further they are becoming entrenched in their belligerent positions.

Certainly, these stereotypes must be broken in order to reach an agreement
between the parties. But the problem is that such clichés can be destroyed only
by actions—neither simple words nor crafty propaganda can do it. That is, the
sides will have to find a way to build some trust by mutually beneficial and reciprocal actions. They will have to show each other that they can stick to their
commitments and fulfill their obligations. Unfortunately, so far there seems to
be no political will to do so on either side. Both sides prefer the language of
ultimatums and threats. When they speak this way they believe that they look
tougher on the international scene and earn some political capital at home.
But continuing to do so may spell out the death of any hope to reach an agreement.

The Psychological Point of View

This theory, with the emphasis on the personalities of the people involved
in negotiations, may give us some hints as to what can be done to improve the
chances of these talks for success.

If under President Clinton the negotiations were moving at least somewhere (at least the sides were talking) under President George W. Bush the

talks broke down and stopped. His personality has a lot to do with this fact. His uncompromising character and plain-speaking style contributed significantly to the breakdown of the negotiations.

He sincerely believes that the "bad guys" have to just give up and quietly disappear from the face of the Earth. The only thing he agrees to negotiate on with those people is the terms of their surrender (and even there he would not give them a lot of leeway). When for some reason they refuse to surrender he gets a shot of noble indignation and resorts to threats and name-calling. Compromise is not a part of his political toolbox. In his black-and-white world white must always win over black and to compromise with black means sullying the white. (It is actually a very interesting and specific feature of the American English where the word "compromise" means to damage something—like in "to compromise security.") Even in our everyday life we would not probably deal with a person who constantly insults us and, at the same time, demands from us different things without giving anything in return. Therefore, it will be a safe bet to say that while he is in power—any success is extremely unlikely.

On the other side—Mr. Kim Jong-Il—remains mostly a mystery for the rest of the world. He may be as much a hawk as President Bush (only in the DPRK sense of this world—a Communist hawk). Or he may be a moderate politician taken hostage by his own military. Unfortunately, cornered by the Bush administration policies from the very beginning, he had no chance to actually demonstrate his character traits. Besides that, the closed nature of the North Korean state prevents us from getting more reliable personal information about him (except, of course, for the unverifiable propaganda that the Western secret service gladly provide to the Western media).

That is, in order to find his personal vulnerabilities and points of psychological contact it is necessary first to talk to him in a normal tone of voice close and personal. His stern father, Kim Il-sung, showed that he was able to make compromises after talking to moderate people—namely, President Carter. Who knows, maybe his son is capable of doing the same. Too bad nobody tried to talk to him like that. That is why the first recommendation would be to appoint as an intermediary a moderate politician who has respect, authority, and trust at the international level. Former Presidents Carter or Clinton, for example, could serve as such intermediaries. But it is necessary to choose the one who does not have any prejudice against Kim Jong-Il, which is difficult after the tsunami of propaganda directed personally against the North Korean leader. Certainly, at the same time, President Bush would have to refrain from further insulting and threatening proclamations against North Korea.

Another hawkish politician who may have a negative effect on the talks is the new prime minister of Japan—Shinzo Abe. It is not to say that he has to be entirely removed from the negotiations (after all, Japan has a right to be represented and to protect its interests). But his personal contacts with North Korean officials and his political rhetoric have to be carefully monitored. Or another—more moderate—Japanese official has to talk on behalf of Japan on the issue.

The most reasonable and calm parties involved in the talks are Hu Jintao of China, Roh Moo-hyun of South Korea, and Vladimir Putin of Russia. They do not have any particular emotional attachment to any person or idea. They are just working hard trying to prevent a war, a nuclear fallout, and a refugee crisis right on their borders. They made quite a few suggestions for solving the problem. And one of the few correct things that President Bush started doing by the end of 2006—he started relying more and more on these participants of the talks to put pressure on DPRK. But again, pressure means action—nor just words. These three gentlemen can talk to Kim Jong-Il as much as they want trying to convince him to give up nuclear weapons. But everything will be in vain if real actions are not undertaken. That is, all the parties involved must, so to speak, "bite the bullet" and provide some money, reach some agreements and actually start doing something to convince Pyongyang to cooperate. And here the lead must be taken by the Chinese and the South Koreans—the allies and brothers of the North. They are rich, powerful, and technologically advanced enough to provide substantial incentives and guarantees to DPRK to once again set in motion the negotiations that hopelessly stalled by the end of 2006.

Problem-solving and Joint Decision-making Points of View

Problem-solving and joint decision-making perspectives are the only approaches that can produce a positive result. All the sides have to realize that, in essence, all of them have one common problem that brought them to the negotiating table—security. Americans, Japanese, South and North Koreans are fighting over the same matter—safety of their people and their states. If they realize it they can get together and try to solve the problem jointly. After all, Henry Kissinger managed to broker peace between two mortal enemies—Israel and Egypt. It is just necessary to decompose the problem into elements and define sides' interests.

The United States of America is concerned with two things:

- a possibility of a nuclear attack from North Korea on their territory or the territory of their allies;
- a possibility that nuclear technology and materials will get into the hands of terrorists by the way of North Korea.

The Japanese and South Koreans are also concerned with a possibility of a nuclear attack on their territories. All these concerns can be easily and entirely eliminated by a simple solution—denuclearization of the North. But it is easier said than done. As it was mentioned above, any heavy-handed approach will produce the result exactly opposite from the intended one.

Now, it is necessary to figure out what North Korea is afraid of and what it needs to start cooperating with the international community. North Korea also has two major concerns:

- a possibility of a military attack from the United States on their territory;
- a possibility of domestic political turbulence and violence incited by American subversive actions.

That is they are interested first of all in the survival of their political regime and the country as it exists at the present time.

The Chinese and the Russians are just interested in avoiding a war, nuclear fallout, and a refugee crisis right on their borders. So, they will be satisfied with any peaceful solution that leads to a more stable region. And the denuclearization of the Korean peninsula is a good starting point—something they will be glad to work toward.

The most vulnerable side in the entire puzzle is North Korea. They are small, poor, isolated, and surrounded by enemies (as they perceive it). The least vulnerable (or rather, so far, not vulnerable at all) is the United States. Therefore, it is up to the U.S. to establish trust and make the first steps in the sequence. They have to do three things:

- drop their insistence on complete, verifiable, and irreversible disarmament as a precondition for negotiations;
- to sign an official pact that would clearly state that as long as North Korea officially and practically maintains its nonnuclear status the US will not attack it;
- remove North Korea from the list of state sponsors of terrorism and stop financing subversive actions on their territory (removal from the terrorist list will be important for phase II—aid and assistance).

North Korea has to reciprocate in the following way:

- declare that they are going to come back to their nonnuclear status (that is, eventually joining NPT once again);
- verifiably freeze all of their nuclear research and military programs (in exchange for shipments of alternative types of fuels—heavy oil, for example);
- "verifiably" means to allow IAEA inspectors back into the country.

That would be phase I. Phase II has to make sure that the agreement this time is actually implemented and the entire process is irreversible. The whole idea does not make any sense without phase II—full and verifiable denu-clearization of the North. But this time it has to be done right—in an orderly manner—without putting the carriage before the horse. This is where the international community has to come into play because even the richest country on Earth cannot afford to do it on its own.

First of all, an international fund holding billions of dollars (up to $10 billion for LWRs, nuclear fuel removal, oil, food, etc.) has to be established and be completely filled up before phase II can even start. Everybody has to chip in—even Europeans—if they really care about world peace and security.

Second, LWRs must be built and operational before North Korea's old reactors are dismantled. It will provide an uninterrupted supply of electricity to the North's economy. In this case they will have nothing to complain about in this respect.

Third, the old DPRK's nuclear reactors and their other nuclear facilities have to be completely dismantled, nuclear fuel must be removed, taken out of the country and either safely stored or reprocessed outside of North Korea (for example, in Russia).

Fourth, for the first few years the country must be given food and fuel assistance to sustain its economy and social order. Later on, technological assistance must be provided to take the country away from its dependence on such international aid. This is why the removal from the terrorist list is so important—otherwise, such help may be legally impossible.

Five, it is vital to integrate North Korea into the regional economy with the help of the Chinese, Russians, and South Koreans. South Korean joint ventures, the Chinese pipeline, and Russian electricity projects are very good starting points for this process. It is also necessary to allow Pyongyang access to the International Monetary Fund, World Bank, and other international financial institutions.

Six, it is necessary to set up normal trade and diplomatic relations with the South (like it was done with Vietnam). It will establish trust and a sense of security between the countries and create an open channel of communication to solve problems.

Seven, it is important to promote social and economic reforms in DPRK not through pressure and subversive actions but through economic integration and friendly influence exerted by China and South Korea. Some could say that all this is too idealistic. Not at all. It is enough to look at Vietnam and the United States. The former enemies normalized their trade and diplomatic relations and are having active and mutually beneficial business ties. In 2006 Vietnam was approved as an official member of the World Trade Organization and became fully integrated into the world market system. The example of Eastern Europe also shows that political reforms are often conjoint with economic integration and the disappearance of the environment of fear.

All these steps have to eventually bring North Korea back into the world community as it happened with Vietnam or East Germany. Whether the Koreas will be reunited or not it is for them to decide. But even if it will not happen soon—at least, we will have a safe and secure environment on the peninsula for a foreseeable future. Certainly, all this will require a lot of patience, time, and money. But this is the only possible and right way to do it. Surely, there will be problems on the way. The reaction of North Korean leadership (especially the military) to the attempts to disarm them and integrate them into the "terrible capitalist" world is unpredictable. On the other side, the tendency of the American Congress to play politics and try to earn domestic political capital by appearing tough on the "enemies" instead of actually thinking about solving problems is another big obstacle on the way to a "happy end" because it is exactly the American parliamentarians who will have to approve the funding for all the programs above. And we can only hope that this time all the sides will use common sense and put safety and security ahead of their political ambitions and considerations of power.

Unfortunately, some recent events showed that the considerations of domestic politics may still play the decisive role in this problem. In the beginning of 2007 the United States were supposed to unfreeze $24 million of North Korean money in exchange for their mothballing of the Yongbyon reactor. The Americans also established the deadline for the North to stop the reactor—the end of April. But what followed can be characterized only as political theater. First, Americans dragged out the release of the money until the last minute and then blamed Pyongyang for not stopping the reactor on time and not observing the deadline. But even when the U.S. was forced by the pressure from the international community to release the money from Banko Delta Asia in Macao—they threatened with sanctions any bank in the world that would dare actually take money from there. Consequently, nobody did. The North did not get the money and the agreement failed once again. All this quite clearly shows that at least the Bush administration is not interested in and in reality is not working toward a solution of the problem. It seems that they are not actually afraid of North Korea but prefer to keep it as a nuclear scarecrow out there (as something to replace the Soviet Union as the face of the enemy) for domestic political purposes—to justify to the American people their tight and aggressive policies in the United States and overseas and, consequently, to justify even bigger military appropriations bills.

Certainly if the conclusion above is true, the future of the talks can be only characterized as fuzzy and gloomy.

7

The Iranian Nuclear Problem
Multilateral Negotiations

THE PROBLEM OF THE IRANIAN NUCLEAR PROGRAM is different from the one of North Korea. In this case not everything is so clear-cut. For example, Iran is a member of the nuclear Non-Proliferation Treaty (NPT) and never officially abandoned its nonproliferation obligations. Tehran also many times officially proclaimed their rejection of the very idea of acquiring nuclear weapons. Some Iranian officials even claim that weapons of mass destruction in general are against the religion of Islam. Finally, all the intelligence services in the world believe that Iran, unlike North Korea, has no nuclear weapons at their disposal and it does not even have any radioactive material—weapons-grade plutonium or highly-enriched uranium (HEU)—to make the weapons. Their long-range missile technology is practically nonexistent. Their medium-range missile technology is a cheap derivative of an old North Korean missile. And the question is: What's the big deal with Iran? Why are so many countries on Earth so worried about its nuclear technology which is, according to official Iranian claims, an entirely peaceful energy program? The problem here is rather political. What makes people worry is the nature of the Iranian government and even more—the ties and alliances that government maintains.

Iran is an Islamic republic and its official ideology is Islam. There is nothing wrong with that. And as it will be discussed in the culture chapter later on in this book—it is, probably, the best and most appropriate type of government for that country. It definitely enjoys a high level of support of its population. It keeps the country quite stable from the political and security points of view and provides for a solid economic growth. But the problems start to emerge when it comes to their foreign policy dogmas, politicians who are currently conducting that policy, and some of the associates they support on the international arena.

One of the officially proclaimed foreign policy doctrines of Iran is that the state of Israel has no right to exist. It was proclaimed quite a few times by several Iranian leaders that they were ready to work tirelessly to make sure that the Jewish state disappears forever from the political world map. After Mahmoud Ahmadinejad was elected President of Iran in June of 2005 the world's worries about stability in the region only increased. He made several statements that showed his extreme anti-Israeli position—calling for destruction of the state of Israel. Finally, there is a long-standing association between Iran and such international extremist Islamic organizations as Hezbollah and Hamas. Although some countries do not recognize them as terrorist organizations, pretty much everybody agrees on at least their extremist character and propensity to violence. The Israelis like nobody else know how brutal these two organizations can be. And since the two do not recognize Israel as a legal international entity and proclaim the destruction of the Jewish state as their main political goal—their alliance with Iran makes the situation in the region extremely tense.

So, some countries fear that if Iran masters nuclear weapons technology it can transfer it to its allies who in turn could use it against Israel. The next possible course of events is that in case of an Israeli crackdown on Hezbollah and Hamas or a large-scale Arab-Israeli conflict Iran could use its medium-range missiles tipped with nuclear warheads to strike Israel. So far, both of these suggestions are in the realm of fantasy but to be on the safe side almost everybody in the world would prefer to have Iran as a state that does not have nuclear weapons technology.

At the same time, Iran, as anybody else in the world, can use nuclear technology for electrical power production. They are allowed to have it under Article 4 of the Non-Proliferation Treaty (NPT). But everybody knows that the borderline between peaceful and military nuclear research is blurry. Therefore, the situation is very delicate. On the surface it is not dangerous. But the presence on the background of some extremist organizations makes the situation potentially explosive—in the most direct sense of this word.

As usual, before the analysis it is important to see how the issue has been developing so far and what elements of the situation are important for further examination.

Development of the Issue

In order to understand all the issues involved in the problem it is necessary to start in 1951 when Mohammad Mossadeq, a strong nationalist leader, was

democratically elected the prime minister of Iran. He almost immediately—
in April—nationalized the country's oil industry, which was mostly owned by
Western interests. In August 1953 Mossadeq was overthrown in a coup engi-
neered by the British and American intelligence services. General Fazlollah
Zahedi was proclaimed the prime minister and the Shah returned to the country. In 1959 the Shah started thinking about a nuclear program. So, in 1967
the United States supplied him with a 5-megawatt research nuclear reactor. In
the same year the Tehran Nuclear Research Center (TNRC) was established,
run by the Atomic Energy Organization of Iran (AEOI).

But, at the same time, the West did not want to see Iran possessing nuclear
weapons. Therefore, in 1968 Iran signed the Non-Proliferation Treaty (NPT)
and in 1970 ratified it. In exchange for their cooperation the Iranians received
an avalanche of nuclear-related knowledge and technologies coming to them
from the West.

In 1975 Henry Kissinger, US Secretary of State at that time, signed the National Security Decision Memorandum 292 entitled "U.S.-Iran Nuclear Cooperation" that outlined the US administration's negotiating strategy for the
sale of nuclear energy equipment to Iran which was supposed to bring US
companies more than $6 billion. But the Americans were not the only ones
who wanted to profit from the Iranian desire to acquire nuclear technology. In
the same year, a German firm—Kraftwerk-Union A.G.—signed a contract
worth between $4 and $6 billion to build a nuclear power plant in Bushehr.
Feeling the heat of competition, the Americans again threw their hat into the
ring. In 1976 President Gerald Ford signed a directive giving Tehran a chance
to buy and operate a US-built reprocessing facility for extracting plutonium
from nuclear reactor fuel. That is, while dealing with a puppet regime, Western governments and companies hurried to profit from the Iranian oil money
offering them all types of nuclear technologies—even those that were supposed to directly lead to nuclear weapons (at least, it is usually the main purpose for the plutonium reprocessing equipment). At that time they were not
asking why Iran would need nuclear energy while it had so much oil. At that
time Henry Kissinger strongly believed that nuclear energy was absolutely
necessary for the growing Iranian economy. At that time Dick Cheney, Donald Rumsfeld, and Paul Wolfowitz were among the key masterminds behind
the US-Iranian nuclear cooperation.

But everything changed in 1979. By then, the Shah managed to alienate almost everybody except for his overseas sponsors. People and business communities of the country were not happy that he almost entirely gave the control
over the Iranian riches to the foreign interests. Religious leaders were unhappy
with his reckless pro-Western reforms without any regard for the local culture.
So, during the late 1960s the Shah became increasingly dependent on the Secret

Police (SAVAK) in controlling those opposition movements critical of his re-form policies. The reign of terror unleashed by SAVAK provoked strikes and mass demonstrations all over the country. The flame of public discontent was also stoked by Ayatollah Ruhollah Khomeini, a religious leader who by then had lived in exile for fourteen years. His main political tool was a set of recoded sermons distributed in the country on regular audiocassettes. Thanks to those messages, he became a spiritual leader of the resistance movement.

After many riots and street battles with police, on January 16, 1979, the Shah and his family fled the country. In two weeks—on February 1st—Ayatollah Khomeini triumphantly came back to Iran. And on April 1st, following a referendum, Iran was proclaimed the Islamic Republic. Almost immediately, rumors of an upcoming renationalization of the oil industry started to circulate (which indeed happened in January 1980).

Just four months after that—in July of the same year—the German Kraftwerk-Union company stopped building the power plant in Bushehr, officially, as a result of overdue Iranian payments on the project. Around the same time, Americans stopped shipping spare parts for F-14 Tomcat jet fighters sold previously by the U.S. to the Shah. Simultaneously, the U.S. froze $567 million of Iranian assets in American banks. That is the West increased pressure on the Islamic regime.

Soon after his escape from Iran the Shah was admitted into the U.S. for a cancer treatment. And although his disease was real, that news provoked an outrage in the Islamic Republic. The Iranians demanded his extradition back into the country for trial and did not believe in the reality of his illness. All this provoked the infamous hostage crisis that lasted for 444 days—November 4, 1979, to January 20, 1981. After that, the animosity between the U.S. and Iran reached its highest point.

But for Iran the situation became even worse on September 22, 1980—when Iraq attacked it and an eight-year-long Iran-Iraq war started. America immediately sided with Iraq and imposed a naval blockade of the Persian Gulf, by so doing, curtailing Iran's oil export capabilities. The war itself also severely damaged the Iranian oil industry and the infrastructure of the country. So, Iranians started searching for alternative sources of energy—once again exploring the idea of nuclear power.

Even during the war they kept working on some of their nuclear projects. They also cooperated with international organizations in this area. For example in 1983 IAEA experts inspected Iran's nuclear facilities and reported on proposed cooperation agreement to help Iran manufacture enriched uranium fuel for their future power stations. At that time, it was not considered to be a crime.

But, certainly, the actual work started only after the war was over in July 1988. Since Western companies and governments did not want to cooperate with the Islamic regime the country started to look for help elsewhere. In 1990 Iran and Russia began negotiations regarding the reconstruction of the Bushehr project. In 1995 they signed an $800 million contract to resume work on the partially completed power plant. In response, the United States imposed sanctions on Iran as a punishment for their determination to pursue their nuclear development program.

In 1996 China and Iran informed the IAEA about their plans to construct a nuclear enrichment facility in the Islamic Republic. And in 1996 China sold to Iran some enrichment plant equipment and even provided gas for the uranium enrichment process.

But the current stage of the crisis can be traced back to the year 2002. In January of that year President George W. Bush included Iran in the "axis of evil" causing anti-American outrage in Tehran. In September of the same year, the Russians started construction works on the site in Bushehr despite American objectives. In August 2002 some defectors accused Iran of the existence of two undeclared nuclear sites in the country—at Natanz and Arak. The US immediately ceased the opportunity and accused Iran of attempting to make nuclear weapons. Iran rejected all the claims and accusations and declared that it strictly observed all the NPT's provisions.

But as a result of that discussion in June 2003 the head of IAEA Mohamed El Baradei asked Iran to sign an addendum of the Non-Proliferation Treaty, which would allow for unannounced inspections of nuclear facilities by the IAEA officials. The addendum was signed in December 2003 and sent to Majlis (the Iranian Parliament) for ratification. In October 2003 Iran started negotiations with IAEA about the nuclear inspections stipulated in the addendum. As a result of the talks the Islamic Republic was supposed to stop its uranium enrichment program and declare all the nuclear-related sites in the country—they did both on October 31st. Soon after that—on November 11th—IAEA officially declared that there was no evidence that Iran was attempting to build nuclear weapons.

But when the actual inspections began, some problems emerged. In June 2004 El Baradei accused Iran of less than satisfactory cooperation during the IAEA's investigation of its nuclear program. In response to the pressure—on July 27, 2004—the Iranians broke the IAEA's seals placed on their uranium centrifuges. Just four days later they announced that they were planning to build more centrifuges to enrich uranium. At the same time, they emphasized the peaceful character of their program. They said that the uranium would be enriched up to no more than 3.6 percent U-239 level—that is, the point where it is enough to run a nuclear power plant but not enough for a nuclear weapon (the nuclear weapons threshold is over 93 percent of U-239).

But the West did not trust the Muslims. The political rhetoric in the West became more harsh and threatening. Rumors of either American or Israeli precision air strikes against Iranian nuclear facilities appeared in the media. In response, in August 2004, Kamal Kharrazi, Iranian Foreign Minister, said that his country would use force against Israel or any other country that would attempt a preemptive strike against its nuclear facilities. Next month, Iranian officials announced that they would not accept any limitations on Iran's uranium enrichment plans by any international body because the right for nuclear power is a sovereign right of the Iranian nation and the enrichment program is an important ingredient of their peaceful energy development agenda.

As usual, excessive pressure led to a boomerang effect. On September 19, 2004, Majlis refused to ratify the addendum to the Non-Proliferation Treaty sent to them a year earlier. The idea of unannounced IAEA inspections of Iranian nuclear sites was dead.

At the same time, Tehran tried to maintain diplomatic communication lines with at least the European countries. In October 2004, the Iranians announced that they were willing to negotiate with the so-called EU-3 (France, Germany, and Great Britain) general nuclear security issues. In November they even voluntarily but temporarily suspended their uranium enrichment process as a gesture of good will. In response, the Europeans made a proposal to provide Iran with civilian nuclear technology (light-water reactors) in exchange for the termination of the uranium enrichment program. It meant that the fuel for the reactors would have to also come from the West. Iran refused, citing fears of dependency on its Western partners who had already proven to be very unreliable in the past.

Nevertheless, the November 2004 agreement between Iran and the EU-3 was a remarkable document. In that document Iran officially denounced nuclear weapons and reaffirmed its commitment to the NPT process. It also agreed to fight terrorism—but specifically only Al-Qaeda and Mujahedin-e Khalq. The EU-3 officially recognized the right of Iran to develop a peaceful nuclear program under Article 4 of NPT. But still there was one big outstanding issue—security. Iran needed security guarantees from his negotiation partners and the Europeans agreed to provide them for Iran. But the United States immediately showed the European what they were really worth on the world political scene. Americans immediately reminded them that they were in no position to guarantee anything and if the United States wanted to attack Iran they would do it whether Europeans liked that or not. Since the security was the main issue for Iran—a very promising accord collapsed. It was the highest point in negotiations—since that time the sides have not come closer to a full-scale agreement.

The situation got even more tense from the diplomatic point of view in June 2005 when an ultraconservative politician—Mahmoud Ahmadinejad—won presidential elections in Iran (with almost 62 percent of the votes). His rhetoric proved to be as extreme as that of President Bush. He openly called for the destruction of the State of Israel (like Bush called for the destruction of the Islamic regime in Iran) and threatened to use force against anybody who would threaten Iran or Iranian interests. But what scared most of the world (even Iran's partners—such as China and Russia) was the fact that his rhetoric strongly reminded everybody of the style used by the leaders of Hezbollah and Hamas. At that time, very few people had any doubts that had those organizations asked for military assistance in their fight against Israel and the West—the new Iranian President would have given them everything (possibly even nuclear weapons). In short, the world got scared and reacted accordingly—with irrationally angry rhetoric. Threats were flying in the face of Iran like desert wind carrying sand. Ahmadinejad responded in kind. In that situation no reasonable communication was possible. Negotiations practically broke down.

Under those circumstances, in August 2005, the Iranian government resumed the uranium enrichment process at the Isfahan site. During an IAEA meeting in Vienna on August 9, 2005, Ayatollah Ali Khamenei—Iran's supreme spiritual leader and the country's highest authority—informed the international community that he issued a fatwa (a holy Islamic order) forbidding the production and use of nuclear weapons. In general, several Iranian leaders (including Ahmadinejad) many times officially proclaimed that the weapons of mass destruction in general and nuclear weapons in particular would go against the rules of Islam. Therefore, as they said, Iran—as the Islamic Republic—simply could not pursue nuclear weapons. They constantly emphasized that their nuclear program was 100 percent peaceful.

But the West (in this case including even Russia) wanted to be on the safe side. Probably remembering actions and proclaimed goals of Hezbollah and Hamas (Iran's protégés), in August 2005 the IAEA adopted a resolution calling once again upon Iran to suspend its uranium enrichment processes. That resolution also charged El Baradei with writing a report on Iran's nuclear program by mid-November.

On September 17, 2005, President Ahmadinejad delivered a speech before the Sixtieth Session of the United Nations General Assembly. In that speech he once again highlighted the peaceful character of Tehran's nuclear program and reiterated that Iran had the right to develop a civil nuclear power program under the terms of the Non-Proliferation Treaty. Nevertheless, a couple of days later the Europeans again officially demanded from the International Atomic Energy Agency (IAEA) to bring Iran's case before the United Nations Security Council.

Finally, in mid-November 2005 El Baradei released his report saying that Iran was still blocking inspections. He especially highlighted the Parchin site where, as he suspected, some military nuclear secrets might have been hidden.

The year 2006 started with two events—the inauguration of Iran's new President—Mahmoud Ahmadinejad—and removal of the IAEA's seals at the Natanz nuclear research facility. The Iranians chose to add the uranium enrichment capabilities of this site to the capacity of the Isfahan facility restarted several months earlier.

The Russians decided to try to break the impasse in the talks caused by uncompromising positions and hot political rhetoric of the Iranians and the Western countries (the EU-3 and the US). The Russians admitted that Iran's apprehension in terms of its dependency on other countries for nuclear fuel was justified by the previous history and experience. So, they suggested a compromise. They said that they would be ready to create a joint Russian-Iranian uranium enrichment venture. The facility itself would be located on the Russian territory (or in a neutral country, such as Kazakhstan) but right on the border with Iran. The Iranians would have an equal stake with the Russians (50/50) in all respects—management, decision-making, profit. The facility would be under the supervision of IAEA. The Russians also guaranteed to the rest of the world that they would thoroughly monitor the usage of nuclear fuel. They would know exactly how much fuel was sent to Iran and, after it is spent, they would make sure that every gram of it would be shipped back to Russia for consequent reprocessing or burial. Certainly, the Russians were ready to do all that if the Iranians would be willing to resume IAEA's inspections of their nuclear facilities to make sure that they would not be working on any military projects. It was almost an ingenious idea—an easy way out for everybody, a compromise solution that everybody was waiting for. It would be, practically, an Iranian facility but under international supervision and without any possibility of it being used for military purposes. But weird things started to happen.

First of all, Iran (for whom it would be an easy way out) diplomatically expressed its general interest in the idea but did little to implement it. The Europeans got up in arms, rejected the Russian idea, and once again suggested their reactors and their fuel to Iran. Americans bluntly rejected the idea and demanded from the Russians to stop their work on the Bushehr site. Russians, certainly, refused. The reaction of China to the proposal (if there was any) was so low-profile that it was even difficult to detect at all. It seemed like there were other considerations at play in that situation—that the successful resolution of the problem was not the primary concern for most participants of the talks. This situation will be examined in detail later in this chapter. It is important to find an explanation for such a behavior of some countries—it may shed some light on certain elements of the problem and, consequently, help to find some elements of the solution.

Soon after restarting the Natanz facility, the IAEA voted 27-3 to report Iran to the UN Security Council. The UN Security Council in turn set a thirty-day time period with the deadline on April 28, 2006, for Iran to stop its nuclear fuel program. Iran refused to comply. At the same time, nuclear talks in Austria between EU-3 and Iran failed as well.

Since the Russians had sided with the West while voting against Iran in both the IAEA and the UN, the Iranians retaliated by announcing that the offer to enrich uranium in Russia was no longer an option and that they were starting their own large-scale uranium enrichment operation immediately. The result of their work was announced in April 2006 by President Ahmadinejad. He claimed that Iranian scientists successfully enriched uranium to the level necessary for a nuclear power plant.

In September 2006 at a press conference in the UN headquarters the President of Iran once again reiterated that the Iranians considered nuclear weapons as something contradicting the most deeply held values of the Islamic religion. He also reminded the world that nuclear weapons research was against the law in the Islamic Republic. But the West entirely disregarded his statements.

At the same time, Iran was actively working on its nuclear program and making big steps in its development. In October 2006 Iran launched the second cascade of 160 centrifuges for enriching uranium. In November Ahmadinejad claimed that Iran was going to build one hundred thousand centrifuges more. Exactly at the same time, the Iranians launched their new forty-megawatt Arak reactor. They also asked for IAEA's assistance in providing safety oversight for that facility. And in January 2007 the President of Iran said that Tehran was about to start the industrial-scale production of fuel for nuclear power stations.

Finally, in December 2006 the UN Security Council unanimously adopted Resolution 1737 in which it was supposed to specify sanctions against Iran for its noncompliance with the previous Security Council's resolutions. What came out of it will be discussed later in this chapter but one thing can be said here—that resolution had amazingly little to do with the Iranian nuclear weapons threat.

As its reaction to that resolution Tehran appointed a special governmental committee and charged it with reconsidering Iran's relations with IAEA. So far, they are not talking about the full withdrawal from the organization. It is not clear either what particular aspects of their work with IAEA will be reconsidered. As the first step of that committee in January 2007, thirty-eight specific IAEA inspectors were prohibited from working in the country and inspecting Iranian Nuclear facilities.

Participants and Actors

Let's now consider the positions and interests of each of the country involved in the negotiations process. It will help us understand their actions and find effective approaches to each party while searching for a solution acceptable for everybody.

The United States of America

The Americans have several concerns over Iran's nuclear program. First and most of all they are afraid that nuclear weapons can get in the hands of radical Islamic terrorist organizations. Unlike the case of North Korea, it is necessary to note that in the case of Iran such a course of events is indeed possible. Iran really takes to heart the idea of helping its Muslim brethren all over the world, which is understandable. The problem is that Iran does not care that their brethren may be quite unscrupulous in their methods and techniques. Even mass murder of innocent civilians and little children, as it happened on September 11, 2001, in New York or on September 1, 2004, in Beslan, Russia, is considered to be an acceptable way of conducting operations. And Iran supports them no matter what they do pretty much like the US is supporting Israel no matter what it does. That is, in case of a large-scale Arab-Israel conflict or if the US attacks Iran, Tehran might seriously consider giving nuclear weapons to terrorist groups with a specific purpose in mind—to strike America.

The good thing is that the Iranians do not have a nuclear weapon yet and are not even close to having one. Besides that, they do not have a missile technology to deliver a nuclear warhead to the US either. Therefore, if they would want to bring an atomic bomb into the United States they would have to use the miniature bomb technology—something like a suitcase bomb—a super-complex piece of equipment they will, probably, never have. Americans are also worried that a so-called dirty bomb will be brought into the United States. But for this scenario a country does not even have to have a nuclear program—radioactive materials can be easily obtained on the market all over the world. Certainly, other means of delivery can be used as well. For example, a merchant ship can serve as a carrier for a big nuclear device that could be detonated in a major American port. This is, perhaps, the only viable scenario for the use of nuclear weapons on American territory by terrorists. And the Americans have to do a much better job securing their ports. But the best way to ensure that something like that never happens is to make sure that Iran simply does not have military nuclear technology at all—the idea full-heartedly supported by the rest of the world.

But it is important to emphasize the difference between military and civilian nuclear know-hows. The gap between the 3.6 percent U-239 civilian and the 93 percent U-239 usable military technologies is quite big. Under a proper organization and international supervision a civil nuclear program can be absolutely safe. That is pretty much the only correct course of action to make sure that the international supervision and proper organization are in place. Therefore, every step that leads to a breakdown of international negotiations and international cooperation is logically counterproductive.

The next two US concerns are that Iran would be able to strike American military targets outside of the United States and to hit Israel. Iran's missiles will, probably, not be able to reach American bases in Europe (except for some parts of Germany). But they can easily reach Americans in the Middle East region and definitely can strike Israel. Several remarks can be made here. Besides the fact that Iran still does not have nuclear weapons, it is important to note that the US provides a very sophisticated air-defense system for its own troops in the region as well as for Israel. That system is capable of shooting down all the primitive Iranian missiles long before they could reach their targets. Besides that, as was mentioned in the previous case study, it is very difficult to marry a nuclear warhead to a missile. Therefore, these worries do not have to be on the front line of the issue. If Iran had ever wanted to deliver a nuclear weapon to Israel—a terrorist group would have, probably, been their choice of delivery means. Although, in case of American troops in Iraq or Afghanistan—a World War II bomber would suffice. But again, it is exactly the presence of American troops on the Iranian border what could theoretically trigger such an event. Therefore, if Americans are really worried about such a possibility, good advice would be to simply remove the troops from the Iranian border.

The Americans are also worried that if Iran eventually gets nuclear weapons it might spark a nuclear rush in that very politically and religiously diverse region.

So far, the options the United States has are similar to those in the North Korean case:

- Military action (including precision air-strikes, naval blockade, and full-scale war);
- Hard-line approach or containment (including different types of sanctions);
- Regime change in Iran using special covert subversive operations in the country;

- Accepting status quo;
- Negotiations.

All types of military action are extremely unlikely. Full-scale war is quite improbable, especially as long as the United States is tied-up in Iraq with no end in sight. Secondly, the Iranian army is big (over half-a-million people), quite sophisticated, and extremely well-motivated. It is not going to collapse as fast as the Iraqi army did because the level of corruption among Iranian military is much lower. Such a war could be too costly if feasible at all for America.

The naval blockade of the Persian Gulf is another option. It is a little bit more likely and has already been used by the US against Iran in the past. But there are big problems associated with this option as well. First of all, under the incumbent Iranian president any such blockade is likely to turn into a full-scale war. Second, the international community will never accept such an action as legitimate. Finally, it will have such a drastic effect on the world economy and the United States in particular (by limiting the oil supply and raising oil prices) that it would be first of all a strike against America itself.

Finally, the air strikes option is the most likely one among all the military variants but still is quite unlikely in reality. First of all, like in the case of the naval blockade, air strikes would, probably, trigger a big war. Iran already warned that in this case it would hit American targets in the region and definitely Israel. Secondly, the air strikes may be ineffective. Iran has quite a few nuclear research facilities scattered all over the country. Some of them may be secret and well-hidden. There is no guarantee that every single one of them will be identified, successfully hit, and entirely destroyed. Finally, the Iranians are preparing for such an eventuality. They, for example, recently, bought some sophisticated air-defense systems from the Russians. Therefore, air raids may become pretty costly.

The political hard-line option is also ineffective and counterproductive. First of all, the United States and many other countries have been running different types of sanctions against Iran already for decades. All this does not seem to have had any impact on the regime or its nuclear program that has been flourishing under those sanctions. Actually, it is the sanctions that give an invaluable propaganda tool for Iran to use among its own people and other Muslim nations. Finally, the tough punitive sanctions that the United States are pushing for are likely to further alienate Iran, enrage its people, and push the country even further on the nuclear defense path.

America is also actively pursuing the option of special covert subversive operations in Iran. It funds heavily Iranian antigovernment groups inside as well as outside the country. So far, it has been a waste of taxpayers' money and it, probably, will be that in the future. In order to understand why, I would refer the reader to the culture chapter later on in this book. In short, the American idea that they can be successful in overthrowing the Iranian government system is as wrong as was their idea that they would be greeted as liberators in Iraq. The poor historical record of the American subversive operations in the world over the last fifty years (they can pretty much just claim Chile in 1973) gives little hope to the proponents of such an approach. Over this period of time such operations produced a lot of blood (like in Latin America) but little impact.

The status quo option is not good either for the United Sates or for Iran. Americans do not like the idea that Iran may eventually develop nuclear weapons and deliver them using terrorist organizations or to strike US forces in the Middle East region. The Iranians are tired of living under sanctions, international political pressure, and a threat of war. Therefore, the situation will have to move somewhere. It can develop in two directions. Either alienated and scared Iran indeed starts developing nuclear weapons (in secret and out of sight of international inspectors) or the international community will manage to convince the country that it will be safe and will have more opportunities for further economic development without nuclear weapons and in cooperation with other countries. But for the latter option the negotiations is the only way. Therefore, negotiations are the only sure way to achieve a successful outcome.

Iran

Under the currently existing system the real power in the country belongs not to the President or the parliament but to the council of Ayatollahs who have to validate all the major decisions made at the political level of the power structure. Islam is the guiding principle for the whole society and the state power system. It is, perhaps, the best way to organize the power structure in an Islamic country. The absolute majority of the Iranians are devoted Muslims and cherish their way of life and love their country. After the revolution and the Iran-Iraq war their country fell behind in economic development but recently made substantial progress in this area.

Therefore, Iran perceives three main types of interests in the entire issue. They are:

- The survival of their culture and way of life (including their way of governing themselves);
- Security of their country;
- Economic development.

The whole nuclear program was started, as they argue, for the purpose of economic development. Recently, their economy was growing rapidly. They started feeling a need for more energy production to maintain that pace of growth and the use of nuclear technology seemed to be the best way to reach the goal. They argue that it would be unwise for them to use only their vast oil resources for energy production because, first of all, oil is their main source of state income and they want to save more of it for generations to come and, secondly, because oil is a "dirty" way of making electricity—the one that damages the environment most of all. Besides that, currently Iran uses up to 30 percent of its own oil for domestic power production. That is if they develop an alternative way of making electricity—they could put more oil up for sale on the international market.

The Iranians argue that by working on their nuclear program they violate no provisions of the nuclear Non-Proliferation Treaty and that, in general, they, as any sovereign nation on Earth, have a right to have their own civil nuclear power program. Article 4 of NPT indeed gives them that right officially. Whether their program in reality is entirely peaceful or not is difficult to say because international inspectors have not been working in the country for quite some time already.

They also insist on complete self-reliance in this area of their economy. They do so because they perceive not only a military but also an economic threat coming from the West. They indeed have quite a negative experience dealing with their foreign partners. Just two examples already mentioned above demonstrate it quite well.

When they bought F-14 Tomcat jet fighters in the United Sates they also (as it is always done) purchased a service contract along with the planes. Americans were supposed to provide them with spare parts and help Iranian technicians to service the planes. But as soon as the American puppet Shah regime was overthrown—the flow of spare parts and technical support stopped. And expensive planes were standing at hangars as useless pieces of junk. The same happened when the Germans abandoned the construction of the nuclear plant in Bushehr—another Western promise broken, another partner who withdrew without fulfilling all the obligations entirely (at least, this is how they see it).

So, when they refuse to accept a European offer of both reactors and fuel from Europe—it is understandable. They know that it would make them dependent and in case of any political problem—they would suffer again. This time they chose the most reliable partner of all—themselves.

They also have a right to feel threatened by the United Sates. They saw what happened just on their border—in Iraq. They hear threats from overseas and see American soldiers positioned in the neighboring countries. They also know very well about all the American subversive covert operations in their country. They feel it. The terrorists murder people and detonate bombs in Iran killing civilians quite regularly.

In November 2006, the world mass media circulated stories that the American special forces were running a terrorist training camp in Ashraf, Iraq (just 100 kilometers from the Iranian border) where they trained about three thousand terrorists from Mujahedin-e Khalq (MeK), an Iranian terrorist organization, hoping that those would be successful at overthrowing the Iranian government. There were even reports that some of those terrorists were trained in secret camps on American territory—in Nevada. It is interesting that MeK is officially recognized in the US as a terrorist organization which does not prevent the Americans from working with them. And the funniest thing is that the U.S. Congress allegedly has no knowledge of such operations although this information can be easily accessible on *GlobalSecurity.org* or in *CQ Weekly* as well as through many other media outlets. And MeK is not the only organization the US works with in Iran. Such groups as National Liberation Army of Iran (NLA), People's Mojahedin of Iran (PMOI), and National Council of Resistance (NCR) are also on the list of American beneficiaries. That is the U.S. is doing with those organizations exactly the same that Iran is doing with Hamas or Hezbollah. In this case, it is a little bit hypocritical to criticize Iran for ties with terrorists. (After all, Al-Qaeda was created not in Tehran.) Certainly, all this does not help to promote mutual understanding and trust between Iran and the United States.

Therefore, for the Iranians to feel safe and to negotiate with confidence, it is necessary to provide them with the following conditions:

- They would need to receive strong security guarantees from the United States in some form of pact or an agreement;
- Guarantees that their state structure and form of government would not be challenged and undermined from the West in any way;
- All the subversive operations in Iran and on its borders would have to be stopped;
- The international community would have to officially (in writing) recognize their right to pursue a peaceful civil nuclear power program.

On the other hand, Iran has to also do a lot to convince the international community of its peaceful intentions and to build some confidence in its negotiational partners.

If North Korea is pretty much a small harmless closed country, Iran is much bigger and stronger, it cooperates with extremist organizations and has political influence ambitions in the region. Therefore, as quite a powerful state, they will also have to provide some guarantees to other countries.

First and most of all, they would have to reconsider their relationships with such organizations as Hezbollah and Hamas. It is one of the most difficult points in the entire issue. Hezbollah is a Shiite organization that carried out more than two hundred terrorist attacks since 1982 and killed more than eight hundred people. They receive up to $60 million a year from Tehran. Hamas, on the other hand, is a Sunni group but it still gets from Iran between $20 and $30 million every year.

But the problem is that the Iranians do not recognize these two organizations as terrorist structures. They would argue that they are freedom fighters struggling against oppression of Muslims. They would also point out that both of the organizations are actually political parties that participate in legitimate political processes in some countries (such as Lebanon or Palestinian territories). Their diplomats could argue that those movements provide valuable services to the poor Arab population—such as education or medical care. And it will be true. Up to 90 percent of the work that, for example, Hamas is doing is in social, welfare, cultural, and educational activities. Consequently, the Iranians would say that their money goes exclusively for those peaceful purposes and not for terrorist operations. Certainly, all this is correct except for the last statement. Definitely, money given by the Iranians to these organizations finance educational as well as military projects. And this is a serious problem.

Unfortunately, recently, because of all the noise around the Iranian nuclear issue, perhaps, the most important problem in the region—Iranian support for extremism—was put on the back burner. But this problem needs a serious international effort and cooperation. It cannot be solved easily. A global set of negotiations and a following treaty against support for terrorism could make at least some progress in this area. But this idea will not, probably, find any support among some countries that officially proclaim the fight against terrorism as their main foreign policy objective—namely, the United States, Great Britain, and Israel. The problem is that these countries just love to conduct what they call "covert operations" (a euphemism for terrorist activities) in other countries whose governments they do not like. The Palestinians behave exactly the same way as the Israelis do against them. And the Iranians conduct their fight in exactly the same way as the US and Britain conducted their operations in the Middle East in some cases for centuries. It is a simple game of tit-for-tat. Therefore, until both sides stop training murderers and killing civilians for political purposes—it is difficult to suggest any viable course of action in this respect.

At the same time, there are a couple of things that Iran can and, probably, will have to do in order to help the negotiations succeed:

- It has to accept international supervision of its nuclear program;
- It would also have to provide security guarantees for Israel and the American forces in the region—at least, sign a pledge that it will not strike them first;
- It would also have to officially denounce all the terrorist operations conducted by Muslim extremists and pledge to join the fight against terrorism (as it did in the November 2004 accord with the EU-3).

Russia

This country has, perhaps, the most balanced and helpful position on the issue. It happens to be so because Russians have the deepest and most serious motives to try to solve the problem in a peaceful and mutually beneficial way.

The Russians have three main concerns and, consequently, three concerns arose during these talks:

- The Russians want to make sure that there will be no large-scale military conflict on their southern borders;
- They want to make sure that Islamic terrorists do not have access to nuclear weapons;
- They want to guarantee the security of their economic interests in Iran for a foreseeable future.

The Russians share with Iran a maritime border in the Caspian Sea. They have quite good trade and commercial relations with Iran that are growing in size and importance. In the years 2005 and 2006 only in the area of construction engineering the volume of trade between the two countries reached $1 billion dollars.

Within the last decade or so the Russians started worrying about the appearance on their borders of a series of belligerent, aggressive, and undemocratic states with nationalistic tendencies in their policies, especially, on their Western borders (namely, Latvia, Lithuania, Estonia). Besides that, Poland started making problems for the transit of the Russian exports (mostly oil and natural gas) onto the European market. All that forced them to look for alternative ways of delivering their goods to the West.

One of the projects the Russians have is a big transport corridor that would start in the Russian city of Astrakhan on the Volga River, over the Caspian Sea and through Iran into the Persian Gulf. This way, as they hope, would help them to bypass a barrier of belligerent states in Eastern Europe and to open a new trade gate for Russian products. Certainly, all these plans can come into being only if peace is preserved in the region.

As everybody knows, the Russians had their own share of problems with Islamic terrorism on their territory. Until now they have been working hard to make sure that in their main Islamic republics and regions (such as Tatarstan, Dagestan, or Chechnya) radical Islamic movements do not get a foothold. For them, a radical Islamic terrorist organization with a nuclear weapon is the worst of nightmares. Therefore, they like nobody else are ready to work to make sure that Iran (with its questionable connections) does not get a hold of the nukes.

At the same time, the Russians realize the futility of all the approaches to the problem except negotiations. They recognize the right of Iran to have its own peaceful civil nuclear power program. And they understand that in this situation only Iran's good will and cooperation along with some form of international supervision can make sure that Iran does not develop nuclear weapons. That is why they are so negotiation-oriented and oppose any use of force or tough punitive actions.

Finally, Iran was a solid source of high-tech contracts for the Russian economy. After the collapse of the Soviet Union, Russia was struggling to save its main high-tech industries—such as weaponry, space, and nuclear power. The main challenge was the lack of funding. In these circumstances big foreign contracts were literally lifesavers for many Russian companies. And Iran provided its share of nuclear power and arms contracts for the Russians. Therefore, they cherish their commercial relations with Iran and do not want to alienate it. They also, certainly, are not going to vote for any sanctions that might damage their ongoing cooperation with Tehran.

That is, probably, why the Russians were undertaking the most sincere efforts and following the most peaceful path while dealing with the Iranian issue. They were also the most creative party among all the countries involved in the talks. Their suggestion of creating a uranium enrichment joint venture on the Iranian border had the potential to solve the problem had other countries followed their lead.

They made sure that the power station they built in Bushehr was 100 percent IAEA requirement compliant and absolutely NPT safe. And it seems that they have reached their goal. In late November 2006 the head of IAEA Mohamed El Baradei officially announced that his organization has no problem with the Bushehr site and that the station was built under his agency's supervision and was completely safe and secure.

The Russians also many times reiterated their opposition to the regime change policy conducted by the United States. They suggested involving Iran into discussions on the regional issues as an equal partner and, by so doing, promote cooperation and trust.

At the same time, the Russians do not want Iran to feel complete impunity. They still want their southern neighbor to cooperate with the international community and to allow IAEA to monitor its nuclear activities. Therefore, they are actively cooperating with their Western colleagues to make sure that Iran feels the pressure. But they prefer that pressure to be soft, nonthreatening, and purely diplomatic.

EU-3

This group includes three European countries—France, Germany, and Great Britain. Their attitudes and, consequently, interests are similar in some respects and vary in others.

Their main common concern is the very idea of nuclear nonproliferation. The spread of nuclear weapons all over the world including countries that sponsor terrorism is something totally unacceptable for them. Secondly, they worry that if eventually Iran acquires nuclear weapons and manages to some-how marry them to its rockets—a medium-range missile theoretically can (in ten or fifteen years) reach some parts of Germany (but not France or Great Britain) from Northern provinces of Iran.[1] Finally, all of them on the surface seem to worry about a possibility of terrorists obtaining an access to the nuclear weapons technology. But in many respects these countries are very different.

Contemporary *Germany* is considered by many a pacifist nation. It is also a nonnuclear state. Therefore, they really take seriously the idea of peace and nonproliferation. They have never been the subject of a large-scale terrorist at-tack on their soil but after having seen some quite scary events around them—they prefer to be on the safe side and not to give terrorists nuclear WMDs. It is unlikely that Iran would fire a nuclear missile at them (there is no reason) unless it would want to hit one of the American military bases on the German territory. But amazingly, Germans did not discuss a possibility for transferring American bases from the territory of their country. Therefore, it seems they do not have too much confidence in further development of Iranian nuclear and missile technologies.

Germans also have their own specific historical sensitivity points. When the new President of Iran, Mahmoud Ahmadinejad, called for the destruction of Israel and denied the historical fact of the Holocaust they were outraged. Therefore, they consider the Iranian leader an extremely dangerous man—similar to some from their own history. And they are determined to do a lot to stop him from acquiring the nukes. They can imagine like nobody else what would have happened if Hitler had been allowed to obtain an atomic bomb. But they are still mostly against drastic military actions and prefer peaceful sanctions.

There is also one interesting detail here—Germany's relationship with Israel. Recently, Israel started putting political pressure on Germany to play a more active role in the anti-Iranian coalition. The Israelis literally say this: "You did the Holocaust—you must deal with Iran now." And this type of argumentation seems to be getting to the Germans. For example, Joschka Fischer, former Foreign Minister of Germany, in his May 2006 article wrote that the Germans had a moral obligation to Israel and had to be more aggressive with Iran. Such an argument presents an interesting challenge for purely rational actor theoreticians.

At the same time, it is useful to remember that the Germans were the ones who started building the Bushehr power plant. They used to have and are still hoping to have profitable commercial relations with Iran. And those commercial interests sometimes outweigh all the other concerns.

France also shares its neighbor's concern over Iranian missiles, terrorists, and nonproliferation. But its attitude have some special nuances. France has a huge Islamic population in its territory. Therefore, they will not want to alienate them by "prosecuting" (as some might see it) their Muslim brothers. The long French-Muslim relationship (since the time of their colonization of Northern Africa) taught them how to deal with Muslims. They are quite sure that Iran is not going to hit them with nuclear weapons—no reason and too many Muslims living in the country. They traditionally consider the Islamic world as their sphere of influence. That is why they are still maintaining good relations with Iran no matter what the current Iranian President says.

The French did not have any experience with Islamic terrorism in their territory since the 1960s. Since that time that experience was almost forgotten and, besides that, according to today's standards those acts of terrorism were, to put it mildly, small-scale.

French exports to Iran have nearly doubled in the early 2000s, totaling 2 billion euros ($2.4 billion) in 2003. Such big French companies as Renault, Gaz de France, and Total are successfully working in Iran.

Another interesting point is that the French are leading designers and builders of nuclear power plants in Europe. They and the Germans used to share the monopoly on nuclear technology in the Middle Eastern region. It was the French who built the nuclear reactor in Osirak, Iraq—the one that was destroyed by the Israeli Air Force in 1981. It is also interesting that the German company that started building the Bushehr plant is now practically a French corporation.

In the late 1980s, the Kraftwerk Union A.G. became a part of the Siemens Company. The new name for the organization was Siemens Nuclear Power. In the early 1990s, Siemens Nuclear Power developed together with the French company Framatome ANP (a subsidiary of the French AREVA Group) the European Pressurized Water Reactor project. Later, Siemens Nuclear Power was integrated into the Framatome ANP. Today, Siemens A.G. owns just about 34 percent of Framatome ANP. On March 1, 2006, Framatome ANP got the new name AREVA NP (NP stands for Nuclear Power) to show its relationship to the French AREVA Group. Headquarters of AREVA NP is in Paris, France. Today, the AREVA Group is a French nuclear company and the world market leader for civilian nuclear technology.

Therefore, now the French look at the Russian monopoly in this respect on the Iranian market with a great deal of jealousy and want a piece of the action. This is where the offer of light-water reactors comes from (although, they are no safer than contemporary Russian equipment and still can be used to obtain material for nuclear weapons). They also want to sell nuclear fuel to the Iranians for a long time. And this is where the rejection of the Russian joint venture idea comes from. They still hope to push the Russians out of the Iranian market and take their place. That is they are using a world security issue to try to promote their own commercial interests in the area even if such a promotion makes a positive outcome of the negotiations less probable. They are ready to use for their own purpose the international community (including even the Americans whom they usually don't like too much as political partners).

But the most interesting position on the issue is the *British* one. On the surface they are also concerned over the same issues but their actions say otherwise. First of all, British territory is out of reach of any existing or "soon-to-come" types of missiles launched from Iran. But the most important fact is that, behind all the antiterrorist rhetoric, London still remains one of the main hubs of terrorist financial and organizational activities in the world. British banks gladly keep accounts and transfer money for "Islamic charities" and other organizations even knowing quite well the reputations of many of them. The paths of many terrorist acts in the world lead back to London. British government readily gives refuge to known and even convicted terrorists from other countries. Such well-known terrorist leaders as Akhmed Zakayev, Omar Bakri Mohammad, Abu Hamza al-Masri and many others live comfortably in London under protection of the British government.

The death in late 2006 of Alexander Litvinenko—another shady figure with close connections to international terrorists (namely to Akhmed Zakayev) who safely lived in London under the protection of the British government—showed that it is, probably, in the territory of Great Britain (not in Iran) where the terrorists are trying to build an atomic bomb. The problem is that he died of exposure to polonium-210—an isotope that in old Soviet times was employed in a radioactive mix intended for use in nuclear explosion devices. But British prefer to close their eyes on such events and, instead, choose to partic-

234

ipate in the Iranian issue where they create an outward appearance of a concern over the problem of international nuclear terrorism.

There are two explanations for this type of behavior. First of all, the British traditionally use terrorist and criminal organizations for their "operations" abroad and it seems that the coming of "the age of terrorism" did not make them rethink their tactics. They supported KLA in Kosovo. Until now they (along with the Americans) generously financed terrorist organizations in the Caucasus Mountains region (including Georgia's *Khmara*) and even in Europe (including Ukraine's *Pora* and Belarus' *Zubr*). Second, shady money always provided a great deal of wealth for big British banks. And at this time when the British economy is not doing so well the government has no intention of damaging one of the most successful British industries—banking. That is, again, political and commercial interests outweigh everything else. Under these circumstances we can expect more rhetoric of solidarity from the British rather than real actions.

On April 27th, 2006 six former Foreign Ministers (Madeleine Albright of the USA; Joschka Fischer of Germany; Jozias van Aartsen of the Netherlands; Bronislaw Geremek of Poland; Hubert Védrine of France; and Lydia Polfer of Luxembourg) published a common editorial in the *International Herald Tribune* in which they warned the US against a military strike and recommended direct talks between the US and Iran. They challenged the Americans to take initiative in their hands and make bold steps toward a fair settlement of all the outstanding issues with Tehran. It is interesting that no British representative signed the article although the Brits are official participants of the six-party talks.

Overall, the Europeans tend to put more blame for the stalemate in the Iran issue on the Americans. Even Joschka Fischer in his quite anti-Iranian May 2006 article blamed Washington for the failure of the November 2004 agreement between the Europeans and Iran. Specifically, he mentions American attempts at the regime change in the Islamic Republic and the Iraq war as the main reason that made the Iranian leaders pull out of that accord.

But in general, it seems that the interest toward the problem is dropping in Europe. When a meeting was called on the issue in December 2006, Russian Foreign Minister Sergey Lavrov, was shocked that his partners looked at him as somebody who bothered them with an insignificant issue. They literally for two weeks did not return his calls and behaved in such a way that was supposed to clearly show that the problem they were disturbed with was far from the main worries of the day. The meeting was even once officially called off but later reinstated. Their final agreement to participate cannot be characterized as anything but reluctant.

To summarize, the Europeans are not concerned too much about the Iranian problem. They are quite sure that Tehran has no reason and no capabilities to hit them with nuclear weapons. They have substantial economic interests and projects in the Islamic Republic. They also have limited worries about terrorism. The French and Germans have not recently had any serious experience with terrorism in their territory. For the British it is a normal tool of foreign policy and a source of income. Besides that, all three states have a substantial Muslim population living in their countries—the people they are not going to alienate by being tough on Iran. Their participation in the whole process is rather symbolic.

On the other hand, one has to understand the environment of extremist and aggressive ideology of political correctness in contemporary European Union. It is like Communist ideology in the Soviet Union—Iran must live by their standards, otherwise they (as Europeans) do not fulfill their historical mission. This ideology also requires people to be concerned (or, at least, look concerned on the surface) about world problems even if they do not care at all about the issue. That is why Europeans have to formally participate in such a global-scale discussion. The second reason for them to participate is to maintain the image of superpowers—the states everyone has to consult with before making a decision. The third reason is to show solidarity with the United Sates (at least to some extent). They want to mend fences with the US after their disagreement over the war in Iraq. They also want to reaffirm the North Atlantic solidarity in a time when even NATO is slowly becoming a shaky structure. And the fourth and final reason for their participation in the process is to try to protect and even promote their own economic interests in the area.

Therefore, we cannot actually expect any real participation or good ideas from the Europeans in this case. We can expect a lot of didactic political rhetoric and attempts to sell their products under the cover of negotiational initiatives. They may agree on some sanctions but are not strong enough to damage either their relations with Iran or their economic interests in the region.

China

China's role in these negotiations is similar to Russia's in the North Korean case. It has very little leverage over Iran and not too much interest in the issue in general. The Chinese are quite sure that Iran is not going to attack them and they have very little experience with Islamic terrorism (just a little bit in their Western provinces). China imports just about 13 percent of its oil from Iran— it is a substantial but not crucial share of their oil supply. And with a new oil pipeline coming from Russia their dependence on the Iranians may become even less. Their main interests are to preserve their commercial interests in Iran and to maintain their reputation of a superpower by participating in the talks conducted by "the big boys." Consequently, they are not going to support any drastic measures including tough economic sanctions, especially, if such sanctions are likely to affect their economic interests in that country.

Israel

The Jewish state is not an official party to the negotiations but if any country has the ultimate interest in the talks—it is Israel. For the Israelis it is a matter of survival. The president of Iran officially was talking about wiping their country off the face of the Earth. They also know what terrorism means and how dangerous their neighbors can be. They remember Iraqi missiles falling on their heads during the 1991 Gulf War. They also know that they are well in reach of Iran's missiles. Finally, they are quite sure that if Iran ever gets an atomic bomb—they will, probably, be the first target. But they simply cannot be represented at the negotiating table because Iran would never talk to them. So, they rely on the United States to express their concerns and protect their interests at the talks.

At the same time, they have to do something to express their opinion and try to affect the problem. What they did—they left the entire diplomatic side of the issue to the Americans and left the tough threatening position for themselves. They many times threatened to bomb Iranian nuclear facilities. They called for military action against the Islamic state. They sincerely believe that they can scare the Iranians into not attacking them. Maybe they are right. At least the history of Arab-Israeli conflicts shows that it is not a good idea to attack them. But such a position has also the other side.

By threatening Iran they may scare their enemy into doing something foolish (like actually acquiring nuclear weapons)—especially, after their prime minister Ehud Olmert practically officially admitted in December 2006 that Israel has nuclear weapons. They are also providing the justification for Iran to continue their political line. It is an excellent propaganda tool for use among Arab and other Muslim nations to stir up anti-Israeli emotions.

But the worst thing happened when in January 2007 the world's media reported that Israel started training for atomic air strikes against Iranian nuclear targets. It was reported that the Israelis were ready to use tactical small-power nuclear "bunker-busters" to destroy Iranian targets in Natanz, Isfahan, and Arak. The Israelis did not put too much effort into denying the rumors. And although many experts consider it just a scare tactic, such reports can kill the entire peace process in the region. Who would blame Iran after that for wanting to get nuclear weapons? Such a propaganda trick also calls into question the commitment of Israel to finding a peaceful solution to the problem. Such a buzz can be spread around for only one purpose—to destroy the negotiation process altogether. On the other hand, it may be just a regular irrational fear reaction.

Certainly, the core issue in the tension between the Israelis and the Muslims is the Palestinian problem. It is far beyond the scope of this book to suggest any way of solving that puzzle but definitely Israel has to do more to solve the problem in such a way that its security and its image in the eyes of the Muslim world is enhanced.

Theoretical Analysis

The Rational Actor Model

We will not be constructing in this part of the work any matrices. As it was mentioned above, they are very perceptional, relative, and imprecise. We will try to examine the situation from a purely rational point of view—no emotions, just indisputable facts and clear logical conclusions.

Fact number one: Iran does not have a nuclear weapon or material for it yet but can eventually obtain both if allowed to conduct its program unchecked for a long time. The same can be said about their missile program. So far, it is quite primitive but can be improved over the years ahead.

Fact number two: Iran has close connections with extremist organizations and has no intention to curtail them. Therefore, a danger of a transfer of nuclear technology to the terrorists does exist.

Fact number three: so far, the IAEA did not find any evidence that Iran pursues a military nuclear program (although, they did not find any evidence saying otherwise either).

Fact number four: the Americans and the Israelis would like to use military force against Iran but, probably, would not be able to pull it off. Any strike would likely turn into a full-scale war and is unlikely to guarantee anything.

Fact number five: after decades of sanctions and covert operations the Iranian regime is running strong and successfully developing its nuclear program. These approaches do not seem to have been working so far.

Now we can use regular logic to come up with recommendations. Status quo is not good for anybody. The Americans and the Israelis are afraid of the Iranian nuclear program. The Iranians are tired of living under sanctions and under a threat of American or Israeli strikes or an invasion.

Under current conditions—fear, threats, no international control, and the invasion of Iraq as a foreign policy precedent—it is very likely that eventually Iran (even if it is not already doing it right now) will start seriously thinking about nuclear weapons as a way to guarantee its security. And if they eventually acquire such weapons—the nukes may actually get into the hands of terrorists.

It is also clear that there is no way the international community can deny Iran the civil energy nuclear power program—neither does it have the right to do so. Therefore, everybody in the world has to realize that it is something inevitable. But, at the same time, it is important to realize that civil and military nuclear programs are two different things and under a proper organization and international supervision one does not necessarily have to lead to the other.

Therefore, the only way to make sure that there is no danger coming from either Iranian missiles or Iranian extremist associates—is to make sure that Iran simply does not have a military nuclear program at all. Previously, we ruled out all the other options for dealing with the problem—all except for negotiations. Consequently, talks are the only way to solve the problem. But the proper content for the talks will be discussed in one of the following theoretical sections.

Cognitive and Learning Theories

What have the main parties—the Americans and the Iranians—learned so far? Unfortunately, their experience dealing with each other has been less than positive.

The Iranians have learned that they could rely only on themselves and could not possibly trust the Westerners. The Germans stopped building the power station, the Americans stopped supplying them with spare parts when the Iranians decided to get rid of the Shah. The only conclusion that can be made is that the West is unreliable and uses its technical expertise as a political weapon. Consequently, only complete self-reliance can provide complete independence.

Besides that, the experience with the Shah regime showed that Americans and British can install a puppet government if the reins of Islamic power are relaxed. Therefore, a strict order must be maintained and the dissident groups (many of which are terrorist ones) must be closely monitored and regulated. The Shah government also forever destroyed the myth of the benevolence of the Western powers. If they install a marionette government—they are going to suck from that country everything, giving in return nothing. Therefore, no pro-Western propaganda is likely to work effectively in Iran. Practically everybody in the country understands (except for some people who hope to come to power under a new puppet regime) that a new occupation is not going to bring anything good. And the example of Iraq is just confirming this impression.

Finally, the Iraq war showed the seriousness of threats directed at Iran from the United Sates. Therefore, the Islamic Republic is going to take its security and sovereignty extremely seriously and fight to the death for their way of life and independence.

Americans, on the other hand, went through the experience of 9/11 and realized that the situation could have been much worse had the terrorists had nuclear weapons. They experienced the wrath of Islamic terrorist groups many times in many places—bombings of embassies in Kenya and Tanzania, the bombing of the destroyer Cole, kidnappings and killings of America citizens. And they know that had their adversaries had an atomic bomb—they would have had no hesitation in using it. It is not even necessary to talk about the horror of such an event. Therefore, they are also ready to do everything to prevent it from happening. If we take into account the dangerously extremist character of the leaders of the two countries—Bush and Ahmadinejad—we will end up with a very precarious situation when two intransigent adversaries are poised to strike each other and each of them sincerely believes that only he is right.

Luckily for the United States, it has nuclear weapons. Unfortunately for Iran, it doesn't. But this is exactly why it may start thinking about getting one.

Also, both parties learned that the other side will provide unconditional support for their mortal enemies—America for Israel, Iran for Hezbollah and Hamas. And the whole Palestinian issue stands right in the middle of the controversy. And each party blames the other for this tragedy. In Iran America is blamed for violence committed by Israel. Iran is blamed in America for the violence committed by extremist Islamic groups. And the sad part is that, to some extent, is it is true in both cases. But the media in both countries make the situation even worse.

Actually, the role of the media in the conflict is quite important. Instead of providing truthful information and food for thought—they mostly feed people with propaganda, fabrications, and disinformation, distorting the real situation and, by so doing, destroying any hope for finding a rational common ground as the result of negotiations. Large-scale demonization campaigns are at full swing in both countries.

It is not even necessary to say how the "Big Satan" is portrayed in Iran. But the situation in the United States is no better. On American news channels (such as CNN or MNBC, for example) so called "experts" without any conscience in their eyes state as a fact that Iran is working on nuclear weapons without having any proof. At the same time, some more honest and objective media (*The New Yorker*, for example) reported that actually the CIA came up with a conclusion that Iran had no nuclear weapons program at all. All this reminds us of the so-called intelligence war going on right before the 2003 Iraq invasion. At that time, some honest American intelligence officers clearly stated that Iraq did not have WMDs but the administration silenced them and the media played cheerleader for the war effort. It seems like the vicious propaganda machine is at work again—the history is repeating itself too soon.

Even IAEA caught Americans lying about the issue. In September 2006 the organization criticized the August 2006 US House of Representatives report on Iran. According to the IAEA's statement, that document contained utterly false and unconfirmed information. For example, the information that Iran had HEU was false. The IAEA specified that Iran had capabilities to enrich uranium only up to the 3.6 percent U-239 level and had only enriched uranium of that grade. But the report falsely stated that Iran already possessed the 90 percent U-239 grade of uranium. Under this pressure of nasty propaganda no reasonable discussion can be conducted. Certainly, American people may be scared into supporting another war again.

Another perceptional problem is that both countries consider themselves missionaries who are supposed to fight for some ideals no matter what. The Iranians see themselves as fighting for oppressed Muslims all over the world. The Americans believe that their mission is to bring Western-style democracy to the rest of the world. Unfortunately, when people get such ideas in their heads—they become extremely intransigent because they are willing to make what they call "sacrifices" for the common good. Indeed, those sacrifices are nothing more than irrational foolish actions committed under the influence of the euphoria of the idea. Sadly, it is exactly in this situation when people commit crimes against humanity because they think that it is them who represent humanity and the other side is somehow inhuman.

The perception of Israel is also important. Their fears are understandable and correct. Throughout their history they learned that it is necessary to be tough to survive. And that is why they keep threatening Iran any chance they get. Certainly, fear is a powerful emotion but we have to realize that in this particular case threats are not effective. They only confirm the perception of danger on the other side and stir up hatred toward the threatening party. Negotiations are the only way here but they cannot go on in the atmosphere of fear and hatred. These are irrational emotions. But the other side must be rational, calm, and feel secure to consider and accept proposals and make concessions. Otherwise the impasse is inevitable. That is why, without realizing it, the Israelis are behaving in a very counterproductive way—actually working against their own interests of safety and security.

In general, the perception of fear, threat, and distrust are the main obstacles in the negotiation process. Without changing this atmosphere no agreement is possible. But it can be done only through real actions—and not empty promises or propaganda tricks.

The Psychological Point of View

This theory, with its emphasis on the personalities of the people involved in negotiations, may give us some hints as to what can be done to improve the chances of these talks for success.

In this particular situation it is enough to highlight just two leaders—Presidents Bush and Ahmadinejad. Both of them are extremists and both may be dangerous. Both of them seem to have the missionary bug in their heads. The dangerousness of President Bush was definitively proven by the Iraq war. The dangerousness of President Ahmadinejad is still mostly perceived from his rhetorical exercises. Certainly, nobody knows what he would have done had he had a chance to actually wipe Israel off the face of the Earth. He may be as dangerous as his counterpart but may be just following a long-standing Middle Eastern rhetorical tradition of extreme claims and overblown exaggerations. This is where cultural analysis may help.

Probably, everybody remembers the Information Minister of Iraq who, during the 2003 invasion, was speaking on behalf of the Iraqi government. The whole world was laughing at his claims that the Americans were destroyed and an unbelievable number of them were killed. Some were even outraged by the propaganda directed at Iraqi people. But what those people did not understand was that the gentleman just followed the Middle Eastern rhetorical tradition and actually his claims were never taken seriously by his countrymen. They knew that according to that tradition when it comes to war, claims like that were the only acceptable form of rhetoric. The pronouncements like "we annihilated millions of enemies" is a standard declaration that can be found in ancient documents going thousands of years back in history. Nobody believed them anyway. The same can be said about proclamations about one's enemy. One must promise to wipe his enemies off the face of the Earth even if tomorrow they are going to kiss each other (although, we have to remember that the kiss is also nothing more than a traditional form of rhetoric).

Certainly, there is no sure way to tell whether Ahmadinejad's comments were made for domestic rhetorical consumption or they indeed reflected his ideology. But it is always important to ask yourself a question "When are revolutionary goals simply rhetoric and when are they controlling and deeply felt commitments?" (Fisher, 1980, p. 49) And it is possible to answer this question only after communicating with one's counterpart normally—calmly and for quite an extensive period of time. This is exactly what has been missing so far in the Iranian nuclear problem negotiating process. But anyway, serious progress in these talks is unlikely while these two gentlemen are in power in their countries.

But the Americans have a chance to change their counterpart in negotiations even without violent actions. The December 2006 local elections in Iran showed that Ahmadinejad had some domestic political problems and that the moderate politicians were getting more popular again. That is, the United States has to seriously think about the signals they send to Iran. Instead of scaring them to death they would have to hint to a possibility of significant progress if another person—more moderate—stands at the helm of the Islamic state. In other words, they have to reach out to the moderates in the country. Instead, the Americans decided exactly at the same time to increase their military presence in the Persian Gulf by sending there a second aircraft carrier group. It was a very foolish thing to do. First of all, it was a noncredible threat that undermined the American position in the region. Secondly, it was a step that only played in favor of Ahmadinejad and other radical leaders in the country by providing them with real material for their political campaigns.

Problem-solving and Joint Decision-making Points of View

This approach emphasizes interests of all the sides and solutions that simultaneously address interests of all the participating parties in a mutually beneficial manner. Therefore, we will also try to address main interests of main parties to the Iran negotiations.

The Americans have three main interests in the situation:

- To prevent nuclear weapons from falling into the hands of terrorists;
- To maintain a global nonproliferation regime and, by doing so, prevent nuclear weapons from falling into the hands of anti-American governments;
- To protect Israel—their ally in the region.

The Iranians have their own three interests in this situation:

- To guarantee the survival of their culture and way of life (including their way of governing themselves);
- To protect the security of their country and safety of their people;
- To ensure the further economic growth for Iran for which the development of the civil nuclear power program they consider to be essential.

Israel has only one interest—but a big one—security or, to some extent, the very survival of the country.

Therefore, if we take what can be called "the reasonable person approach" toward the issue—the suggested sequence of steps may look like this.

The United Sates and Iran would have to simultaneously sign a series of official documents and make strong commitments in several areas. The Americans would have to give the following guarantees to the Iranians:

- To guarantee safety and security of the Iranian state by signing some form of a nonaggression pact with its government;

- To guarantee that the state structure and the form of government in Iran would not be challenged and undermined by the US authorities;
- To guarantee the complete cessation of all the subversive operations in Iran and on its borders.

The international community would also have to officially recognize the right of Iran to pursue a peaceful civil nuclear power program.

Iran would have to make the following commitments:

- To take an official obligation upon itself not to develop nuclear weapons and to reaffirm their strong commitment to NPT (although, they never quit the agreement in the first place);
- To accept international supervision of all types of its nuclear programs and allow free access of IAEA inspectors to all the nuclear site's on their territory;
- To provide security guarantees for Israel and the American forces in the region—to sign an agreement that the Islamic Republic will not attack either Americans or Israelis unless they attack first.

Certainly, these are just absolutely basic commitments that must be made to move the process at least somehow ahead. But undoubtedly it would be nice to see also the following step in order to make the process stronger:

On the part of the United States:

- To restore full diplomatic relations with Iran;
- To remove all the unilateral sanctions imposed on Iran by the US government.

On the part of Iran:

- To agree with the concept of "the two states"—Palestine and Israel—in relation to the main problem in the Middle East;
- To pledge to join the global fight against terrorism and not only against Mujahedin-e Khalq or Al-Qaeda;
- To cooperate with the United States to curb Shiite violence in Iraq;
- To sign a comprehensive security treaty with other countries in the region which would outlaw nuclear weapons.

But if we take a close look at the elements above, many of them were already present in the November 2004 accord—commitment to NPT, denunciation of nuclear weapons, suspension of the enrichment process, fight against terrorism, recognition of Iran's right to a peaceful nuclear program. But it was the

United States who wrecked the agreement by refusing to provide security guarantees to Iran. That is, the experience shows that the agreement is possible and Iran can be convinced to cooperate but the main question is whether the Americans will go along.

Unlike the case of North Korea everything looks much easier—there is no need for large-scale financial expenditures or complex technological building projects. Iran can do everything on its own. But there is still one big outstanding issue that makes the whole problem extremely complex. The issue is the Iranian ties with Hezbollah and Hamas. It is very unlikely that Tehran will ever renounce its ties with these organizations. In their view, by cooperating with them they carry out their religious mission and help the oppressed Muslims all over the world. And in some respects there is nothing terrible in all that. We have to remember that those two entities also have political wings that provide valuable services to many needy people.

The main task is to make sure that the nuclear technology and materials will not get into the hands of the militant members of those organizations. The only way to do it is to make Iran issue an official guarantee that the Islamic Republic will make sure that such a technology will never be knowingly provided by them to the terrorists.

Some people would say that this suggestion is ridiculous—that such a promise will mean nothing because it is impossible to verify. And they will be right to a large degree. Problems of credible commitment, trust, and verification have been haunting the negotiation process for thousands of years and are the most difficult problems to solve. And under the level of mistrust between the main parties in this situation—it would be very difficult indeed.

But there is a little hope here. Fortunately, we deal with deeply religious people here. For them, there are some things they will not be able to step over. For example, an oath given to Allah is something they are very unlikely to violate. That is in this case a fatwa (a holy Islamic order) would be a good way to ensure their compliance with their promise.

Actually, on August 9, 2005 Ayatollah Ali Khamenei—Iran's spiritual leader and highest authority—already issued a fatwa forbidding the production and use of nuclear weapons. After that, some Iranian leaders (including Ahmadinejad) many times officially proclaimed that the weapons of mass destruction in general and nuclear weapons in particular would go against the rules of Islam. But nobody in the West trusted them.

And this is where again the cultural differences come into play. For example, in the United States, where even Jewish members of Congress are sworn into office on the Bible, a religious oath means nothing. Therefore, for them, a fatwa does not mean anything either. But for the Islamic people it is a law they would have a hard time violating.

In general, it seems that a cultural signaling game has been going on for quite some time between the U.S. and Iran but the problem is that these two countries have been using different cultural frequencies and, therefore, did not hear each other.

For example, the United States has been issuing threats meaning to show its determination and resolve but showing, in the Iranian eyes, only its wickedness and aggressiveness. On the other side, the Iranians kept issuing fatwas and other Islamic decrees and promises meant to show that they indeed had no intention to develop nuclear weapons but kept missing the American target audience altogether. This is a good example of negotiators speaking different cultural languages and not understanding each other.

But what the West is missing is a set of very interesting and encouraging signals coming from Iran in the area of its relations with radical Islamic movements. For example, in December 2006 a Hamas leader Khaled Meshaal suggested a *hudna* with Israel for ten years. Hudna is an Arabic word meaning "truce" or "armistice." According to the Islamic law, a hudna imposes very serious obligations on every Muslim no matter with whom such a truce is made. It is not simply a political obligation but rather a moral and religious duty of every Muslim. That is if hudna comes into effect, Israel can be quite sure about its safety and security (certainly, if the Israelis in their turn stop assassinations in Palestinian territories).

Even more, Khaled Meshaal said that Hamas de facto recognizes the existence of the state of Israel and even hinted at a possibility to recognize it legally if the Palestinian state is established in its official 1967 borders. It is a sensational development that was entirely missed by the Western media because nobody in the West believes in religious oaths. But it might have been a breakthrough in the Palestinian issue. Therefore, often West can blame only itself for its own cultural insensitivity and deafness.

But the main point here is that such a proclamation could not be possibly made by Hamas without close consultation with Iran. Basically, it means that Iran cleared that statement and, by doing so, gave a clear signal to Israel and the United States that it was willing to put pressure on its friends—Hezbollah and Hamas—and ensure their cooperation with the international community. Still, the West prefers to ignore those signals.

That is again—all the elements are in place—the conditions of the 2006 November accord, the fatwas, the Hezbollah and Hamas signals. But the West manages to miss all of them. And this is where the question of intent inevitably arises. Do the Americans indeed want to reach an agreement with Iran or just want to keep it as a scarecrow for their domestic political purposes?

There is still another problem to solve. Even if the technology is not given to terrorists—it is possible for them to obtain (to steal or buy) nuclear material for their future weapons. That is why the issue of the enrichment facilities is important. Even if the official Tehran is not going to give the terrorists a weapon—some overzealous team of rogue technicians can steal some HEU and give it to the "bad guys." Therefore, it would be more safe to make sure that the enrichment process is conducted somewhere out of Iran.

That is why the Russian suggestion was so important and interesting. To remind us, they suggested organizing a uranium enrichment facility for Iran on the Russian (or Kazakh) territory but not far from the Iranian border. That facility would be a 50/50 Russian-Iranian joint venture under international supervision. The Russians actually went one step further and suggested organizing a regional uranium enrichment facility on their territory where all the neighboring countries that wanted to pursue their own nuclear power program would be able to obtain fuel for their power plants. It would be a good solution for many future problems that may arise on the Eurasian continent if other countries decide to develop their own nuclear power infrastructure.

The unwillingness of Iran to be dependent on Western countries has strong historical justifications. That is why they want to be able to produce nuclear fuel for their own power plants. But, perhaps, if the facility is right on their border and in a non-Western country, if they have a majority interest in the enterprise as well as a strong management control—maybe in this case they will agree on such an option.

But the problem here is mostly not in Iran but in the West again. The United States immediately rejected the idea as unacceptable without any further explanation. Such a reaction calls into question America's desire to solve the problem at all. Probably, they just want to keep it going as a pretext for their domestic politics and their interference in the region? After all, they do not have any objections against oil and natural gas pipeline projects coming from Iran into Georgia and Azerbaijan. These pipelines are mainly intended to harm the Russian economy but will also inevitably benefit the Iranian government. That is, those projects will bring the Iranians the money they could use to strengthen their regime and develop nuclear weapons. But the Americans strongly support those pipelines. It seems that making problems for the Russians is a higher political priority for the United States than solving the Iranian nuclear problem. Also, such events as the deliberate American attack on the Iranian consulate and arrest of Iranian diplomats in Erbil, Iraq on January 11, 2007 can be seen only as an attempt to make sure that no negotiations between the two counties are possible. (And in the eyes of the outside world this attack is no better than the Iranian takeover of the American embassy in 1979.) Generally speaking, the Iraq war is slowly turning into another complication in the whole nuclear crisis. Certainly, the Iranians are involved in Iraq but the Americans, instead of negotiating this issue and cooperating in this respect, prefer to demonstrate what can only be characterized as inadequate reactions—like, for example, the January 2007 order to the US military personnel to kill Iranian agents in Iraq.

The Europeans rejected the Russian uranium enrichment idea too and immediately offered Iran their own reactors (with their own fuel, of course) as a possible alternative solution. They argue that their reactors are safer in terms of nuclear nonproliferation. It is simply not true. For example, the type of equipment the Russians use in Bushehr is as safe (if not safer than) any contemporary Western design. Besides that, experts agree that it is possible to "use light water reactors to produce plutonium for nuclear weapons" (Niksch, 1996). Therefore, it is quite clear that the Europeans are just using these negotiations as a method of market competition against the Russians.

And the proof for this is the December 2006 UN Security Council Resolution number 1737. That resolution was supposed to introduce sanctions against Iran but boiled entirely down to the list of companies that would be prohibited from doing business in that country. The inventory of companies introduced by the Europeans was intended to push the Russians from that market. The Russians started fighting for their interests. At the end, a compromise was reached. In a special provision the Russians managed to take most of their companies from under the scope of the resolution. But on the other hand, the resolution stipulated that only the ongoing contracts at that time would be allowed to be finished but the future cooperation with the Islamic Republic would be hampered for the Russians. That is, what is going to happen on the Iranian market after the fall of 2007—when the Bushehr power station is finished—is a wide open question. But the very fact that the whole debate was not about the nuclear program but about that list of companies showed the real focus of the whole process for the Europeans. And the next logical question is: Do the Europeans really want any progress or do they find the issue convenient to use as their international business competition tool?

Ultimately, it can be said that the Iranian problem can be solved under two conditions—if different countries manage to overcome their cultural differences and, most importantly, if there is a real will on both sides to solve the problem in a fair and mutually acceptable manner.

Note

1. Iranian 3-stage Shahab-4 missile will eventually have a maximum range of 1,800 miles and will be able to reach some Eastern German cities, such as Dresden or Munich (but not Berlin). But France and UK will still remain out of its reach. But all the experts agree that it will probably take ten to fifteen years for that missile to appear and became operational.

IV
CULTURE

8

Culture and Negotiations

Theoretical Debate

Hardly anyone will ever say that culture has no effect on international negotiations. There are tons of books and articles written on the subject. And it would be hardly worthwhile writing another piece on the topic unless the author of this book saw a serious problem in the way the issue is covered in those writings and perceived by many people.

Most of the texts on the subject matter of culture and negotiations or culture and international communication will give you a useful advice on how to say hello in a foreign language, how to dress and behave properly, how to shake hands and bow, what gestures not to use while talking, who to send to negotiate as the main representative of one's side (man or woman, young or old, technician or politician) and many other interesting pieces of information like that. But all this just shows the preoccupation of the Western civilization with checklists—an easy way to memorize and learn a limited number of simple skills and facts that would help a Westerner to look respectful and knowledgeable. But if we look really closely, all the things above (however important they may be) ultimately boil down to the issue of cultural awareness to a set of outward customs that are simply supposed to make that person look nice. But indeed, all this provides just a superficial polish under which there is the same old rugged "Western imperialist" interior (this is how many people in the world would actually define it).

At the same time, many scholars and practitioners warn against a simplistic understanding of culture—that is, against boiling everything down to *national customs*:

> Too often in the past, cultural variables were thought of as "quaint customs" that one merely had to "learn about" in order to succeed in foreign settings—don't show the bottom of your shoes to people in Arab lands, remember to bow when meeting the Japanese, take a gift when you are entertained in someone's home, and don't make this or that gesture that means something-or-other lewd in such-and-such country. The idea that knowledge about customs makes it possible for different cultures to overcome differences is simplistic. (Roth, Hunt, Stavropoulos, and Babik, 1996, p. 154)

Most, for example, British and American foreign service officials receive very good cultural training in the sense described above—they can say hello in twenty-five different languages, dress impeccably, and behave flawlessly. But still they are considered to be the most difficult (and, to be honest, utterly disliked) negotiators in the world. And the question is: Why?

The answer is quite simple: superficial rituals and dress codes are not culture. Culture is a complex and deeply seeded psychological structure that runs the lives of millions of people who share similar history, language, physical environment, religious beliefs, etc. There are different definitions of culture but the two chosen for the purpose of this book come from books written by Glen Fisher—an American international relations practitioner and educator. He writes that culture is "the human being's unique way of coping with the environment (both physical and social) and surviving" (Fisher, 1988, p. 44). He also defines culture as "a pretested *design*, a store of knowledge and an entire system of coping skills that has been crafted by humans who have gone before, a design that has been socially created, tested, and shared, and one that can be transmitted to the child" (Fisher, 1988, p. 44). That is, culture allows people to survive and when we trample somebody's culture—we threaten the very survival of their kind. The reaction will be swift and brutal.

Besides that, cultural training is not just supposed to make sure that we do not offend anybody. It is supposed to help us understand each other and, by so doing, to help us find effective and mutually beneficial solutions to our problems. That is, cultural training has to inject deep cultural understanding and respect—which is something often missing from the process.

To give you an illustration, when, let's say, an American negotiator enters a negotiating room and sees on the other side of the table his or her counterpart—a mullah in traditional attire—the American may have an immediate feeling of repulsion (like in the movie *Enemy Mine*—a fear of an alien lizard, dangerous and unknown). And what's the use that he or she said hello in perfect Farsi and dressed and behaved correctly if the other side is seen as something retarded coming right from the time of the dark ages. The negotiations will go nowhere if the whole attitude is visible. It is likely that the demands of the "superior" beings will be out of the acceptance range of the "inferior" ones.

It is important to realize that the two sides at the negotiating table are absolutely equal, that their demands are as important to them as ours to us, and that their positions are as reasonable as ours. In order to realize that, we have to understand how their positions were formed and where they are coming from—not in our misperception but in their reality. But for that we have to admit the reality, value, and independence of their culture—something many negotiators refuse to do. They believe that if they somehow admit the value of somebody's culture—they will betray their own nation. They do not understand that, indeed, everything is the other way around—the deeper they comprehend and respect the other side's culture the better negotiating results they will achieve and the better they will be able to protect the interest of their own country. The deep knowledge of others will allow them to be more persuasive and effective as negotiators.

The main problem with the simple truths above is that many international communication practitioners (including negotiators)—especially, from Great Britain and the United States—approach every international communicative act with an indestructible believe of their moral and intellectual superiority. They sincerely believe that only their way of life is right, their positions are correct, their goals are moral. They do not even want to acquire any knowledge about the deep structure of the way of life of "the other." Indeed, why would one want to acquire something inferior if he or she already possesses something superior? One just has to teach "the other" how to live correctly. And the reasoning and emotions of the other side may be disregarded as "backward" and unenlightened. After all, only enlightened people know the real value of the human life and the purpose of it. All the others have not quite grown up to the level of the developed nations and have to learn the "universal" interpretation of human values and discard their "retarded" ones. So, those people actively argue against learning other peoples' ways as something detrimental to them and openly refuse to respect other cultures until those cultures accept "the appropriate" interpretations of human values. These people are called *universalists.*

The universalists sincerely believe that they possess the ultimate knowledge and understanding of such concepts as freedom, fairness, democracy, and human life. Consequently, those who do not share their beliefs are either stupid or evil people. Consequently, all the positions and suggestions of the other side are either dumb or wicked. It is quite clear what kind of negotiating environment is established at such talks and what kind of results can be expected.

Universalism is predominantly a Western phenomenon—mostly American and West European. It is sad to say that the majority of international communication educators (practitioners) representing those nations are universalists. They come to the negotiating table not with the idea of finding a mutually beneficial solution but with the missionary idea of showing others how everything must be organized in a certain area—trade, environment, arms control, etc. So, negotiations turn into a high-pressure monolog of one side while the other is supposed to be quiet and learn and ultimately accept the "advanced" solutions suggested to them.

This is how Glen Fisher (a very experienced international communication practitioner and educator) describes the main complaints forwarded against, in this case, American negotiators by the representative from other nations:

- Americans carry a leadership role in their heads and tend to see American objectives as coinciding with those of a larger world community including the counterpart's country. While this assumption may or may not be accurate, the outlook affects American style. The French and Mexicans, for example, tend to be unimpressed, while the Japanese are more appreciative.
- Americans see themselves as models of modernity and technological success and, therefore, as advisors. This seems to give them a license to prescribe, an approach that is taken whether invited or not in many negotiations.
- Among other kinds of "imperialism," Americans have been accused of "moral imperialism." This may be the identification of a particularly hard-to-take attitude of self-righteousness Americans are perceived sometimes as carrying into negotiations.
- Americans also see themselves playing an international role as problem-solvers working in everyone's best interests. They therefore expect a degree of deference to this role in negotiation and assume that everyone's final position will be arrived at during negotiation. But an American's sense of problem-solving may be interpreted as an attempt to manipulate. (Fisher, 1980, p. 45)

And all this happens only because in this case Americans (but it may also be British) negotiators *sincerely* believe that it is not worth knowing other cultures deeply, that some rituals will suffice, and that in reality their mission is not finding a mutually accepted solution but instilling in the other side "the right" understanding of this world's "real" values. And after the other side will be enlightened—they will finally understand that only the right way has been suggested to them and will gladly accept it. That is, it is not a way of compromises and slow moves toward each other. Those people honestly believe that the other side will reject its own interests and culture, cross over and accept the "real" solutions." And when it does not happen—there appears to be a sense of noble indignation on the universalists' side—how dare they not accept the ultimate truth! No wonder the Iranian and North Korean negotiations are going nowhere, that people of Latin America and Russia become more and more alienated, protectionist, and nationalistic, the problems with the Muslim world become more complex and dangerous. All this happens because Western communicators often become thoroughly confused as to what role culture plays in international negotiations and as to what culture actually is.

It is not to say that all the universalists are bad people. Many of them honestly believe that it is possible to unify the world under a certain code of universal values and, by so doing, to promote worldwide happiness and understanding—an illusion similar to Communism. The main difficulty is to find that universal interpretation of those "human nature" values.

The main problem in the arguments of the universalists is that they claim such values as freedom, fairness, democracy, and respect for human life as universal "human nature" values. They argue that if you ask people all over the world whether they want freedom, democracy, fairness, and a long happy life—everybody would say "yes." Consequently, they proclaim these values universal and try to build their communication strategies based on these values.

Indeed, it is very difficult to argue that, probably, everybody in the world would really respond to such a question positively. But representatives of every nation would mean different things while answering this question. The main problem is that "freedom", "fairness", "democracy", "respect for human life" are not values themselves but simply terms, words, or even better *labels* representing different things for different nations. We can always find in a dictionary a linguistic label—a set of symbols and sounds—that is used by the linguists and interpreters to represent in one language something found in another one. But no dictionary in the world would explain to us what this nation actually means when they use this term within their culture and how close their understanding of this linguistic label is to ours. Consequently, when the universalists proclaim the universality of values, indeed, they proclaim nothing more than some relative universality of labels. Therefore, their approach can be called simply *ethical or cultural labelism.*

For example, if the English word "democracy" is usually translated into Japanese as みんしゅしゅぎ (minshushugi) it does not mean that this particular combination of symbols and sounds means what an American or a British means by "democracy." Indeed, these are just labels matched by linguists to somehow provide for the transfer of meanings between the languages. All this has also nothing to do with the outward appearance of their state structure either. They may have a state governing body the name of which would be translated as "parliament" into English but the deep cultural meaning of that body and the role it plays in that society will be different. Indeed "the way institutions are *interrelated within a cultural system* affects the way that people are programmed to think about any specific institution. . . . Simply comparing institutions cross-nationally, isolated from the context of their systems, is rather naïve, like trying to compare pieces from different jigsaw puzzles without taking into account all the other pieces from the respective puzzles that give meaning to the individual piece" (Fisher, 1997, pp. 59–61).

To avoid a simplistic interpretation of the whole issue we have to consider what is called the *implicit social role* that the government plays in a certain society (Fisher, 1997, pp. 85–96). For example, if in the U.S. the main implicit social role of the government is to provide safeguards for individual freedom and self-fulfillment for each American citizen while in Russia—and to a large extent in Japan (Fisher, 1997, pp. 151–52, 154, 157–58, 161–62) and China— the implicit social role of the government is "to restrain people, to curb the impulses which undermined group well-being . . . to attend to the citizens needs and in turn to provide guidance, check performance, and demand obedience" (Fisher, 1997, pp. 91). Therefore, if a Japanese answers that he or she indeed likes みんしゅしゅぎ (minshushugi) or a Russian likes Демократия (demokratiya)—they actually mean exactly the opposite from what an American means by "democracy." It is interesting that when the word "democracy" (民主主義) had to be constructed in Japanese it was created out of the "written characters to produce something like 'peopleness' or populism" (Fisher, 1980, p. 62)—not even close to what democracy means to an American. Consequently, the perception of interests derived from such culture-bound notions will be different for different nations. The actions that are considered to be "in the best interest of democracy" in Russia will be practically opposite from what can be considered "in the best interest of democracy" in Great Britain.

Unfortunately, human beings always assign moral values to such political concepts. That is those who are in favor of freedom and democracy as we understand them—they are moral people. Those who are not—their behavior is immoral. Such a position kills negotiations from the outset—we cannot negotiate morality. But these misconceptions come from simple ignorance about the way other cultures operate and how they form their moral standards. The main idea of this chapter is that in order to really learn other cultures and, consequently, to be able to find truly mutually beneficial solutions during negotiations, each negotiator "must delve below" superficial cultural knowledge and try "to find foundational principles that can be used to ground moral decisions" (Ferre and Willihnganz, 1991, p. 13). This is exactly what this chapter will attempt to do—to show those foundational principles that underlie the interpretation of certain moral values by different nations. Only after we comprehend how other people form their notions of "right" and "wrong," "good" and "bad"—can we claim that we at least somehow understand their culture because of how exactly these concepts constitute the basis for the philosophy of the culture.

But the universalists openly refuse to respect other cultures' ideas that are different from their own. For example, Kruckeberg (1996) supports Lear's (1984) point of view that "if we have to respect the rationality and autonomy of every culture, then it turns out that there is one culture whose rationality and autonomy we cannot respect—our own" (p. 86). They believe that "Indeed, there are constants in most fundamental human values. Also, there are basic concepts of good and evil that transcend cultural boundaries" (Kruckeberg, 1996, p. 89). "It is easy to assume that if there are any moral truths, they must be timelessly true, perhaps because morality tends to present itself as universalizable" (Lear, 1984, p. 165).

The problem with the last argument is quite clear—the universalists never say who is going to interpret what constitutes those "timeless truths." For them the answer is obvious—they, the Western-civilization universalists, get to do it because they possess the ultimate and universal knowledge of what those truths are. They know from the depth of their hearts that what they believe in is universally true and the only moral way to live. But people from other cultures may disagree:

> When . . . philosophers and social scientists talk so uncritically about the universality of moral beliefs, what they are doing is ignoring the cultural meanings embedded in foreign practices and beliefs and substituting their own, more familiar ones. What allows them to do this without apparently meeting contradictions by the facts is their confused view of the meaning of a "prohibition against murder" as quasi-empirical, quasi-conceptual entity. (McDonald, 1986, pp. 146–47)

What the universalists are doing is substituting the whole psychological structure of another culture with their own cultural projections and continuing to comfortably operate in this environment truly believing at the same time that they understand what the other side is supposed to think. That is, they establish their world as the model for everybody else. And they not always do it subconsciously. Actually, there is a whole body of literature that tries to justify such an approach theoretically. They try to show Western moral superiority and, consequently, to establish Western notions of "right" or "wrong" as universal. For them, the Western ethos is the most ethical ethos in the world and all other people have to subscribe to the same set of moral norms and act

according to them. This is what international communication scholars write
about such literature:

> The views expressed in this literature establish United States customs as the
> "norm" and those of practitioners in other countries as "other." This approach
> leads to development of ethics codes that attempt to impose U.S. standards on
> practitioners from other countries and on U.S. nationals working elsewhere. Such
> an approach is problematic because U.S. standards are highly specific and legalis-
> tic and leave little room for cultural variation. It also establishes the U.S. method
> of conducting business as the most ethical without calling into question U.S.
> practices. For example, this literature might be viewed as suggesting not only that
> U.S. and Japanese practitioners might handle an airplane crash differently, but
> also that the U.S. tendency to protect the company name and wealth from law-
> suits is more ethical than the Japanese desire to apologize and make restitution to
> affected families. (Roth, Hunt, Stavropoulos, and Babik, 1996, p. 154)

That is "the radical universalists give absolute priority to demands of the
cosmopolitan moral community over other perceived lower moral communities" (Kruckeberg, 1996, p. 85; see also Donnelly, 1989).

But it is important to note that not everyone in the West are universalists.
There is a strong group of international communication practitioners and
scholars who believe that "it is dangerous to establish one mode of practice as
the norm and thereby label all other practices as deviant" (Roth, Hunt,
Stavropoulos, and Babik, 1996, p. 152). For example, Donaldson (1989) argues that simply transferring one's values into the international arena is a
"recipe for error and cultural arrogance" (p. 12).

These people conduct a spirited debate with the universalists trying to re-
fute their main arguments. For example, to the universalists' argument that "if
there are any moral truths, they must be timelessly true, perhaps because
morality tends to present itself as universalizable" (Lear, 1984, p. 165), the *internationalists* respond that "history strongly suggests that someday we will
view some of our present practices as ethically flawed . . . [one] should not automatically assume that he or she understands another society's practices well
enough to criticize them, let alone attempt to change them" (Jaksa and
Pritchard, 1994, p. 19). Indeed, slavery and racial segregation used to be the
norm of the American society—now we consider them as immoral and unethical. Who knows how future will change our current beliefs. Maybe in two
hundred years the ideas we are ready to die for now will be also considered immoral and unethical.

But the internationalists do not stop here—they continue to argue with universalists. Probably, the reader remembers the universalists' argument that "if
we have to respect the rationality and autonomy of every culture, then it turns

out that there is one culture whose rationality and autonomy we cannot respect—our own" (Kruckeberg, 1996, p. 86). As it usually happens with the universalists—it is very difficult to find any rationale for their claims. In this particular case it is not clear how respect for other cultures leads to disrespect of your own. It seems the other way around, if you respect other cultures—you can count on reciprocal respect of your culture by others. If every culture is special—you can be proud of your culture as being also special and unique.

"Successful [cultural] immersion does not come at the expense of one's own background, but rather functions as an important compliment to it." This quote came from the term paper of one of the undergraduate students whose professor the author of this book was proud to be. It is really amazing how professors and diplomats cannot understand something so obvious for an 18-year-old.

But the universalists continue:

> Our moral beliefs present themselves as basic truths about how human beings should act, but we are now supposed to respect incompatible moral beliefs just so long as they are actually embodied in a culture. By the standards of rationality available in our tribe these two stances are incompatible: being forced to accept that alternative incompatible moral outlooks . . . cannot help but undermine the confidence of reflective moral agents. (Lear, 1984, p. 147)

It seems that there are some misconceptions here. First of all, nobody ever was talking about giving up our own culture for another one. Secondly, nobody also has ever talked about "forcing to accept" somebody's "moral outlooks". Usually, we talk about respect and noninterference but not full acceptance. Finally, we do not have to change our own culture—we just have to understand, respect, and learn how to deal with some elements of another one. And nobody forces us to do it. If you do not want—don't do it. But afterwards, please, do not ask why negotiations failed and why the other side did not respect you and your position.

Quite often, so-called universal human rights are used by the universalists as an argument in support of the universality of what is right and what is wrong. Donnelly (1989), for example, argues that prohibition against degrading or inhuman treatment, arbitrary deprivation of life, and an equitable share of the means of subsistence are the universal values accepted all over the world. Donaldson (1989) identified ten minimal human rights applied and honored by all internationally. They include such rights as physical security, right to minimal education, right to political participation, and others. Donnelly (1989) writes: "It may be necessary to allow limited cultural variations in the form and interpretation of particular human rights, but we must insist on their fundamental moral universality" (p. 124). For the universalists "such rights would seem universal by definition" (Kruckeberg, 1996, p. 88). Such a simplistic argument cannot but shock any really thinking person.

The problem with this argument is still the same—the universalists never say who is going to interpret these human rights labels. That is who is going to define what is a violation of a certain human right and what is not—what, for example, constitutes "degrading or inhuman treatment, [or] arbitrary deprivation of life." For the universalists the answer is obvious—they get to do it because they possess the ultimate and universal truth.

But it seems that unwillingness to learn about other cultures extends into unwillingness to learn about other things as well—including the idea of human rights. It is obvious that the universalists are not aware of all the problems associated with the so-called universal human rights at the international arena. For example, "in 1982 and 1983 the US was alone in voting against a declaration that education, work, healthcare, proper nourishment, and national development are human rights. . . . The United States insisted that it does not recognize a 'right for food' " (Sardar and Davies, 2002, p. 70; see also Blum, 2001). Since universalism is a predominantly American phenomenon, the question is: What set of human rights will the universalists be using as their frame of reference—the one recognized by their own country or a more comprehensive one suggested by the UN? But it seems that the 'right for food' is in jeopardy of being not an important part of their own interpretation of the "universal human nature."

The ideology of ethical universalism "defines what is democracy, justice, freedom; what are human rights and what is multiculturalism; . . . In short, what it means to be human. The rest of the world . . . must simply accept these definitions. . . ." This ideology "defines human rights as it wishes, then uses emotive language of human rights as a stick to beat any country that does not fall in line . . . " (Sardar and Davies, 2002, pp. 201–2).

On Behalf of the universalists Spaemann (1989) argues that "common features" of the universal human nature are "self evident" (p. 5). Sardar and Davies (2002) brilliantly responded to this argument—not everything is that simple:

> That all are created equal is both a "self evident" truth and meaningless if it remains "self evident" rather than explored, questioned and permitted to express differences and diversity. All people are indeed created equal, but live with the actual inheritance of human inequalities, the legacy of real history. Equality of opportunity, equal right to exercise the liberty to be themselves, equal freedom to define and live out their beliefs as they understand them, requires more than just treating everyone the same. The libertarian rhetoric of equal rights and self evident equal creation can be as doctrinaire, illiberal, intolerant and inequitable as any ideological system. (pp. 205–6)

People who actually lived and worked abroad for long periods of time will definitely disappoint the universalists by saying that human rights have no universal interpretations at all. For example, the absence of the universal free health care system in the United States (and especially, its system of HMOs) is considered a gross violation of human rights (in particular, the right for physical security) by the rest of the world. The American two-party system and the role of money in this political system is considered a gross violation of human rights (in particular, the right for political participation) by the rest of the world. The same can be said about such labels as "minimal education" (secular versus religious, free versus paid), "capitalism" (American model versus Rhine model),[1] etc.

That is why the notion of universal human rights is, probably, the last one the universalists would be advised to use.

A big problem with most universalists seems to be that they sincerely do not understand that they simply cannot possibly see and comprehend human values of all the human beings living all over the world. But this is the mandatory requirement for finding and proclaiming universal human values—theoretically and scientifically, one has to know and deeply understand all (or at least most of) the moral standards and values on the globe in order to detect and select common ones. How can a person—who lives, let's say, in northern Iowa—know and profoundly understand all the deeply seeded cultural interpretations of all the moral values of the Chinese, Australians, South Africans, Brazilians, and Russians at the same time? It is simply impossible. And it is not necessary. If you want to negotiate with representatives of different nations—go culture by culture and learn as you go—there is no need for a universal knowledge but there is a need for case-specific comprehension and deep understanding.

The universalists simply do not understand their own psychological and social limitations as human beings. What human beings usually do is they take their own values—the ones they know and understand because they were brought up in a certain culture—and merely project their interpretation of these values onto other people without realizing it. But the main problem with the universalists' argument is that they never saw what the source of their theory is—where all those "universal" interpretations come from. But the internationalist point of view looks at each culture specifically and sees that everything is based on physical environment, history, religion, cosmology, and even composition of neighbors of each nation. In short, everything is rooted in reality. But again, where the universalists' standards theoretically come from is not clear at all.

Norms and values are adopted "*out of awareness*" and are accepted "as common sense, even as human nature" (Fisher, 1997, p. 10). This is where the illusion of the commonalities of the moral values as well as the infamous concept of the so-called "universal human nature" come from. But actually "*There are fewer universal commonalities in human thought process than most people think*"

(Fisher, 1997, p. 28). There is a "need to be wary of those who claim universality for certain beliefs. . . . The supposed commonalities of human nature prove evanescent where mindsets and perception habits are concerned. . . . Even someone who might be judged as needing psychiatric help in one society may be considered quite sane in another. Culture and personality studies conducted by anthropologists have documented stark contrasts in the most fundamental aspects of human experience: cosmology, ethics, meaning of death, family roles, governance. . . . The importance of this kind of radical variation in values and behavior can hardly be overestimated" (Fisher, 1997, pp. 28–29). "The counsel of the psychological anthropologist applies: while people may be alike in basic human qualities, they do not necessarily think alike" (Fisher, 1980, p. 38).

The value system of each society formulates "an ethic which, when shared by the society and internalized by individuals, functions to control behaviors" (Fisher, 1997, p. 105). This system defines such concepts as shame, sin, guilt, honor, dignity (Fisher, 1997, p. 105). This system also establishes the limits of morality: "These limits differ markedly, of course, from one society to another, . . ." (Fisher, 1997, p. 67). The process of formation of the value base "involves selective knowledge, prejudices, attitudes, and opinions of participating masses of people" (Fisher, 1997, p. 11). Consequently, "The common sense or obvious consideration domestically becomes not so common or obvious internationally. . . . What is right and wrong or reasonable and unreasonable takes on different coloration" (Fisher, 1997, p. 18). That is, "culture is variable; there is no one universally preferred or natural way of life, and standards for evaluating cultures must, to a large extent, be comparative and relative. What is appropriate in the desert might not work in New York" (Fisher, 1997, p. 44).

But unfortunately, people do tend to proclaim their interpretation of everything as universal: ". . . the normal and unconscious assumption is that the habitual ways of thinking of one's own society are a matter of *human nature* and therefore have universal application" (Fisher, 1997, p. 30). Indeed, these people merely project what is called their own "mindset" on the rest of the world. "Mindset" is a "fixed mental attitude formed by experience, education, prejudice, etc." (Fisher, 1997, p. 2). Going abroad, negotiators simply project their own mindset onto the other side without actually understanding the foreign mindsets. "We too comfortably find ourselves relying on our domestic experience and normal ethnocentric common sense rather than focusing directly on new dimensions of problem solving that are demanded by international realities" (Fisher, 1997, p. 2). This naïve but self-confident ethnocentrism has been witnessed and well documented by many all over the world: "unfortunately, the practitioner too easily and naively assumes that such foreign mindset factors as need to be taken into consideration will be understood on the basis of one's previous experience in 'understanding people'. . . . Normal ethnocentrism itself tends to produce self-assurance in this regard for both amateurs and professional" (Fisher, 1997, p. 3).

Such negotiators don't understand that "an ethos or way of customary thinking is aligned with some degree of cultural uniqueness" (Fisher, 1997, p. 168). That is, moral standards are unique for each culture. And even the most of what they call basic human perceptions—such as human rights—can be skewed: "the perception of threat, human rights, or appeals to world opinion, it frequently turns out that assumptions held in one country regarding these matters are not matched in another" (Fisher, 1997, pp. 1–2). For example, American ethos is considered only "superficially egalitarian" (Hodge, 2000, p. 50) and, consequently, not applicable to the world human rights issues at all by many nations.

For example, the "projecting much more of an American frame of reference" onto foreign events led to such disastrous miscalculations as the Vietnam war (Fisher, 1997, p. 30). Robert McNamara admitted that "We . . . acted according to what we thought were the principles and traditions of this nation. We made our decisions in light of those values. Yet we were wrong, terribly wrong. . . . " (Fisher, 1997, p. 7). Or here is another example. When admitting the Shah of Iran into the United States, Americans assumed that this "*humanitarian*" action "would *naturally* be understood in Iran" (Fisher, 1997, p. 9). But it seems that there is nothing natural about understanding another nation's values and, consequently, actions.

The universalists argue that there is a "consensus" on the moral positions that underlie the notion of "virtue" (Kruckeberg, 1996, p. 89; see also Donnelly, 1989, pp. 121–22). What they don't say (or don't understand) is that this so-called consensus may exist to only some extent among a very small group of countries that share the same cultural, historic, and religious background. That is the entire consensus on "ethics of universal solidarity" is basically based on the white man Anglo-Saxon protestant ideology—the ideology that is far from being universal.

Indeed, how can a person, who comes from a life of privilege, understand a black boy, who has clawed his way up from the horror of the suburban Nigerian slums, and is now sitting across the negotiating table? Without deeply learning his culture and his mindset it is simply impossible. But unfortunately that learning is not usually done because it is assumed in advance that the black gentlemen on the other side of the table must subscribe to the same cultural and, consequently, political standards as his white counterpart:

> [T]hey seem not to be able to imagine life itself in any guise other than the one they themselves are enmeshed in. . . . It is quite unrealistic to expect that someone brought up on a diet of exclusively American media should comprehend the

dynamics of Arab culture or appreciate the struggle needed to survive in an African village. . . . In the land of the free, the underlying ethic of too much discourse is that one is free only to do things "our way." As Henry Ford said of his motor car: "You can have it in any color you like as long as it's black." In this case, of course, the singular option is white. (Margaret Wertheim as cited in Sardar and Davies, 2002, p. 135)

Sometimes, the universalists claim that a certain "moral consensus" is seen in the results of some research programs that were conducted overseas. It is very difficult to put a lot of stock in this claim. First of all, it entirely contradicts a huge body of sociological and anthropological research that states otherwise. Second, as was mentioned above, the actual product of such kind of research is simply a bunch of meaningless labels that are interpreted in a rather arbitrary way. Third, the results of a research program conducted in a Third World country and funded by a rich country will always be suspect to all reasonable people.[2] Fourth, in some countries (especially, in Eastern civilizations) people may tend to agree with researchers simply out of politeness. Finally, people may not simply be able to explain how their value system differs from another one. Here is just one example: "Unfortunately, if one asks foreign colleagues to explain the underlying philosophy and fundamental assumptions that apply to the way their government functions, the chances are that the answer, even if the question is taken seriously, will be a confusion of schoolbook pronouncements and unstudied rationalizations. Most people do not routinely dwell on the way that they are programmed to think about government and its operations. It is not necessary, the logic of government is taken for granted" (Fisher, 1997, p. 90). The same can be said about values and ethics in general. People of a certain culture are usually not capable of clearly explaining their cultural value base. They just subconsciously know it. But formulating, categorizing, explaining, and clearly thinking about it, this is something they may not be simply capable of. That is "I know what it is but I can't explain it to you". Therefore, superficial surveys simply cannot produce any valuable data when it comes to such deep and complex issues as morals. (Merely saying "I like 'Демократия' or '民主主義'" does not mean anything.)

Another universalists' argument is globalization—world is becoming more homogeneous. They usually make this conclusion based on superficial observations. But what they do not realize is that only 10 percent of the culture is visible and 90 percent is invisible for an outsider (Hodge, 2000, p. 32). So, to concentrate on less than 10 percent of visible similarities and ignore 90 percent of deep culturally-seeded reasons for differences is not appropriate. Certainly, many people in the world now wear Nike sneakers and Levi's denim jackets. But the main idea is that "Deep cultural values . . . are more resistant to change than superficial cultural expressions are" (Hodge, 2000, p. 33). That is why people accept easier superficial things—such as blue jeans, baseball caps, or even elections—but inside still remain who they are (Russians, Arabs, Chinese, or Brazilians). That is, the world only seems to be getting more homogeneous but indeed it is just a dangerous and deceptive illusion.

Donnelly (1989) argues: "It may be necessary to allow limited cultural variations in the form and interpretation of particular human rights, but we must insist on their fundamental moral universality" (p. 124). Obviously, the universalists expect to be thanked for "allowing" the rest of the world "limited" cultural variations. This looks more like a set of private school rules rather than equality and freedom. Tempered universalists say that it is possible to "take into account the moral taste of host countries" (Kruckeberg, 1996, p. 88). That is, first of all, they just have to *take into account* local cultures but not *use* them as their guiding systems. Second, the very expression "moral taste" shows that the universalists again boil down the whole issue to simple local customs. But the main problem is not in observing superficial rituals but in knowing, respecting, and observing local deeply rooted codes of ethics. People may dress and act right but still they will be imposing their cultural judgments on others.

The amazing self-confidence and aggressiveness of the universalists can be explained by the fact that they do not fear any repercussion. They (usually representatives of the so-called superpowers) are absolutely sure that nobody will ever dare come to their countries and try to impose on them somebody's cultural values. They are very sure of that one-way flow of force. That is their "confident self image [is] based on a sense of moral, economic, or military *superiority* (or all three) ..." (Fisher, 1997, p. 106). But if something like that had ever happened, in this case, they would have immediately remembered that their cultures and countries are unique and that nobody has a right to interfere with their cultural, economic, and political judgments. The universalists often say that "The best possible life for everyone is achievable only when everyone follows the rules of morality, rules that quite frequently may require individuals to make genuine sacrifices" (Kruckeberg, 1989, p. 11). But it seems that they are the ones who in this case violate their own rules because it is they who are not willing to sacrifice anything. They do not want to sacrifice even temporarily the smallest part of their culture. They want to live comfortably while everybody else in the world is supposed to behave in a way they define for them.

But if we do not understand why a certain nation sees something as right (or wrong) for them, why they are so passionate about the choices they make, why they are even ready to die for what they believe in—how can we find a solution which would satisfy them as much as us and leave them happy as a result of negotiations (and not bitter and resentful against us)? If we do not know how

they feel about what democracy is, how are we going to understand their negotiational position, which is formed "in the best interest of democracy" as
they see it? If we do not understand their deeply seeded philosophical notion
of fairness, how are we supposed to understand what they mean when they say
that we are being unfair? All this requires digging deep into the hearts and
minds of our counterparts—a long and difficult learning process—the labor
for our souls, so to speak. It is hard and that is why many people are not simply willing to do it. But it is absolutely necessary if we want to understand the
other side, conduct negotiations as a joint problem-solving process, and ultimately find mutually beneficial solutions. And the result of the learning
process itself may be extremely rewarding and enriching. It may show us a
whole treasure chest of new negotiating strategies and available solutions covered by the dirt of ignorance otherwise. The author realizes that it is difficult
to understand exactly what he is talking about without examples. So, in the
next section he will try to give some specific examples of cultural differences
in interpretations of seemingly most common theoretical concepts as well as
to explain the significance of those differences for the negotiation process.

Certain "Universal" Values

The Value of Human Life

This is one of the values the universalists consider undisputable. They consider it the ultimate universal value. It is necessary to disappoint them again—
the very notion of the human life and what counts as a "valuable" human life
varies dramatically across cultures and nations.

In some cultures life is measured not from the moment of birth but from
the moment of conception. Consequently, in their opinion, the human fetus
is already a complete human being and killing this embryo is as big a crime
as killing a full-grown person. Many religions of the world consider abortion
an immoral act and a mortal sin. Therefore, at the international level, the
question of what is human life is not an idle issue but a matter of practical
significance. It may be important, for example, in the area of political communication because in one country a female candidate who had an abortion
in the past may be doomed to failure while in another country it would not
matter at all. Such matters may be important when one chooses the right negotiator for a certain issue. A female negotiator who had an abortion in the
past may not be the right choice to negotiate human rights issues with, let's
say, a radically Roman Catholic country. She may be accused of hypocrisy
and may actually lack credibility on the issue in the eyes of the other side.
Cultural universalists are likely to miss such cultural nuances. They assume

it is not important because they think that it does not matter. At the same time, people of that particular culture may believe and think otherwise. But most likely the question of whether such a factor as abortion is important or not will not even come to universalists' minds because they cannot even imagine that something like that can be different from what they think is important.

Here is another example. In case of a serious business-related problem "The Japanese, however, are conditioned to ask forgiveness and even to express a willingness to resign . . . or die" (Roth, Hunt, Stavropoulos; Babik, 1996, p. 153). The Japanese, who are very afraid to "lose face" and under extreme circumstances can even commit a ritual suicide ("hara-kiri"), are very delicate partners to work with. We have to be very careful with our policies and communications with Japanese colleagues, partners, employees, and students so that we do not cause what we would perceive as an inadequate reaction but they would perceive as a matter of honor. "For example, suicide is not uncommon among Japanese students who fail to make the grade" (Hodge, 2000, p. 49).

It is obvious that the notion of human life is quite different between the Japanese and Americans. And the existence of such a phenomenon as the "kamikaze" proves this point once more. Some Westerners accuse Japanese of being cruel and inhumane. It is not true. They are not insensitive—they simply have a different idea as to the reason what one lives for.

Another problem is the notion of what is considered a "valued" human life. Some extremists proclaim the lives of "infidels" worthless. But don't be quick to condemn them. How are they different from some Western leaders who call the death of thousands of innocent civilians "collateral damage" and the death of one of their own citizens a "senseless and brutal act of terrorism"? Many countries in the world still use capital punishment and consider it a valuable tool of crime fighting. And every nation in the world glorifies its own soldiers who kill many enemy fighters (somebody's sons and fathers). When our allies get killed we call it "mass murder" when our allies kill we call it "isolated cases of arbitrary deprivation of life." As was mentioned above, while many people die of hunger—the need for food is still not recognized as a basic human right by some. In general, we know that every government would authorize killings if it is deemed necessary. For example, until now in the United States there is a standing order for the Air Force pilots to shoot down any civilian airliner with all the people onboard if it flies too close to the White House. It seems that McDonald is right when he writes: "a 'prohibition against murder' [is] a quasi-empirical, quasi-conceptual entity" (McDonald, 1986, pp. 146–47).

And the universality of values is exactly the thing which is used to justify killings of so-called "evil" people because "evil person" is usually defined as somebody who does not adhere to the "universal" (read—personally and culturally preferred by somebody else) moral standards or set of values. "When we encounter different cultural symbols, people merely seem different, perhaps, even colorful. But when they express different values, they seem unnatural, dangerous, or evil" (Hodge, 2000, p. 33).

But the bottom line of the very idea of human life boils down to the notion of the meaning of life—its main purpose. And the question, "What do people live for on this Earth?" would be answered entirely different by people of different nations. Some would say success, some—God, some—pleasure, some—family, some—their country and society, some—spiritual development, etc. What is the right answer? Unless we can find one—we cannot even talk about the universal meaning of human life.

Freedom and Democracy

One of the most difficult concepts is the notion of freedom and, in particular, the freedom of speech. The American idea is that freedom of speech is when every member of a society can express his or her point of view freely (say whatever they want). But most Europeans and Asians have quite a different point of view on this matter. They believe that freedom and, especially, freedom of speech is not only the right to say what you think but, more importantly, it is the right to be heard. In their opinion, the American notion of freedom of speech is the principle of "a voice crying in the wilderness"—you can say whatever you want but nobody cares.

In general, applying the Western notion of freedom to other cultures is extremely destructive: "This notion of 'freedom'—or more appropriately, libertarian individualism which promotes every individual's potential for fulfillment . . . the withdrawal of all collective, communal, and social responsibility—undermines everything that indigenous cultures, traditions, and history stand for" (Sardar and Davies, 2002, p. 125).

The same can be said about the notion of democracy. Actually, it is a very complex notion and requires quite an extensive explanation.

In fact, the author of this book was always interested in what the word "democracy" meant for different nations. In his long and extensive conversations with representatives of different nations he tried to dig deeply into their souls (not necessarily minds) to comprehend their understanding of this concept. And here he will try to explain some of his findings. Let's start with the Muslims.

After many discussions the author realized that for most of the mainstream Muslims the notion of "democracy" can be expressed and explained in one world—Islam. Their deep cultural logic goes like this.

The God—Allah—is absolutely good, benevolent, fair and all-merciful. He created people for happiness. Unfortunately, people do not live up to God's Providence. So, he set up some rules for them. But the only idea behind those rules is to make sure that people live good lives and become better as their lives go on. So, if everybody—the society as a whole—lives according to his rules (the rules of Islam) it would be a perfect society that would consist of good and caring people who treat each other fairly. Consequently, a state has to be a reflection of such a model—it should be an Islamic state ruled by the laws of Allah. Since God is absolutely good, benevolent, fair, and all-merciful—the state based on God's laws will also be good, benevolent, fair, and all-merciful. Therefore, the state's laws must be at least closely connected with the Islamic law—the Shariah. But all the laws in the world would never work if the people who interpret and apply them are sinners. Thus, the people who rule the country have to not only know and understand the Islamic law perfectly but be able to apply it correctly—they also have to be deeply spiritual people who are in constant communion with God and understand God's will through prayer and spiritual readings. And such people exist—they are Mullahs. They are the best people to decide what is right and what is wrong on God's land—because they are in communion with Allah and are supposed to understand his will. And in this case the state will be a likeness of God's kingdom on Earth where all good people who live by God's good rules will be caring about each other, helping each other, and be happy, each separately and all together as a society. At least, this is the idea.

The idea of separation of church and state does not receive a lot of support among Muslims. In this case, they say, the country is run by politicians and everybody knows what they are. So, who would you like to be at the helm of your state—a bunch of professional liars or a group of righteous men who rule in council with each other, with holy prayer and in communion with a benevolent, fair, and all-merciful God? In this case, at least theoretically, the comparison is not in favor of the Western notion of democracy. And it is important to know that they hold this belief dear and on any occasion they automatically resort to this model in case of need. For example, mullahs become Islamic nations' leaders in a time of crisis. This is how Ayatollah Khomeini emerged in Iran. That is why, for instance, Muqtada al-Sadr (however controversial his role may be) immediately became Iraq's new Shia leader when the country fell in turmoil after the American invasion.

That is why we have to understand that for Iranians, for example, the structure of their state—where the final say belongs to a council of holy men—is the ultimate model of democracy and they do not want anything else. All other forms of government (including American) are the ultimate form of tyranny for them. The opinion of a handful of dissidents does not reflect the view of the entire nation. Consequently, we have to be very respectful of their state structure and to the ruling elite because they are not middle-aged retrogrades but the model of democracy for the rest of the world (in their sincere opinion).

Another example may be Russia where the notion of democracy is different from Muslim and from American ones. In Russia people put a much greater emphasis on interpersonal relationships rather than on official regulations and procedures. In order to understand the Russian notion of democracy it is necessary to understand the concept of "sobornost" that can be loosely translated as "togetherness" or "cathedralness"—the image of a huge temple where the whole nation is gathered in spiritual unity as one big parish. This tradition goes all the way back over a thousand years ago to the Novgorog republic political tradition and to the form of political decision-making called "veche." This tradition emphasized consensus over the rule of majority. The rights of minorities must be strictly observed and guaranteed. It is impossible to conduct a successful political campaign in Russia without taking into account this part of the Russian mentality. And a miserable failure of all the parties for which American practitioners did PR during the 2003 Russian parliamentary elections (they did not even cross the 5 percent barrier and were not represented in the Russian parliament at all) is definite proof of this point. In that case, the American PR consultants emphasized in their campaign such "universal" values as individual freedom and success, wealth, and the sanctity of private property that turned out to be big turnoffs for the Russian public gradually becoming more and more traditional.

For the same reason, the Russians completely reject the American interpretation of the value of "fairness" which in the American version reads "let the best [read—'the strongest'] guy win." In Russian culture, loser (not winner) is the national hero. And all the losers are supposed to be taken care of and their rights and safety must be guaranteed. No American will ever understand it. Some good advice—read Dostoyevsky.

In general, soon after 1991, when foreign interpretations of ethical values were imposed on the Russians, all those interpretations were rejected by the moral organism of the Russian society as an incompatible transplanted organ. Now the Russians again are coming back to their traditional understanding of what is moral and what is not in their own country. And it is especially noticeable in the area of democracy. In the early 2000s, the Russian political system came back to practically one party system (the "United Russia" party rules while all the others have no chance) under the leadership of a strong and charismatic leader—Vladimir Putin. Many in the West interpreted that as a rollback against democracy. Indeed, it was a return to the Russian tradition of democracy, which can be expressed in a slogan—one party, one leader. This is exactly as much democracy as the Russians can take—otherwise, the whole country starts falling apart. Only strong leaders throughout Russian history were loved and lionized—the weak were hated and soon forgotten (if not killed). This is what the Russians like and this is what the Russians need for the survival of their nation. It has been so—it will be so. And even possible successors of Putin (who is himself a former KGB officer) are either former military or law enforcement officers: Sergey Ivanov, Boris Gryzlov, Sergey Shoygu, and Sergei Mironov respectively are a former KGB officer, a former high-level police officer, a former high-level military officer, and a former paratrooper. Nobody has to have any misconceptions—one of them will be voluntarily and happily elected by the Russians to a large extent exactly because of their background. That is why, when a Westerner starts talking to the Russians about a need for more democracy (in the Western sense, of course) in their country—they look at him or her as either not a very smart person (who has no idea about the Russian cultural tradition) or as an enemy (who intentionally wants to destroy their country). In either case, they may not be that far from the truth.

There is another very interesting detail showing how Russian and Western notions of democracy differ. In the fall of 2006 the Russian parliament abolished the electoral threshold—the minimum percentage of voters that must show up for an election in order for those elections to be recognized as valid. Since that time on—whatever number comes—it is going to be good. It happened because Russians had trouble with elections—people did not come. Nobody cared about them. The problem is that the Russians do not associate elections with democracy. Actually they (as well as many other nations on the planet) are always puzzled with "the American preoccupation with voting" (Fisher, 1997, p. 94). For some reason, Americans consider elections a symbol of democracy. Actually, it is a formal requirement for them—however ridiculous and unfair some elections may be (like in Afghanistan or Iraq)—they sincerely believe that after that the democracy has finally triumphed.

Indeed, if one thinks philosophically—what is the logical connection between quantity and quality in the process of voting? What should guarantee that if many people vote for somebody—he or she will be a good leader? More often in the West we can see situations when thinking people can regretfully say "he is a terrible and incompetent leader but more people voted for him." It is an axiom that there are more dim-witted people in the world than geniuses. The smart ones are always in the minority. That is, we will always have a system where dummies will outvote Einsteins. Again, the philosophical connection between quality and quantity in the whole process is unclear. Besides that, voting is the system which is easy to manipulate (probably, the easiest one to manipulate) either through direct fraud or through media manipulation. No wonder this system is so much loved by those who want to be able to manipulate others.

The Russians would, probably, prefer what can be called the Communist Party system—when bureaucrats had to go through decades of grueling management careers. They were supposed to be climbing the ladder of power from the very bottom to the very top. And at every stage they were supposed to be selected by their colleagues for the next phase as the most deserving ones. It is not to say that it always worked perfectly—but usually it did. That is why (until Gorbachev came into power) the Soviet leaders were not young and flashy (hardly fit for an election campaign) but quite effective. Therefore, for the Russians a really democratic leader is not necessarily the one voted into the office but the one who, first of all, cares about ordinary people (mostly those who would be called "losers" in American society) and, second, who climbed all the way up from simple origins into the elite due to his or her hard work and talent.

And even the Japanese state, that is on the surface structured as a parliamentary democracy, in its essence has little to do with democracy as it is understood in the West.[3]

In general, it is important to make a clear distinction between *ideal* and *real democracy*. The ideal democracy is just an abstract idea that can come in different shapes and forms (Communist, Liberal Market, etc.). But the real democracy is what we have in practice on the ground. That is, real democracy is ideal democracy but adjusted by reality for local cultural, historical, environmental, and economic conditions. Everybody likes to discuss principles of ideal democracy forgetting that such a thing simply does not and cannot exist in this world. Necessary deviations, that are justified by the factors indicated above, create different types of real democracies that are far from being ideal. And those deviations make different forms of real democracy sustainable because the ideal democracy in reality is not viable—it cannot survive the real world. For example, the American political system has, probably, the largest deviation in the world from the principles of the ideal Liberal Democracy. We can point at such gross violations of democratic principles as the role of money in America's political system, the two-party system, the existence of the electoral college, the role of private media and their ownership in the political process, the outrageous power of lobbying, the way the courts may interfere in political decision-making, disenfranchising of poor and minority voters, the absence of universally accessible health care and higher education for all the citizens, and interference of the government with school programs. But these deviations help to make the country economically and socially stable. They will work only in the United States—any other country under all these conditions would have socially collapsed a long time ago.

So, when we talk about democracy we have to expect that we are going to see culture-specific deviations in every country and there is nothing wrong with that. But what is wrong is to criticize them for that because those deviations make at least some forms of democracy sustainable in that particular nation. Otherwise, if we try to implement any form of ideal democracy, that country is likely to collapse. So, those people, who are talking about using the principles of ideal democracy for a certain country, either try to intentionally destroy that particular state or they are not very smart because they do not see the deviations that make their own democracies viable and sustainable.

Finally, for the Chinese a really democratic society is the one organized as a big family with its own patriarchs and obedient and respectful children. But here we have to note that the notion of family is different for different nations as well.

Some universalists say that "in all cultures, parents have duties toward their children, children have duties to their parents" (Spaemann, 1989, p. 5). The problem is we cannot even compare such duties in the American society (where children are supposed to leave home at 18 and become absolutely independent and see their parents twice a year—on Christmas and Thanksgiving) and many South European, African, Middle Eastern, or Chinese societies (where many generations may live their whole lives under one roof and strongly rely on each other's support in all matters—independence in such society is not a core value). In the latter type of society a person who would want to become absolutely independent from the family would be considered a pariah, an immoral individual who wants to relinquish his or her societal duties. In such cultures the whole society is based on the family network support. Kids are taught to be dependent on their families and take care of the others. It is exactly opposite from the American way where children are taught to be independent from a very early age. That is, the universalist point of view is as wrong as it can be. The family values in the American and more traditionalistic[4] types of societies are not similar—they are actually opposite. It is not to say that one is better than the other—they are simply different. That is why in such societies striving for ultimate independence and individual freedom is not a symbol of democracy but rather a sign of a sick and immoral mind. But respect, help, and discipline are considered to be ingredients of a democratic society.

A Specific Example—The Japanese Culture of Negotiating

For some reason the concept of the *national character* "has not enjoyed the highest reputation among social scientists. But it might actually serve the negotiator's purposes better, for it can call attention both to the patterns of personality that negotiators tend to exhibit as products of their own society and to the collective concerns and outlooks that give a nation a distinctive 'character'. . . ." (Fisher, 1980, p. 37). Looking at those collective concerns and outlooks we indeed can find some common patterns that underlie any social and international type of behavior: "We start by recalling the anthropological proposition that patterns of personality do exist for groups that share a common culture, that in the process of being socialized in a given society, the individual picks up the knowledge, the ideas, the beliefs and values, the phobias and anxieties of the group. Some of this is taught explicitly; most of it is absorbed subconsciously" (Fisher, 1980, p. 37).

Actually, some experts (Fisher, 1997) believe that "80 percent of the explanation for a person's acquired behavior is to be found in cultural patterns imposed by that person's social group and normally absorbed and internalized without much effort. The remaining 20 percent fits into the category of the uniquely individual" (p. 45). That is, the national character may account for about 80 percent of human behavior in a social situation.

So, here we will try to use this anthropological approach and explore how the Japanese national character affects their style of negotiating—their negotiational strategies, approaches, methods, and behaviors.

We have to start with the fact that even the most basic and taken-for-granted concepts of the Western world are not working in Japan. For example, all the Americans and Europeans consider decision-making a primary function of a manager. It is not even discussed—it is assumed subconsciously. Consequently, when two or more managers meet and negotiate they are involved in a group decision-making process. But the Japanese do not look at this process that way and believe that the whole concept of Western decision-making is not appropriate to the negotiating process at all:

> In explaining the problem to an American audience, the president of a Japanese corporation suggested that perhaps the term "decision-making" is not applicable to the Japanese, that the concept as understood in the West involves so many difficult philosophical comparisons and contrasts in basic assumptions that it should not be used. Something like "direction-taking" might be better, for this would allow one to consider the consensus-building process in Japanese problem-solving and would avoid the notion of a decision being a finite and isolated act of executives that can set off a series of subsequent actions in an organization to support the will of management. (Fisher, 1980, pp. 32–33)

Actually, to understand the Japanese approach toward negotiations it is necessary to understand the concept of *haragei*—"consensus-oriented talking around a point of bargaining" (Fisher, 1980, p. 63). That is, for the Japanese, negotiations are not a straightforward shot for a goal but a comprehensive discussion of a whole complex of problems related to the issue under consideration. The whole straight linear approach to talks seems too simplistic to them. And in order to understand it we have to go deeper into their pattern of national thinking and compare it with, for example, the American way of doing things: "The Japanese tend to look at problems as 'a total system.' The result is that the Japanese are uncomfortable with the American custom of reaching an agreement through a series of stages . . . a complete grasp of the whole system is required before any concessions or decisions are made. The contrasting American style of problem-solving requires the bargaining situation to be broken down into a series of subissues. Each issue is discussed, concessions are made, and an agreement is reached. The final agreement is a sum of concessions" (Hawrysh and Zaichkowsky, 1989, pp. 38–39).

Consequently, their comprehensive approach is reflected in the fact that they usually look more forward in their deliberations than their Western counterparts: "The Japanese often have business plans that extend 30 years or more into the future. They tend to see the future in terms of historical context and thus cast plans in terms of long-term historical trends or goals. Americans' sense of the future is much more immediate; looking more than a year or two into the future is rare" (Hodge, 2000, p. 68).

This comprehensive approach is also reflected in what Westerners often call "situational ethics." In order to find straightforward simple effective solutions for business problems the West invented a simple straightforward effective ethical system in which everything is categorized—black vs. white, good vs. bad. The Japanese, on the other hand, trying to look at each problem from a more all-encompassing point of view, realize that their actions (so clearly categorized in Western ethics) may have different consequences under different circumstances. This is where Western negotiators often have "problems with Japanese 'situation ethics.' That is, as the Japanese appear to take different positions in different settings, the Americans sees duplicity and lack of individual integrity rather than normal behavior in a consensus society. The Japanese, on the other hand, have a problem trying to anticipate the effect of Christian-based ethics and the importance of principles in American positions. . . . This does not eliminate a sense of right and wrong or the subjective feelings that go with ethical issues; it just makes it harder to understand it all cross-culturally" (Fisher, 1980, p. 46).

Consequently, by not making simplistic moral judgments the Japanese are capable of taking a more flexible point of view on the negotiation process and, therefore, trust their partners a little bit more. "The Japanese seem more willing to develop trust even in the face of unexpected, inconsistent behavior on the part of the other party" (Hawrysh and Zaichkowsky, 1989, p. 36) while the

Americans, for example, look at surface behavioral acts of their counterparts, interpret them in quite simplistic (almost Freudian) ways and guide their future negotiational techniques based on those previous (and often scarce) observations.

Another trait of the Japanese national character is their notion of "individual" and "group." There is a Japanese saying "the nail that sticks up gets hit down" (Hodge, 2000, p. 38). An individual, in their point of view, is not supposed to be the individual in the Western sense—something special—but rather a valuable member of the society. The value of each individual is determined not by how different he or she is but how much he or she contributes to the common cause. Actually "the Japanese equivalent of 'individualistic' has a negative nuance while in English it is positive" (Fisher, 1980, p. 61). The group dynamic in that society always prevails over personal needs and character traits.

To appreciate the Japanese notion of "the individual" it is important to understand that "The person is not an individual in the western sense" (Hawrysh and Zaichkowsky, 1989, p. 35). Like in all high-context cultures in Japan "the perception of the individual is inextricably bound to his or her relationships and the context in which they occur. . . . They are quite serious when they say 'friendship first and business second' " (Hawrysh and Zaichkowsky, 1989, p. 35). That is why it is important "to allow sufficient time for a strong personal relationship to develop during long dealings. The importance of the nontask stage in the Japanese negotiation process becomes obvious given these requirements, for it is in this stage that the personal relationship develops" (Hawrysh and Zaichkowsky, 1989, p. 36).

That is, for the Japanese, negotiation is not a competitive contest between two or more individually brilliant and tough negotiators but rather a discussion between two or more entities—cultural assemblies—each of which is expressing a position that benefits that entire group. But it is first necessary to find that unified position that would express the interests of the entire group. Therefore, all the decisions are usually made by consensus. A fight between separate individuals would tear the society apart, therefore, all the individuals are expected to subject their personal positions to the interests of the whole group. Actually they are brought up to be dependent on the group and see nothing wrong with that: "Japanese do not necessarily find a dependency relationship undignified or undesirable. Japanese culture provides for this in the *amae* concept in personal relationships, as when a student is dependent on a teacher, a child on its parents, or an employee on his employer" (Fisher, 1980, p. 43).

But all this harmony-seeking process understandably takes a lot of time and requires a natural evolution process for a consensus to ripen up which frustrates many Western negotiators: "The Japanese are far less concerned about adhering to some acceptable time schedule, instead preferring to focus on the end result, allowing agreements to evolve over time. Given the differing cultural perceptions of time it becomes apparent how US complaints of delays in negotiations and wasted time would not be understood by the Japanese mind" (Hawrysh and Zaichkowsky, 1989, p. 38).

Consequently, since group dynamics prevail over personal positions "In negotiating with the Japanese it is important to remember that it is not sufficient to convince just one person, the whole group must be won over. The US emphasis on independent action often means they are outnumbered at the bargaining table as well as making it difficult for them to appreciate the strategic advantage of group appeals rather than individual ones" (Hawrysh and Zaichkowsky, 1989, p. 39).

Since unity is important the culturally reaffirming show of unity is important as well. If you call the attention to just one person it may violate the group harmony—if you praise or admonish somebody, some person in the group may lose his or her face. In Japan "calling attention to individual successes and failures can cause loss of face for some members and severely damage the dynamics of group performance" (Hodge, 2000, p. 32).

Consequently, all the discussions and disagreements are left for backstage communications. At the official level everything is supposed to be "civilized" (as the Japanese see it): "Westerners who negotiate with Japanese feel that the whole idea of holding a formal session specifically to negotiate is somehow foreign to many Japanese. . . . They [Japanese] see such as the occasion to ceremonially adopt what has already been worked out in a patient consensus-gathering process. To openly disagree at a formal stage is distasteful and embarrassing, like enduring a husband and a wife spat at . . . dinner party. Certainly, the Japanese are not prepared to change their position in such a setting" (Fisher, 1980, p. 17).

That is, it is a little bit unwise to expect open and frank discussions at formal meetings. Those sessions can serve as opinion-exchange forums where the sides express their positions and retire to their headquarters to ponder the latest developments and to form new group positions to be presented at the next conference.

As a result, the role of the negotiating team leader in Japan is regarded not as the Western "chief negotiator" but as the main representative of his or her company or country and a wise coordinator and manager rather than a decision-maker. Here leadership and status are achieved by professional competence but mostly by seniority and experience: "the team leader might be only marginally competent in the specific subject matter under negotiation, but still be the obvious head. He holds his position by being the representative of a consensus process through which the negotiating position has been derived. His technical command may depend on subordinates, but his symbolic authority is high" (Fisher, 1980, p. 22). And there is nothing wrong with that because "in Japan, new initiatives depend heavily on middle-level technical experts, and their superiors tend to accept their judgments. Their accumulation of data and information serves both the deliberation process and implementation" (Fisher, 1980, pp. 32–33). Therefore, we can be sure that all the technical aspects have been worked out very carefully and that the team leader has taken everything into consideration.

Accordingly, the Japanese subconsciously value counterpart negotiators that exhibit the same qualities that they consider important. Therefore, good advice for the organizations that want to choose appropriate negotiators for their talks with the Japanese may be the following: "Selection of negotiators is closely tied to corporate status which in turn is based on age, seniority, and knowledge of the subject. . . . Long-term thinking, good listening skills, pragmatism, and a broad perspective are often more important than detailed knowledge or skills—though this is changing rapidly" (Hodge, 2000, p. 121).

All the above is reflected in the strategies that the Japanese employ during talks. For example, Japanese usually come to negotiate in teams while Americans can send in just one person—in either case this may create some confusion. Besides that, as was already mentioned, Americans in this case are outnumbered by their counterparts which may entail for them some unfavorable negotiational dynamics.

Besides that, the whole strategy of negotiating is different for the Japanese. They do not consider negotiations as a win-or-lose game but rather as a cooperative and friendly attempt at arriving at mutually beneficial solutions. Therefore, any type of aggressive and high-pressure strategies and tactics is unacceptable and insulting for them:

> Winning at the bargaining table is unacceptable if it involves loss of face for either party. Americans, however, regard this sensitivity as a sign of weakness. Instead, Americans tend to admire the tough, thick-skinned business executive. As a result, tactics employed in the exchange process to gain advantage by exploiting weakness or faults of opponents, quite acceptable in American boardrooms, are seen as disruptive to the proper spirit of negotiation in Japan. Such tactics are not used by the Japanese and are resented when employed by Americans. (Hawrysh and Zaichkowsky, 1989, p. 38)

Consequently, "bold use of bargaining power such as 'final offer' strategies are viewed by the Japanese as crude attempts at persuasion and are often met with withdrawal from formal negotiations. The Japanese live as well as negotiate by the proverb *No aru taka wa tsume wo kakusu*, or 'An able hawk hides its talons'" (Hawrysh and Zaichkowsky, 1989, p. 38).

The strategy of intentional ambiguity is also quite often employed by skillful Japanese negotiators: "This notion of ambiguity is central to the Japanese style as it helps make tentativeness legitimate.... Here ambiguity is useful because the administrator may take the interim step of 'deciding' how to proceed. The process of 'proceeding' in turn generates further information. In this way the ambiguity provides the way of legitimizing the loose rein that a manager permits in certain organizational situations where agreement needs time to evolve or where further insight is needed before conclusive action can be taken" (Hawrysh and Zaichkowsky, 1989, p. 36).

Sometimes this ambiguity is expressed in the form of silence that gives Japanese negotiators an unexpected cultural advantage: "silence can be an effective tool for extracting concessions from Americans at the negotiating table. Left in a prolonged silence, American negotiators can be tempted to offer concessions or volunteer information just to fill what for them is an uncomfortable breach of social norms" (Hodge, 2000, p. 89).

Generally speaking, the whole Japanese style of negotiating is very different from the Western one. First of all, they are very careful with words. They try to ponder carefully every statement they make and in general they are not as "wordy" as their Western counterparts: "For Asians—especially the Japanese—taking the time to ponder on what the other side has just said is a sign of courtesy and interest. Jumping in with a comment right after someone has finished speaking means you haven't considered what the other person has just said. Asians don't communicate back and forth like a tennis match. They value communicating a lot with few words...." (Hodge, 2000, p. 89). Actually, good rhetorical skills, so valued in the West, may raise suspicions of insincerity among Japanese negotiators: "The Japanese leaders are not required to have highly developed rhetorical skills and may even be distrusted for too much verbal facility" (Stewart and Bennett, 1991, p. 157).

Finally, the Japanese are much more reserved and polite in their communications, which is often mistaken by their Western counterparts for insincerity: "The Japanese word *tatemae*, for instance, refers to the 'surface communication' that maintains harmony and prevents the relationship from deteriorating" (Hodge, 2000, p. 63). For Americans *tatemae* may seem as concealment, dishonesty, and hypocrisy—for Japanese it is just courtesy and harmony. In this case an "open discussion of differences might irreparably damage a relationship...." (Hodge, 2000, p. 63).

Certainly, all the above is reflected in surface behavioral acts exhibited by Japanese negotiators. It is interesting that gestures, outward behaviors, and rituals—the points that Western cultural training is mostly concentrated on—are called by Fisher (1980) simply "noise" because they are not that important (p. 53). The meaning of this term is quite clear—the noise rarely exhibits deep cultural meanings but, nevertheless, can seriously hamper international negotiations. Therefore, the study of noise is also important. For example, interestingly enough Fisher (1980) writes:

> Perhaps the most unnerving form of Japanese "noise" is silence! Long pauses are normal in Japanese conversation both before responding and in the middle of a developing thought. To an American in such a situation, fifteen seconds can be a very long time, and panic tends to set in to fill the conversation vacuum. Further, Japanese forms of polite behavior tend to confuse Americans even though they rarely find themselves having to match bow for bow. Japanese politeness seems artificial to the Americans, as is also the case of the more formal European and Latin America behavior. Japanese attempts to avoid giving offense leave Americans with little feedback—they do not know how their messages are being received. Most difficult of all is knowing when the answer is "no." In fact, an internationally wise Japanese has written a book for American businessmen to help them understand Japanese ways. The title is *Never Take Yes for an Answer*. Japanese use of smiles and even laughter to signal shyness or embarrassment visibly confuses Americans. (p. 55)

Indeed, such a behavioral detail as the use of "no" is, probably, the most highlighted and discussed point by negotiation scholars and practitioners and one of the most frustrating (for Westerners) aspects of negotiating with the Japanese. In fact, the Japanese do have some problems with using "no" as an answer—they'd rather "convey the message indirectly by saying, 'It is very difficult,' or, 'Maybe.' Bad news is delivered piecemeal and indirectly until one gets the picture" (Hodge, 2000, p. 63).

In general, it is always a good idea to try to imagine how we look in the eyes of our counterparts. It may provide us with some useful hints. And in the case of the Japanese such an impression may be quite unexpected for us: "When you experience what seems to be the overbearing intensity of Arabs or Italians, remember that that is probably how Americans seem to the Japanese" (Hodge, 2000, p. 150). Usually, "Arguments and overt expression of frustration or anger are considered detrimental to the spirit of friendship that should surround any interpersonal interaction" (Hawrysh and Zaichkowsky, 1989, p. 37). Therefore, the American overly expressive communication style (as they see it) may be really offensive to the Japanese. They also sometimes complain about the use of humor and "senseless joking" by the Americans in the situations and about the subjects that are not appropriate for such a lighthearted treatment in their point of view.

This part of the chapter is far from pretending to give the reader the exhaustive list of guidelines as to how to negotiate with the Japanese. The only goal for this section was to demonstrate a specific example of how cultural variables affect negotiational dynamics, strategies, styles and, possibly, outcomes.

Cultural Analysis

Now it is time to make sense out of all this richness of material presented above. If everything is so deep, complex, and confusing, can we ever have any hope to understand other nations and conduct effective negotiations with them? The answer is—definitely yes.

The problem is not to try to become an American, Japanese, Russian, Nigerian, or Brazilian if you are not. The main thing is to analyze their culture and understand how they approach certain issues and how they see certain things. Then, one has to learn how to "conduct yourself with 'an accent'" (Hodge, 2000, p. 186). That is, we do not pretend to be them but try to adjust our negotiational methods, styles, and arguments to our counterparts. But in order to be able to understand them, first, we have to effectively analyze them and find the right approach. Are there any guidelines for such an analysis? There are some but they mostly emphasize the *intercultural* domain. At the same time, when we deal with negotiations we mostly deal with *international* issues. The difference is that in this case the aspects of politics, different economic systems, and different legal patterns of thinking also come into play. And the cultural variables have a tremendous effect on all these aspects.

Fortunately, there is a writer who addressed these complex issues in his books. His name is Glen Fisher. Everybody who is interested in the effect of culture on international relations—including negotiations and other types of communications—would be strongly advised to read his writings. You can find some of them in the bibliography part of this book. The following analysis guidelines were collected piece-by-piece mostly from his writings and the credit for them should primarily go to him.[5]

Cultural Analysis Guidelines

In order to understand a foreign mindset we have to answer the following general questions:

- What are the main elements of a certain foreign mindset?
- What are the political aspects of that mindset?

- What are the economic and business elements of that mindset?
- How does the law—as a pattern of national problem-solving—function in that particular society?

Certainly, it is necessary to break down these general questions into more specific ones in order to be able to understand a certain deeper mindset. So, the following questions may actually serve as a set of guidelines for conducting such an analysis.

The Main Elements of a Certain Foreign Mindset

1. *What significant values and assumptions about dealing with nature and its resources result from coping with the group's physical environment?*
   Behavioral patterns are very often closely connected to the physical and natural environments nations live in. Certainly, the methods of survival will be different in a hot desert and frozen tundra. Consequently, human attitudes toward nature, lifestyles, and surviving skills will be different as will be the crisis coping mechanisms.
2. *How does the human environment and the way culture defines social structure mold mindsets?*
   Here we may deal with such concepts as societal hierarchy, interrelationships between individuals and collective needs, power distance, and many similar problems.
3. *How does the society's collective past experience survive in the form of a culturally transmitted memory?*
   This is where we have to deal with the problem of self-image of a certain nation formed by culturally shaped images and stories transmitted in that society as historical facts.
4. *What knowledge or information base will people bring to the issue or event?*
   This is where we deal with past as well as contemporary myths, images, and even media messages perceived in that particular society as common sense truths. That is, here we have to study their knowledge base—what they actually *do* know and what they *think* they know about this world.
5. *Is there a unique "deep cultural lens" at work?*
   This is where we deal with moral values, religious issues, national philosophy and ideology. Is the issue under negotiation usually learned as a group or individual item? Is there an emotional charge associated with this issue? Is this pattern of thinking institutionalized in this particular culture and nation or does it just function as an internal personal set of behavioral guidelines? Such issues as the influence of reli-

gious figures on government affairs or an officially adopted national legislation on the problems of abortion or divorce may fall under this category.

6. *What should one take into account regarding the process by which mindsets come to be engaged?*

Mindsets usually come to be engaged in relation to a certain specific problem. So, it is important to understand the context of each issue in a certain nation. Are there any hidden agendas? Is there a difference in the style of logic between us and them? Do group decision-making dynamics affect the way the mindsets work in relation to this particular issue?

Political and Legal Aspect

1. *What is the implicit purpose of the government in that country?*

Here we deal with the national subconscious idea of how the government ought to work—how government affairs should be handled, what the structure of the government should be, who should be in charge, what elements of social life the government should be a guardian of, what the role of the government should be vis-à-vis other institutions, etc.

2. *What is the public sense of political process?*

Here we deal with the national subconscious idea of how the political process ought to work—the forms and rules of political decision-making, the political legitimacy problem, the idea of fair politics and fair political tools and methods, and the role of ideology in politics.

3. *What is the role of public officials in the nation's political system?*

Here we may consider different styles of political leadership preferred in each nation—for example, charismatic, traditional, or legal rational. We also may consider the role that government officials are expected to play—public servants vs. masters of the land.

4. *How does the law serve as a pattern of national political thinking?*

What is the source of the law (religion vs. secularism, sin vs. guilt)? What is the national perception of the law—for example, a set of moral obligations or just an expression of an ideal? To whom does the law actually apply?

5. *How do political institutions serve as the embodiment of the political culture?*

How do specific governmental institutions carry out specific functions prescribed by that nation's cultural outlooks?

Economic and Business Aspects

1. *What is the implicit purpose of economic activities and institutions in a certain society?*

   Here we have to deal with such notions as ownership, property rights, profit-making, and taxation. Several questions are extremely important in this respect. For example, for whose benefit should the economic activities be mostly conducted (collective vs. personal gains)? What is the main societal purpose of business activities—personal advancement, profit-making or service to the society?

2. *How is work looked upon?*

   Is it, for example, considered a social duty or providence's punishment?

3. *What is the effect of social structures on economic activities?*

   How social classes affect the nation's economic activities—the activities prescribed and allowed for certain classes and classes derived from certain activities, the class-activity mobility issue. Other issues are also important in this respect—like, for example, interrelationships between tradition and bureaucracy, wealth and social status.

4. *What are the notions of economic justice and equity—at home and abroad?*

   Is it OK to provide everybody with approximately equal opportunities and then let them fight it out or is it necessary to distribute actual benefits of economic activities equally among the nation's or world's citizens? To what extent can the opportunities and the distribution be equalized? How can it be done if it is allowed at all? To what degree can economic activities be interfered with for the purpose of establishing economic justice and equality?

Certainly, these are main questions to be addressed in a prenegotiation cultural analysis. Many other questions can be added to this list to make it even more useful. For example, Fisher (1980) highlights the following ones: "Is competition 'good'? Does the well-being of the individual or that of the group take precedence when property rights, profit, law or government policy come into discussion? What loyalties are to be honored first in determining how official position is to be used? How is national interest defined and when does it take priority? . . . When is an issue a religious one? When does unthinkable immoral behavior in one society become thinkable in another?" (p. 49)

But one important remark must be made here. These guidelines can be useful only if all the questions above are answered sincerely and honestly—the way the answers actually are but not the way we want them to be. And second, the answers must be based on actual knowledge not on our stereotypes and misconceptions about other nations. Only in this case can we get out of such an analysis extraordinarily interesting insights into other nations' mindsets and use those insights while forming our negotiational strategies, tactics, methods, and approaches.

Conclusion

Before every negotiation it is necessary to conduct cultural analysis that is supposed to start with understanding that such labels as "freedom," "democracy," "human life," "family" have absolutely different, very often opposite, meanings for the representatives of different nations. Without this simple understanding we are not only dangerously close to chauvinism and nazism (the feel of national superiority) we are also dangerously close to business and political failure.

It may be possible to create what can be called a general protocol of moral understanding or simply primitive ethical guidelines for separate culture groups—such as, for example, the Protestant Anglo-Saxon culture group, or the North-Mediterranean or Catholic South-European culture group, or Orthodox Christian East European Slavic culture group. But even in this case it is quite clear that they will be extremely difficult to implement, especially, when politics or national interests come into play.

In general, every international negotiator "must accept that all civilizations have the same right to exist, the same freedom to express themselves, and the same liberty to order their society guided by their own moral vision. Moreover, all the people of the world have the right and freedom to disagree . . ." (Sardar and Davies, 2002, p. 169).

Cultural universalism is always counterproductive and confusing. First of all, instead of pulling people together, as many idealist universalists think, it actually separates them even more. Secondly, it misleads us into believing that we actually know and understand how other people see the world. But, how can we understand other nations if we are "interpreting the reality of other societies through the distorting prism of European concepts"? (Sardar and Davies, 2002, p. 167)

"Western civilization constructed not only terrestrial empires and colonies but also an intellectual empire in which it alone exemplified the proper meaning and use of reason, objectivity and adherence to universal concepts and principles . . ." (Sardar and Davies, 2002, p. 142).

If we reject the cultural universalism—some useful advice can be given to international negotiators.

First of all, it is important to remember that the perception of a country's interests is a derivative of that nation's culture. For example, Americans can negotiate in the interest of just one company (or a small group of companies). For instance, the whole American foreign policy in relation to Latin America in the early 1950s was conducted in the interest of just one company—the United Fruit (Kunczik, 1997, pp. 246–51). The Russians will always at least try to negotiate in the interest of the whole nation. The Muslims will be talking keeping in mind first of all the interest of their faith. Small nations will be negotiating in the interest of survival while big ones—in the interest of their power and competition with other big nations. This simple understanding will help to comprehend how their interests are formed and what may be the bottom line for them. That is if you know how position is formed—you can find efficient ways to affect it.

Second, it is not a good idea to mix negotiational subjects. If the main subject of negotiations is trade or arms control—it is a good idea to keep it this way and not to mix in such issues as democracy, freedom, or human rights because this is exactly where most misunderstandings usually occur.

Third, it is a good idea when choosing people you are going to negotiate with to choose not those with whom you would like to talk (a handful of dissidents who happen to agree with you) but those who actually represent their nations and actually make decisions in that country. That is, no matter how strongly many American politicians disrespect Iranian ayatollahs—they would be the ones to talk to about the Iranian nuclear issue.

Fourth, it is important to choose arguments and negotiational tools the other side will understand—not the ones you think will be effective. That is, a smart negotiator would try to understand the deep cultural meaning and all the related cultural issues pertaining to the subject of negotiations. Then, he or she would use the ideas and notions of that culture (not the concepts of his or her own culture) to present the necessary negotiational position. The knowledge of their religious writings and other literature may help to pick up some proper arguments from there. Simplistic pronouncements from American civics textbooks will hardly impress them. Culturally specific arguments are always the most powerful ones. But if the heads of the representatives of the other side are just mysterious black boxes for you—you will be forced to poke around in that blackness without any system or clear direction.

Finally, we must respect everybody. Even if we do not exactly understand why their society is structured or is functioning in a certain way—we have to realize that it is their long history, physical environment, and many other factors that formed their society and kept it the way it is. We do not have to be condescending and wait until they "grow up" to our "enlightened" state of society. They did not come "right from the middle-ages" but, probably, in their opinion—we did. If they are different—it does not mean that they are re-tarded. "[T]his does not mean they are simply 'proto-Americans.' They have their own values and traditions, and they can get very touchy if others do not respect these" (Hodge, 2000, p. 160). This is where many negotiations start failing.

Some people would say that it is unfair to criticize Western (mostly American and British) negotiators all the time and forget about the other side. On one hand, it is a fair statement. Often the Americans and the British also suffer from cultural stereotypes and misconceptions. Representatives of other nations also often lack cultural awareness and understanding when they are talking to the representatives of these two countries. This chapter was written not specifically for Western negotiators but for representatives of every nation with a simple idea—other cultures must be thoroughly studied and understood before negotiations can start—whatever culture it may be, American or Nigerian.

On the other hand, there are several important circumstances that make the American side the main target of criticism. First of all, the American culture dominates movie screens, stores, and the mass media all over the world. Americans cannot complain that their culture is underexplored and unknown. Second, cultural universalism is mostly an American (and British—generally, white-man Anglo-Saxon protestant) phenomenon. There are very few representatives of other nations who would argue that everybody in the world have to think and feel exactly like them. Third, for some reason, when, let's say, Russians talk to Chinese or Nigerians to Brazilians, there have never been any complaints of cultural insensitivity. Other countries among themselves manage somehow to respect each other and talk to each other as equals. Finally, the sheer size and power of the United States is reasonably expected to attract a lot of criticism. America is the only hyperpower and its actions in all areas are examined with special attention. A small country delegation's cultural insensitivity will, probably, harm only that country. But the position of the American delegation in any talks may have much more far-reaching consequences. That is why there is so much criticism and scrutiny.

But if America wants to continue to play its role as the shining beacon for the rest of the world and to be the model for the future—it will have to learn how to respect other nations and to deal with them fairly. Otherwise, it may lose its moral authority. Why do we demand fair and respectful negotiations from Third World countries when the largest and most powerful country on Earth still has not quite learned how to do it?

It is imperative to make an important note at the end. Certainly, there are some practices that, probably, most people on Earth would find appalling and repulsive—like violence against women or child labor. But we have to remember two things. First of all, all those practices are not culture-specific (they happen in every culture), but they are always rooted in economic circumstances and as those circumstances change—they change as well. That is the best way to fight them, not force, threats, or condescending and patronizing moral lectures—but economic aid and development. Second, as history shows, countries tend to develop on their own toward a better humanitarian situation as time goes on. Certainly, they may be moving much slower than we would want them to but it is important to be patient here. Any excessive pressure usually creates a boomerang effect—accusations of cultural imperialism and support for the traditional ways of doing things. So, the best way to promote change is education and personal example. But for this we ourselves have to be flawless and serve as models for the future. But how can we be such models if we ourselves disrespect other nations, choose arrogance and ignorance over education and understanding, and often use threats and violence to solve problems? We have to learn how to understand others better and only then will negotiations be much easier. Go culture-by-culture. Use their culture-specific moral standards as your guidelines. And try to never impose your moral vision on others. This is good advice for neither lazy nor arrogant people.

Notes

1. On the differences between the American and the Rhine models of capitalism, please see Albert, 1993; Marshal and Tucker, 1992; and Sennett, 1998.

2. It is important to note that it is always possible to find an extremely small group of Westernized (or pretend-to-be-Westernized) people in every society who find it more profitable to live in a symbiotic relationship with the incoming outsiders. But they do not represent by any means their entire society. Unfortunately, it is namely this type of people that is usually chosen by Western researchers as their research subjects (mostly, because of the accessibility issue and their language skills). Consequently, the research results always come out severely skewed. Exactly, these tiny groups of people serve as the "living proof" for all the universalist ideas—however absurd it may be.

3. One can read about it, for example, in Okabe Kazuaki's article available at www .tabunka.org/newsletter/true_democracy.html.

4. *Traditionalistic*—adhering to tradition especially in cultural or religious practices. (Hyperdictionary.com. Available: www.hyperdictionary.com/dictionary/traditionalistic).

5. The ideas presented here are mostly adopted and adapted from Fisher, 1997. The author would like to thank Mr. Fisher for his generous permission to use his material.

Conclusion

THIS BOOK IS THEORETICAL AND PRACTICAL IN NATURE at the same time. The new—communication-oriented—two-level-game model offered in this volume can help international communication practitioners as well as scholars to raise some useful theoretical claims and point out professional applications for use by professional negotiators.

That is, what the author tried to do from the theoretical point of view was to take an analytical approach that has been used primarily in one field—international relations—and explore its relevance and application to the analysis of international negotiations from a communication perspective. This particular analytical approach—the two-level game—is part of a larger approach of the rational actor models and the game theoretic models. The application of a new version of this approach to the field of communication may be helpful in the analysis of international negotiations.

The Theoretical Novelty and Significance of the New Model

In theoretical respects, the new model makes three changes in the traditional assumptions of the two-level-game theory. It recognizes the dynamism of interests as the basis for actors' actions in the game. It emphasizes the role of information in forming and adjusting these interests. And it relaxes the unitary actor assumption. The result is a model where communication—by providing information in these conditions—lies at the very heart of the two-level negotiation process and where the institutional structure is a significant factor that affects some important aspects of this process.

The New Model—Its Novelty and Significance

This book conceptualized the negotiation process as the game of interests. Interests were defined as actors' perceptions of a certain situation arising from actors' values. Since information plays the key role in the process of shaping perceptions, informational exchange is the main game process in the new model.

More attention was paid to the availability and role of information in the new model than in the previous ones. Several roles of information were highlighted— identity (actor) formation, interest formation, and interest adjustment. These aspects helped better understand how communication and information actually shape the negotiation process.

In the new version, the game is not one of calculations based on the best guesses of the opponent's positions and actions. The new game has two main processes. The first one is the exchange of information with the purpose of forming and adjusting actors' interests. The second process is the one of the choice and use of political tools (such as side-payments and ratification procedures) in order to reconfigure the structural context of the game to receive an advantage.

In the new version, actors negotiate, communicate, exchange information, exchange side-payments, and choose ratification procedures. They interact and communicate. They try to move the vertical interest border to the left or to the right by affecting each other's perceptions, forming actors, and making payments. The side "wins" that moves the border in the direction it needed to the degree it needed. It is a game of wit and political skills.

The new version of the game is much more realistic. By assuming exclusively bounded rationality and rejecting the unitary actor assumption, this volume moves the game analysis closer to real world situations. It is also a step toward a deeper understanding of the negotiation process and a step away from a purely abstract and detached model.

The conceptualization of interests is another novelty introduced by the transformed model. First, a difference was shown between situational interests and fundamental values. It is an important difference because in different situations people act not only according to their values but also according to the actual circumstances of the moment. What they have to do at that moment may contradict their values. In other instances, they may simply make perceptional mistakes and act against their values without realizing it. Sometimes ideology takes over, overcoming even such a basic interest as survival. That is why we often cannot use fundamental values alone to calculate human actions.

Since the model assumes exclusively bounded rationality, it is very difficult to calculate sides' interests solely on the rational basis. And people rarely actually do so. They may collect available information, process it as well and as quickly as possible and take whatever they *perceive* as the best available course of action. However, people in reality may sometimes act even against their fundamental values and beliefs. The purely rational approach cannot usually explain such actions. But the new approach's explanation is quite simple—people simply perceived the situation in a way that allowed them do what they did. That is why interests are *perceived*. And perceptions are flexible, as the communication literature tells us. Consequently, interests are also dynamic. People's interests can be influenced (by giving them side-payments or more information) by different agents who can shape and adjust them. The concept of a dynamic interest opens many possibilities, including the possibility of creating actors on purpose using the identity or actor formation function of information (what sometimes is called in political communication the *grass-tops activity*).

One of the important novelties of the new model, in terms of the two-level-game theory, is that interests serve as the basis for all of the game interactions. Instead of contrapositioning actors according to their actor group affiliation—P, C, or E—the new model contraposes them according to their interests. This is more realistic and more common sense. People fight not because they belong to different branches of government but because they perceive different situations in different ways—that is, they have different interests.

The new model ties together more closely concepts such as interests, information, and institutions. Previous models did this too but in a rather loose way. In the new model they are interwoven and affect each other quite strongly. Information and communication affect the processes of actor formation, interest formation, and interest adjustment. Interests and actors, in turn, are aggregated into institutions that, in turn, regulate the distribution and the flow of information. This, consequently, affects the processes of actor formation, interest formation, and interest adjustment. In this case it becomes clearer why these three concepts are particularly important and how they interact with each other.

In the new model, the process of approval replaces the old emphasis on ratification. This is suggested to be more realistic and it makes more sense from the structural point of view. In this perspective, ratification is just one (usually final) instance in a long and difficult internal approval process. This concept captures all the usual elements of an entity's structure—P + C + E. That is, this approach is more sound from a theoretical as well as practical point of view than the emphasis on ratification.

Another novelty of the approach offered in this book is how side-payments are treated. Besides their traditional form of the exchange of values, the new model emphasizes intangible or symbolic side-payments that have a clear communication character. Symbolic side-payments may convey a message of readiness to negotiate and flexibility. They may be made to take care of or to shape the perceptions held by some important constituencies. Often politicians have to appear to have squeezed out of the opponent an important concession, otherwise, they will be perceived by their constituencies as weak and ineffective leaders. In this case, the side-payment is a "face-saving" device, a way out of a deadlock. The side-payment may also be a symbolic message of respect that can calm down the opposition and help to neutralize one of the *counter* cells in the new game's diagram. This kind of message can change sides' perceptions of each other from "enemies" to "strategic partners" with whom a future agreement is possible. That is why the side-payment is a communication tool. And this tool can help the two-level-game players to move the vertical interest border at each actor group level.

In general, the significance of this model is that it offers a more dynamic, realistic, and versatile perspective regarding the negotiation process. It specifies several concepts and introduces several new ones. It moves the whole character of the game away from abstract modeling and toward the analysis of the real life cases of interest struggles. That is why it should be more useful in assisting with understanding, explaining, and analyzing real world situations. On the other hand, it still retains some possibilities for a game of numbers—numerical analysis. That is, regardless of its qualitative and human-perception-oriented character, the new model is constructed in such a way that it still contains many features that allow it to be used for hypothesis testing, outcome estimation, and, in the future, even probably forecasting. That is, it holds many features of a game-type theory.

In one respect the new model offers a very counterintuitive and almost heretical proposition. Traditionally, in political science the situation at the Chooser level was of paramount importance because the legislators have to give their final approval for a signed agreement—to ratify it. If they do not ratify it—the initiative is dead. The new model argues that the situation at the C level may be less important for the negotiation outcome than it was considered previously. This book argues that the perspective that the situation at the Chooser level is of paramount importance is somewhat superficial. There are other variables that account for the outcome at the legislative level—pressure from the Endorsers, the type of ratification procedure, pressure from the supporters at the executive level, and the ability of supporters to neutralize the opponents through the use of side-payments. The ratification can be problematic not because of the supreme importance of the members of the legislature but because there were no supporters for the initiative, there were no side-payments made, or the ratification procedure was chosen incorrectly. This suggests that if actors know how to use political tools available to them—they will be able to shape legislators' perceptions and often interests and, by so doing, push their initiative through (or kill a document if they want to). The Choosers are not that all-powerful after all—they heavily depend on their constituencies, money, and political favors. If they are often allowed to act in real life as if they were all-powerful—it is mostly because other people cannot or do not know how to affect them. This book offers one possible insight on the political tools available to exert pressure on the legislators. That is why the situation at the Chooser level is the most volatile and most easily changeable. And that is why the situation at the Chooser level before any internal political action begins is not decisively important. Skillful politicians may be able to change it to their benefit.

The Analytical Benefits of the New Model— Questions and Recommendations

The new intra-entity analytical dimension of the new model opens new practical possibilities for policymakers or decision-makers. Using this model, they can actually analyze real life internal approval processes and consider their future course of action. For example, these are the questions directly derived from and based on the new model that a politician has to ask him or herself before introducing a new initiative for negotiations:

1. What administrative body is responsible for the area in which the initiative is introduced (State Department, the Pentagon)?
2. What is the attitude of the officials of this particular organization in relation to this initiative (*for-* and *counter-* interest-holders and how many on each side)?
3. Does this initiative require ratification?
4. What is the formal procedure of (requirement for) the ratification process?
5. Is it possible to change it if necessary and, if yes, how?
6. What is the attitude of the members of this body (the Choosers) in relation to this initiative (*for-* and *counter-* interest-holders and how many on each side)?
7. Is there a substantial interest group of supporters (the Endorsers) to back up the initiative?
8. If not, can it be recruited or created?
9. What are the main concerns of our opponents (if a group has been already identified in such a way)?
10. Is it possible to accommodate them, that is, to make side-payments?

Based on the dynamics of the new model a set of recommendations for a politician who wants to introduce a new initiative for negotiations can also be suggested:

1. Create (recruit or mobilize) a substantial group of supporters (Endorsers) for the cause you champion. The larger the group and the more powerful it is—the more chance for success you have. But it is important to have one in order to have any chance for success.
2. Listen to the opposition, find out its main complaints about your position. Be ready to negotiate, to share the power, to accommodate concerns of your opponents to the largest possible degree without compromising your position. Try to choose the smallest side-payments with the largest effects—that is, at the smallest cost but which tips the balance in a certain situation in your favor.
3. Learn and understand the situation at the Proposer level. Try to move the vertical interest border to the right as far as possible, that is, recruit executive supporters, lobby, make your position known to them, and make them understand it.
4. Choose the simplest and easiest process of approval available. The fewer people you need to approve your proposal—the better.
5. If all four positions above are carefully taken care of, the situation at the Chooser level should not be a problem. Supporters will exert their pressure on the Choosers. Side-payments will neutralize opponents. Supporters at the Proposer level will apply their pressure on the Choosers as well. Nevertheless, complacency is very dangerous here. Therefore, do not disregard this area either. Study the situation at the Chooser actor group level, make your position known, recruit and mobilize supporters, lobby, try to convert as many Choosers to your position as possible. But the main thing is—to make side-payments—try to adjust your opponents' interests.

All these questions and recommendation have to increase the probability of the successful outcome of the internal approval process.

A General Approach toward International Negotiations— the Complex Analysis

As a general methodology for studying negotiations the author of this book suggests what can be called *the complex analysis*. This approach stipulates and prescribes the examination of all the elements of the negotiational process from all the available theoretical points of view. That is, it considers negotiations as a multifaceted complex of different factors, elements, and ingredients all of which must be closely examined in order to find the best available solution to the problem at hand. And this general approach entails some general observations that will summarize this book quite well.

For example, this volume has shown quite well that the traditional point of view that theory and practice live in different realms is not correct. Actually, theory helps to guide practice while practice helps to conceptualize and advance theories. The case studies demonstrated that different theoretical approaches are not just futile exercises in philosophy—they can actually serve as effective and valuable analytical tools for negotiation practitioners. And it is important to be versed in all of them to be able to conduct a really thorough and professional analysis.

Another idea of this volume is that however complex the world of political chess may be—it is always useful to try to look also at the arrangement of the pieces on each side separately—the domestic politics. The position of each piece can tell us a lot about the interests of each side, its defensive philosophy and offensive strategy. Domestic politics not only always affect but often directly drive international negotiations. So, without a solid understanding of internal dynamics and structural elements of each side—it is impossible to foresee and prevent many problems that cannot only impede but entirely kill any positive development.

It is also important to note that dogmatism—ideological, cultural, or conceptual—is something that must be avoided at any cost by a negotiations analyst. Critical and free thinking in this field is not a recommendation but a requirement. Very often it is necessary to throw out old stereotypes, to revise old assumptions and concepts, to revise some items in the knowledge base that have seemed undisputable until now. Rigidity does not allow for creative thinking and creative thinking is absolutely necessary in order to use such methods as joint decision-making and problem-solving. And as it was shown above, these are the two most effective and useful types of approaches toward the process of international negotiations.

Finally, cultural knowledge and sensitivity are crucial for success of any international talks. One can be the best negotiation theoretician in the world, but if he or she does not know, understand, and respect the culture of the other side—they have to be kicked out of the negotiating table. Anyway, with the participation of such an individual the talks will go nowhere.

This is actually one of those circumstances when the situation is indeed extremely simple—black and white. Cultural arrogance and ignorance will lead to hatred and failure. Cultural knowledge and understanding will provide a skilled negotiator with a deep understanding of the process of the other side's

interest-formation, will help to find culturally specific arguments and approaches, and simply win the sympathy of the other side (that can be crucial
in many cultures). That is why the author considers the culture chapter of this
book one of the most important parts of this volume.

But, at the same time, it is wrong to think that every set of negotiations can
be brought to a successful conclusion. Besides quite obvious cases, when the
win-sets of the parties do not overlap or when the conditions are not ripe yet,
there are some cases when actually the participants of the talks come into negotiations without any intention to even work toward a successful outcome.
They are not interested in any mutually beneficial and acceptable solutions—
they are interested in PR.

More and more often international negotiations are used as a tool of international public relations. The author of this work analyzed the North Korean
and Iranian sets of negotiations from the position that their participants have
been actually looking for positive outcomes. But often it is quite clear that the
sides are not really interested in the outcome but rather in the process itself.

A good example of such negotiations may be the talks conducted between
Iraq and the United States before the 2003 invasion. Now everybody knows
that President Bush had no intention of reaching any agreement with Saddam
Hussein. He just wanted to pretend that he exhausted all the diplomatic ven-
ues before going to war. That is the negotiations were used as an international
PR tool to fake his good will.

After looking at some of the negotiations covered in this book, similar suspicions arise. Often sides behave in a counterproductive way and it is not clear
whether they do it by mistake or as a result of some emotional distress or because they actually don't want to reach any agreement. Often they reject useful
initiatives and support some actions that are clearly going to kill the progress.

For example, it is not clear why President Bush does everything against reaching agreements with North Korea and Iran. Is it because he is honestly confused
or is receiving a bad advice or because he is indeed just buying time to get out
of Iraq and finally attack Iran and North Korea? Or, maybe, the whole deal is intended for domestic consumption—to create a scarecrow for his own nation to
keep his party in power and to assure public support for his political agenda.
The same question can be addressed to his counterparts—Iran and North
Korea. Are they really interested in the talks or just buying time to develop nuclear weapons? Perhaps, only history will answer these questions.

But what can be said for sure is that no knowledge and analysis are going to
help if there are no sincere intentions to reach a mutually beneficial agreement. Good will is the main condition for the success of any talks.

Appendix

Numerical Data Analysis and Hypotheses Development

THIS APPENDIX WILL TRY TO PAVE THE WAY for a possible practical use of the new model. This model can be extended through quantitative analysis to help communication practitioners to analyze negotiation situations with greater precision. At the same time, it is important to offer a word of caution here. It is not implied in any way that the calculations below and their results are supposed to prove this model right or wrong. They do not constitute a statistical test of the new model. What is shown in the appendix part of this work is not intended to be a test for this theory. It is just an idea how a relatively large-N statistical study, based on the new model, can be organized in the future.

Numbers will be used for two purposes. First of all, numbers are very illustrative. It is difficult to show clearly the interrelations between variables, differences in their effects, and their importance for the overall process without using numbers. At the same time, no inferential statistics will be used and no significant relationship claims will be made. The use of numbers will be purely descriptive. The only type of numerical analysis used in this study will be simple nonparametric odds ratios or risk estimates. This is a very widespread and widely used type of analysis. Information about its mechanisms and typical uses can be found in many statistical textbooks. (Bohrnstedt and Knoke, 1994; Siegel and Castellan, 1988; Poindexter and McCombs, 2000; Tate, 1998).

The second reason for using numbers in this study is that one way for a new theory to develop is to provide testable hypotheses for future research. By creating a numerical model and showing a clear algorithm for using it, this part of the book will provide a point of view on the way of modeling this kind of intra-entity relationship numerically in case somebody will ever want to conduct a follow-up study based on this new version of the theory in the future. But even in the current form (with small samples), the new model will be applicable to real life situations because it describes very solid, clear, and a simple algorithm for numerical analysis.

One of the best ways to explore the new model from the quantitative point of view may be the use of logistic regression. This method of statistical analysis may help to find the effect of each variable in the model on the outcome of negotiations and actually calculate the odds of success for each initiative. The model would look as follows:

$$g = \beta_0 + \beta_1 X_1 + \beta_2 X_2 + \beta_3 X_3 + \beta_4 X_4 + \beta_5 X_5 + \beta_6 X_6$$

Where:
The outcome variable is dichotomous—if a bill passed (1) or failed (0);
X1: situation at the Proposer (P) level (scale from 1 to 7 discussed below);
X2: situation at the Chooser (C) level (scale from 1 to 7 discussed below);
X3: presence of Endorsers (E)—dichotomous ("yes": 1, or "no": 0);
X4: type of ratification procedure—dichotomous ("simple majority": 1, vs. "qualified majority": 0);
X5: first dummy variable for the categorical variable called "side-payments made"—dichotomy ("yes": 1, or 0 for "not necessary" and "no");
X6: second dummy variable for the categorical variable called "side-payments made"—dichotomy ("not necessary": 1, or 0 for "yes" and "no").

The following formula would produce the odds for the positive outcome in each case:

$$\text{odds}(X_i) = \exp\left(g[X_i]\right)$$

Simple exponentiation of each coefficient from the equation above would produce the odds ratio decrease or increase between different levels or groups within each variable.

Certainly, it is naive to think that it is possible to calculate a kind of universal coefficient that would assist in calculating the odds of success or failure in any situation in any area of human life. But it is possible to use this equation within limits of certain areas of studies or a certain organization. The algorithm for using the model would be as follows:

1. Collect data for a certain area of interest or a certain organization and calculate the formula coefficients.
2. Put the parameters of a current situation of interest or a set of negotiations in the formula and calculate current odds for success.

3. Analyze the situation and find the elements that have to be worked on in order to increase the chances of a certain outcome.
4. Recalculate the odds periodically as the situation progresses until statistical coefficients reach the threshold odds values established in advance.
5. After the final outcome is known, add this situation to the data set and recalculate the equation coefficients, that is, update the data set for future use.

One word of caution, it is necessary to have a very extensive data set before using this formula. Relatively large numbers of variables and complexity of the formula require several dozen situations for the logistic regression to work. It is not possible for every organization. Although, it is definitely possible for federal agencies (like the U.S. Department of States), large corporations, and other large institutions.

Unfortunately, in the case of this particular study, the use of logistic regression is not possible either, mostly because of a very small sample size the author is going to use—just eighteen units—eighteen internal approval processes.

These eighteen internal approval processes come from eight major sets of negotiations. These eight sets of talks will constitute a kind of convenience sample that will represent different types of negotiations (monetary, trade, oil, civil aviation, defense, etc.) between different countries (UK, France, USA, Germany, and others) for a fifty-year time span (1943–1993). Such a wide scope of issues, countries, and time periods should make this sample more interesting. The talks included in the analysis are the Bretton Woods Monetary Agreement, the International Trade Organization (ITO), the Anglo-American Oil Agreement, the International Civil Aviation Agreement, the European Coal and Steel Community (ECSC), the European Defense Community (EDC), the North American Free Trade Agreement (NAFTA), and the Maastricht Treaty on European Monetary Union.

There is no special meaning in the composition of the data set presented in this appendix. This is a sort of sample data set used for the purpose of technology demonstration. These eight sets of talks were chosen because all of the negotiation situations reflected in them were very illustrative in terms of two-level-game interactions and because the material for analysis was readily available in the multitude of international negotiation literature sources.[1] The cases were analyzed and coded based on the information from different available sources and put together in a series of *predictor-outcome cross-case displays*. From those displays it is easy to see the final data set shape across all the cases and to compare those cases against each other. The reader will not see here detailed discussions of each case (they can be found in other sources indicated here and it is beyond the scope of this book). But what will be demonstrated is the final cumulative analysis of the entire data set pertaining to the dynamics of the new model of the two-level-game theory.

Variables

The variables for analysis come directly from the new model. They are conceptualized in the form that would allow for fast and parsimonious analysis. The independent variables are:

1. *The situation at the Proposer (P) level*—described on a scale as "very unfavorable," "unfavorable," "somewhat unfavorable," "neutral," "somewhat favorable," "favorable," and "very favorable."
2. *The situation at the Chooser (C) level*—described on a scale as "very unfavorable," "unfavorable," "somewhat unfavorable," "neutral," "somewhat favorable," "favorable," and "very favorable."

These variables were analyzed in the following fashion. For example, the code of "very unfavorable" means that a situation at a certain actor group level was such that an *absolute majority* of actors at this level was *against* a certain initiative, proposal, or agreement. Consequently, the code of "favorable" means that a situation at a certain actor group level was such that the *majority* of actors at this level was *for* a certain initiative, proposal, or agreement. The code "somewhat favorable" means that proponents of a certain initiative, proposal, or agreement outweighed the opponents at this actor group level but just a little bit. The code "neutral" means that neither opponents nor supporters of a certain initiative, proposal, or agreement at a certain actor group level had any advantages.

1. *The presence of supporters at the Endorser level*—simple dichotomy "yes" or "no."
2. *The type of ratification procedure used*—dichotomy "simple majority" or "qualified majority."
3. *The usage of the side-payments by the actors*—"yes," "no," or "not necessary."

The dependent variable is the success or failure of the approval process of a certain agreement in a certain country. That is, the dependent variable is dichotomous—"pass" or "fail." The unit of analysis is the approval process of one agreement in one country.

Success does not necessarily mean that the agreement was signed, ratified, and came into force. There might be many special circumstances that could prevent it from happening and those circumstances might have come mainly from the outside of the negotiation process. Like, for example, if the internal approval process in one of the participating entities failed and that entity withdrew from the agreement before the other side even had a chance to put the document forward for ratification. Success means that had it been only up to the "non-withdrawal" country—the ratification would have definitely happened. Success means that the sum of P + C + E was good enough to pass the initiative. Success means that the overall chances for passing this initiative within this particular country were overwhelmingly high.

The unit of analysis here is the process of internal approval of one initiative, agreement, or document in one country. This means that if there are three countries involved in the process of negotiations there may be three units of analysis. Unfortunately, we don't have complete information about all the participants of all the agreements, so that if there were twelve parties that signed an agreement it does not mean that there will be twelve entries in the final predictor-outcome cross-case display. As a rule, we have complete information only about major and most influential sides involved in the talks. Very often, we will have complete information about just two or three participants of some negotiations. This is how the data set of eighteen cases came into being.

The Connection between Textual and Graphic Forms of the New Model

Before showing the results of the analysis, it is necessary to explain one important term. It will be said sometime that the actors tried "to push the vertical interest border line to the right." This form will be used for the sake of parsimony. It basically means that the players tried to create a favorable situation for a certain initiative at a certain level. To visualize this metaphor, please, refer to the new model's diagrams in chapter 3.

In the outcome display the expressions like "situation was favorable" or "very unfavorable" are used. It is very important to explain the scale used here. This is not a simple Likert scale although it may look like this. Actually, this scale is an inalienable part of the original model and was derived directly from the model's graphic representation. It should directly connect theoretical and numerical models. This scale gives an excellent opportunity to actually visualize what we mean by, for example, "unfavorable" situation and it also clearly demonstrates the distance between a certain current situation and the positive approval point. This scale, so to speak, evaluates and calculates the situation for each approval process. That is, it links a possible narrative, a textual de-

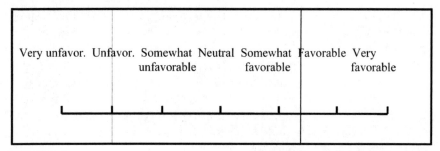

FIGURE A.1.
The connection between the measurement scale and the graphical representation of the new model

scription of the situation, to the graphic model and numeric values. Without this scale the connection between the model and a narrative would be vague and unclear. This scale will serve the purpose of a more exact analysis of the situation. Consider Figure A.1.

Let's say, the rectangular figure represents a situation at the C level in the model in a certain country. The solid vertical line represents the two-thirds qualified majority ratification requirement. The dotted vertical line represents the current situation—"unfavorable."

Then, it is not necessary to move the border all the way up to "very favorable" for ratification. Approximately the one-third point between "somewhat favorable" and "favorable" would suffice. Finally, it can be seen exactly—in units—what distance separates the current situation from the ratification level. It ties the words with the picture and with the numbers. It shows that in discussing a certain situation, it is not just a vague and obscure concept but a certain point on the situational continuum and that all the situations labeled in a certain way are approximately the same. For example, if we code "unfavorable" as 2 and the two-thirds ratification level, consequently, as 5.33, we will get the distance to work on −3.33 units.

It is also important to make a significant remark here. Because the data set size is very small and the sample is not random, it will not even be possible to generalize the conclusions of such a kind of analysis onto the universe of all the two-level negotiations. But what will be done is an attempt to find a way to accurately describe the situation in the data-set. Consequently, it would be good advice for every user of this model—to work within limits of his or her area of interest, organization, or data set, because every extrapolation or generalization beyond the known area would be very problematic.

Ultimately, after analyzing all the eighteen internal approval processes, the author of this work put them together in the final cross-case display summarizing the analysis. The display is shown in Table A.1.

TABLE A.1
The Final Cross-Case Display Summarizing the International Negotiations Data Set Analysis Results

Agreement & Country	Situation at the Proposer (P) level	Situation at the Chooser (C) level	Presence of Endorsers (E)	Type of Ratification Procedure	Side-Payments Made	Result
ITO U.S.	Very favorable	Very unfavorable	No	Qualified majority	Yes	Failed
ITO U.K.	Unfavorable	Very unfavorable	No	Simple majority	No	Failed
Bretton Woods U.S.	Very favorable	Somewhat unfavorable	Yes	Simple majority	Yes	Passed
Bretton Woods U.K.	Very favorable	Very unfavorable	Yes	Simple majority	Yes	Passed
Oil Agreement U.S.	Somewhat unfavorable	Unfavorable	No	Qualified majority	No	Failed
Oil Agreement U.K.	Favorable	Favorable	Yes	Simple majority	Not necessary	Passed
Civil Aviation Agreement U.S.	Very favorable	Unfavorable	Yes	Simple majority	Yes	Passed
Civil Aviation Agreement U.K.	Somewhat unfavorable	Somewhat favorable	Yes	Simple majority	Not necessary	Passed
ECSC France	Very favorable	Somewhat favorable	Yes	Qualified majority	Yes	Passed
ECSC Germany	Very favorable	Favorable	Yes	Qualified majority	Yes	Passed
EDC France	Very unfavorable	Very unfavorable	No	Qualified majority	No	Failed
EDC Germany	Favorable	Favorable	Yes	Qualified majority	Not Necessary	Passed
NAFTA Mexico	Very favorable	Very favorable	Yes	Simple majority	Not Necessary	Passed
NAFTA Canada	Somewhat unfavorable	Somewhat unfavorable	Yes	Simple majority	Yes	Passed
NAFTA U.S.	Favorable	Unfavorable	Yes	Simple majority	Yes	Passed
Maastricht Treaty France	Very favorable	Somewhat favorable	Yes	Qualified majority	Yes	Passed
Maastricht Treaty Germany	Somewhat unfavorable	Unfavorable	Yes	Qualified majority	Yes	Passed
Maastricht Treaty U.K.	Unfavorable	Very unfavorable	Yes	Simple majority	Yes	Passed

Nonparametric Point of View and Odds Ratio Calculations

It was necessary to come up with an alternative way of numerical analysis of the situations in the data set that consist of just eighteen internal approval processes. So, two things had to be done before the analysis. First of all, it was necessary to choose an appropriate set of procedures. Second, it was necessary to simplify the data and, by so doing, make it manageable.

Nonparametric procedures would be most appropriate because they do not require large data-set sizes. Since the focus of the whole model is on the odds of success of a negotiation proposal, the procedure called the "risk analysis" would be very appropriate in this case because it actually estimates the odds ratios.

Now, it is possible to simplify the data set in order to be able to work with it. The first thing to do is to recode all the variables into simple binomial dichotomies. In the new form the data will look as follows:

1. Dependent variable called "result:" "passed"—1; "failed"—0.
2. Situation at the Proposer (P) level: "favorable"—1; "unfavorable"—0.
3. Situation at the Chooser (C) level: "favorable"—1; "unfavorable"—0.
4. Presence of Endorsers (E): "yes"—1; "no"—0.
5. Type of ratification procedure: "simple majority"—1; "qualified majority"—0.
6. Side-payments made: "yes"—1; "no"—0 (includes "no" and "not necessary").

Table A.2 is the code table for the new form of the data set.

Now, each variable from Table A.2 can be cross-referenced in the model with the outcome variable to identify with what decrease or increase in odds of outcome "1" on the "result" variable each independent variable is associated.

It will be hypothesized that:

1. A favorable situation at the Proposer (P) level will be associated with an increase in odds for the positive outcome of negotiations.
2. A favorable situation at the Chooser (C) level will be associated with an increase in odds for the positive outcome of negotiations.
3. The presence of Endorsers (E) will be associated with an increase in odds for the positive outcome of negotiations.
4. The simple majority type of ratification procedure will be associated with an increase in odds for the positive outcome of negotiations.
5. The presence of side-payments will be associated with an increase in odds for the positive outcome of negotiations.

TABLE A.2
The Final Cross-Case Display Summarizing the International Relations Data Set Analysis Results: the Dichotomous Form

Agreement & Country	Situation at the Proposer (P) level	Situation at the Chooser (C) level	Presence of Endorsers (E)	Type of Ratification Procedure	Side Payments Made	Result
ITO U.S.	Favorable (1)	Unfavorable (0)	No (0)	Qualified majority (0)	Yes (1)	Failed (0)
ITO U.K.	Unfavorable (0)	Unfavorable (0)	No (0)	Simple majority (1)	No (0)	Failed (0)
Bretton Woods U.S.	Favorable (1)	Unfavorable (0)	Yes (1)	Simple majority (1)	Yes (1)	Passed (1)
Bretton Woods U.K.	Favorable (1)	Unfavorable (0)	Yes (1)	Simple majority (1)	Yes (1)	Passed (1)
Oil Agreement U.S.	Unfavorable (0)	Unfavorable (0)	No (0)	Qualified majority (0)	No (0)	Failed (0)
Oil Agreement U.K.	Favorable (1)	Favorable (1)	Yes (1)	Simple majority (1)	No (0)	Passed (1)
Civil Aviation Agreement U.S.	Favorable (1)	Unfavorable (0)	Yes (1)	Simple majority (1)	Yes (1)	Passed (1)
Civil Aviation Agreement U.K.	Unfavorable (0)	Favorable (1)	Yes (1)	Simple majority (1)	No (0)	Passed (1)
ECSC France	Favorable (1)	Favorable (1)	Yes (1)	Qualified majority (0)	Yes (1)	Passed (1)
ECSC Germany	Favorable (1)	Favorable (1)	Yes (1)	Qualified majority (0)	Yes (1)	Passed (1)
EDC France	Unfavorable (0)	Unfavorable (0)	No (0)	Qualified majority (0)	No (0)	Failed (0)
EDC Germany	Favorable (1)	Favorable (1)	Yes (1)	Qualified majority (0)	No (0)	Passed (1)
NAFTA Mexico	Favorable (1)	Favorable (1)	Yes (1)	Simple majority (1)	No (0)	Passed (1)
NAFTA Canada	Unfavorable (0)	Unfavorable (0)	Yes (1)	Simple majority (1)	Yes (1)	Passed (1)
NAFTA U.S.	Favorable (1)	Unfavorable (0)	Yes (1)	Simple majority (1)	Yes (1)	Passed (1)
Maastricht Treaty France	Favorable (1)	Favorable (1)	Yes (1)	Qualified majority (0)	Yes (1)	Passed (1)
Maastricht Treaty Germany	Unfavorable (0)	Unfavorable (0)	Yes (1)	Qualified majority (0)	Yes (1)	Passed (1)
Maastricht Treaty U.K.	Unfavorable (0)	Unfavorable (0)	Yes (1)	Simple majority (1)	Yes (1)	Passed (1)

A cross-tabulation of the P-level variable with the outcome variable is shown in Table A.3.

TABLE A.3
A Cross-tabulation of the P-Level
Variable with the Outcome Variable

		Result	
		0	*1*
P-level	*1*	1	10
	0	3	4

The odds of the positive outcome of negotiations increase by a factor of 7.5 when the situation at the P-level is favorable. The Chi-Square value for this matrix is about 2.85 that would be significant at the 0.1 level of confidence.

A cross-tabulation of the C-level variable with the outcome variable produced a matrix with an empty cell ("favorable"—"failed"). This empty cell prevents us from calculating the odds ratio. In order to be able to calculate it, the imputed value of 1 will be used for that cell.[2]

TABLE A.4
A Cross-tabulation of the C-Level
Variable with the Outcome Variable

		Result	
		0	*1*
C-level	*1*	1	7
	0	4	7

The odds of the positive outcome of the negotiations increase by a factor of 4 when the situation at the C-level is favorable. The Chi-Square value for this matrix is about 1.35 that would not be significant at any level of confidence.

A cross-tabulation of the E variable with the outcome variable is shown in Table A.5.

TABLE A.5
A Cross-tabulation of the E-Level
Variable with the Outcome Variable

		Result	
		0	*1*
E	*1*	0	14
	0	4	0

Unfortunately, the odds ratio for this matrix cannot be calculated. The use of imputed values is impossible also. Two imputed values would distort the real picture too much and produce an entirely artificial odds ratio value. Besides that, it is clearly seen here that the presence of endorsers in the data set is perfectly correlated with the success of the negotiations. It will be necessary to find another way of working with this variable.

A cross-tabulation of the type of ratification procedure variable with the outcome variable is shown in Table A.6.

TABLE A.6
A Cross-tabulation of the Type of Ratification Variable with the Outcome Variable

		Result	
		0	1
Type of ratification procedure	1	1	9
	0	3	5

The odds of the positive outcome of the negotiations increase by a factor of 5.4 when a simple majority as the ratification procedure is used. The Chi-Square value for this matrix is about 1.95 which would not be significant at any level of confidence.

A cross-tabulation of the side-payment variable with the outcome variable is shown in Table A.7.

TABLE A.7
A Cross-tabulation of the Side-Payment Variable with the Outcome Variable

		Result	
		0	1
Side-payment	1	1	10
	0	3	4

The odds of the positive outcome of negotiations increase by a factor of 7.5 when side-payments were used. The Chi-Square value for this matrix is about 2.85 that would be significant at the 0.1 level of confidence.

In case of two variables—"C-level" and "type of ratification procedure"—the Chi-Square test failed to produce a significant result. Therefore, these two particular odds ratio coefficients should not be taken too seriously because these two particular values may have been received due to chance. But this is not important here. It is necessary to recall that it is not the purpose of this analysis to claim any statistical significance. It is impossible to do it anyway with such a small and nonrandom sample. The main purpose of this numerical exploration is to illustrate the elements and the mechanisms of the new model. And it seems that general direction of the numerical findings were consistent with the hypotheses:

1. A favorable situation at the Proposer (P) level was associated with an increase in odds for the positive outcome of negotiations.
2. A favorable situation at the Chooser (C) level indeed was associated with an increase in odds for the positive outcome of negotiations.
3. The presence of Endorsers (E) was associated with an increase in odds for the positive outcome of negotiations.
4. The simple majority type of ratification procedure was also associated with an increase in odds for the positive outcome of negotiations.
5. The presence of side payments indeed was associated with an increase in odds for the positive outcome of negotiations.

It is not possible to conclude that the hypotheses were supported because the sample is too small and nonrandom. It is not even actually a regular sample. It was not drawn from any larger population and is not supposed to represent anything. It is actually a little universe by itself—a population of particular real world situations to be explored. It was mentioned above that such would be the best point of view for any organization or institution because large samples can be feasible only in rare cases. That is why the significance of those Chi-Square coefficients is not really important here because the values of the odds ratio coefficients are calculated for the whole population of case studies in this data set. These will not be extrapolated onto any larger universe and, consequently, the chance deviations do not come into play here.

At the same time, the low Chi-Square coefficients show that the differences between observed and expected values in the matrices are not very big. That is, there are no real striking patterns in the data distribution between the cells. But, again, this may have happened due to a very small size of our data set. It is extremely difficult to receive any significant coefficients at all with just eighteen units of analysis. And the fact that two of the coefficients—"P-level" and "side-payments"—turned out to be significant even with this amount of data available (even though just at the 0.1 confidence level) shows that at least these two coefficients may really mean very much for the final outcome variable.

But it is appropriate to recall here again that this analysis does not have any ambition to support or reject any hypotheses from the empirical point of view. The only purpose of this numerical analysis is to see if the general trends will be consistent with the theoretical positions of the new model. So far, the numbers provided quite a good illustration of what this model is all about. Now it is time to create the numerical model for the negotiation outcome odds calculation.

The Numerical Model for the
Negotiation Outcome Odds Calculation

The analysis below is called numerical rather than statistical because, first of all, there is no general population to generalize the results on and, secondly, because what you will see is just a numbers game intended to show how such an analysis can be done theoretically in the future.

Each of the above calculated coefficients represented either an increase or a decrease in odds of the positive outcome of negotiations. Consequently, the model will be the sum of increases or decreases in odds for the positive outcome of negotiations. Certainly, such an approach has its own problems. First of all, it is impossible to determine each coefficient's effect on the dependent variable *controlling for the effect of other variables.* In this model, each coefficient represents *only the direct effect* of each independent variable on the dependent one—the indirect effects are not taken into account here. Consequently, this model also does not take into account any spurious correlations either. But in order to see if there are any, several variables were cross-referenced.

For example, it is logical to suggest that the less favorable the situation at the C level the more side payments are to be made. A cross-tabulation of the C-level variable with the side-payment variable is shown in Table A.8.

TABLE A.8
A Crosstabulation of the Side-Payment Variable
with the C-Level Variable

		C-level	
		0	*1*
Side-payment	*1*	8	3
	0	3	4

It is also logical to suggest that the less favorable the situation at the P level the more side-payments are to be made. A cross-tabulation of the P-level variable with the side-payment variable is shown in Table A.9.

Appendix

TABLE A.9
A Cross-tabulation of the Side-Payment
Variable with the P-Level Variable

		Side-Payment	
		0	*1*
P-level	*1*	3	8
	0	4	3

It would also be logical to suggest that the less favorable the situation at the C level the simpler the ratification procedure would be chosen. A cross-tabulation of the C-level variable with the ratification procedure variable is shown in Table A.10.

TABLE A.10
A Cross-tabulation of the C-Level
Variable with the Ratification
Procedure Variable

		Ratification Procedure	
		0	*1*
C-level	*1*	4	3
	0	4	7

Finally, it is logical to suggest that the more complex the ratification procedure is the more side payments are to be made. A cross-tabulation of the type of ratification procedure variable with the side-payment variable is shown in Table A.11.

TABLE A.11
A Cross-tabulation of the Side-Payment Variable with the Type
of Ratification Variable

		Side-Payment	
		0	*1*
Type of ratification procedure	*1*	4	6
	0	3	5

The distribution of data in the cells shows that there are no apparent relationships between these variables. Besides that, the Chi-Square test values for all these matrices were well below significance at any level of confidence (the highest one was 1.6). But again, it may have happened only due to chance because of a very small data-set size.

That is why, again, this model cannot be used for verification of the theoretical model offered in this work. It is supposed to serve as just a rough illustration of the interrelations between the variables and differences in their effects in relation to a particular data set. It is also supposed to illustrate the general algorithm of how this model can be used to estimate the odds of a success or a failure of an intra-entity approval process.

In general, the sum of the main variable odds ratio coefficients will produce an estimate of the odds for the positive outcome ("passed") of the intra-entity approval process:

Situation at the Proposer (P) + level	Situation at the Chooser (C) + level	Presence of Endorsers + (E)	Type of ratification + procedure	Side payments made

Situation at the Proposer (P) level:　　+7.5 for "favorable" (1/1 cell)
　　−7.5 for "unfavorable" (0/0 cell)

Situation at the Chooser (C) level:　　+4 for "favorable" (1/1 cell)
　　−4 for "unfavorable" (0/0 cell)

Type of ratification procedure:　　+5.4 for "simple majority" (1/1 cell)
　　−5.4 for "qualified majority" (0/0 cell)

Side payments made:　　+7.5 for "yes" (1/1 cell)
　　−7.5 for "no" (0/0 cell)

The only problem in this situation is the value for the E variable. It is not possible to calculate the absolute value of the effect of this variable on the outcome in terms of the odds ratio coefficient. But what is possible is to calculate the minimum relative effective value of this variable for this particular data set. It will be done by finding the minimum positive effect coefficient for this variable that has offset the worst odds ratio coefficients combination in the data set.

The worst-case scenario happened in Germany during negotiations of the Maastricht Treaty:

Situation at the Proposer (P) level:　　−7.5—"unfavorable"
Situation at the Chooser (C) level:　　−4—"unfavorable."
Type of ratification procedure:　　−5.4—"qualified majority".
Side-payments made:　　+7.5 for "yes"

The sum of these coefficients is −9.4, but the outcome was positive. It means that the effect of the E variable offset the sum of effects of other variables. In order to produce the value of at least +1 on the outcome variable, the effect of the E variable should be at least +10.4. This value would be the least *relative* effective value for this particular case and, through interpolation, for our data-set in general. Consequently, the effect coefficients for the data set will be as follows:

Situation at the Proposer (P) level:	+7.5 for "favorable" (1/1 cell)
	−7.5 for "unfavorable" (0/0 cell)
Situation at the Chooser (C) level:	+4 for "favorable" (1/1 cell)
	−4 for "unfavorable" (0/0 cell)
Presence of Endorsers:	+10.4 for "yes" (1/1 cell)
	−10.4 for "no" (0/0 cell)
Type of ratification procedure:	+5.4 for "simple majority" (1/1 cell)
	−5.4 for "qualified majority" (0/0 cell)
Side payments made:	+7.5 for "yes" (1/1 cell)
	−7.5 for "no" (0/0 cell)

The sum of coefficients and, consequently, the positive outcome odds for this sample are shown in Table A.12.

Now, when the outcome cumulative values have been received, it is possible to find the threshold values for the cumulative coefficients representing positive and negative outcomes of negotiations (the "Outcome" column in Table A.12). In case of the positive outcome, the smallest positive value is 1 (Maastricht Treaty/Germany). But this value must be discarded because it was assumed artificially while calculating the smallest possible value for the E+ coefficient. The next smallest positive value is +4.8 (Civil Aviation Agreement/UK). The closest to the zero point negative value is −4.8 (ITO/US). It means that, for the data set, every agreement that has a cumulative result coefficient value of − *4.8 or lower* is likely to fail. On the other hand, every agreement that has a cumulative result coefficient value of +4.8 *or higher* is likely to succeed. The agreement with a cumulative result coefficient value within the interval of +/− 4.8 is in the gray area with an uncertain outcome. Therefore, *within the limits of our data set*, it is possible to make tentative and conditional but still a conclusion that supporters of a certain initiative have to make sure that at the moment of final approval the cumulative result coefficient value for their initiative is at the +4.8 level or higher. At the same time, the opponents of that initiative have to work toward the cumulative result coefficient value of −4.8 or lower.

The above described approach offers a valuable tool for many communication practitioners and politicians to evaluate the odds for success or failure of

TABLE A.12

The Final Cross-Case Display Summarizing the International Relations Data Sets Analysis Results: the Final Numerical Model

Agreement & Country	Situation at the Proposer (P) level	Situation at the Chooser (C) level	Presence of Endorsers (E)	Type of Ratification Procedure	Side-payments Made	Result
ITO U.S.	+7.5	−4	−10.4	−5.4	+7.5	−4.8
ITO U.K.	−7.5	−4	−10.4	+5.4	−7.5	−24
Bretton Woods U.S.	+7.5	−4	+10.4	+5.4	+7.5	+26.8
Bretton Woods U.K.	+7.5	−4	+10.4	+5.4	+7.5	+26.8
Oil Agreement U.S.	−7.5	−4	−10.4	−5.4	−7.5	−34.8
Oil Agreement U.K.	+7.5	+4	+10.4	+5.4	−7.5	+19.8
Civil Aviation Agreement U.S.	+7.5	−4	+10.4	+5.4	+7.5	+26.8
Civil Aviation Agreement U.K.	−7.5	+4	+10.4	+5.4	−7.5	+4.8
ECSC France	+7.5	+4	+10.4	−5.4	+7.5	+24
ECSC Germany	+7.5	+4	+10.4	−5.4	+7.5	+24
EDC France	−7.5	−4	−10.4	−5.4	−7.5	−34.8
EDC Germany	+7.5	+4	+10.4	−5.4	−7.5	+9
NAFTA Mexico	+7.5	+4	+10.4	+5.4	−7.5	+19.8
NAFTA Canada	−7.5	−4	+10.4	+5.4	+7.5	+11.8
NAFTA U.S.	+7.5	−4	+10.4	+5.4	+7.5	+26.8
Maastricht Treaty France	+7.5	+4	+10.4	−5.4	+7.5	+24
Maastricht Treaty Germany	−7.5	−4	+10.4	−5.4	+7.5	+1
Maastricht Treaty U.K.	−7.5	−4	+10.4	+5.4	+7.5	+11.8

their ideas. It is very intuitive and easy to use. Each coefficient is a decrease or increase in odds for a successful outcome of an internal approval process due to effect of a certain variable. The final outcome is the sum of all these coefficients. The threshold values can be seen in the data set itself. This nonparametric approach has its advantages and limitations.

An advantage of this approach is that it gives a unique opportunity to work with small samples and, consequently, can be used by any person, company, or organization. Another advantage is that it does not require an expansive computer software and ability to read and interpret a computer statistical output—all calculations can be done by hand. Finally, nonparametric procedures provide exact—not asymptotic—results.

In terms of disadvantages, it is impossible to extrapolate the results beyond the limits of a certain data set. And, probably, the main one is that this procedure provides only direct effects of independent variables on the outcome variable, not taking into account the effect of other variables in the model or spurious correlations. Consequently, values of some coefficients become inflated or deflated. For example, in the model the P-level coefficient is inflated while the side-payment coefficient is strongly deflated. (This will be demonstrated in the next section.) The nonparametric method provides just an approximation of a good large sample logistic regression model. That is why, certainly, the best way to use the model presented in this book is to collect a really large data set and use a regular logistic regression analysis, which would produce a much better analysis outcome. (The problem is that large negotiation data sets with all the information necessary for the new model simply do not exist yet. And those that do exist do not contain all the information necessary to code the data according to the requirements of the new model.)

Finally, the nonparametric approach does not identify the effect of the vertical moving interest border in the model. It happened because it was necessary to recode the two scale-type variables into dichotomies and, by so doing, made them static. It is a major drawback as far as the purpose of this book is concerned. That is why the next section will explore the effect of each coefficient on the model deeper, correct some distortions, and explore further the effect of the degree of favorability of the situation at the P and C levels on the final outcome variable. Only after that can the model be considered to be practically fully explored.

Effect of Each Separate Variable

The first question is: How far does the vertical moving interest borderline at the P level need to be moved in order to start producing an increase in odds for

TABLE A.13
The P-Level 7-Point Scale Odds-Ratio Calculations

P-level situation	Failed (probability)	Passed (probability)	Frequency	Odds of Success
1 "very unfavorable"	1 (1.000)	0 (0.000)	1	0
2 "unfavorable"	1 (0.500)	1 (0.500)	2	1
3 "somewhat unfavorable"	1 (0.250)	3 (0.750)	4	3
4 "neutral"	0 (0.000)	0 (0.000)	0	—
5 "somewhat favorable"	0 (0.000)	0 (0.000)	0	—
6 "favorable"	0 (0.000)	3 (1.000)	3	infinity
7 "very favorable"	1 (0.125)	7 (0.875)	8	7

the positive outcome? Table A.13 should answer the question. In this table, the same kind of coding is used as in the initial form of coding—7-point Likert-type scale. It will help us to see where and how along this continuum the situation changes.[3]

As can be seen, within limits of the data set, as long as the vertical moving interest border stays at the 2 level ("unfavorable"), there is approximately a 50/50 chances for success. But as soon as this border is moved to the third level ("somewhat unfavorable"), there is an increased chance for a successful outcome by a factor of 3 and then the chances for a successful outcome skyrocket into infinity. Consequently, the "somewhat unfavorable" level can be considered as a kind of threshold for this particular variable for this particular data set.

Consequently, it is quite clear that the strong effect coefficient for this variable calculated previously was inflated because, practically, the lower third of the whole scale does matter to the final outcome and the other two thirds don't. This inflation will be seen even better in comparison with the side-payment coefficient that will be discussed below.

The next question is: How far does the vertical moving interest borderline at the C-level need to be moved in order to start producing an increase in odds for the positive outcome? The answer is in Table A.14.

As can be seen, within limits of our data set, as soon as the vertical moving interest borderline is moved to the second level ("unfavorable"), the chances for a positive outcome increase by a factor of 3 and then the chances for a successful outcome skyrocket into infinity. Consequently, the "unfavorable" level can be

TABLE A.14
The C-Level 7-Point Scale Odds-Ratio Calculations

C-level situation	Failed (probability)	Passed (probability)	Frequency	Odds of Success
1 "very unfavorable"	3 (0.600)	2 (0.400)	5	0.667
2 "unfavorable"	1 (0.250)	3 (0.750)	4	3
3 "somewhat unfavorable"	0 (0.000)	2 (1.000)	2	infinity
4 "neutral"	0 (0.000)	0 (0.000)	0	—
5 "somewhat favorable"	0 (0.000)	3 (1.000)	3	infinity
6 "favorable"	0 (0.000)	3 (1.000)	3	infinity
7 "very favorable"	0 (0.000)	1 (1.000)	1	infinity

considered as a kind of threshold for this particular variable for this particular data set.

It can also be seen that the variation on this particular variable does not have practically any effect on the outcome variable. As soon as the "unfavorable" line is crossed, there are very high chances for success. That is why it can be assumed that the coefficient for this particular variable calculated previously may be inflated as well. In a logistic regression model, this coefficient might have been overshadowed by the effects of other variables and, consequently, might have not been significant at all. That is, probably, why the Chi-Square coefficient for that particular matrix was not significant either.

There is not much to say from the data set about the E variable coefficient. As it was explained above, it was calculated from the worst-case scenario of the Maastricht Treaty/Germany case. But what can be said is that this variable is perfectly positively correlated with the outcome variable and it has, definitely, one of the strongest if not the strongest effect in the model. This coefficient shows that if communication practitioners or policy decision makers do not communicate with their opponents, don't find out what is important for them, and don't compromise—they practically have no chances for success.

The effect of the type of ratification procedure variable is very intuitive and makes perfect sense. By simply changing the ratification procedure from qualified majority to simple majority, it is possible to increase chances for a positive outcome by a factor of 5.4. And it is understandable: the simpler the approval procedure—the fewer problems can occur along the way. It is, probably, the only coefficient in the model that is neither inflated nor deflated in value. At the same time, it is important to remember that the Chi-Square coefficient for that particular matrix was not significant. Therefore, this coefficient can be considered just as a fair approximation to the real data-set value.

The last coefficient in the model—the side-payment—must be seriously deflated. It can be determined citing several reasons. First of all, its value of +7.5 is equal to that of the P-level coefficient. But two-thirds of the variation of that variable do not have any effect on the outcome variable. That is why it seems unlikely that these two variables have the same effect on the final outcome. It seems that the side-payment variable coefficient is deflated because of the dichotomous form in which it was presented in the model calculations. This form distorts the real sense and significance of the side-payment in the model. And the main problem is the "not necessary" category. The dichotomous version approaches the problem of side-payments mechanistically—they either were made or not—and it does not take into account the situation itself. In several cases side-payments were not made only because they were not necessary. Even without them the situation was favorable enough. This was reflected in the initial coding. But it was lost in the dichotomous form. This form masks a very important fact that side-payments were very important because they were made only in very difficult situations and really saved many agreements. Secondly, the dichotomy creates an impression that this variable does not have a serious effect on the outcome because in the dichotomous form it is possible to get an impression that often side-payments were not made but the outcome was positive anyway. But again, this situation occurred only in cases where these side-payments were not absolutely necessary. It means that in the table expressing the model in the dichotomous form in cases where side-payments were not necessary—a value of "zero" instead of -7.5 should have been input. It would have shown that in those cases the absence of a side-payment did not have any *negative* effect on the odds of the positive outcome but it simply did not have *any* effect at all.

In order to correct this distortion and find out the real significance of side-payments for the outcome of the negotiations, it is necessary to recode this variable back into trichotomy. Table A.15 shows the distribution of frequency values in a three-category matrix (2: "was made"; 1: "not necessary"; 0: "was not made").

The Cramer's V coefficient for this matrix is 0.841 with the p value of 0.002 which shows a very strong and highly significant relationship between these two variables. The squared coefficient shows that this variable alone can account for more than 70 percent variation of the dependent variable. That is why it is possible to say that it is one of the most important and strong variables in

TABLE A.15
A Crosst-abulation of the 3-Level Side-Payment
Variable with the Outcome Variable

		Result	
		0	*1*
Side-payments	*2*	1	10
	1	0	4
	0	3	0

the model and that the value of its coefficient in the model above was definitely and strongly deflated.

U.S. Negotiations of Voluntary Restraint Agreements in Steel

Now it would be interesting to apply these coefficients to the steel VERs case study and see if the cumulative coefficients for the outcome variable will be consistent with the real world outcome of this particular internal approval process. It would be like checking a new negotiation situation against an already existing data set and, consequently, against existing coefficients estimated from that data set.

The situation in terms of the Section 201 escape clause option was as follows:

Situation at the Proposer (P) level: −7.5 for "unfavorable"

Situation at the Chooser (C) level: +4 for "favorable"

Presence of Endorsers: +10.4 for "yes"

Type of ratification procedure: −5.4 for "qualified majority"

Side-payments made: −7.5 for "no"

The cumulative outcome coefficient: −6.

This coefficient is consistent with the real world result of the internal approval process for the Section 201 escape clause option—it failed—the cumulative coefficient is below the -4.8 threshold value for failures.

The situation in terms of the VERs option was as follows:

Situation at the Proposer (P) level: +7.5 for "favorable"

Situation at the Chooser (C) level: −4 for "unfavorable"

Presence of Endorsers:	+10.4 for "yes"
Type of ratification procedure:	+5.4 for "simple majority"
Side-payments made:	+7.5 for "yes"
The cumulative outcome coefficient:	+26.8.

This coefficient is consistent with the real world result of the internal approval process for the VERs solution—it passed. This coefficient is also well above the +4.8 threshold value for successes. It means that such coefficients, regardless of their limitations, in general theoretically could be used as *very rough* estimates of the odds for success of a certain internal approval process in a similar structure and under similar circumstances. The American decision-makers might have used such a methodology (if they had one) to estimate which of the proposals had a better chance for domestic approval success and, consequently, which of them should have been presented at the international level.

Discussion

Analysis of the data in the data set illustrated the model quite well. Regardless of some special characteristics of this data set, the general mechanisms and elements of the model were clearly seen working during the data analysis process. The general direction of the estimates of the numerical coefficients of the effects of each variable on the outcome of the internal approval process was consistent with the hypothesized effects' directions.

It can be concluded from the numerical analysis of the data that, first of all, it seems that all the variables in the model are those that really can help to explain the variability of the dependent variable. Second, each variable separately indeed contributes to a general understanding of the problem of how and why possible outcomes of the internal approval processes came into being.

It may be appropriate to remember here that in the data set the situations at the P and C levels were marked at the moment of time right before any political moves were made. Then, three tools were utilized, namely—recruitment of Endorsers, the choice of the best appropriate form of ratification, and side-payments. As long as the vertical moving interest border stayed at the P and C levels at that particular moment at the "very unfavorable" position, the odds for any favorable outcome were extremely low. And it is understandable—there is a certain amount of work any political tool can do. From that far-left position it was almost impossible to move the vertical interest borderline to

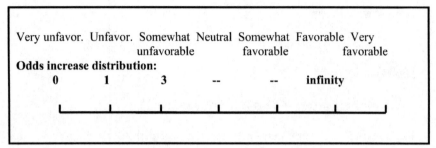

FIGURE A.2.
The Proposer level odds increase distribution

the right far enough for a successful ratification. At the "unfavorable" points (at the P and C levels) the chances for a positive outcome started to increase. And they were very high at all other higher levels. And it is clear, again, that from these positions it is much easier to move the vertical borderline farther to the right. It basically means that the variation of positions on these two variables does matter too much for the final outcome and that any shift to the right facilitates the positive outcome—that is exactly what the model suggests. Moreover, the surprisingly smooth and steady increase in odds for a successful outcome over the range of values on these two independent variables makes a very demonstrative and illustrative argument for the offered model.

Graphically, it is illustrated on Figures A.2 and A.3.

Unfortunately in the data set the variation on these two variables, that had any significant impact on the dependent variable, was limited basically to just the lower part of the scale. But it is necessary to remember that word of caution that was offered above. It is not appropriate to try to extrapolate results from any data set onto anything else beyond its scope or field. What is observed here is an effect of this particular set of cases and any other set from

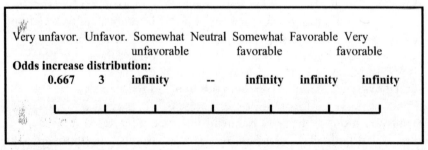

FIGURE A.3
The Chooser level odds increase distribution

any other area may produce very different results. That is why, for communication practitioners and politicians it is absolutely necessary to create their own data sets, analyze them, and draw their own conclusions based only on those results.

Although all the above coefficients do not have to be taken too seriously for the reasons abundantly explained already, it is interesting to see how the two figures above seem to underscore the importance and effectiveness of the communication point of view on international negotiations. Traditionally, the political struggle within a country's government was explored by scholars and exploited by fiction writers. The political situation in a country's parliament and the parliamentary ratification procedure were the idols worshiped by generations of political scientists. They even suggested that the interest groups and negotiators would tailor their political position based on the position taken by the P and C actors. So, the Proposer and the Chooser (the incumbent politicians) almost dictated the rules of the game. But the analysis above shows almost the opposite picture and implies serious limitations on the power of politicians. It shows that the initial reaction of the Ps and Cs may not even be that important after all (unless, of course, the situation at these two actor group levels is very bad—that is "very unfavorable"). The main question is not what they think initially but what they will think at the final moment of the institutional approval process (that may be years away). That is, the main element in the game is the communication aspect. The main issue is not what the situation is as of right now (static) but what we can do about it (dynamic). If we communicate—recruit endorsers, make side-payments, simplify ratification procedure (if necessary), we can change everything. (That is, probably, why big corporate interest groups are more powerful than politicians—they can make them do whatever they want.) The real leverage in the negotiation process is communication—not incumbency. And this is a dramatic shift from all previous conceptualizations of the process of international talks.

The other three variables—presence of supporters, type of ratification procedures, and side-payments—also had each its own impact on the final outcome variable. The strongest effect was exerted by the Endorsers variable that had a perfect positive correlation with the positive outcome. As was expected, quite a strong effect of side-payments was observed as well. The effect of the type of ratification procedure on the final outcome was not particularly strong but visible.

In short, numerical analysis clarified and at least illustrated the main elements and dynamics of the new model. And what we have seen in this appendix is consistent with what was expected according to the new model.

Notes

1. The sources were: Anderson, 1981; Baum, 1958; Blair, 1976; Cooper, 1947; Cox and Kernell, 1991; Dell, 1995; Diebold, 1952 and 1959; Dobson, 1991; Doern and Tomlin, 1991; Eckes, 1975; Ehrmann, 1957; Featherstone, 1988; Fursdon, 1979; Gardner, 1980; George, 1991; Giavazzi and Giovanni, 1989; Gillingham, 1991; Gros and Thygesen, 1992; Grosser, 1961; Jonsson, 1987; Katzenstein, 1978; Kock, 1969; Kuisel, 1983; Lerner and Aron, 1957; Lusting, Bosworth, and Lawrence, 1992; Mallalieu, 1956; Miller, 1980; Milner 1997; Milward, 1984; Sampson, 1975; Schmitt, 1962; Schott, 1989; Shonfield, 1965; Shugart and Carey, 1992; Smith, 1950; Stoff, 1980; Thayer, 1965; Tint, 1972; Tsoukalis, 1993; Van Dormael, 1978; Vernon and Spar, 1989; Waltz, 1979; Williams, 1966; Willis, 1968.

2. For the use of imputed values see: Tate, R. (1998). *An introduction to modeling outcomes in the behavioral sciences.* Edina, MN: Burgess.

3. This methodology was described in: Tate, R. (1998). *An introduction to modeling outcomes in the behavioral sciences.* Edina, MN: Burgess.

Bibliography

Acuff, F. L. (1993). *How to negotiate anything with anyone anywhere around the world.* New York: AMACOM.

Albert, M. (1993). *Capitalism against capitalism.* London: Whurr Publishers.

Allison, G. T. (1971). *Essence of decision: Explaining the Cuban missile crisis.* Boston: Little Brown

Anderson, I. (1981). *ARAMCO, the United States, and Saudi Arabia.* Princeton, NJ: Princeton University Press.

Anderson, J. A. (1987). *Communication research: Issues and methods.* New York, NY: McGraw-Hill.

Axelrod, R. M. (1984). *The evolution of cooperation.* New York, NY: Basic Books.

Axelrod, R., and R. O. Keohane. (1986). Achieving cooperation under anarchy: strategies and institutions. In A. K. Oye (Ed.), *Cooperation under anarchy.* Princeton, NJ: Princeton University Press.

Bagli, C. V. (1997, January 18). Norfolk wins a big round in the battle over Conrail. *The New York Times,* p. A35.

Baldwin, R. E. (1985). *The political economy of U.S. import policy.* Cambridge, MS: MIT Press.

Barnaby, F., and N. Ritchie. (2004). *North Korea: Problems, Perceptions, and Proposals.* Oxford, Great Britain: Oxford Research Group. [On-line]. Available: www.oxfordresearchgroup.org.uk/publications/books/northkorea.htm.

Bartos, O. J. (1978). Simple model of negotiation: A sociological point of view. In I. William Zartman (Ed.), *The negotiation process: Theories and applications.* Beverly Hills, CA: Sage.

Bateman, J. C. (1958) A new moral dimension for communication. *Public Relations Journal,* 14 (August), 16–17.

———. (1957). The path to professionalism. *Public Relations Journal, 13* (March), 6–8.

Baum, W. (1958). *The French economy and the state*. Princeton, NJ: Princeton University Press.

Bettenhausen, K., and K. Murnighan. (1985). The emergence of norms in competitive decision-making groups. *Administrative Science Quarterly* 30, 350–72.

Bies, R. J. (1987). The predicament of injustice: The management of moral outrage. In L. L. Cummings and B. M. Staw (Eds.), *Research in organizational behavior: Vol. 9.* (289–319). Greenwich, CT: JAI Press.

Blair, J. (1976). *The control of oil*. New York, NY: Pantheon.

Blum, W. (2001). *Rogue state*. London: Zed Books.

Bohrnstedt, G. W., and D. Knoke. (1994). *Statistics for social data analysis*. Itasca, IL: F. E. Peacock.

Botan, C. (1992). International public relations: Critique and reformulation. *Public Relations Review,* 18 (2), 149–59.

Bowen, G. L. (1989). Presidential action and public opinion about U.S. Nicaraguan policy: Limits to the 'rally round the flag' syndrome. *Political Science and Politics* 22 (December), 793–800.

Bryant, A. (1993, December 23). Board endorses air union's bid to buy United. *The New York Times,* p. A1.

Bull, H. (1995). *The anarchical society: A study of order in world politics*. New York, NY: Columbia University Press.

Bunn, G. (1992). *Arms control by committee—managing negotiations with the Russians*. Stanford, California: Stanford University Press.

Cameron, K. S. (1984). The effectiveness of ineffectiveness. In B. M. Staw and L. L. Cummings (Eds.), *Research in organizational behavior* (Vol. 6, p. 276). Greenwich, CT: JAI.

Christians, C. G. (1989). Ethical theory in a global setting. In T. W. Cooper (Ed.), *Communication ethics and global change* (pp. 3–19). White Plains, NY: Longman.

Christians, D. G., and J. W. Carey. (1989). The logic and aims of qualitative research. In G. H. Stempel III and B. H. Westley (Eds.), *Research methods in mass communication* (2nd ed.). Englewood Cliffs, NJ: Prentice-Hall.

Colosi, T. (1984). A model for negotiation and mediation. In D. B. Bendahmane and J. W. McDonald, Jr. (Eds.), *International negotiation*. Washington, DC: Foreign Service Institute, US State Department.

Committee on Armed Services. (1988, May 16 and 17). *Hearings before the defense policy panel of the committee on armed services* (U. S. Congress. House of Representatives). Retrieved April 28, 1998, from the U.S. Department of State Electronic Reading Room: www.foia.state.gov/

Committee on Foreign Relations. (1992a). *Report on the START treaty U.S.* (U. S. Congress, U. S. Senate, U.S. Government Printing Office). Retrieved April 28, 1998, from the U.S. Department of State Electronic Reading Room: www.foia.state.gov/

———. (1992b). *Hearings on the START treaty* (U. S. Congress, U. S. Senate, U.S. Government Printing Office). Retrieved April 28, 1998, from the U.S. Department of State Electronic Reading Room: www.foia.state.gov/

Condon, J. C., and F. S. Youself. (1975). *An introduction to intercultural communication*. New York, NY: Bobbs-Merrill.

Conybeare, J. A. (1984). Public goods, prisoner's dilemma and the international political economy. *International Studies Quarterly* 28, 5–22.

———. (1991). Voting for protection: An electoral model of tariff policy. *International Organization* 45 (Winter).

Cooper, J. (1947). *The right to fly.* New York, NY: Holt.

Cooper, T. W. (1989). Global universals: In search of common ground. In T. W. Cooper (Ed.), *Communication ethics and global change* (pp. 20–39). White Plains, NY: Longman.

Coser, L. A. (1956). *The functions of social conflict.* New York, NY: The Free Press.

———. (1967). *Continuities in the study of social conflict.* New York, NY: The Free Press.

Coughlin, C. C. (1985). Domestic content legislation: House voting and the economic theory of voting. *Economic Enquiry* 23 (July), 437–48.

Cowhey, P. F. (1993). Domestic institutions and the credibility of international commitments: Japan and the United States. *International Organization* 47 (Spring).

Cox, G., and S. Kernell (Eds.). (1991). *The politics of divided government.* Boulder, CO: Westview.

Cross, J. G. (1978). Negotiation as a learning process. In I. William Zartman (Ed.), *The negotiation process: Theories and applications.* Beverly Hills, CA: Sage.

Culbertson, H. M. (1973). Public relations ethics: A new look. *Public Relations Quarterly* 17 (Winter), 15–25.

———. (1994, August). Cultural beliefs: A focus of study in cross-cultural public relations. Paper presented at the meeting of the Association for Education of Journalism and Mass Communication, Atlanta, GA.

Daniels, A. C. (1989). *Performance management.* Tucker, GA: Performance Management Publications.

Deetz, S. A. (1997). Communication in the age of negotiation. *Journal of Communication* 47 (4), 118–35.

Dell, E. (1995). *The Schuman plan and the British abdication of leadership in Europe.* New York, NY: Oxford University Press.

Derwinski, E. J. (1984). The art of negotiation within the congress. In D. B. Bendahmane and J. W. McDonald Jr. (Eds.), *International negotiation.* Washington, DC: Foreign Service Institute of the U.S. Department of State.

Deutsch, K. W., et al. (1957). *Political community in the North Atlantic area: International organization in the light of historical experience.* Princeton, NJ: Princeton University Press.

Diebold, W. (1952). *The end of ITO.* Princeton, NJ: International Finance section, Economics Department, Princeton University.

———. (1959). *The Schuman plan: a study in economic cooperation, 1950–1959.* New York, NY: Praeger.

Dobson, A. (1991). *Peaceful air warfare.* Oxford: Oxford University Press.

Doern, G. B., and B. Tomlin. (1991). *Faith and fear.* Toronto: Stoddart.

Donaldson, T. (1989). *The ethics of business.* New York: Oxford University Press.

Donnelly, J. (1989). *Universal human rights in theory and practice.* Ithaca, NY: Cornell University Press.

Dozier, D. M., and W. P. Ehling. (1992). Evaluation of public relations programs: What the literature tells us about their effects. In J. E.Grunig (Ed.), *Excellence in public relations and communication management* (pp. 159–84). Hillsdale, NJ: Lawrence Erlbraum Associates, Publishers.

Druckman, D. (1978). Boundary role conflict: Negotiation as dual responsiveness. In I. W. Zartman (Ed.), *The negotiation process: Theories and applications*. Beverly Hills, CA: Sage.

Easton, D. (1965). *A systems analysis of political life*. New York: John Wiley and Sons.

Eckes, A. (1975). *A search for solvency: Bretton Woods and international monetary system, 1941–1971*. Austin, TX: University of Texas Press.

Ehrmann, H. (1957). *Organized business in France*. Princeton, NJ: Princeton University Press.

Einhorn, R. J. (1985). *Negotiating from strength—Leverage in U.S-Soviet arms control negotiations*. Washington, D.C.: Georgetown University.

Elfstrom, G. (1991). *Moral issues and multinational corporations*. New York: St. Martin's Press.

Fairman, M. (1961). A saint for Madison avenue. *Public Relations Journal* 17 (November), 14–16.

Fearon, J. D. (1995). Rationalist explanations for war. *International Organization* 49 (3), 379–414.

Featherstone, K. (1988). *Socialist parties and European integration*. Manchester: Manchester University Press.

Federation of American Scientists. (2004). *DPRK: Nuclear Weapons Program* [Online]. Available: http://fas.org/nuke/guide/dprk/nuke/.

Ferre, J. P., and Willihnganz, S. C. (1991). *Public relations and ethics: A bibliography*. Boston, MS: G. K. Hall & Co.

Finer, H. (1964). *Dulles over Suez*. Chicago, IL: Quadrangle.

Fisher, G. (1980). *International negotiations: A cross-cultural perspective*. Yarmouth, ME: Intercultural Press.

———. (1997). *Mindsets: The role of culture and perception in international relations*. Yarmouth, ME: Intercultural Press.

Fisher, R., and W. Ury. (1983). *Getting to yes: Negotiating agreement without giving in*. New York, NY: Penguin.

Fiske, J. (1982). *Introduction to communication studies*. New York, NY: Methuen.

Fiske, S. T., and S. E. Taylor. (1991). *Social cognition*. New York, NY: McGraw-Hill.

Frieden, J. A. (1991). Invested interests: The politics of national economic policies in a world of global finance. *International Organization* 45 (Autumn).

Fursdon, E. (1979). *The European defense community: a history*. New York: St. Martin's.

Gardner, R. (1980). *Sterling-dollar diplomacy in current perspective*. (2nd ed.) New York, NY: Columbia University Press.

Gaubatz, K. T. (1996). Democratic states and commitment in international relations. *International Organization* 50 (1), 109–39.

George, A. L., and McKeown, T. J. (1985). Case studies and theories of organizational decision making. *Advances in Information Processing in Organizations* 2, 21–58.

George, S. (1991). *Britain and European integration since 1945.* Oxford: Basil Blackwell.

Giavazzi, F., and A. Giovanni (Eds.). (1989). *Limiting exchange rate flexibility.* Cambridge, MA: MIT Press.

Gillingham, J. (1991). *Coal, steel, and the rebirth of Europe, 1945–1955.* Cambridge: Cambridge University Press.

Gilpin, R. (1987). *The political economy of international relations.* Princeton, NJ: Princeton University Press.

Gilson, S. C. (2000). Analysts and information gaps: Lessons from the UAL buyout. *Financial Analysts Journal* 56(6), 82–110.

Goldblat, J. (1994). *Arms control: A guide to negotiations and agreements.* Thousand Oaks, CA: SAGE Publications.

Gowa, J. (1989). Rational hegemon, excludable goods, and small groups: An epitaph for hegemonic stability theory. *World Politics* 41 (April), 307–24.

Grieco, J. M. (1993a). Anarchy and the limits of cooperation: A realist critique of the newest liberal instiutionalism. In D. A. Baldwin (Ed.), *Neorealism and neoliberalism: The contemporary debate.* New York, NY: Columbia University Press.

———. (1993b). Understanding the problem of international cooperation: The limits of neoliberal institutionalism and the future of realist theory. In D. A. Baldwin (Ed.), *Neorealism and neoliberalism: The contemporary debate.* New York: Columbia University Press.

Gros, D., and N. Thygesen. (1992). *European monetary integration.* New York: St. Martin's Press.

Grosser, A. (1961). *La Quatrieme Republique et sa Politique Exterieure.* Paris: Armand Colin.

Grunig, J. E. (1992). Communication, public relations, and effective organizations: An overview of the book. In J. E.Grunig (Ed.), *Excellence in public relations and communication management* (pp. 1–28). Hillsdale, NJ: Lawrence Erlbraum Associates, Publishers.

Grunig, J. E., and L. A. Grinug. (1992). Models of public relations and communication. In J. E.Grunig (Ed.), *Excellence in public relations and communication management* (pp. 285–325). Hillsdale, NJ: Lawrence Erlbraum Associates, Publishers.

Grunig, J. E., and T. Hunt. (1984). *Managing public relations.* New York: Holt, Rinehart & Winston.

Grunig, J. E., and F. C. Repper. (1992). Strategic management, publics and issues. In J. E. Grunig (Ed.), *Excellence in public relations and communication management* (pp. 117–57). Hillsdale, NJ: Lawrence Erlbraum Associates, Publishers.

Grunig, L. A. (1992). Activism: How it limits the effectiveness of organizations and how excellent public relations departments respond. In J. E. Grunig (Ed.), *Excellence in public relations and communication management* (pp. 503–30). Hillsdale, NJ: Lawrence Erlbraum Associates, Publishers.

Grunig, L. A., J. E. Grunig, and W. P. Ehling. (1992). What is an effective organization? In J. E. Grunig (Ed.), *Excellence in public relations and communication management* (pp. 65–90). Hillsdale, NJ: Lawrence Erlbraum Associates, Publishers.

Haas, E. B. (1958). *The uniting of Europe: Political social and economic forces, 1950–1957.* Stanford, CA: Stanford University Press.

Haas, E. B. (1983). Words can hurt you; or, who said what to whom about regimes. In S. D. Krasner (Ed.), *International regimes.* Ithaca, NY: Cornel University Press.

Habeeb, W. M. (1988). *Power and tactics in international negotiation.* Baltimore, MD: John Hopkins University Press.

Hage, J. (1980). *Theories of organizations: Form, process, and transformation.* New York: Wiley.

Hardin, R. (1982). *Collective action.* Baltimore, MD: John Hopkins University Press.

Hatch, E. (1983). *Culture and morality: The relativity of values in anthropology.* New York: Columbia University Press.

Hawrysh, B. M., and J. L. Zaichkowsky. (1989). Cultural approaches to negotiations: Understanding the Japanese. *International Marketing Review* 7(2), 28–42.

Heckman, R., and A. Guskey. (1998). The relationship between alumni and university: Toward a theory of discretionary collaborative behavior. *Journal of Marketing Theory and Practice* 6(2), 97–112.

Hodge, S. (2000). *Global smarts: The art of communication and deal making anywhere in the world.* New York: John Wiley & Sons.

Hodgson, K. (1992). Adapting ethical decisions to a global marketplace. *Management Review* (May).

Hopmann, P. T. (1995). Two paradigms of negotiation: Bargaining and problem solving. *Annals of AAPSS* 542, 24–47.

Hopmann, P. T. (1996). *The negotiation process and the resolution of international conflicts.* Columbia, SC: The University of South Carolina Press.

Hudson, M., and Stanier, J. (1998). *War and the media: A random searchlight.* New York: New York University Press.

Hunt, T., and A. Tirpok. (1993). Universal ethics code: An idea whose time has come. *Public Relations Review* 19(1), 1–11.

Jaksa, J. A., and M. S. Pritchard. (1994). *Communication ethics: Methods of analysis* (2nd ed.). Belmont, MA: Wadsworth.

Jervis, R. (1970). *The logic of images in international relations.* Princeton, NJ: Princeton University Press.

Jervis, R. (1976). *Perception and misperception in international politics.* Princeton, NJ: Princeton University Press.

Jervis, R. (1986). Representativeness in foreign policy judgments. *Political Psychology* 7(3), 483–505.

Johnson, D. W. (1974). Communication and the inducement of cooperative behavior in conflicts: A critical review. *Speech Monographs* 41 (March), 64–78.

Jonsson, C. (1989). International negotiations and cognitive theory: A research project. In F. Mautner-Markhof (Ed.), *Process of international negotiations.* Boulder, CO: Westview Press.

Jonsson, C. (1990). *Communication in international bargaining.* London: Pinter Publishers.

Jonsson, C. (1987). *International aviation and the politics of regime change.* New York: St. Martin's Press.

Jurgensen, J. H., and J. Lukaszewski. (1987). Ethics: Content before conduct. *Public Relations Journal* 44 (July), 47–48.

Kartchner, K. M. (1992). *Negotiating START: Strategic arms reduction talks and the quest for strategic stability.* New Brubswick, NJ: Transaction Publishers.

Katz, D., and R. L. Kahn. (1978). *The social psychology of organizations* (2nd ed.). New York: Wiley.

Katzenstein, P. (1976). International relations and domestic structures: Foreign economic policies of advanced industrial states. *International Organization* 30 (Winter), 1–45.

Katzenstein, P. (Ed.). (1978). *Between power and plenty.* Madison: University of Wisconsin Press.

Kazuaki, Okabe. (n.d.). Why the Japanese system isn't true democracy? *The Newsletter of United for a Multicultural Japan* 2(3). [On-line]. Available: www.tabunka.org/newsletter/true_democracy.html.

Keohane, R. O. (1984). *After hegemony: Cooperation and discord in the world political economy.* Princeton, NJ: Princeton University Press.

Keohane, R. O., G. King, and S. Verba. (1994). *Designing social inquiry: Scientific inference in qualitative research.* Princeton, NJ: Princeton University Press.

Kindleberger, C. P. (1986). International public goods without international government. *The American Economic Review* 76(1), 1–13.

Kissinger, H. (1969). The Vietnam negotiations. *Foreign Affairs* 47, 211–34.

Kock, K. (1969). *International trade policy and the GATT, 1947–1967.* Stockholm: Almqvist and Wiksell.

Krasner, S. D. (1976). State power and the structure of international trade. *World Politics* 28(3), 317–47.

———. (1983). Regimes and the limits of realism: Regimes as autonomous variables. In S. D. Krasner (Ed.), *International regimes.* Ithaca, NY: Cornell University Press.

Krasner, S. D. (1978). *Defending the national interest: Raw material investments and U.S. foreign policy.* Princeton, NJ: Princeton University Press.

Kruckeberg, D. (1989). The need for an international code of ethics. *Public Relations Review* 15 (Summer), 6–17.

———. (1993). Universal ethics code: both possible and feasible. *Public Relations Review* 19 (Spring), 21–31.

———. (1996). Transnational corporate ethical responsibilities. In H. M. Culbertson and N. Chen (Eds.), *International public relations: A comparative analysis* (pp. 81–92). Mahwah, NJ: Lawrence Erlbaum Associates.

Kuisel, R. (1983). *Capitalism and the state in modern France.* Cambridge: Cambridge University Press.

Kunczik, M. (1997). *Images of nations and international public relations.* Mahwah, NJ: Lawrence.

Lakoff, G., and M. Johnson. (1980). *Metaphors we live by.* Chicago: The University of Chicago Press.

Lancy, D. F. (1993). *Qualitative research in education: An introduction to the major traditions.* New York: Longman.

Lapham, L. (1997). *Waiting for the barbarians.* London: Verso.

Larson, D. W. (1985). *Origins of containment: A psychological explanation.* Princeton, NJ: The Princeton University Press.

Lawler, E. J., and J. Yoon. (1995). Structural power and emotional process in negotiation: A social exchange approach. In R. M. Kramer and D. M. Messick (Eds.), *Negotiation as a social process*. Thousand Oaks, CA: Sage.

Lear, J. (1984). Moral objectivity. In S. C. Brown (Ed.), *Objectivity and cultural divergence* (pp. 135–70). Cambridge: Cambridge University Press.

Lebow, R. N. (1985). Conclusion. In R. Jervis, R. N. Lebow, and J. G. Stein (Eds.), *Psychology and deterrence*. Baltimore, MD: Johns Hopkins University Press.

Leeds, B. A. (1999). Domestic political institutions, credible commitments, and international cooperation. *American Journal of Political Science* 43(4), 979–1002.

Lehman, H. P., and J. L. McCoy. (1992). The dynamics of the two-level bargaining game. The 1988 Brazilian debt negotiation. *World Politics* 44 (July).

Lerner, D., and R. Aron. (1957). *France defeats the EDC*. New York, NY: Praeger.

Lindeborg, R. A. (1994). Excellent communication. *Public Relations Quarterly* 39 (Spring).

Linklater, A. (1998). *The transformation of political community: Ethical foundations of the post-westphalian era*. Columbia, SC: The University of South Carolina Press.

Linowes, D. F. (1977). International business and morality. *Vital Speeches of the Day* 43(15), 475–78.

Lohmann, S. (1997). Linkage politics. *Journal of Conflict Resolution* 41(1), 38–67.

Lusting, N., B. Bosworth, and R. Lawrence. (1992). *Assessing the impact of North American free trade*. Washington, DC: Brookings Institution.

Mallalieu, W. (1956). *British reconstruction and American policy, 1945–1955*. New York: Scarecrow.

Marshal, R., and M. Tucker. (1992). *Thinking for a living: Education and the wealth of nations*. New York, NY: Harper Collins.

Mayer, F. W. (1992). Managing domestic differences in international negotiations: The strategic use of internal side payments. *International Organization* 46 (Autumn).

McBride, G. (1989). Ethical thought in public relations history: Seeking a relevant perspective. *Journal of Mass Media Ethics* 4(1), 5–20.

McDonald, H. (1986). *The normative basis of culture: A philosophical inquiry*. Baton Rouge, LA: Louisiana State University Press.

McElreath, M. (1997). *Managing systematic and ethical public relations*. Boston, MS: McGraw Hill.

McLeod, D. M., W. P. Eveland Jr., and N. Signorielli. (1994). Conflict and public opinion: Rallying effects and the Persian Gulf war. *Journalism Quarterly* 71(1), 20–31.

Mechling, T. B. (1976–1977). The mythical ethics of law, PR and accounting. *Business and Society Review* 20 (Winter), 6–10.

Merriam, S. B. (1998). *Qualitative research and case study applications in education*. San Francisco: Jossey-Bass.

Miles, M., and M. Huberman. (1994). *Qualitative data analysis*. Thousand Oaks, CA: Sage.

Miller, A. (1980). *Search for security*. Chapel Hill: The University of North Carolina Press.

Miller, J. (1978). *Living systems*. New York: McGraw-Hill.

Miller, K. (1995). *Organizational communication: Approaches and processes*. Belmont, CA: Wadsworth Publishing Co.

Milner, H. V. (1992). International theories of cooperation among nations. *World Politics* 44, 466–96.

———. (1997). *Interests, institutions, and information: Domestic politics and international relations*. Princeton, NJ: Princeton University Press.

Milner, H. V., and P. B. Rosendorff. (1997). Democratic politics and international trade negotiations. *Journal of Conflict Resolution* 41(1), 117–46.

Milward, A. (1984). *The reconstruction of Western Europe, 1945-51*. London: Methuen.

Mitrany, D. (1975). *The functional theory of politics*. London: St. Martin's Press.

Moran, R. T., and W. G. Stripp (Eds.). (1991). *Successful international business negotiations*. Houston, TX: Gulf Publishing Company.

Morgan, C. T. (1990). Issue linkage in international crisis bargaining. *American Journal of Political Science* 34(2), 311–33.

Mueller, J. E. (1970). Presidential popularity from Truman to Johnson. *American Political Science Review* 64 (May), 18–23.

———. (1973). *War, presidents and public opinion*. New York: John Wiley and Sons.

Niksch, L. A. (1996). *North Korea's Nuclear Weapons Program*. Washington, DC: Federation of American Scientists. [On-line]. Available: www.fas.org/spp/starwars/crs/91-141.htm.

Nisbett, R., and L. Ross. (1980). *Human inference: Strategies and shortcomings of social judgment*. Englewood, CA: Prentice-Hall.

Nye, J. S., Jr. (1997). *Understanding international conflict*. New York, NY: Addison Wesley Longman, Inc.

Olasky, M. N. (1978). *Corporate public relations: A new historical perspective*. Hillsdale, NJ: Lawrence Erlbaum Associates.

Oye, K. A. (1986). Explaining cooperation under anarchy: Hypotheses and strategies. In K. A. Oye (Ed.), *Cooperation under anarchy*. Princeton, NJ: Princeton University Press.

Pahre, R. (1997). Endogenous domestic institutions in two-level games and parliamentary oversight of the European Union. *Journal of Conflict Resolution* 41(1), 147–74.

Patton, M. Q. (1990). *Qualitative evaluation methods*. (2nd ed.). Thousand Oaks, CA: Sage.

Pauly, J. J. (1991). A beginner's guide to doing qualitative research in mass communication. *Communication Monographs*, 125.

Pearce, J. A., II, and R. B. Robinson Jr. (1982). *Strategic management: Strategy formulation and implementation*. Homewood, IL: Irwin.

Pelline, J. (1993, December 23). United OKs employee buyout in landmark action. *The San Francisco Chronicle*, p. D1.

Pocock, J. G. (1984). Verbalizing a political act: Toward a politics of speech. In M. J. Shapiro (Ed.), *Language and politics*. Oxford: Basil Blackwell.

Poindexter, P. M., and M. E. McCombs (2000). *Research in mass communication: A practical Guide*. New York: Bedford/St. Martin's Press.

Potter, W. J. (1996). *An analysis of thinking and research about qualitative methods*. Mahwah, NJ: Lawrence Erlbaum Associates.

Pruitt, D. G. (1995). Networks and collective scripts: Paying attention to structure in bargaining theory. In R. M. Kramer and D. M. Messick (Eds.), *Negotiation as a Social Process*. Thousand Oaks, CA: Sage.

Putnam, R. D. (1988). Diplomacy and domestic politics: The logic of two-level games. *International Organization* 42 (Summer), 427–60.

Radford, K. J. (1977). *Complex decision problems: An integrated strategy for resolution.* Reston, VA: Reston Publishing.

Remmer, K. (1998). Does democracy promote interstate cooperation? Lessons from the Mercosur Region. *International Studies Quarterly* 42, 25–52.

Robbins, S. P. (1990). *Organization theory: Structure, design, and applications.* Englewood Cliffs, NJ: Prentice Hall.

Rogers, E. M. (1995). *Diffusion of innovations.* New York: The Free Press.

Ross, L. (1977). The intuitive psychologist and his shortcomings. In L. Berkowitz (Ed.), *Advances in experimental social psychology.* New York: Academic Press.

Roth, N. L., T. Hunt, M. Stavropoulos, and K. Babik. (1996). Can't we all just get along: Cultural variables in codes of ethics. *Public Relations Review* 22 (Summer), 151–61.

Rubin, J. Z., and B. Brown. (1975). *The social psychology of bargaining and negotiations.* New York: Academic Press.

Said, Mohamed el-Sayed. (2002, January). Cultural coexistence and the absence of law. In Ashild Kjok (Ed.), *International Symposium on Terrorism & Human Rights. Terrorism and human rights after September 11: Toward a universal approach for combating terrorism and protecting human rights* (pp. 142–45). Cairo, Egypt: Cairo Institute for Human Rights Studies.

Sallot, L. M., G. T. Cameron, and R. A. Weaver. (1997). Professional standards in public relations: A survey of educators. *Public Relations Review* 23 (Fall).

Sampson, A. (1975). *The seven sisters: The great oil companies and the world they made.* New York: Viking.

Sardar, Z., and M. W. Davies (2002). *Why do people hate America?* New York: Disinformation.

Saunders, H. H. (1984). The pre-negotiation phase. In D. B. Bendahmane and J. W. McDonald Jr. (Eds.), *International negotiation.* Washington, DC: Foreign Service Institute of the U.S. Department of State.

Schelling, T. C. (1963). *The strategy of conflict.* New York: Oxford University Press.

———. (1966). *Arms and influence.* New Haven, CT: Yale University Press.

Schelling, T. C., and M. H. Halperin. (1961). *Strategy and arms control.* New York: Twentieth Century Fund.

Schmitt, H. (1962). *The path to European Union: From the Marshall Plan to the common market.* Baton Rouge: Louisiana State University Press.

Schott, J. (1989). *Free trade areas and US trade policy.* Washington, DC: Institute for International Economics.

Seib, P., and K. Fitzpatrick. (1995). *Public relations ethics.* Fort Worth, TX: Harcourt Brace College Publishers.

Sennett, R. (1998). *The corrosion of character: The personal consequences of work in the new capitalism.* New York, NY: W. W. Norton & Company.

Sharpe, M. L. (1986). The professional need: Standards for the performance of public relations. *International Public Relations Review* 10 (November), 10–16.

Shockley-Zalabak, P. (1999). *Fundamentals of organizational communication: Knowledge, sensitivity, skills, values.* New York: Longman.

Shoemaker, P. J., and S. D. Reese. (1996). *Mediating the message: Theories of influence on mass media content* (2nd ed.). White Plains, NY: Longman.

Shonfield, A. (1965). *Modern capitalism: The changing balance between public and private power.* Oxford: Oxford University Press.

Shugart, M., and J. Carey. (1992). *Presidents and assemblies.* New York: Cambridge University press.

Siegel, S., and N. J. Castellan. (1988). *Nonparametric statistics for the behavioral sciences.* New York: McGraw-Hill.

Silkenat, J. R., and J. M. Aresty (Eds.). (2000). *The ABA guide to international business negotiations.* Chicago: American Bar Association.

Sillars, A. L. (1981). Attributions and interpersonal conflict resolution. In J. H. Harvey, W. Ickes, and R. F. Kidd (Eds.), *New directions in attribution research: Vol. 3.* Hillsdale, NJ: Lawrence Erlbaum.

Simon, H. A. (1979). Rational decision making in business organizations. *American Economic Review* 69(4), 493–513.

Simon, H. W. (1976). *Persuasion: understanding, practice, and analysis.* Reading, MA: Addison-Wesley.

Sitkin, S. B., and R. J. Bies. (1993). Social accounts in conflict situations: Using explanations to manage conflict. *Human Relations* 46(3), 349–70.

Smith, H. L. (1950). *Airways abroad.* Madison: University of Wisconsin Press.

Smith, R. D. (1996). Communication as a social process. *Public Relations Review* 22(2), 199–200.

Snidal, D. (1985). The limits of hegemonic stability theory. *International Organization* 39(4), 579–614.

Spaemann, R. (1989). *Basic moral concepts* (T. J. Armstrong, Trans.). London: Routledge.

Spector, B. I. (1978). Negotiation as a psychological process. In I. W. Zartman (Ed.), *The negotiation process: Theories and applications.* Beverly Hills, CA: Sage.

Stake, R. E. (1981). Case study methodology: An epistemological advocacy. In W. W. Welsh (Ed.), *Case study methodology in educational evaluation.* Proceedings of the 1981 Minnesota Evaluation Conference, Minneapolis, MN: Minnesota Research and Evaluation Center.

Stein, A. (1990). *Why nations cooperate.* Ithaca, NY: Cornell University Press.

Stein, J. G. (1988). International negotiation: A multidisciplinary perspective. *Negotiation Journal* 4, 221–31.

Stewart, E. C., and M. J. Bennett. (1991). *American cultural patterns.* Yarmouth, ME: Intercultural Press.

Stoff, M. (1980). *Oil, war, and American security: The search for a national oil policy, 1941–1947.* New Haven, CT: Yale University Press.

Strange, S. (1983). Cave! hic dragones: A critique of regime analysis. In S. D. Krasner (Ed.), *International regimes.* Ithaca, NY: Cornell University Press.

Strauss, A., and J. Corbin. (1990). *Basics of qualitative research: Grounded theory procedures and techniques.* Newbury Park, CA: Sage.

Strauss, R. S. (1987). Foreword. In J. E. Twiggs (Ed.), *The Tokyo round of multilateral trade negotiations: A case study in building domestic support for diplomacy.* Washington, DC: Georgetown University Institute for the Study of Diplomacy.

Talbott, S. (1984). *Deadly gambits.* New York: Alfred A. Knopf.

Tate, R. (1998). *An introduction to modeling outcomes in the behavioral and social sciences.* Edina, MN: Burgess Publishing.

Taylor, M. (1987). *The possibility of cooperation.* New York: Cambridge University Press.

Thayer, F. (1965). *Air transport policy and national security.* Chapel Hill: University of North Carolina Press.

The U.S. Department of State. (1982a). *Memorandum of conversation, 1982.* Retrieved April 28, 1998, from the U.S. Department of State Electronic Reading Room: www.foia.state.gov/.

———. (1982b). *Letter to allied Foreign Ministers on the Secretary's meeting with Gromyko, 1982.* Retrieved April 28, 1998, from the U.S. Department of State Electronic Reading Room: www.foia.state.gov/.

———. (1984). *Gromyko's speech in Stockholm. Memorandum for the President, 1984.* Retrieved April 28, 1998, from the U.S. Department of State Electronic Reading Room: www.foia.state.gov/.

———. (1985a). *Arms control memorandum (part 7), 1985.* Retrieved April 28, 1998, from the U.S. Department of State Electronic Reading Room: www.foia.state.gov/.

———. (1985b). *Arms control memorandum (part 1), 1985.* Retrieved April 28, 1998, from the U.S. Department of State Electronic Reading Room: www.foia.state.gov/.

———. (1990a). *U.S.-Soviet summit joint statement on START, 1990.* Retrieved April 28, 1998, from the U.S. Department of State Electronic Reading Room: www.foia.state.gov/.

———. (1990b). *Theme paper: U.S.-Soviet relations, 1990.* Retrieved April 28, 1998, from the U.S. Department of State Electronic Reading Room: www.foia.state.gov/.

———. (n.d.). *Gorbachev's Private Agenda.* Retrieved April 28, 1998, from the U.S. Department of State Electronic Reading Room: www.foia.state.gov/.

Thompson, L., E. Peterson, and L. Kray. (1995). Social context in negotiation: An information-processing perspective. In R. M. Kramer and D. M. Messick (Eds.), *Negotiation as a social process.* Thousand Oaks, CA: Sage.

Tint, H. (1972). *French foreign policy since the Second World War.* London: Weidenfield and Nicolson.

Tsoukalis, L. (1993). *The new European economy.* (2nd ed.) Oxford: Oxford University Press.

U.S. Congressional Research Service. (1991a). *CRS report for Congress—START: Effects on U.S. and Soviet forces.* (The Library of Congress). Retrieved April 28, 1998, from the U.S. Department of State Electronic Reading Room: www.foia.state.gov/.

———. (1991b). *CRS report for Congress—START: Chronology of major events.* (The Library of Congress). Retrieved April 28, 1998, from the U.S. Department of State Electronic Reading Room: www.foia.state.gov/.

Van Dormael, A. (1978). *Bretton Woods: Birth of a monetary system.* New York: Holmes and Meier.

Vernon, R., and D. Spar. (1989). *Beyond globalism.* New York: Free Press.

Walters, R. S. (1994). *U.S. negotiations of voluntary restraint agreements in steel, 1984: Domestic sources of international economic diplomacy* (Case Study No. 107). [Electronic File]. Washington, DC: Institute for the Study of Diplomacy, School of Foreign Service, Georgetown University. Available: http://data.georgetown.edu/sfs/programs/isd/.

Walton, R. E., and R. B. McKersie. (1965). *A behavioral theory of labor negotiations: An analysis of a social interaction system.* New York: McGraw-Hill.

Waltz, K. (1979). *Theory of international politics.* Reading, MA: Addison-Wesley.

Warmer, G.A. (1965). Public relations and privacy. In O. Lerginger and A.J. Sullivan (Eds.), *Information, influence, and communication: A reader in public relations* (pp. 440–65). New York: Basic Books.

Williams, P. (1966). *Crisis and compromise: Politics in the Fourth Republic.* Garden City, NY: Anchor.

Willis, F. R. (1968). *France, Germany, and the New Europe.* Stanford, CA: Stanford University Press.

Yin, R. K. (1994). *Case study research: Design and methods.* (2nd ed.) Thousand Oaks, CA: Sage.

Young, O. R. (1980). International regimes: problems of concept formation. *World Politics* 32(3), 331–56.

———. (1975). Strategic interaction and bargaining. In O. R. Young (Ed.), *Bargaining: Formal theories of negotiation.* Urbana: The University of Illinois Press.

Young, P., and P. Jesser. (1997). *The media and the military: From the Crimea to desert strike.* New York: St. Martin's Press.

Zaremba, A. J. (1988). *Mass communication and international politics: A case study of press reactions to the 1973 Arab-Israeli war.* Salem, WI: Sheffield Publishing.

Zartman, I. W. (1978). Negotiation as a joint decision-making process. In I. W. Zartman (Ed.), *The negotiation process: Theories and applications.* Beverly Hills, CA: Sage.

———. (1984). Negotiation: Theory and reality. In D. B. Bendahmane and J. W. McDonald Jr. (Eds.), *International negotiation.* Washington, DC: Foreign Service Institute of the U.S. Department of State.

———. (1989). In search of common elements in the analysis of the negotiation process. In F. Mautner-Markhof (Ed.), *Process of international negotiations.* Boulder, CO: Westview Press.

Index

About the Author

Alexander G. Nikolaev is an associate professor of communication in the department of culture and communication at Drexel University (Philadelphia, PA). He earned his doctorate from the Florida State University where he also taught for four years. His areas of research interest and expertise include such fields as public relations; political communication; organizational communication; international communication; international negotiations; international news coverage; and discourse analysis. He authored several articles in these areas in trade and scholarly journals as well as some book chapters in the United States and overseas. He edited *Leading to the 2003 Iraq War: The Global Media Debate* with E. Hakanen. He also has years of practical work experience in the fields of journalism and public relations in the United States and Eastern Europe. His current research focuses on international political rhetoric, international news coverage, international negotiations, and transformation and applications of the two-level-game theory.